BRITISH AND AMERICAN PLAYWRIGHTS
1750–1920

General editors: Martin Banham and Peter Thomson

Harley Granville Barker

Harley Granville Barker, one of the most versatile figures in twentieth-century theatre, was the leader of the campaign to reform the English stage in the Edwardian period. His work as an actor, director, playwright, and manager set new standards of production and gave Shaw his first successful showings; his later career as a critic, after he abandoned the stage, opened new interpretations of Shakespeare and led the way to the establishment of a national theatre.

This volume presents three of Granville Barker's best plays: *The Marrying of Ann Leete* (about a young woman rebelling against convention), *The Voysey Inheritance* (digging at middle-class hypocrisy), and *Waste* (banned by the Lord Chamberlain, the tragedy of a politician caught in a sexual trap). Written between 1899 and 1907, and collected here for the first time in a scholarly edition, they reveal Barker as an exciting, subtle, and innovative dramatist.

OTHER VOLUMES IN THIS SERIES

TOM ROBERTSON edited by William Tydeman
W. S. GILBERT edited by George Rowell
HENRY ARTHUR JONES edited by Russell Jackson
DAVID GARRICK AND GEORGE COLMAN THE ELDER
  edited by E. R. Wood
WILLIAM GILLETTE edited by Rosemary Cullen and Don Wilmeth
GEORGE COLMAN THE YOUNGER AND THOMAS
  MORTON edited by Barry Sutcliffe
ARTHUR MURPHY AND SAMUEL FOOTE edited by George
  Taylor
H. J. BYRON edited by J. T. L. Davis
AUGUSTIN DALY edited by Don Wilmeth and Rosemary Cullen
DION BOUCICAULT edited by Peter Thomson
TOM TAYLOR edited by Martin Banham
JAMES ROBINSON PLANCHÉ edited by Don Roy
A. W. PINERO edited by George Rowell
CHARLES READE edited by Michael Hammet
SUSAN GLASPELL edited by C. W. E. Bigsby

Also by Dennis Kennedy:
Granville Barker and the Dream of Theatre (CUP, 1985)

'I read it straight through at once from start to finish. It is immensely
readable as well as wonderfully informative ... Barker was something of
a God to me, and I am delighted that his importance in the history of the
English theatre should now be more fully acknowledged.'
                                                    – Sir John Gielgud

'The story, with many amazing illustrations, of the great lost leader of
modern British Theatre.'
                – Sir Peter Hall, choosing his book of the year in *The Observer*

Plays by
Harley Granville Barker

THE MARRYING OF ANN LEETE
THE VOYSEY INHERITANCE
WASTE

Edited with an introduction and notes by
Dennis Kennedy

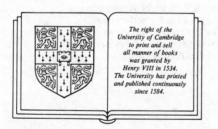

The right of the
University of Cambridge
to print and sell
all manner of books
was granted by
Henry VIII in 1534.
The University has printed
and published continuously
since 1584.

CAMBRIDGE UNIVERSITY PRESS

Cambridge
London   New York   New Rochelle
Melbourne   Sydney

Published by the Press Syndicate of the University of Cambridge
The Pitt Building, Trumpington Street, Cambridge CB2 1RP
32 East 57th Street, New York, NY 10022, USA
10 Stamford Road, Oakleigh, Melbourne 3166, Australia

First published 1987

Printed in Great Britain at
the University Press, Cambridge

British Library cataloguing in publication data

Granville Barker, Harley
Plays by Harley Granville Barker. – (British and American
playwrights, 1750–1920)
I. Title   II. Kennedy, Dennis
III. Granville Barker, Harley. The marrying of Ann Leete
IV. Granville Barker, Harley. The Voysey inheritance
V. Granville Barker, Harley. Waste   V. Series
822'.912   PR6013.R29

Library of Congress cataloguing in publication data

Granville Barker, Harley, 1877–1946.
Plays.
(British and American playwrights, 1750–1920)
Contents: The marrying of Ann Leete – The Voysey inheritance –
Waste.
I. Kennedy, Dennis, 1940–   .   II. Title.   III. Series.
PR6013.R29A6   1987   822'.912   86-26434

ISBN 0 521 30642 6 hard covers
ISBN 0 521 31407 0 paperback

CE

GENERAL EDITORS' PREFACE

It is the primary aim of this series to make available to the British and American theatre plays which were effective in their own time, and which are good enough to be effective still.

Each volume assembles a number of plays, normally by a single author, scrupulously edited but sparingly annotated. Textual variations are recorded where individual editors have found them either essential or interesting. Introductions give an account of the theatrical context, and locate playwrights and plays within it. Biographical and chronological tables, brief bibliographies, and the complete listing of known plays provide information useful in itself, and which also offers guidance and incentive to further exploration.

Many of the plays published in this series have appeared in modern anthologies. Such representation is scarcely distinguishable from anonymity. We have relished the tendency of individual editors to make claims for the dramatists of whom they write. These are not plays best forgotten. They are plays best remembered. If the series is a contribution to theatre history, that is well and good. If it is a contribution to the continuing life of the theatre, that is well and better.

We have been lucky. The Cambridge University Press has supported the venture beyond our legitimate expectations. Acknowledgement is not, in this case, perfunctory. Sarah Stanton's contribution to the series has been substantial, and it has enhanced our work. Later volumes in the series have benefited from the care and attention of Kevin Taylor.

Martin Banham
Peter Thomson

TO MIRANDA, MEGAN, and JESSICA

CONTENTS

ILLUSTRATIONS

ACKNOWLEDGMENTS

Roma Woodnutt of the Society of Authors has been most cooperative as the literary representative of the Granville Barker Estate. For permission to reproduce the illustrations I am grateful to the BBC Hulton Picture Library, the Curators of the Bodleian Library, and the Mander and Mitchenson Theatre Collection. My research has been especially facilitated by the staffs of the Bodleian Library, the British Library, and by Jean Blanco of the University of Pittsburgh Library; and has been generously supported by the Office of Research of the University of Pittsburgh.

I owe thanks to many other people. Particularly: Martin Banham and Peter Thomson, the general editors of the series, for advice and encouragement; Sarah Stanton, Kevin Taylor, and Chris Lyall Grant of Cambridge University Press; Margery Morgan for leading the way; Eric Salmon for much help, published and private; John Barton for discussing his production of *Waste* with me and for generously lending his performance script; William Coats; Erica Magnus; Hazel Carr Leroy, my graduate research assistant, whose work was careful and whose dedication was admirable; Anthony Parise, again; Ann Tyrrell Kennedy, as always.

University of Pittsburgh   D.K.

I Harley Granville Barker in 1907.

INTRODUCTION

Harley Granville Barker was a minor dramatist in at least one sense: he wrote few plays. After a period of youthful apprenticeship he published only seven full-length stage works, one of which was a collaboration and two of which have never been produced. His reputation as a playwright is based primarily on three comedies and a tragedy written in the first decade of the century – and based on very sketchy viewing. During the author's life (1877–1946), *The Marrying of Ann Leete* had a grand total of two performances, before a private audience in 1902. *Waste*, banned by the censor, suffered a similar fate in 1907 and waited thirty years for a public presentation. *The Madras House* fared slightly better: it got ten performances at its première in 1910 and a revised version ran in 1925. Of all the plays, only *The Voysey Inheritance* achieved a reasonable acceptance in the theatre in its time.

Yet despite this slender output Granville Barker can now justly be seen as a major figure, one of the most important playwrights of that crucial, transitional era we call Edwardian. As an artist he links the dreamy 1890s, when art existed for its own sake, to the harsh 1920s, when the horrors of war had unmasked the moral poverty of *la belle époque* and bred new experiments in aesthetic form and social concern. Coming between Victoria and Kaiser Bill's bombs, Barker's Edwardian plays – like the first poems of Ezra Pound, written in the same period – seem to partake of both the nineteenth and the twentieth centuries. They connect the world of Maeterlinck and the early Yeats to the world of Pirandello and T. S. Eliot.

Indeed some of Barker's dramatic techniques and accomplishments are so advanced that they have become valued only in recent years. The Aristotelian conviction that the best drama moves forward in an unrelenting and single line of action, which is complete in itself and which somehow purges or erases itself on the confines of the stage, has dominated western theatre since the seventeenth century. Playwrights like Maeterlinck and Beckett, who rely on precise ellipsis and static images; or like Chekhov and Pinter, who are discursive and anecdotal; or like Shaw and Brecht, who are episodic and didactic, have had to create their own audiences in the face of great resistance. Granville Barker shares qualities with all of them. It is significant that the first serious attempts to understand his plays were written about 1960, when criticism was being sharply awakened to alternatives to the tradition of dramatic style and content.[1] More significantly, it was not until 1975 that *The Marrying of Ann Leete*, one of the more difficult of the plays, was resurrected on the stage. When David Jones directed it for the

Royal Shakespeare Company in London – its first performance for seventy-three years and its first public presentation – he began a minor revival that has given Barker a fairer viewing. The National Theatre produced *The Madras House* for Barker's centenary in 1977, *Waste* and *The Voysey Inheritance* were broadcast on BBC television (the announcer for the latter in 1979 asserting that its author was now recognized 'as one of the great dramatists of the century'), and *Waste* was successfully presented by the RSC in 1985 at both the Barbican and in the West End. Published commentaries have aided the revival, staking claims for Barker's central importance to twentieth-century theatre.

But to insist on this importance remains provocative. To many observers Granville Barker has seemed a mildly interesting period writer, intriguing in flashes but ultimately dry, talky, a bit over-refined, and curiously untheatrical. In fact a common opinion holds that Barker was not creating true drama at all: 'Not so much plays as conversations', said James Agate, trying hard to give a compliment. The plays have been curtly dismissed by several important critics of twentieth-century drama, including Alardyce Nicoll (who also dismisses their writer as 'the pet of a creative literary coterie'). For John Russell Taylor, in the influential *Revels History of Drama in English*, Barker is 'that strange enigma, a practical man of the theatre who seems to have little instinct as a dramatist'.[2] These judgments, coupled with the earlier neglect of the work, would suggest that we are dealing with a minor dramatist after all.

If his value as a playwright is controversial, his general importance is safer to assess. Harley Granville Barker may well have been the most important theatre artist in England in the first years of our century, and one whose influence has continued. As an actor, director, manager, and critic his versatility has always seemed surprising and his accomplishments extraordinary. Through his auspices, for example, Shaw's plays were rescued from their own theatrical darkness and given their first major showings. From 1900 to 1913, Granville Barker acted in, directed, or presented eighteen separate Shaw works, the great majority either world premières or first public performances in London. Barker effectively invented the position of the modern director in England, and operated a series of impressive theatre managements under his artistic control. In his first great burst of accomplishment, at the Court Theatre from 1904 to 1907, he staged thirty-two plays for nearly a thousand performances and established a standard of acting and production that was entirely superior to any then in use. Later his direction of *The Winter's Tale, Twelfth Night*, and *A Midsummer Night's Dream* at the Savoy Theatre revolutionized English Shakespearian production. He attended to a wide variety of scripts from Euripides to Galsworthy, and stimulated a new generation of English playwrights. He wrote convincingly of the need for a subsidized national theatre and by the time of the First World War was close to bringing it into being. He was then acknowledged throughout Europe and America as a theatrical innovator of major consequence.

But even in this area Barker's reputation is alloyed, for at the height of his fame everything changed. The outer facts are simple: he met a woman and abandoned the theatre. Since the woman was American, rich, and ten years his senior, since she and Barker were both already married (she to the railway heir Archer Huntington, he to the actress Lillah McCarthy), and since she disliked the theatre, most actors, and especially Bernard Shaw, the story has assumed the proportion of tragic myth. In the received version the great artist, the hope of a revitalized stage, was seduced by luxury into betraying the cause he had fought for so magnificently. In his later life Barker achieved a different kind of fame as an intelligent and sensitive critic, particularly in the famous *Prefaces to Shakespeare*. But to those he had led in the fight for a new theatre this scholarly success, attached to a snobbish hyphenated name, was a pale image of the old power. Lewis Casson, one of the earliest and most loyal of the followers from the Court Theatre, gave the classic expression to the theme: Barker was a hero who 'gave up the struggle, threw off the dust of battle, and became a mere professor. To us it was almost a desertion, and we found it hard to forgive him.' That was written in the foreword to C. B. Purdom's standard biography, published in 1955, which sees Barker's life as the tragedy of a divided man who did not know himself. 'Barker sacrificed himself to an illusion', Purdom wrote. 'No one is to blame but himself, for he defeated himself.'[3]

They are harsh and unyielding words, and go a long way to explain Barker's curious reputation. The 'illusion', in the biographer's view, was the attempt to remain an artist after closing off the true source of his art, which was day-to-day work on the stage. It is a judgment of some justice, but vastly oversimplified and one-sided. Partly through the recent work of Eric Salmon,[4] we are now able to see more clearly into Barker's motives. First, it is important to stress that Helen Huntington did not seduce him with her money: though she appeared at an opportune time, he fell deeply in love with her and remained so for the rest of his life. Next, Barker had been saying for a number of years before his second marriage that he wanted to leave active stage work and devote himself to writing, since he found it impossible to do both. Most of all, he was conscious that the war was destroying the foundations of the national theatre that he had spent fifteen years preparing. He had practiced his art in the conviction that the only hope for theatrical excellence was a subsidized repertory theatre free of the constraints of the marketplace where actors and plays alike were treated as commodities to be bought, sold, and discarded. Through personal effort and example, Barker had demonstrated that such a repertory theatre was possible; in fact, he thought it was nearly a reality when Europe erupted. Reflecting in 1923 on the reasons for his retirement, he wrote to St John Ervine:

> As to the producing of plays, I made up my mind sometime before 1910 that it was futile to plough the sand i.e., in this connection, to make a production and then disperse it, the play to semi-oblivion, the actors to demoralisation. On the personal count I had made up my mind even earlier to give up acting when I was 30 and producing when I was 40. I made – or contributed to – one attempt after another to create a theatre which should be an institution of some permanence. In 1914 this seemed on the verge of accomplishment.[5]

The war, the affair with Helen, and his fortieth birthday conspired to force an exit. He had had enough of a lonely fight, which now seemed doomed to fail. When he remarried in 1918 he was free from debt and financial worry for the first time in his life. The man of the theatre would become a man of letters.

Of the many ironies that color Barker's life, the most disturbing has to do with his career as a dramatist. From the start he felt himself pulled in two directions: the busy world of an actor, director, and manager is not conducive to the reflection needed for a writer. In fact, Barker found that he had little time for anything outside the rehearsal room during the period of his most intense production activity. Fully occupied with the Court Theatre, the first chance he had to work on *Waste* was on his honeymoon with Lillah McCarthy. (Perhaps she should have suspected her new husband even then; writing a tragedy about sexual relations is not the most obvious form of marital celebration.) *The Madras House* could be started only when he was recuperating from typhoid fever and, back in harness again, he had great difficulty finishing it in time for the scheduled opening. So it is not surprising that he wrote little before the First World War. But after he left the stage and had unlimited time for writing, his dramatic output, as we have already noted, was pitiably small. He revised three of his earlier plays; he also translated some sixteen Spanish and French comedies, most of them with Helen – a substantial achievement, though they are much less interesting than his own work. New original pieces, however, amounted only to *The Secret Life* in 1923 and *His Majesty* in 1928. Neither of them has been performed. Though Barker lived until 1946, he did not complete another play.

This disturbing fact has lent support to the charge that Granville Barker was not a committed dramatist and that he lost touch with his best impulses when he retired to the study. John Russell Taylor went so far as to claim that the last two plays were intended as closet drama; 'they verge on completely subjective fantasy', he wrote, 'and in any case were written to be read rather than acted'.[6] It is the ultimate irony for a man of the theatre, to be condemned for not understanding how a play works on the stage or – worse – for not caring. How could such a judgment come to pass?

From the beginning of his life, Granville Barker had no opportunities or hopes outside the theatre. His father, Albert James Barker, was an irrelevancy; but his mother, Mary Elizabeth Bozzi-Granville, part actress and part Italian, was a powerful influence. Under the name of Miss Granville she supported the family with recitals of popular poems throughout England and was especially admired for her onstage birdsong. Sometimes the young Harley was introduced in the act, wearing a sailor suit. Like many children of theatrical families before him, Barker's education was chiefly informal and chiefly literary. In 1891, at age thirteen, his mother placed him for a few months in Sarah Thorne's theatre school in Margate. In 1895 he was acting on tour with the Shakespeare troupe of Ben Greet, where he played Paris to Lillah McCarthy's Juliet. He also wrote his first play, *The Comedy of Fools*, composed in collaboration with Berte Thomas, an actor whom he had met in Margate.

Having no luck in placing it, the authors destroyed the manuscript. In the next four years, however, while Barker was struggling as an actor in London, he and Thomas completed three more plays which have survived, though unpublished. They are not very successful, and only one was produced (*The Weather-Hen*, in 1899); yet they show the young dramatists, discontented with the accepted standards of English playwriting, were searching for a new style. Their chief interest is also their chief drawback: oversubtle dialogue that reveals inner states but obscures action. Barker, the dominant partner from the beginning, was influenced most by the introverted irony of George Meredith's novels and by the Symbolist use of intense but static images found in the plays of Maurice Maeterlinck.

An example from the most difficult of these collaborations can show how the writers were attempting to forge a new method of theatrical communication, closer to the techniques of music than to Victorian drama. *Our Visitor to 'Work-a-Day'* was written in 1898 and 1899 with Barker in almost complete charge. From his partner we have a picture of Barker nearly possessed as he improvised dialogue while Thomas tried to copy it down, understanding almost nothing of its meaning.[7] I once had occasion to read act 5 quickly to check a reference, and found myself in Thomas's position: detached from the rest, the act made almost no sense at all. The language is so referential and dislocated that no consensus reality appears to be operating behind the words, as if the characters knew something that we do not. Though it is unjust to quote this passage from act 4 out of context, it can represent how the speakers seem to be possessors of a secret denied to the audience:

VIVIEN: Finger prints.
YEO: His?
VIVIEN: The Man's way out.
YEO: From ————?
VIVIEN: You always knew me.
YEO: Bird of prey.
VIVIEN: You wit.
YEO: Probably she will bear it well.
VIVIEN: Griselda.
YEO: Your coming here is mean.
VIVIEN: I hate him.
YEO: Pray.

Yet even where the meaning is not clear, the dialogue is striking for the power of the characters' thoughts welling up behind the words, the words themselves tumbling the thoughts and tripping them up, creating a reality out of the words as music creates one out of sound. The play as a whole, in spite of its problems and failures, is a marvel of subtext and innuendo where broken rhythms indicate broken lives.

The Marrying of Ann Leete was also completed in 1899, the first play that Barker undertook alone. Though it would not be published for a decade, it was a clear sign that its young author was capable of extraordinary achievement. *Ann Leete* is adventurous, challenging, unique, and yet it is easy to understand why it was little admired in its time. Like its predecessor it uses techniques of indirection that were unknown in the mainstream theatre of London. Even the audience of the St James's Theatre, which A. W. Pinero and Oscar Wilde had trained up to high comedy and the literate society problem play in the 1890s, would hesitate to applaud Barker's subtlety. Not that there was a chance of public performance: *Ann Leete* was a piece for the independent producing societies if there ever was one.

At the time of Barker's apprenticeship the alternative to the regular stage was in the small group of private clubs organized for the purpose of presenting non-commercial or censored plays to a membership of committed subscribers. J. T. Grein's Independent Theatre, modeled on Antoine's Théâtre Libre, struggled throughout the nineties to establish an English foothold for the new drama of Europe and of Shaw. William Archer and individual actresses like Florence Farr, Elizabeth Robbins, and Janet Achurch (along with her husband Charles Charrington) had also fought the difficult battle of bringing Ibsen to London. In 1895 Shaw called them 'the Impossibilists'. Later Barker himself would refer to them as 'the Secessionist Movement':[8] they had seceded from the commercial realm to found a new state of art.

In the year of *Ann Leete*'s composition, a new idealistic group was established by some of the members of the Fabian Society. They called it, simply, the Stage Society and intended to produce unusual plays, using professional actors on their off days and nights. Granville Barker was soon an important participant, acting in three of the six programs of the opening season and directing a fourth. He became indispensable, especially to Shaw, who had found at last both a London venue and an ideal juvenile lead for his plays. Within the next few years Barker acted Marchbanks in *Candida*, Kearney in *Captain Brassbound's Conversion*, Napoleon in *The Man of Destiny*, Frank in *Mrs Warren's Profession*; and he directed (or co-directed with the author) both *The Man of Destiny* and *The Admirable Bashville*. 'My only misgiving with regard to you', Shaw wrote his young friend in 1901, 'is as to whether the Stage, in its present miserable condition, is good enough for you: you are sure to take to authorship or something of that kind.'[9]

The Stage Society's purpose was admirably apparent in January 1902. In that month both *Mrs Warren's Profession* and *The Marrying of Ann Leete* were presented for the usual two private performances each: the one banned by the censor from the public stage, the other banned by the playwright's attempt at a new style of drama. A. B. Walkley, London's reigning theatre critic, thought *Mrs Warren* passable enough. He chided Shaw for not writing a play but 'a series of explanations', yet found no difficulties in understanding the author's intentions and rather liked the performance (*Times* 7 Jan. 1902:9). Walkley had admired Barker a few years earlier, for the composition of *The Weather-Hen* and for acting the title role in William Poel's production of *Richard II*. Indeed he thought Barker was 'not a bad Frank' in *Mrs Warren*. But *The Marrying of Ann Leete* was another matter entirely, and the critic was at a loss. He thought that Winifred Fraser, who played Ann, 'appeared to be suffering under the same disadvantage as the audience in not knowing what in the world the author was driving at'. The dialogue was 'wild catch-as-catch-can' which demanded 'an explanatory pamphlet':

> It must be difficult to write a play in four acts ... and throughout
> them all to keep your audience blankly ignorant of the meaning of
> it ... Granville Barker calls his piece a comedy. It might more
> suitably be termed a practical joke. (*Times* 28 Jan. 1902:7)

The other papers were not much kinder. 'Almost incomprehensible', said *The Daily Chronicle* of the same date (p. 6). *The Stage*, while recognizing some merit, thought 'the motive of the play is obscure' (30 Jan. 1902:21). Even Arthur Symons, who admired much about the work, noted that the Stage Society audience, which could be highly enthusiastic, received it coldly (*Academy* 62, 1 Feb. 1902:123). *The Daily Telegraph* (28 Jan. 1902:5), however, had no reservations: 'But never, surely, did audience leave a theatre more completely mystified.'

Looking at it now, close to a century after its composition, the work appears subtle but far from obscure. Or rather, it is perhaps easier now to see how it uses a surface obscurity as its method of conveying action: interested in the gradual growth of and the changes in its protagonist's mind, the play concentrates on inner life. Like *The Cherry Orchard*, written a few years later, *Ann Leete* avoids the big scenes of the well-made play and of romantic melodrama. Instead it gives us moments of great passion and high decision under ironic control, moments which appear to be inconsequential because they appear to be ordinary. By the play's end Ann knows very well what she has done and why, but the process of learning has been slow, and it is the process that Barker takes as his subject. Like the sprouting of a seed – to use the play's own imagery – the process has been partly hidden both from her consciousness and from the audience. Barker's irony is thus a most difficult kind: rather than knowing more than the protagonist, the audience is placed in the middle of confusing and contradictory situations which reveal their meaning only gradually and through effort. We are in the position of the characters of the drama, understanding some matters, misunderstanding others. Needless to say, this is precisely like life, though the style is not 'life-like' in the accepted conventions of nineteenth-century Realism.

As if to alert us to its technique, the play opens in literal obscurity: in the dark and with a scream. As the stage gets lighter, our eyes become accustomed to a formal garden with late eighteenth-century figures moving about, almost somnambulistically, after an all-night revel. Though their talk is crisp and sharp, it has a dreamlike quality to it, an attention to pure sonorities that is reminiscent of *Our Visitor to 'Work-a-Day'*:

> GEORGE: Morning! These candles still smell.
> SARAH: How lively one feels and isn't.
> CARNABY: The flowers are opening.
> ANN: (*in a whisper*) Couldn't we go in?
> SARAH: Never run away.
> ANN: Everything looks so odd.
> SARAH: What's o'clock .. my lord?
> LORD JOHN: Half after four.
> ANN: (*to* SARAH) My eyes are hot behind.
> GEORGE: What ghosts we seem!
> SARAH: What has made us spend such a night?
> CARNABY: Ann incited me to it. (*He takes snuff.*)
> SARAH: In a spirit of rebellion against good country habits ..
> ANN: (*to her sister again*) Don't talk about me.

> SARAH: They can see that you're whispering.
> CARNABY: .. Informing me now she was a woman and wanted
> excitement.
> GEORGE: There's a curse.
> CARNABY: How else d'ye conceive life for women?

Some of the figures appear to question their own reality, wondering if so sophisticated an existence can be called life. Their sleepless night and aimless morning suggest that the scene is a dream and the characters distant in emotion as well as time.

But as dawn turns to day the dream becomes a harsh, even cruel, reality. Carnaby Leete, Ann's father and owner of the estate, is a pleasant but scheming Parliamentarian, declining in fortune and in health, desperately trying to reclaim his political star. Earlier in his career he left the Tories and sealed an alliance with the Whigs by marrying his elder daughter Sarah to Sir Charles Cottesham. Sensing another change of political climate, he now subtly attempts to rearrange a connection with the Tories by marrying Ann Leete to Sir John Carp. The outer subject of the play is thus clearly political, as it so often is in Barker's work. As a dramatist he was particularly drawn to the turncoat politician, the man who remains faithful – or seems to remain faithful – to some private allegiance while betraying his party, family, or class. (Such figures reappear in *Waste* and the one-act *Vote by Ballot*; *The Voysey Inheritance* and *The Madras House* contain non-political versions; and the motif is given its largest expression in *His Majesty*, where the main action is an abdication.) Throughout *Ann Leete* we are reminded of how important public affairs are to most of the characters, which lends an additional cynicism to their ultra-civilized lives.

Carnaby's concerns are enlarged by references to the changing conditions of the bigger world: the French Revolution has blown democracy across the Channel and the ancient ruling families of England cannot ignore the scent. His own son George, for example, in a dramatic attempt to escape his father's influence, has married himself to the daughter of a local farmer, a desperate democratic act. George is a 'cropped republican' whose hair, as well as his clothing, signify his advanced political opinions, as Barker's costume note to the 1902 typescript makes clear. (It is reprinted here as Appendix A.) Further, it is readily apparent that the condition of women in the play is meant to point to the end of the nineteenth rather than the end of the eighteenth century. Ann is a Victorian or Edwardian New Woman a hundred years removed: 'You want a new world .. you new woman', her brother says. In 1899, then, Barker wrote of the dawn of his new century by setting the play in a historical period with parallels to the present. Like Brecht's alienation effect, the device allows the audience to see the immediate more clearly by granting some distance to the real subject.

But what is the real subject? As the play goes forward the public theme recedes into insignificance; what emerges is a private concern that is characteristic of the dramatist's method. For what finally matters in the action is not the rise of democracy or the shifting alliances of party politics or even the position of women, but the secret processes of Ann Leete's mind. The play uses her 'marrying', which is an external event, to convey the changes of an inner life. The perennial problem of drama is how to render the invisible visible – how to take a mystery and make it a seen object. Chekhov, facing the problem with freshness and distinction, found a solution that altered the course of theatre after him. In Chekhov the inconsequential meanderings of a character like Vanya take us to the delicate center of the self, while the outer action of the play, the dispossession of Sonya and Vanya of their just inheritance, seems to occur on its own, almost without human prompting. Working independently and at the same time (*Ann Leete* was written in the year of *Uncle Vanya*), Barker experimented with what might be called 'recessive action', a technique that attempts to reproduce the hidden movements of the human heart. Thus the apparent obscurity that gave such trouble to the original audience is neither willful nor obstructive: it is the very life of the play itself. As the drama starts in a darkness that gives way to light, so Ann grows from ignorance to understanding.

And like the *anagnorisis* of Oedipus, the knowledge she gains is about herself. She begins the play, newly arrived in the adult world, uncritically accepting the nature of her father's protection; she is in the ancient position of woman in a patriarchal society, her consequence deriving from youth and sexual innocence, her value assigned by her usefulness as a barter commodity between men. As she gradually advances in intellectual maturity, she observes the unhappiness wrought on her sister by paternal care. Sarah's marriage, which in the second act disintegrates into a mockery of a divorce, is a sterile reproach to Ann's future. Her brother George's alternative, while blessed with fertile outcome, seems equally unattractive: he has brought his simple country wife into society, and suffers the continual embarrassment of living in his father's world while having rejected his father's way. Ann is caught in a moral dilemma that is close to the condition of a tragic protagonist, for she must reject her father's desires and her siblings' examples to assert her own identity, but in so doing must reject Lord John Carp as well. In the first act she thinks she loves him; by the third her isolation is complete as she says no to the entire world about her, the only world she knows and the only one supposedly available to her.

If the play shares a theme with *A Doll's House*, the influence stops at this point. Ibsen's Nora, recognizing a similar state of worldly affairs, refuses to participate further and slams the door. Ann Leete somehow understands that saying no is not a solution, and goes on, absurdly, to say yes, grasping

what is at hand. She remains a comic protagonist because she will not accept
isolation any more than she will accept her father's dying world.
Unexpectedly and suddenly she turns to the simplest and most 'natural'
character in the play, the gardener, whose very name is about to blossom:
'John Abud .. you mean to marry. When you marry .. will you marry me?'
Her action avoids the sentimental because she knows fully that it means
giving up her comfortable and convenient world for unknown territory, a
harsh landscape of choice. Socially it is an awkward decision; the gardener
lives with nature, midwife to plants and flowers, but depends for
employment on landowners like Carnaby. Thus Ann will lose her status and
yet still see the members of her class leading privileged lives. Nonetheless
her choice is not only courageous but devastatingly complete. After the
wedding party in her father's polished hall, she and Abud walk nine muddy
miles to his simple cottage to start their life together, Adam and Eve waking
in God's mind, making the world green again by force of youthful
righteousness.

   The final scene in that cottage, powerful in its compression and its
unspoken overtones, plays like a critique of the end of *A Doll's House*. It is
highly charged with the sexual anticipation of a bridal night and charged as
well with the imminent expectation of new life. Ann's action turns out to be
much more than a gesture, even though her family conclude she is mad. For
her the choice is luminous with promise, a happiness that comes from
simplicity and hope:

> ANN: Papa .. I said .. we've all been in too great a hurry getting
>   civilised. False dawn. I mean to go back.
> ABUD: He laughed.
> ANN: So he saw I was of no use to him and he's penniless and he
>   let me go. When my father dies what will he take with him? ..
>   for you do take your works with you into Heaven or Hell, I
>   believe. Much wit. Sally is afraid to die. Don't you aspire like
>   George's wife. I was afraid to live .. and now .. I am content.

The play began in the dark, and now closes at night in a room that is almost
dark – a single candle lights it. Ann opens the door that leads upstairs to her
new bed and new life, reversing Nora's rejection of the patriarchal world.
As Abud holds the candle to light the cold stairs, Ann accepts the night
because she is sure of the day. She will be subservient to her husband – she
is in the eighteenth century – but on her own terms and by choice. For her
the world is no longer patriarchal. Her marrying is not her father's but her
own.

All the plays Granville Barker composed with Berte Thomas, together with
Agnes Colander, an unpublished play he wrote alone in 1900 and 1901,

share with *Ann Leete* an interest in the condition of women. They all have female protagonists as well (though *Our Visitor to 'Work-a-Day'* may be an exception; it is difficult to tell who is meant to be the chief figure there). So it was a considerable change that occurred in 1903, when at age twenty-five Barker began work on *The Voysey Inheritance*, a play solidly in the hands of men. Law, finance, and power are the outward concerns, much more noticeably than politics is the outward concern of *Ann Leete*. Indeed how Edward Voysey can fit into the world of men is the major dramatic question of the piece.

The Voysey Inheritance is easily the most accessible of Barker's plays. It was performed 115 times in the Edwardian period, has been revived reasonably often, and has been in print more or less continuously since its first publication in 1909. Unlike *Ann Leete* it follows the more obvious conventions of nineteenth-century Realism: it is set in the present, it examines a current family problem, and it uses dialogue that avoids the oblique, elliptical style of the earlier plays. Its comedy is also more obvious and accessible, especially in characters like the booming army major and the deaf Mrs Voysey. Yet Barker returned to *Ann Leete* for a structural model for this play. Again he gives us a protagonist who is opposed by his father and placed in a moral dilemma of serious proportions. Again the protagonist refuses the simple course and refuses the examples of his elder brothers. And again the protagonist finds a solution to his dilemma by accepting a mate under difficult conditions. *The Voysey Inheritance* is also a 'sexual' comedy, interested finally in how marriage, sex, and sexual relationships can be seen as indices of human worth.[10]

Edward Voysey is tossed into the middle of a fiscal and familial mess in act 1, a mess he is particularly unwilling and unable to face. His father, 'sixty or more and masterful', has spent a life secretly defrauding the clients of his small solicitor's firm, using the funds in his trust for speculation and personal profit. He reveals the extent of the thievery to Edward, the junior partner, as preparation for his son's 'inheritance', claiming that his own father had passed it to him years before. The business, always near the brink of disaster, has been kept intact by the old man's financial genius, a matter of some pride to him. Edward is horrified at the disclosure, and temperamentally incapable of assuming the mantle of the middle-class buccaneer. His father nonetheless badgers him to accept the challenge out of family-duty – Edward fully aware of the irony in the idea – and then inconveniently dies. Edward enjoys telling the mourning family in act 3 that their comfortable life is built on crime, and looks forward to the inevitable 'smash' that will put him in prison but release him from an onerous and terrifying guardianship of empty honor.

Max Beerbohm called the third act 'the finest scene of grim, ironic comedy in modern English drama' (*Saturday Review* 11 Nov. 1905:621) for its unrelenting portrayal of middle-class hypocrisy. Beerbohm, like many critics at the first performance, immediately recognized the high virtue of the work. William Archer, who insisted that he could not understand any of Barker's earlier plays, thought *Voysey* a masterpiece.[11] Of a revival seven years later, also directed by the author, *The Observer* (8 Sept. 1912:9) went so far as to say that it was 'the finest comedy of modern times ("The Playboy of the Western World" and "Man and Superman" not excepted)'. Clearly the play did not suffer the fate of *Ann Leete*.

The scenic realism and bitter humor recommended the piece to Edwardian audiences, who could readily identify with the outer subject. The portrayal of a London lawyer's office and of Chislehurst family life lent an almost Naturalist authenticity that had been absent from Barker's previous work. Solicitors in private firms were not much regulated in the period, and crooked ones were common enough. Shaw's own grandfather, a solicitor himself, was ruined when his partner absconded with £50,000 of his money and a large sum belonging to his clients. A similar event occurs in H. G. Wells' novel *Kipps*, published in the year of *Voysey*'s première. There is throughout a strenuous condemnation of middle-class values – Edward at one point identifies his responsibility as that of being 'the servant of men whose ideal in life is to have a thousand a year ... or two thousand ... or three' – and some of the discussions about money and the right to it have a Marxist slant.

But if the outer events of the play were easily accessible, the deep subject caused the usual trouble. Fatigued by its length and its discursiveness, many spectators felt the conclusion weak and indecisive. 'Certainly the man who could write the first three acts of *The Voysey Inheritance* must be something of a genius', said Arnold Bennett in a letter, 'but the man who could write the fourth and fifth acts must be something of a fool.'[12] Subsequent readers have often agreed; after the savage comedy of the wicked solicitor the last act particularly seems uncompelling. Alice Maitland, who has made a career of refusing Edward's proposals, changes her mind, convinces him to marry her, and agrees to share the Herculean burden of saving the firm. Edward wishes only to abdicate from responsibility and take the consequences; if he did so, however, he would bring ruin not only to the family but to his innocent clients as well. Alice thought him a 'well-principled prig' before; now the challenge of his inheritance has given him 'a man's work'. She convinces Edward to become a kind of socialist Robin Hood, fiddling with the accounts as his father did but in order to correct his father's injustices. The monumental (and illegal) task excites her and gives her purpose. Together they will attack old Voysey's mess, finding personal salvation in holy dedication to a secret cause.

The ending seems tame because the play is not about middle-class hypocrisy but about the transforming effect of the inheritance on Edward.

All of Barker's comedies end with a scene in which a man and woman discuss the nature of their commitment to each other, trying to forge a future out of the chaos of their pasts. How can we live in a fallen world and not be tainted by its moral corruption? The answer in *Voysey* is the same as in *Ann Leete* and *The Madras House*: by an act of overwhelming personal integrity that may betray conventional wisdom but that transmutes the nature of the world itself. For Barker this commitment is symbolized by sexual relationship. Edward, saying no to his father, is trapped in himself; when he says yes to the woman he loves he learns he can also say yes to the difficulty of his position in life. The final scene, then, gives us the new partners planning a raid on the future, sanctified by their sexual agreement. We do not know what the future will be for Edward – he may still be found out and go to prison – but we know that he will face it with an authority created by his dedication to a cause and to a mate.

The Voysey Inheritance appeared in the second season of the famous Vedrenne–Barker performances at the Court (or Royal Court) Theatre in Sloane Square. In three years of operation, Barker, together with his business manager, J. E. Vedrenne, presented what became known as the 'Thousand Performances': an unparalleled series of new English plays, advanced European drama, and experimental productions of Euripides. Starting with thrice-weekly matinees on days when professional actors were free, by mid-1905 the enterprise was using the theatre nights and afternoons, with a stock company playing for a committed audience of forward-looking Londoners, many of whom had abandoned the regular theatres. Barker was in artistic control, co-directing Shaw's contributions and directing all the other works. He rapidly proved that good acting, good writing, intelligent programing, and sensitive production could exist on a low budget and with a social conscience. Without subsidy and without subscribers, the Court experiment had elevated the Secessionist Movement from the marginal and eccentric to be a serious alternative to the commercial theatre.

At the center of the Court programs – disturbingly central to many commentators – were the comedies of Bernard Shaw. Of the 988 performances of the Vedrenne–Barker seasons, 701 were of eleven plays by that single author: 'the Shaw Repertory Theatre' was a common jest that hit home. But if Shaw provided the substance (and some of the guarantee fund) for the management, it was Barker who gave the most famous playwright of the twentieth century his first extended opportunity. Amazing as it now seems, Shaw's plays (eleven were in print by 1903, including *Man and Superman*) had rarely been performed publicly in London until Barker took charge of them. Despite the growing sales of the published versions, and some stage success in America and Germany, the commercial London theatres had snubbed Shaw with the consistency of an organized campaign. Unable to understand their style and purpose, managers, as well as many critics who saw the limited productions of the Stage Society, concluded they were not plays at all. For his part Shaw generally held back from the few London performances that were offered, fearing the standard of production was so low that it would ruin his further chances. Barker changed all that. The Court demonstrated that Shaw wrote plays well enough, witty, acerbic provocative, and moving to boot. In fact it was Edward VII, one of the last people who might be expected to enjoy Shaw, who presented something like an official seal of approval: at a command performance of the politically sensitive *John Bull's Other Island* in March of 1905, the King of Great Britain and Ireland and Emperor of India laughed so hard that he broke his chair. Did the Defender of the Faith fall to the floor amid sticks and upholstery? History, alas, does not say.

'Yes, decidedly the Court is our "Shavian" theatre', wrote A. B. Walkley in his review of *The Voysey Inheritance*. 'Mr Shaw's own plays are shown there nightly, and in the afternoons they give you new plays by younger men' with the 'faint aroma' of Shaw (*TLS* 10 Nov. 1905:384). *Man and Superman* was Mr Shaw's play in the evenings when *Voysey* had its matinees, a revival of the production first seen in May; *Major Barbara*, which Shaw wrote for the Court company, would follow in late November. Barker took the role of John Tanner in the first, made up with red beard to look like Shaw; and Adolphus Cusins in the second. The two men were linked fast in the public mind as the leaders of a new theatre, social in interest, intellectual in content, revolutionary in intent. Their connection to the Fabian Society and to the leftist intelligentsia united them further, Barker appearing as the chief disciple of England's most voluble reformer. Indeed, the connections were deeper in some minds: a persistent rumor had it that Shaw was Barker's true father. The facts refuse to support the contention, but rumors have never shown much interest in facts.

Despite the presence of a New Woman and an interest in the Life Force, *The Voysey Inheritance* shows little direct influence from his elder friend. Barker's work concerns itself with the delicate overtones of human existence, whereas Shaw deliberately sounds with a brass band. Shaw liked to compare his own plays to Verdi and Barker's to Debussy. *Major Barbara* – which actually uses a brass band and a big drum – shares with *Voysey* an interest in wealth, poverty, and the robber-baron character, but Shaw scores for grand opera and grand passion. Barker, focusing on Edward's spiritual growth, gives us impressionist harmonies on piano, flute, and a single violin.

The delicate chords are nowhere more apparent than in Barker's next play, *Waste*, completed in 1907 and intended as the centerpiece of the new Vedrenne–Barker season at the Savoy Theatre. Flushed with the success of three years at the Court, the management boldly attempted to extend its ideals to the general public at a larger house in the West End. Barker hoped that he could soon start true repertory scheduling, which had not been possible at the Court, and attract a major subsidy to underwrite the less popular work: he was tired of limited productions enforced by economy, and had his eye on *Peer Gynt* for the Savoy. The move turned into disaster. The managers were squabbling, locked into a disagreement about the fundamental purpose of their enterprise. When autumn came, the revivals of older Shaw plays proved weak and new productions of Galsworthy and Euripides were disappointing. Most disturbing, however, was the case of *Waste*. Scheduled to open in November, it was refused a license by the censor and could not be publicly performed.

The licensing of plays had been a thorn in the side of British drama since 1737, when Henry Fielding's satires of the government prompted Robert Walpole to drive him from the stage by legislative means. From then until 1968 various theatre Acts placed authority to permit or prohibit the production of a script in the hands of the Lord Chamberlain, a court officer of ancient title removed from parliamentary oversight. In practice the chore of reading and passing on the suitability of plays was delegated to an assistant hired by his office; without legal standing, this functionary nonetheless wielded absolute judgment over the nation's new drama. In 1907 the Examiner of Plays was one G. A. Redford, a former bank manager who had no particular qualifications for the position other than an excessive allotment of high Victorian morality. The ban on *Waste* raised a great outcry from the artistic and intellectual populace, and in the next few years a major campaign was waged against Redford and censorship, with Granville Barker as its leader. In the end the Liberal government proved unwilling to alter the status quo, and thus *Waste*, like *Ghosts* and *Mrs Warren's Profession* before it, would stay off the public stage until the censor's office changed its mind.[13]

So instead of being the banner of the new Vedrenne–Barker season at the Savoy, the play could have only two private performances by the Stage Society. The censorship even affected casting. Norman McKinnel, who had rehearsed the lead role under the author's direction, was prevented by his manageress at the last moment from appearing in a banned play, despite the fact that the Stage Society production was perfectly legal. In the emergency Barker himself hurriedly took the part.

The official objections to *Waste* centered on what Redford called 'the extremely outspoken reference to sexual relations'; he further demanded that Barker 'eliminate entirely all reference to a criminal operation'.[14] Since the plot turns on an abortion, this would be difficult to accomplish. The censor's implication was that the offensive parts of the play were gratuitous and could be removed as one removes extra socks from a traveling bag that proves too small. Despite the official objections, however, there was a grave suspicion that Redford was acting in the grand Walpole tradition and banning the play for political reasons. Its convincing analysis of the machinery of Edwardian government could embarrass party leaders on both sides by its exposé of the cynical inner world of parliamentary power.

Walkley's review of the Stage Society production said as much: he admired the play greatly, but approved the censor's decision. 'The subject-matter of *Waste*', he wrote, 'together with the sincere realism with which it is treated, makes it, in our judgment, wholly unfit for performance under ordinary conditions before a miscellaneous public of various ages, moods, and standards of intelligence' (*Times* 27 Nov. 1907:8). The opinion of the critic of the major national newspaper reminds us that though the age was transitional it remained Victorian in its official morality. Whether the true objections were to sexual or to political matters, Barker's play was too powerful and too dangerous to be unleashed on the 'unthinking and still imperfectly educated crowd'. That last phrase may sound like Walkley at his patronizingly worst, but it was writen by J. T. Grein (*Sunday Times* 1 Dec. 1907:4) – the same J. T. Grein who founded the Independent Theatre Society, whose opening production in 1891 had been a private performance of *Ghosts*. It is difficult to believe that Grein would defend censorship in any way, since one of the purposes of his pioneer society was to present prohibited plays; but like many intelligent men of the day he thought the government had a duty to defend the public from itself. William Archer called *Waste* 'our greatest modern tragedy',[15] but it was tossed onto the theatrical scrapheap.

We can take some comfort from the fact that Redford had at least been affected by the play, for the mixture of sex and politics that roused his ire is at its core. Indeed *Waste* has more to do with politics even than *Ann Leete*, and the protagonist is a politician who lives for nothing but public service. 'Hard-bitten, brainy, forty-five, and very sure of himself', Henry Trebell has sharpened his mind and his instincts until he is 'a machine that runs smoothly'. He has drafted an extraordinary bill which would disestablish the Church of England and reallocate its funds to a great new educational system. He has a holy devotion to social reform; he wishes to recapture the ancient and sacred teaching function of the church and apply it to secular use, to build an earthly palace for the kingdom of the spirit. The established religion is moribund, and Trebell would replace it with a religion of knowledge. The center of his creed is a vision of schools 'not built next to the church, but on the site of the church'. He sees a priesthood of teachers, well trained, properly paid, to provide salvation from ignorance.

In the service of an ideal Trebell has made virtues of his aloofness and aloneness. Party loyalties matter little to him, even less than they do to Carnaby Leete. Elected as an Independent, he aligned himself with the Liberals; now he is ready to join the Conservatives, who are expected to return to power shortly, in exchange for a cabinet seat and a promise to carry his disestablishment scheme through Parliament.

Waste opens with one of Barker's most difficult scenes. Julia Farrant, wife of a ranking Tory and herself a considerable influence in the halls of power, has invited Trebell to a weekend house-party designed to help him turn his coat. But Trebell does not appear in the first scene. Instead most of the time is given to the women, listening to music after dinner and discussing political matters second-hand, as if the playwright had set out to give a demonstration of Thorstein Veblen's theory of vicarious leisure. What they talk about is the difficult part: references fly by, to people, political events, social entanglements. It is hard to tell what is fictional, what topical, what important. 'It is a grave flaw in the construction of Mr Granville Barker's otherwise admirable play *Waste*', wrote his friend William Archer in *Play-Making*, 'that it should open with a long discussion, by people whom we scarcely know, of other people whom we do not know at all, whose names we may or may not have noted on the playbill.'[16] Barker has stretched attention to the limit in this extreme instance of tossing the audience into the middle of the play world; it is significant that his revision of the scene in 1927 (reprinted here as Appendix B) lessens the confusion considerably.

But the confusion in the original version serves a worthwhile dramatic purpose. One of the most interesting techniques of the work is the manner in which Barker creates a convincing fictional world by blending the actual with the imagined. A small example occurs early in the scene, when references are made within seconds of each other to Newnham, a well-known college at Cambridge, and to Jude's, an invented college at Oxford. More significantly, we are presented with a political situation firmly based in the actual – the workings of Parliament, party names and philosophies, the way a cabinet thinks. But this is merged with the imagined at a very high level; not only are the characters themselves fictional, as would be expected, but the political condition of the Conservatives and the Liberals has been reversed and the central political concern, disestablishment itself, given an importance it did not have in 1907. Thus at the outset the drama creates a grounding in the actual that is extremely authentic, but by subtly altering facts and adding fictions it can readily go beyond Naturalist reportage into the frightening world of Trebell's inner life. The method may at first seem simply to be that of the mirror, where the world is reflected clearly, though backwards. It is much more, however, like that of the dream, based on experience and observable fact but likely to become at any moment a horrifying distortion of life.

The world's reality, especially its political reality, nonetheless remains important. Though the Church of England was not about to suffer harm in the Edwardian age, the subject was topical enough. Various Liberal governments, influenced by Nonconformists in the nineteenth century, found the established religion an embarrassment; Erastianism was an outmoded relic from the past, inappropriate for a forward-looking democratic party. The Episcopal Church of Ireland, which could claim only one-seventh of the population as members, was disestablished by Parliament in 1871; and an act disestablishing the church in Wales would be passed in 1914, to take effect after the war. But the political power of the Church of England was great – its two archbishops and some twenty-four bishops still sit in the House of Lords – and its ancient endowments much more secure from parliamentary tampering. Yet the income from those endowments, which in the period ran to many millions of pounds annually, could be a temptation to any government. In *Waste* it is the Conservatives who are about to attempt disestablishment, but we should recall that in 1907 a Liberal government was actually in power.

The established church has of course long been accused of being more interested in outward form than in spiritual life. As the old joke has it, an Englishman likes the Church of England because it doesn't interfere with a man's politics or his religion. Some of the power of *Waste* derives from an opposition based on that premise. The only defender of the faith to appear is Lord Charles Cantelupe, a character who is sincerely religious but who nonetheless represents the snob appeal of anglicanism: he is an aristocrat, with 'high church' interests, concerned with appearances and power. The spiritual leader is the atheist Trebell, whose consuming passion for education gives him the zeal of a religious reformer. He wins Cantelupe over to his disestablishment bill when he shows that a church loosed from its ties to the state is freed to be the spiritual agency it wants to be.

Barker's masterstroke was to use the formal dismantling of a religion as the background to an investigation of spiritual need. Even the frivolous Amy O'Connell admits that it is 'some spiritual need or other' that prompts her to flirt with Trebell. Amy, who lives apart from her Irish husband because she refuses to have the children he and his religion demand, desperately seeks love from the iceman Trebell. Her horror at her own fertility is what destroys her; when she becomes pregnant with his child, and finds him cold to her human need, she rushes to end life blindly, secure only in her fear. Many of the other characters look for a kind of salvation in endeavors that have religious overtones. Her husband, a historian of the thirteenth century, finds peace in the Catholic past amid a modern world he despises. Walter Kent seeks a superhuman hero in Trebell, as Frances seeks a human brother in him. Still other characters rely on the quest for power as a train ticket to a worldly paradise.

It is Trebell's own quest, of course, that takes us to the center of the play. Ostensibly – that is, as the world is seen in news stories – Trebell is ruined by a scandal which, though never made public, is used as a weapon against him. Amy has died in a back-alley abortion and, although her husband agrees to keep quiet about the baby's paternity, Trebell's career hangs in the balance. The Tory shadow cabinet, under the benign but cynical leadership of Lord Horsham, soon to be Prime Minister, is not so forgiving. Finding a series of objections to an uncompromising man and his uncompromising bill, the cabinet council decides that the unsavory affair provides a convenient excuse to drop both. In this respect we see the public man ruined by private sin, making the play a 'tragedy' as the press, in its reductive way, understands that awesome word. A number of contemporary reviewers noted the similarity to the Parnell scandal; but so many parallels can be found that the 'tragedy' seems commonplace if not banal.

The real tragedy in Barker's play is far from banal. It is not political disappointment that causes Trebell to shoot himself; rather it is a failure in his spiritual life. When Amy reveals her pregnancy, he is clearly interested in the prospect of having a child. He is horrified by her request for help to end her condition, and is devastated by the abortion. His awareness that he never cared for her only increases the growing darkness in him. His intellect allows him to be cynical even after Amy's death, as when he defends himself to his new colleagues in the third act: 'Oh, cheer up. You know we're an adulterous and sterile generation. Why should you cry out at a proof now and then of what's always in the hearts of most of us?' But what grows inside him is a sense of his own death-in-life. He spends a night in reflection as he waits for Horsham's decision about his political future. When the note arrives in the morning he already feels dead to the world as he knew it; he sees even his great work as barren, and the recognition of that barrenness has driven life from him. The central theme of the play is sterility; its central image is abortion. In his dark night of the soul Trebell looks inward for comfort and finds only a 'spirit which should have been born, but is dead'. As Agnes Colander realizes in Barker's early unpublished play, 'suicide's easy when there's so little left to kill'.

The crisis in the protagonist's political life serves to force the crisis in his secret life, and it is the second that brings the tragedy. Trebell's failure is one of the simplest and most profound of failures: an inability to love. 'Power over men and women and contempt for them!' is Frances' explanation. He is lost in himself with no one to extract him. Ann Leete, in a similar dilemma, leaps over isolation by a courageous affirmation. Unlike Barker's comic heroes, Trebell cannot find salvation because he has not been taken outside of himself. Edward Voysey can say yes to life after being saved by Alice from emotional celibacy; Trebell, lacking sexual salvation, can say yes only to death.

The censorship of *Waste* and the failure of the Savoy venture were serious blows to Granville Barker's dream of establishing a repertory theatre in

London, and it took him some years to recover the momentum of the Court days. The life of a professional actor was not for him; he obviously could not make a living from his playwriting; and there was no place for a freelance director. England's most promising theatre artist was without an artistic home and began to look for opportunities elsewhere. He was briefly tempted by an offer to direct a new theatre in New York; then was forced back on tour to help pay for the Savoy debts, one result of which was a nearly fatal bout of typhoid fever. The enforced idleness of illness has often prompted books from busy men; Barker used his convalescence to write a new play.

The Madras House is a fascinating comedy of Edwardian life, rich in implication and filled with theatrical vigor. More episodic than his other plays, it follows a theme rather than a strong plot. Its four acts are like semi-transparent overlays, each adding new complexity and depth to the subject; its protagonist wanders among them more as an observer than as the driver of an action. Each act is concerned in a different way with the position of women, particularly men's economic relationship to women, in a highly charged sexual environment. The 'house' of the title is a fashion house, and becomes the setting for the third act, where the men of the drapery trade engage in the business of reducing women to sexual automatons for economic exploitation in *haute couture*. As with *Ann Leete* and *Voysey*, the play is ultimately interested in how social and moral attitudes in the world at large come home to roost. The final scene again gives us a glimpse of the protagonist attempting to chart a new life with his spouse through the rough waters of domestic sexuality.

In 1910 Barker was the chief artistic force behind a promising repertory season sponsored by the American impresario Charles Frohman at his London theatre, the Duke of York's. *The Madras House* premièred there, along with Shaw's *Misalliance*, written as a companion piece, and Galsworthy's *Justice*. The best of England's new playwrights were being offered under conditions that Barker had hoped for since the turn of the century. But business was not good, especially for *Misalliance* and *Madras*; instead of nursing them to some degree of success, Frohman acted on instinct and replaced them with safer and blander fare. Soon he chose to end the experiment entirely, after only a few months of trial. To Barker the episode proved that a commercially based repertory was impossible: when Frohman smelled the ill wind from the box office, he was no longer interested in art.

Yet in the remaining years before the First World War Barker reached the height of his reputation. In management with his wife he staged an unprecedented series of plays, including Ibsen, Schnitzler, Masefield, Euripides, and of course Bernard Shaw. Most notable were three astounding productions of Shakespeare at the Savoy in 1912 and 1914.

Barker easily proved himself to be the finest director of the age and the man most qualified to assume charge of a national theatre, were one somehow to materialize.

He had first made his mark as a leader of the campaign for a national theatre when Archer asked him to collaborate on a book that would outline the steps necessary for its creation. Privately printed in 1904 in the hope of a single, philanthropic donor, it was published in 1907 as *A National Theatre: Scheme and Estimates*. The plan is impressive in its detail and admirably economical. The philanthropist did not appear, but most of Barker's work from the time of the Court Theatre on can be seen as a personal attempt to make a London repertory company inevitable. In 1913 and 1914, operating three theatres, running a sustained ensemble of actors, designers, and musicians, producing Euripides, Shakespeare, and modern drama, he had just about achieved his goal. All that was needed was a permanent building and an endowment of a few million pounds – obstacles not so great as they may seem. Barker thought that some form of subsidy was soon to be secured, and others shared his optimism. But as he wrote to St John Ervine in the letter quoted at the beginning of this introduction, 'Then came the war.'

His immediate response was to do a war play, and a typically difficult one; his own adaptation of Thomas Hardy's *The Dynasts*, a verse drama of cosmic scope about the Napoleonic Wars. By 1915, however, few could pretend that the current war would be over quickly, and the London theatre had become devoted to mindless entertainment. Barker sailed for New York again and directed a short repertory season of Shakespeare and Shaw. In the spring he staged huge outdoor productions of Euripides at eastern universities in the U.S., and then retired from active work in the theatre. Conditions, never congenial to his talent, had become impossible. Shaw wrote to Gilbert Murray in July, 'Barker has chucked the theatre. Fact. He has devoted himself to poverty and playwriting.'[17]

That is probably what he expected and intended. But after service in the army, his marriage to Helen Huntington insured he would not be poor; and though he wrote a great deal, few plays resulted. His detachment from the stage seemed to have affected his pen, for when *The Secret Life* was published in 1923 Archer objected. It is much more subtle than previous works: obsessed with the inner life of its characters, the action runs hidden like an underground river. 'In this play', Archer said, 'you seem to be drifting away from, not towards, the theatre that is understood [*sic*] by the people – even the fairly intelligent people.' Barker's answer is significant for us; he knew the difficulties in the way of performance but insisted that the problem was not in the play, but rather that 'there is no English company of actors so trained to interpret thought and the less crude emotions, nor, as a consequence, any selected audience interested in watching and listening to such things'.[18] The difficulties would be overcome, in other words, by the kind of theatrical system the two men had wished for in 1904.

With a long, careful rehearsal period *The Secret Life* could be made to work wonders on the stage, and we can only hope that some day it will be given its chance. Barker's last play, *His Majesty*, though not as difficult, has also never been seen. Indeed the dramatist refused to permit a performance by Harcourt Williams in 1933, fearing that it could not be adequately cast. He still needed a national theatre, free of the pressures of time and commerce, where dramatic art could flourish.

Except for the wildly successful, a life in the theatre is spasmodic, fraught with insecurity. Those who are concerned with simply working can often manage, but those who wish to do extraordinary work cannot be sure of anything. Barker understood this more than anyone of his time; the first half of his life, spent in dedication to the ancient value of the stage, was wasted as Trebell's vision is wasted. But Barker's suicide was metaphorical only: he chose to retire from active work in order to produce considered work, like the *Prefaces to Shakespeare*. That he wrote only two more plays is not surprising, given the condition of the stage and his absolute insistence on quality. Why write plays, no matter how effective, that no one is prepared to perform? A dramatist cannot be content forever with two performances by the Stage Society.

'But the faculties I write with are not on the surface, somehow', he admitted to Helen in 1918. 'I have to dig down.'[19] That last sentence can stand as a monument to Barker's work as a playwright, and is just as apt for his work as an actor, director, critic, and reformer. He sought a theatre where the hidden processes of the spirit could find expression, believing that the power of the stage lies not in external show but in its unique ability to capture essences. 'No great drama depends on pageantry', he noted in *Prefaces to Shakespeare*.[20] 'All great drama tends to concentrate upon character; and, even so, not upon picturing men as they show themselves to the world like figures on a stage – though that is how it must ostensibly show them – but on the hidden man.' Granville Barker's plays remain challenges for us because he wrote for a theatre of the secret life. In many ways the late twentieth century is more capable of doing justice to his work than the early century was, especially in the subsidized repertories of the National Theatre and the Royal Shakespeare Company, operating under conditions close to what Barker always hoped for. But the plays still do not give themselves up easily. To meet them honestly and on their own terms we must ourselves dig down.

A NOTE ON THE TEXTS

For a playwright, Granville Barker once advised, 'pens and paper are needed, and a large waste-paper basket'.[21] Barker must have had a full waste-paper basket all his life; indeed he was not so much a writer as a rewriter, changing, tinkering, and sometimes remaking his plays with almost obsessive care. In a discussion about the quartos of *Hamlet*, Frank Sidgwick, his witty publisher, teased him in 1937 about his own textual variants: 'It would certainly be a novel idea to do your Collected Plays (when you have stopped writing and re-writing) with collations from the Earlier Octavos. But I don't think we shall ever do you in Folio; it doesn't fit the bookshelf in the flat.'[22] For us, a harsh result of Barker's habit of revision is that choosing a text for performance or print is no simple matter. Leaving aside the numerous drafts and manuscript alterations, two of his four Edwardian plays exist in two published versions (*Waste* and *The Madras House*) and one, *The Voysey Inheritance*, was published in three different forms. Only the earliest, *The Marrying of Ann Leete*, has a single life (in *Three Plays* of 1909, which I use as the basis of my text).

The complication for the others is that the revisions are not always improvements, and the later ones were done after the period of Barker's active work on the stage. *Voysey*, for example, which was first produced in 1905, was published in *Three Plays* in 1909. Barker revised the text for a 1912 revival, making slight adjustments in the dialogue and a small alteration in the last scene. The changes are clearly for the better, but are very minor. (This version was published in 1913.) A more significant revision was done much later, for a performance in 1934, and published in 1938. It is superficially brought up to date by references to Rockefeller, Matisse, Picasso, and to the 'threatening' international outlook; the sums of money are often larger; the slang is modernized. Yet the feeling of the whole, especially of the plot and characters, remains Edwardian. Though the writing is sometimes more polished, the version falls between two ages: it wants to belong both to an England heading toward a second global conflict and to an England as yet innocent of world war. For these reasons I have chosen to stick with Barker's original impulses, and have used the 1913 text.

Waste presents a more difficult choice. It was also first published in *Three Plays* in 1909 and afterwards revised, but the 1927 version (which was not seen on the stage until 1936) is a thorough rewriting. Barker himself identified the problem in his dedication to the new edition. 'I doubt if one scrap of the old dialogue survives', he admitted; 'so it is a thing I had –

dramatically – to say twenty years ago, said as I'd say it now. But now I'd have something else to say.' That last sentence is telling; intellectually and stylistically the revision bears more resemblances to his last drama, *His Majesty*, published in 1928, than to the 1909 *Waste*.

The changes are similar to those in the ultimate *Voysey* but are more authoritative and more complete: the same plot and the same characters are used to make a different play. The mechanics of the work are altered in a number of ways. In the third act of the original, for example, Trebell is brought on to meet his antagonist Justin O'Connell by accident (Horsham has a new servant who bungles his instructions); in the revision Trebell forces his way in, hot to speak to the husband of the woman whose death is about to ruin his career. Trebell is made to be fifty-one, six years older than in the early version, and more self-aware; he tends to explain himself with great insight. The difficult first scene is significantly altered – partly to accommodate two decades of changing British life, partly to correct the obscurity of the original. (It is reprinted here as Appendix B, as an example of Barker's stylistic revisions.) What is missing, however, is the brisk, elliptical quality of the 1909 script, in which the protagonist is surprised and shocked by events partly because he has never thought out his life. The later version is dramatically smoother (though, significantly, no shorter), but the roughness of the original, like that of *Ann Leete*, has to my mind a more distinctive ring, and speaks more clearly with Barker's unique voice. Thus I have used the 1909 version here, convinced that it is a more authentic play, peculiarly Edwardian in style and theme, and more theatrically exciting.

Most directors, however, will probably feel inclined to make cuts in *Waste*, to reduce the obscurity caused by some of the less important references and to reduce the playing time. Though Barker argued forcefully against wholesale surgery on Shakespeare, it is comforting to note that he made deletions himself when directing *Waste* in 1907.[23] John Barton dealt with the textual problem in another way: his sensitive production for the RSC in 1985 used a script made up of the best scenes from both versions. While this imaginatively solved some difficulties, to my mind the result was confusing. The qualities of the two are so different that forging them into a single text created temporal and emotional uncertainties that outweighed the benefits. On the whole I believe the play is better served by holding to the earlier version, though I openly admit that it presents difficulties that remain to be solved in production.

In preparing the texts I have silently corrected obvious misprints, and standardized character identifications in stage directions and in speech headings. I have also standardized some punctuation and a few spellings, neither of which were strong points with the dramatist. Barker uses numerous ellipses in dialogue, sometimes with three dots but more commonly with only two. These breaks are meant to indicate changes of tone or brief pauses: as if the characters, in making up their words, were overwhelmed by the thoughts tumbling upon them. I have standardized all the ellipses to two dots, to better convey Barker's distinctive punctuation, and to suggest more clearly that they are best not treated as long pauses.

It may seem perverse to omit *The Madras House* from this collection, since it is often thought to be Barker's most accomplished play, and I do so with great regret. Space limitations make it possible to include only three works, and my justification is that alone among Barker's plays *The Madras House* exists in a responsible recent edition (edited by Margery Morgan and published by Methuen in 1977). Thus with the appearance of this volume all four of Barker's major plays are again available in print for the first time in a generation.

Explanatory footnotes have been limited to a bare necessity. But as the plays often refer deeply to details of English law, finance, politics, and religion, it seemed important to provide a reasonable degree of guidance. I fear that British readers may find some of the notes annoyingly obvious, but trust they will bear in mind that many of the references will not be easily understood by readers elsewhere.

NOTES

1 Particularly important are an essay by Gerald Weales called 'The Edwardian Theatre and the Shadow of Shaw' in *Edwardians and Late Victorians*, ed. Richard Ellmann (New York: Columbia Univ. Press, 1960); and Margery Morgan's *A Drama of Political Man* (London: Sidgwick & Jackson, 1961), which remains a most sensitive reading of the plays.

2 Agate, *A Short View of the English Stage* (London: H. Jenkins, 1926), 86; Nicoll, *English Drama 1900–1930* (Cambridge: Cambridge Univ. Press, 1973), 393–6; Taylor, *Revels History of Drama in English*, gen. ed. T. W. Craik (London: Methuen, 1978), 7:194.

3 Purdom, *Harley Granville Barker* (London: Barrie & Rockliff, 1955), 285. The quotation from Casson is on p. viii.

4 *Granville Barker: A Secret Life* (London: Heinemann, 1983), and Salmon's edition of letters, *Granville Barker and His Correspondents* (Detroit: Wayne State Univ. Press, 1986). On Barker's work as a director, manager, and active playwright, see Dennis Kennedy, *Granville Barker and the Dream of Theatre* (Cambridge: Cambridge Univ. Press, 1985).

5 *Granville Barker and His Correspondents*, 499–500.

6 *The Rise and Fall of the Well-Made Play* (London: Methuen, 1967), 114–15.

7 Morgan, 41.

8 Shaw, *Our Theatres in the Nineties* (London: Constable, 1931), 1:20; GB, 'The Theatre: The Next Phase', *English Review* 5 (1910): 631.

9 *Bernard Shaw's Letters to Granville Barker*, ed. C. B. Purdom (London: Phoenix House, 1956), 8.

10   See Dennis Kennedy, 'Granville Barker's Sexual Comedy', *Modern Drama* 23 (1980): 75–82.

11   *The Old Drama and the New* (London: Heinemann, 1923), 357–8. Archer's original review appeared in *World* 14 Nov. 1905: 823.

12   *Letters of Arnold Bennett*, ed. James Hepburn (Oxford: Oxford Univ. Press, 1968), 2:324.

13   *Waste* was refused license a second time in 1910, according to the records of the Lord Chamberlain's Office (now in the British Library); it was passed in 1920, though not publicly performed until 1936. *Ghosts* was approved in 1914, and *Mrs Warren's Profession* in 1925.

14   Purdom, 73–4.

15   *The Old Drama and the New*, 360.

16   *Play-Making* (London: Chapman & Hall, 1912), 98.

17   *Collected Letters*, ed. Dan H. Laurence (London: Max Reinhardt, 1985), 3:301.

18   *Granville Barker and His Correspondents*, 87, 96.

19   *Granville Barker and His Correspondents*, 338.

20   *Prefaces to Shakespeare* (Princeton: Princeton Univ. Press, 1946), 1:7.

21   *On Dramatic Method* (London: Sidgwick & Jackson, 1931), 6.

22   Sidgwick and Jackson Papers, Bodleian Library, Oxford.

23   The promptbook is in the British Library (C.116.g.11), and indicates cuts in the first three acts, which were restored for the 1909 publication.

BIOGRAPHICAL RECORD

1877   Harley Granville Barker born in Kensington in London, 25 November, son of Albert James Barker and Mary Elizabeth Bozzi-Granville (stage name Miss Granville).

1891   First appearance on stage, with a juvenile company at Harrogate. Trained at Sarah Thorne's theatre school in Margate.

1892   Small parts on the London stage.

1894   Understudy in Florence Farr's season at Avenue Theatre, when Shaw's *Arms and the Man* was first performed.

1895   On tour with Ben Greet's Shakespeare troupe; played Paris to Juliet of Lillah McCarthy. Began playwriting collaboration with Berte Thomas: three unpublished plays have survived.

1899   Member of Mrs Patrick Campbell's company in London. *The Weather-Hen*, a comedy by GB and Berte Thomas, produced at Terry's Theatre. Played Richard II for William Poel. Wrote *The Marrying of Ann Leete*, his first solo play.

1900   Active in Stage Society, founded the previous year: played important roles in Ibsen, Hauptmann, Shaw's *Candida* and *Captain Brassbound's Conversion*; directed bill of poetic one-acts in April.

1901   Directed Zangwill's *The Revolted Daughter*. Directed and played Napoleon in Shaw's *The Man of Destiny*. Joined Fabian Society.

1902   Played Frank in Shaw's *Mrs Warren's Profession*, and directed *The Marrying of Ann Leete*, both for Stage Society in January.

1903   Directed S. M. Fox's *The Waters of Bitterness* and Shaw's *The Admirable Bashville* for Stage Society. Played Marlowe's Edward II for William Poel at Oxford.

1903–5   Wrote *The Voysey Inheritance*.

1904   With William Archer wrote *Scheme and Estimates for a National Theatre* (privately circulated, in hope of a donor). Directed *The Two Gentlemen of Verona* and *Candida* at Court Theatre for J. H. Leigh, Gilbert Murray's translation of *Hippolytus* at Lyric Theatre for New Century Theatre, and Yeats' *Where There Is Nothing* at Court for Stage Society, among others. Wrote *Prunella* with Laurence Housman.

1904–7   Vedrenne–Barker management at Court Theatre. In three seasons presented 32 plays by 17 authors for 988 performances: the 'Thousand Performances'. Many were new works; 701 of the performances were of 11 plays by Shaw, including first performances

28

of *John Bull's Other Island, Man and Superman, Major Barbara, The Doctor's Dilemma,* and *Don Juan in Hell.* Other dramatists included Euripides, Ibsen, Maeterlinck, Galsworthy, St John Hankin, and GB himself (*The Voysey Inheritance* and *Prunella*). GB co-directed the Shaw plays and acted in most of them, and directed all the other works.

1906   Married Lillah McCarthy. Began writing *Waste.*

1907   Short-lived extension of Vedrenne–Barker management at Savoy Theatre in autumn. *Waste* banned; privately presented by Stage Society in November, directed by GB. *A National Theatre: Scheme and Estimates* published.

1908   First visit to U.S. Vedrenne–Barker productions on tour. Nearly died of typhoid fever in Dublin; started *The Madras House* while recuperating.

1909   Directed Galsworthy's *Strife* at Duke of York's Theatre. Gave evidence to Parliamentary Committee on stage censorship.

1910   Chief force behind a brief experiment in repertory at Duke of York's, sponsored by Charles Frohman. Directed *The Madras House* and Galsworthy's *Justice* among others; Shaw directed *Misalliance.* Visit to Germany and Max Reinhardt.

1911   Beginning of Lillah McCarthy–Granville Barker management at Little Theatre, where a number of modern plays were given under GB's direction; Shaw wrote and directed *Fanny's First Play* for the occasion, and it settled in for a long run.

1912   Management moved to Kingsway Theatre, where GB directed *Iphigenia in Tauris, The Voysey Inheritance,* and Galsworthy's *The Eldest Son.* Revolutionary productions by GB of *The Winter's Tale* and *Twelfth Night* at Savoy in autumn.

1913   Directed Arnold Bennett's *The Great Adventure* at the Kingsway, GB's only big popular success. St James's Theatre taken by management, first for Shaw's *Androcles and the Lion,* then for another short repertory venture, all plays directed by GB.

1914   Directed *A Midsummer Night's Dream* at Savoy. Visit to Moscow Art Theatre and Stanislavsky. Directed his own adaptation of Hardy's *The Dynasts* at Kingsway after outbreak of war.

1915   Season of repertory at Wallack's Theatre, New York, including two Shaw works and a remounting of *A Midsummer Night's Dream.* Start of attachment to Helen Gates Huntington, wife of railroad heir Archer Huntington. Open-air productions of *Iphigenia in Tauris* and *The Trojan Women* at eastern universities in U.S. Decided to abandon active work in the theatre. To France to write book on the work of the Red Cross. Returned to U.S. to lecture.

1916   Asked Lillah McCarthy for divorce. Wrote one-act *Farewell to the*

Theatre and some fiction. Returned to England and enlisted; eventually granted a commission in Army Intelligence.

1917 Back in U.S. Divorce granted. Helen Huntington applied for divorce in France.

1918 Married Helen in London. Archer Huntington unexpectedly provided a large settlement.

1919 Bought country estate in Devon. First Chairman of Council of new British Drama League. Devoted himself to full-time writing.

1920 Began translating French plays, and began series of translations of modern Spanish plays with Helen (see list of plays at end of this volume). Started to use hyphenated form of name.

1921 Directed Maeterlinck's *The Betrothal* at Gaiety Theatre.

1922 *The Exemplary Theatre* published.

1923 *The Secret Life* published, GB's first full-length original play since *The Madras House* in 1910. First volumes of *The Players' Shakespeare*, with introductions by GB, which continued through 1927.

1925 British academy lecture, 'From Henry V to Hamlet'. Directed revised version of *The Madras House* at Ambassador's Theatre.

1927 First series of *Prefaces to Shakespeare*.

1928 *His Majesty* published, his last play.

1929 President of Royal Society of Literature; edited *The Eighteen-Seventies* for RSL.

1930 *A National Theatre* published, thorough reworking of book written with Archer in 1904. Second Series of *Prefaces to Shakespeare*. Clark lectures at Cambridge (*On Dramatic Method*).

1931 Moved to Paris. Address to Shakespeare Association (*Associating with Shakespeare*).

1934 *A Companion to Shakespeare Studies*, edited by GB and G. B. Harrison. With Harcourt Williams, directed revised version of *The Voysey Inheritance* at Sadler's Wells Theatre. *The Study of Drama* published.

1936 With Michael MacOwan, directed revised version of *Waste* at Westminster Theatre, its first public performance.

1937 Director of British Institute in Paris. Third series of *Prefaces to Shakespeare*. Romanes Lecture at Oxford (*On Poetry in Drama*).

1940 Assisted Lewis Casson in production of *King Lear* at Old Vic, with John Gielgud in lead. Escaped Paris just before German Occupation for Lisbon and U.S. Worked for British Information Services in New York until 1942 and continued writing on Shakespeare.

1942 Lectured at Toronto on Shakespeare.

1943 Visiting lecturer at Harvard.

1944 Lectured at Princeton (*The Use of the Drama*).
1945 Returned to England at end of war. Fourth series of *Prefaces to Shakespeare* (fifth series published posthumously in 1947).
1946 Returned to Paris. Died of arteriosclerosis on 31 August, aged 68. Buried in cemetery of Père Lachaise.

THE MARRYING OF ANN LEETE

Written 1899

First performed by the Stage Society (a private performance) at the Royalty Theatre on 26 January 1902, with the following cast:

ANN LEETE	Winifred Fraser
LORD JOHN CARP	Julian Royce
GEORGE LEETE (Ann's brother)	Kenneth Douglas
DANIEL TATTON	J. Malcolm Dunn
LADY SARAH COTTESHAM (Ann's sister)	Henrietta Watson
CARNABY LEETE (Ann's father)	H. A. Saintsbury
JOHN ABUD	C. M. Hallard
REV. DR REMNANT	Howard Sturge
MRS OPIE	Helen Rous
DIMMUCK	George Trollope
MR TETGEEN	A. E. George
LORD ARTHUR CARP (Lord John's brother)	Charles V. France
MR SMALLPEICE	J. Y. F. Cooke
SIR GEORGE LEETE (Carnaby's father)	Arthur Grenville
MR CROWE	Sydney Paxton
LADY LEETE (Carnaby's mother)	Bessie Page
DOLLY (George's wife)	Florence Neville
REV. MR TOZER	Ivan Berlin
MR PRESTIGE	Howard Templeton
MRS PRESTIGE	Mrs Gordon Gray

Directed by Granville Barker.

ACT I

The first three acts of the comedy pass in the garden at Markswayde, MR CARNABY
LEETE'S *house near Reading, during a summer day toward the close of the
eighteenth century: the first act at four in the morning, the second shortly after
mid-day, the third near to sunset. The fourth act takes place one day in the following
winter; the first scene in the hall at Markswayde, the second scene in a cottage some
ten miles off.*

    *This part of the Markswayde garden looks to have been laid out during the
seventeenth century. In the middle a fountain; the centrepeice the figure of a nymph,
now somewhat cracked, and pouring nothing from the amphora; the rim of the
fountain is high enough and broad enough to be a comfortable seat.*

    *The close turf around is in parts worn bare. This plot of ground is surrounded by a
terrace three feet higher. Three sides of it are seen. From two corners broad steps lead
down; stone urns stand at the bottom and top of the stone balustrades. The other two
corners are rounded convexly into broad stone seats.*

    *Along the edges of the terrace are growing rose trees, close together; behind these,
paths; behind those, shrubs and trees. No landscape is to be seen. A big copper beech
overshadows the seat on the left. A silver birch droops over the seat on the right. The
trees far to the left indicate an orchard, the few to the right are more of the garden
sort. It is the height of summer, and after a long drought the rose trees are dilapidated.*

    *It is very dark in the garden. Though there may be by now a faint morning light in
the sky it has not penetrated yet among these trees. It is very still, too. Now and then
the leaves of a tree are stirred, as if in its sleep; that is all. Suddenly a shrill,
frightened, but not tragical scream is heard. After a moment* ANN LEETE *runs
quickly down the steps and on to the fountain, where she stops, panting.* LORD
JOHN CARP *follows her, but only to the top of the steps, evidently not knowing his
way.* ANN *is a girl of twenty; he an English gentleman, nearer forty than thirty.*

LORD JOHN: I apologise.
ANN: Why is it so dark?
LORD JOHN: Can you hear what I'm saying?
ANN: Yes.
LORD JOHN: I apologise for having kissed you .. almost unintentionally.
ANN: Thank you. Mind the steps down.
LORD JOHN: I hope I'm sober, but the air ..
ANN: Shall we sit for a minute? There are several seats to sit on somewhere.
LORD JOHN: This is a very dark garden.
        (*There is a slight pause.*)
ANN: You've won your bet.
LORD JOHN: So you did scream!
ANN: But it wasn't fair.
LORD JOHN: Don't reproach me.
ANN: Somebody's coming.
LORD JOHN: How d'you know?
ANN: I can *hear* somebody coming.
LORD JOHN: We're not sitting down.

(ANN'S *brother,* GEORGE LEETE, *comes to the top of the steps, and afterwards down them. Rather an old young man.*)

GEORGE: Ann!

ANN: Yes.

GEORGE: My lord!

LORD JOHN: Here.

GEORGE: I can't see you. I'm sent to say we're all anxious to know what ghost or other bird of night or beast has frightened Ann to screaming point, and won you .. the best in Tatton's stables – so he says now. He's quite annoyed.

LORD JOHN: The mare is a very good mare.

ANN: He betted it because he wanted to bet it; I didn't want him to bet it.

GEORGE: What frightened her?

ANN: I had rather, my lord, that you did not tell my brother why I screamed.

LORD JOHN: I kissed her.

GEORGE: Did you?

ANN: I had rather, Lord John, that you had not told my brother why I screamed.

LORD JOHN: I misunderstood you.

GEORGE: I've broke up the whist party. Ann, shall we return?

LORD JOHN: She's not here.

GEORGE: Ann?

(LADY COTTESHAM, ANN'S *sister and ten years older, and* MR DANIEL TATTON, *a well-living, middle-aged country gentleman, arrive together.* TATTON *carries a double candlestick .. the lights out.*)

TATTON: Three steps?

SARAH: No .. four.

LORD JOHN: Miss Leete.

(TATTON *in the darkness finds himself close to* GEORGE.)

TATTON: I am in a rage with you, my lord.

GEORGE: He lives next door.

TATTON: My mistake. (*He passes on.*) Confess that she did it to please you.

LORD JOHN: Screamed!

TATTON: Lost my bet. We'll say .. won your bet .. to please you. Was skeered at the dark .. oh, fie!

LORD JOHN: Miss Leete trod on a toad.

TATTON: I barred toads .. here.

LORD JOHN: I don't think it.

TATTON: I barred toads. Did I forget to? Well .. it's better to be a sportsman.

SARAH: And whereabout is she?

ANN: (*from the corner she has slunk to*) Here I am, Sally.

TATTON: Miss Ann, I forgive you. I'm smiling, I assure you, I'm smiling.

SARAH: We all laughed when we heard you.

TATTON: Which reminds me, young George Leete, had you the ace?

GEORGE: King .. knave .. here are the cards, but I can't see.

TATTON: I had the king.

ANN: (*quietly to her sister*) He kissed me.

SARAH: A man would.

GEORGE: What were trumps?

TATTON: What were we playing .. cricket?

ANN: (*as quietly again*) D'you think I'm blushing?

SARAH: It's probable.

ANN: I am by the feel of me.

SARAH: George, we left Papa sitting quite still.

LORD JOHN: Didn't he approve of the bet?

TATTON: He said nothing.

SARAH: Why, who doesn't love sport!

TATTON: I'm the man to grumble. Back a woman's pluck again .. never. My lord
.. you weren't the one to go with her as umpire.

GEORGE: No .. to be sure.

TATTON: How was it I let that pass? Playing two games at once. Haven't I cause of
complaint? But a man must give and take.

> (*The master of the house, father of* GEORGE *and* SARAH
> COTTESHAM *and* ANN, MR CARNABY LEETE, *comes slowly
> down the steps, unnoticed by the others. A man over fifty – à la Lord
> Chesterfield.*)

GEORGE: (*to* LORD JOHN) Are you sure you're quite comfortable there?

LORD JOHN: Whatever I'm sitting on hasn't given way yet.

TATTON: Don't forget that you're riding to Brighton with me.

LORD JOHN: Tomorrow.

GEORGE: Today. Well .. the hour before sunrise is no time at all.

TATTON: Sixty-five miles.

LORD JOHN: What are we all sitting here for?

TATTON: I say people ought to be in bed and asleep.

CARNABY: But the morning air is delightful.

TATTON: (*jumping at the new voice*) Leete! Now, had you the ace?

CARNABY: Of course.

TATTON: We should have lost that too, Lady Charlie.

SARAH: Bear up, Mr Tat.

TATTON: Come, a game of whist is a game of whist.

CARNABY: And so I strolled out after you all.

TATTON: She trod on a toad.

CARNABY: (*carelessly*) Does she say so?

TATTON: (*with mock roguishness*) Ah!

> (GEORGE *is on the terrace, looking to the left through the trees.*
> TATTON *is sitting on the edge of the fountain.*)

GEORGE: Here's the sun .. to show us ourselves.

TATTON: Leete, this pond is full of water!

CARNABY: Ann, if you are there ..

ANN: Yes, Papa.

CARNABY: Apologise profusely; it's your garden.

ANN: Oh ..

CARNABY: Coat-tails, Tatton .. or worse?

TATTON: (*ruefully discovering damp spots about him*) Nothing vastly to matter.

LORD JOHN: Hardy, well-preserved, country gentleman!

TATTON: I bet I'm a younger man than you, my lord.

ANN: (*suddenly to the company generally*) I didn't tread upon any toad .. I was kissed.

> (*There is a pause of some discomfort.*)

SARAH: Ann, come here to me.

LORD JOHN: I apologised.

GEORGE: (*from the terrace*) Are we to be insulted?

CARNABY: My dear Carp, say no more.

> (*There is another short pause. By this it is twilight, faces can be plainly seen.*)

SARAH: Listen .. the first bird.

TATTON: Oh, dear no, they begin to sing long before this.

CARNABY: What is it now .. a lark?

TATTON: I don't know.

ANN: (*quietly to* SARAH) That's a thrush.

SARAH: (*capping her*) A thrush.

CARNABY: Charming!

TATTON: (*to* LORD JOHN) I don't see why you couldn't have told me how it was that she screamed.

CARNABY: Our dear Tatton! (*sotto voce to his son*) Hold your tongue, George.

TATTON: I did bar toads and you said I didn't, and anyway I had a sort of right to know.

LORD JOHN: You know now.

SARAH: I wonder if this seat is dry.

LORD JOHN: There's been no rain for weeks.

SARAH: The roads will be dusty for you, Mr Tat.

TATTON: Just one moment. You don't mind me, Miss Ann, do you?

ANN: I don't mind much.

TATTON: We said distinctly .. To the orchard end of the garden and back and if frightened – that's the word – so much as to scream .. ! Now, what I want to know is ..

LORD JOHN: Consider the bet off.

TATTON: Certainly not. And we should have added .. Alone.

CARNABY: Tatton has persistence.

SARAH: Mr Tat, do you know where people go who take things seriously?

TATTON: Miss Leete, were you frightened when Lord John kissed you?

GEORGE: Damnation!

CARNABY: My excellent Tatton, much as I admire your searchings after truth I must here parentally intervene, regretting, my dear Tatton, that my own carelessness of duennahood has permitted this – this .. to occur.

> (*After this, there is silence for a minute.*)

LORD JOHN: Can I borrow a horse of you, Mr Leete?

CARNABY: My entire stable; and your Ronald shall be physicked.

SARAH: Spartans that you are to be riding!

LORD JOHN: I prefer it to a jolting chaise.

TATTON: You will have my mare.

LORD JOHN: (*ignoring him*) This has been a most enjoyable three weeks.

CARNABY: Four.

LORD JOHN: Is it four?

CARNABY: We bow to the compliment. Our duty to his grace.

LORD JOHN: When I see him.

GEORGE: To our dear cousin.

TATTON: (*to* LADY COTTESHAM) Sir Charles at Brighton?

SARAH: (*not answering*) To be sure . . we did discover . . our mother was second cousin . . once removed to you.

CARNABY: If the prince will be there . . he is in waiting.

LORD JOHN: Any message, Lady Cottesham? . . since we speak out of session.

SARAH: I won't trust you.

CARNABY: Or trouble you while I still may frank a letter. But my son-in-law is a wretched correspondent. Do you admire men of small vices? They make admirable husbands though their wives will be grumbling – silence, Sarah – but that's a good sign.

SARAH: Papa is a connoisseur of humanity.

ANN: (*to the company as before*) No, Mr Tatton, I wasn't frightened when Lord John . . kissed me. I screamed because I was surprised, and I'm sorry I screamed.

SARAH: (*quietly to* ANN) My dear Ann, you're a fool.

ANN: (*quietly to* SARAH) I will speak sometimes.

SARAH: Sit down again.

      (*Again an uncomfortable silence, a ludicrous air about it this time.*)

TATTON: Now, we'll say no more about that bet, but I was right.

LORD JOHN: Do you know, Mr Tatton, that I have a temper to lose?

TATTON: What the devil does that matter to me, sir . . my lord?

LORD JOHN: I owe you a saddle and bridle.

TATTON: You'll oblige me by taking the mare.

LORD JOHN: We'll discuss it tomorrow.

TATTON: I've said all I have to say.

GEORGE: The whole matter's ridiculous!

TATTON: I see the joke. Good night, Lady Cottesham, and I kiss your hand.

SARAH: Good morning, Mr Tat.

TATTON: Good morning, Miss Ann, I . .

SARAH: (*shielding her sister*) Good morrow is appropriate.

TATTON: I'll go by the fields. (*to* CARNABY) Thank you for a pleasant evening. Good morrow, George. Do we start at mid-day, my lord?

LORD JOHN: Any time you please.

TATTON: Not at all. (*He hands the candlestick – of which he has never before left go – to* GEORGE.) I brought this for a link. Thank you.

CARNABY: Mid-day will be midnight if you sleep at all now; make it two or later.

---

prince: the Prince of Wales, who became Regent in 1811 and King George IV in 1820.
frank: to mark the cover of a letter with his signature, exercising the Parliamentary postal privilege.
link: a torch.

TATTON: We put up at Guildford. I've done so before. I haven't my hat. It's a day and a half's ride.

> (TATTON *goes quickly up the other steps and away. It is now quite light.* GEORGE *stands by the steps,* LORD JOHN *is on one of the seats,* CARNABY *strolls round, now and then touching the rose trees,* SARAH *and* ANN *are on the other seat.*)

GEORGE: Morning! These candles still smell.

SARAH: How lively one feels and isn't.

CARNABY: The flowers are opening.

ANN: (*in a whisper*) Couldn't we go in?

SARAH: Never run away.

ANN: Everything looks so odd.

SARAH: What's o'clock .. my lord?

LORD JOHN: Half after four.

ANN: (*to* SARAH) My eyes are hot behind.

GEORGE: What ghosts we seem!

SARAH: What has made us spend such a night?

CARNABY: Ann incited me to it. (*He takes snuff.*)

SARAH: In a spirit of rebellion against good country habits ..

ANN: (*to her sister again*) Don't talk about me.

SARAH: They can see that you're whispering.

CARNABY: .. Informing me now she was a woman and wanted excitement.

GEORGE: There's a curse.

CARNABY: How else d'ye conceive life for women?

SARAH: George is naturally cruel. Excitement's our education. Please vary it, though.

CARNABY: I have always held that to colour in the world-picture is the greatest privilege of the husband. Sarah.

SARAH: (*not leaving* ANN'S *side*) Yes, Papa.

CARNABY: Sarah, when Sir Charles leaves Brighton ..

> (SARAH *rises but will not move further.*)

CARNABY: (*sweetly threatening*) Shall I come to you?

> (*But she goes to him now.*)

CARNABY: By a gossip letter from town ..

SARAH: (*tensely*) What is it?

CARNABY: You mentioned to me something of his visiting Naples.

SARAH: Very well. I detest Italy.

CARNABY: Let's have George's opinion.

> (*He leads her toward* GEORGE.)

GEORGE: Yes?

CARNABY: Upon Naples.

GEORGE: I remember Naples.

CARNABY: Sarah, admire those roses.

SARAH: (*cynically echoing her father*) Let's have George's opinion.

> (*Now* CARNABY *has drawn them both away, upon the terrace, and, the coast being clear,* LORD JOHN *walks towards* ANN, *who looks at him very scaredly.*)

CARNABY: Emblem of secrecy among the ancients.
SARAH: Look at this heavy head, won't it snap off?
      (*The three move out of sight.*)
LORD JOHN: I'm sober now.
ANN: I'm not.
LORD JOHN: Uncompromising young lady.
ANN: And, excuse me, I don't want to .. play.
LORD JOHN: Don't you wish me to apologise quietly, to you?
ANN: Good manners are all mockery, I'm sure.
LORD JOHN: I'm very much afraid you're a cynic.
ANN: I'm not trying to be clever.
LORD JOHN: Do I tease you?
ANN: Do I amuse you?
LORD JOHN: How dare I say so!
ANN: (*after a moment*) I was not frightened.
LORD JOHN: You kissed me back.
ANN: Not on purpose. What do two people mean by behaving so .. in the dark?
LORD JOHN: I am exceedingly sorry that I hurt your feelings.
ANN: Thank you, I like to feel.
LORD JOHN: And you must forgive me.
ANN: Tell me, why did you do it?
LORD JOHN: Honestly I don't know. I should do it again.
ANN: That's not quite true, is it?
LORD JOHN: I think so.
ANN: What does it matter at all!
LORD JOHN: Nothing.
      (GEORGE, SARAH *and then* CARNABY *move into sight and
      along the terrace,* LORD JOHN *turns to them.*)
LORD JOHN: Has this place been long in your family, Mr Leete?
CARNABY: Markswayde my wife brought us, through the Peters's .. old Chiltern
    people .. connections of yours, of course. There is no entail.
      (LORD JOHN *walks back to* ANN.)
SARAH: George, you assume this republicanism as you would – no, would not – a
    coat of latest cut.
CARNABY: Never argue with him .. persist.
SARAH: So does he.
      (*The three pass along the terrace.*)
ANN: (*to* LORD JOHN) Will you sit down?
LORD JOHN: It's not worth while. Do you know I must be twice your age?
ANN: A doubled responsibility, my lord.
LORD JOHN: I suppose it is.
ANN: I don't say so. That's a phrase from a book .. sounded well.
LORD JOHN: My dear Miss Ann .. (*He stops.*)
ANN: Go on being polite.

---

entail: limit on the inheritance of property to a specified and unalterable succession of heirs.
republicanism: see Introduction, p. 9.

LORD JOHN: If you'll keep your head turned away.

ANN: Why must I?

LORD JOHN: There's lightning in the glances of your eye.

ANN: Do use vulgar words to me.

LORD JOHN: (*with a sudden fatherly kindness*) Go to bed .. you're dead tired. And good-bye .. I'll be gone before you wake.

ANN: Good-bye.

> (*She shakes hands with him, then walks towards her father who is coming down the steps.*)

ANN: Papa, don't my roses want looking to?

CARNABY: (*pats her cheek*) These?

ANN: Those.

CARNABY: Abud is under your thumb, horticulturally speaking.

ANN: Where's Sally?

> (*She goes on to* SARAH, *who is standing with* GEORGE *at the top of the steps.* CARNABY *looks* LORD JOHN *up and down.*)

LORD JOHN: (*dusting his shoulder*) This cursed powder!

CARNABY: Do we respect innocence enough .. any of us?

> (GEORGE *comes down the steps and joins them.*)

GEORGE: Respectable politics will henceforth be useless to me.

CARNABY: My lord, was his grace satisfied with the young man's work abroad or was he not?

LORD JOHN: My father used to curse everyone.

CARNABY: That's a mere Downing Street custom.

LORD JOHN: And I seem to remember that a letter of yours from .. where were you in those days?

GEORGE: Paris .. Naples .. Vienna.

LORD JOHN: One place .. once lightened a fit of gout.

CARNABY: George, you have in you the makings of a minister.

GEORGE: No.

CARNABY: Remember the Age tends to the disreputable.

> (GEORGE *moves away,* SARAH *moves towards them.*)

CARNABY: George is something of a genius, stuffed with theories and possessed of a curious conscience. But I am fortunate in my children.

LORD JOHN: All the world knows it.

CARNABY: (*to* SARAH) It's lucky that yours was a love match, too. I admire you. Ann is 'to come,' so to speak.

SARAH: (*to* LORD JOHN) Were you discussing affairs?

LORD JOHN: Not I.

GEORGE: Ann.

ANN: Yes, George.

> (*She goes to him; they stroll together up the steps and along the terrace.*)

SARAH: I'm desperately fagged.

---

vulgar words: common or vernacular expressions.
powder: from his hair.

LORD JOHN: (*politely*) A seat.

SARAH: Also tired of sitting.

CARNABY: Let's have the Brighton news, Carp.

LORD JOHN: If there's any.

CARNABY: Probably I still command abuse. Even my son-in-law must, by courtesy, join in the cry .. ah, poor duty-torn Sarah! You can spread abroad that I am as a green bay tree.

(CARNABY *paces slowly away from them.*)

LORD JOHN: Your father's making a mistake.

SARAH: D'you think so?

LORD JOHN: He's played the game once.

SARAH: I was not then in the knowledge of things when he left you.

LORD JOHN: We remember it.

SARAH: I should like to hear it.

LORD JOHN: I have avoided this subject.

SARAH: With him, yes.

LORD JOHN: Oh! .. why did I desert the army for politics?

SARAH: Better fighting.

LORD JOHN: It sat so nobly upon him .. the leaving us for conscience sake when we were strongly in power. Strange that six months later we should be turned out.

SARAH: Papa was lucky.

LORD JOHN: But this second time .. ?

SARAH: Listen. This is very much a private quarrel with Mr Pitt, who hates Papa .. gets rid of him.

LORD JOHN: Shall I betray a confidence?

SARAH: Better not.

LORD JOHN: My father advised me to this visit.

SARAH: Your useful visit. More than kind of his grace.

LORD JOHN: Yes .. there's been a paragraph in the *Morning Chronicle*, 'The Whigs woo Mr Carnaby Leete.'

SARAH: We saw to it.

LORD JOHN: My poor father seems anxious to discover whether the Leete episode will repeat itself entirely. He is chronically unhappy in opposition. Are your husband and his colleagues trembling in their seats?

SARAH: I can't say.

LORD JOHN: Politics is a game for clever children, and women, and fools. Will you take a word of warning from a soldier? Your father is past his prime.

(CARNABY *paces back towards them.*)

CARNABY: I'm getting to be old for these all-night sittings. I must be writing to your busy brother.

Mr Pitt: William Pitt the Younger, Tory Prime Minister under George III, 1783–1801 and 1804–6.
Morning Chronicle: leading political journal until 1803, when *The Times* assumed more importance.
Whigs: political party representative of middle-class trade interests and constitutional monarchy, opposing the Tories.

LORD JOHN: Arthur? . . is at his home.

SARAH: Pleasantly sounding phrase.

CARNABY: His grace deserted?

SARAH: Quite secretaryless!

LORD JOHN: Lady Arthur lately has been brought to bed. I heard yesterday.

SARAH: The seventh, is it not? Children require living up to. My congratulations.

LORD JOHN: Won't you write them?

SARAH: We are not intimate.

LORD JOHN: A good woman.

SARAH: Evidently. Where's Ann? We'll go in.

LORD JOHN: You're a mother to your sister.

SARAH: Not I.

CARNABY: My wife went her ways into the next world; Sarah hers into this; and our little Ann was left with a most admirable governess. One must never reproach circumstances. Man educates woman in his own good time.

LORD JOHN: I suppose she, or any young girl, is all heart.

CARNABY: What is it that you call heart . . sentimentally speaking?

SARAH: Any bud in the morning.

LORD JOHN: That man Tatton's jokes are in shocking taste.

CARNABY: Tatton is honest.

LORD JOHN: I'm much to blame for having won that bet.

CARNABY: Say no more.

LORD JOHN: What can Miss Ann think of me?

SARAH: Don't ask her.

CARNABY: Innocency's opinions are invariably entertaining.

LORD JOHN: Am I the first . . ? I really beg your pardon.

(GEORGE *and* ANN *come down the steps together.*)

CARNABY: Ann, what do you think . . that is to say – and answer me truthfully . . what at this moment is your inclination of mind towards my lord here?

ANN: I suppose I love him.

LORD JOHN: I hope not.

ANN: I suppose I love you.

CARNABY: No . . no . . no . . no . . no . . no . . no.

SARAH: Hush, dear.

ANN: I'm afraid, Papa, there's something very ill-bred in me.

(*Down the steps and into the midst of them comes* JOHN ABUD, *carrying his tools, among other things a twist of bass. A young gardener, honest, clean and common.*)

ABUD: (*to* CARNABY) I ask pardon, sir.

CARNABY: So early, Abud! . . this is your territory. So late . . Bed.

(ANN *starts away up the steps,* SARAH *is following her.*)

LORD JOHN: Good-bye, Lady Cottesham.

(*At this* ANN *stops for a moment, but then goes straight on.*)

SARAH: A pleasant journey.

(SARAH *departs too.*)

---

twist of bass: bunch of split rush or straw used for tying up garden plants.

GEORGE: (*stretching himself*) I'm roused.

CARNABY: (*to* ABUD) Leave your tools here for a few moments.

ABUD: I will sir.

>（ABUD *leaves them, going along the terrace and out of sight.*)

CARNABY: My head is hot. Pardon me.

>（CARNABY *is sitting on the fountain rim; he dips his handkerchief in the water, and wrings it; then takes off his wig and binds the damp handkerchief round his head.*)

CARNABY: Wigs are most comfortable and old fashioned . . unless you choose to be a cropped republican like my son.

GEORGE: Nature!

CARNABY: Nature grows a beard, sir.

LORD JOHN: I've seen Turks.

CARNABY: Horrible . . horrible! Sit down, Carp.

>（LORD JOHN *sits on the fountain rim,* GEORGE *begins to pace restlessly; he has been nursing the candlestick ever since* TATTON *handed it to him.*)

CARNABY: George, you look damned ridiculous strutting arm-in-arm with that candlestick.

GEORGE: I am ridiculous.

CARNABY: If you're cogitating over your wife and her expectations . .

>（GEORGE *paces up the steps and away. There is a pause.*)

CARNABY: D'ye tell stories . . good ones?

LORD JOHN: Sometimes.

CARNABY: There'll be this.

LORD JOHN: I shan't.

CARNABY: Say no more. If I may so express myself, Carp, you have been taking us for granted.

LORD JOHN: How wide awake you are! I'm not.

CARNABY: My head's cool. Shall I describe your conduct as an unpremeditated insult?

LORD JOHN: Don't think anything of the sort.

CARNABY: There speaks your kind heart.

LORD JOHN: Are you trying to pick a quarrel with me?

CARNABY: As may be.

LORD JOHN: Why?

CARNABY: For the sake of appearances.

LORD JOHN: Damn all appearances.

CARNABY: Now I'll lose my temper. Sir, you have compromised my daughter.

LORD JOHN: Nonsense!

CARNABY: Villain! What's your next move?

>(*For a moment* LORD JOHN *sits with knit brows.*)

LORD JOHN: (*brutally*) Mr Leete, your name stinks.

CARNABY: My point of dis-ad-vantage!

---

cropped republican: see Introduction, p. 9, and Appendix A.

LORD JOHN: (*apologising*) Please say what you like. I might have put my remark better.

CARNABY: I think not; the homely Saxon phrase is our literary dagger. Princelike, you ride away from Markswayde. Can I trust you not to stab a socially sick man? Why it's a duty you owe to society .. to weed out .. us.

LORD JOHN: I'm not a coward. How?

CARNABY: A little laughter .. in your exuberance of health.

LORD JOHN: You may trust me not to tell tales.

CARNABY: Of what .. of whom?

LORD JOHN: Of here.

CARNABY: And what is there to tell of here?

LORD JOHN: Nothing.

CARNABY: But how your promise betrays a capacity for good-natured invention!

LORD JOHN: If I lie call me out.

CARNABY: I don't deal in sentiment. I can't afford to be talked about otherwise than as I choose to be. Already the Aunt Sally of the hour; having under pressure of circumstances resigned my office; dating my letters from the borders of the Chiltern Hundreds .. I am a poor politician, sir, and I must live.

LORD JOHN: I can't see that your family's infected .. affected.

CARNABY: With a penniless girl you really should have been more circumspect.

LORD JOHN: I might ask to marry her.

CARNABY: My lord!

> (*In the pause that ensues he takes up the twist of bass to play with.*)

LORD JOHN: What should you say to that?

CARNABY: The silly child supposed she loved you.

LORD JOHN: Yes.

CARNABY: Is it a match?

LORD JOHN: (*full in the other's face*) What about the appearances of black-mail?

CARNABY: (*compressing his thin lips*) Do you care for my daughter?

LORD JOHN: I could .. at a pinch.

CARNABY: Now, my lord, you are insolent.

LORD JOHN: Is this when we quarrel?

CARNABY: I think I'll challenge you.

LORD JOHN: That will look well.

CARNABY: You'll value that kiss when you've paid for it. Kindly choose Tatton as your second. I want his tongue to wag both ways.

LORD JOHN: I was forgetting how it all began.

CARNABY: George will serve me .. protesting. His principles are vile, but he has the education of a gentleman. Swords or .. ? Swords. And at noon shall we say? There's shade behind a certain barn, midway between this and Tatton's.

Aunt Sally: a fairground game in which players throw sticks at a figure of a woman's head, trying to break the pipe in her mouth. Carnaby means that he is the current target of all political attacks.

Chiltern Hundreds: eight 'hundreds' (subdivisions of a county having their own court) in Oxfordshire and Buckinghamshire that contain the Chiltern Hills; the play is set near them. There may also be an oblique reference here to the Stewardship of the Chiltern Hundreds, a nominal office that provides the traditional means of resigning a Parliamentary seat. But though Carnaby has given up his ministry, he has not resigned his seat in the Commons.

LORD JOHN: (*not taking him seriously yet*) What if we both die horribly?
CARNABY: You are at liberty to make me a written apology.
LORD JOHN: A joke's a joke.
> (CARNABY *deliberately strikes him in the face with the twist of bass.*)
LORD JOHN: That's enough.
CARNABY: (*in explanatory apology*) My friend, you are so obtuse. Abud!
LORD JOHN: Mr Leete, are you serious?
CARNABY: Perfectly serious. Let's go to bed. Abud, you can get to your work.
> (*Wig in hand,* CARNABY *courteously conducts his guest towards the house.* ABUD *returns to his tools and his morning's work.*)

ACT II

Shortly after mid-day, while the sun beats strongly upon the terrace, ABUD *is working dexterously at the rose trees.* DR REMNANT *comes down the steps, hatted and carrying a stick and a book. He is an elderly man with a kind manner; type of the eighteenth century casuistical parson. On his way he stops to say a word to the gardener.*

DR REMNANT: Will it rain before nightfall?
ABUD: About then, sir, I should say.
> (*Down the other steps comes* MRS OPIE, *a prim, decorous, but well bred and unobjectionable woman. She is followed by* ANN.)
MRS OPIE: A good morning to you, Parson.
DR REMNANT: And to you, Mrs Opie, and to Miss Ann.
ANN: Good morning, Dr Remnant. (*to* ABUD) Have you been here ever since . . ?
ABUD: I've had dinner, Miss.
> (ABUD'S *work takes him gradually out of sight.*)
MRS OPIE: We are but just breakfasted.
DR REMNANT: I surmise dissipation.
ANN: (*to* MRS OPIE) Thank you for waiting five hours.
MRS OPIE: It is my rule to breakfast with you.
DR REMNANT: (*exhibiting the book*) I am come to return, and to borrow.
ANN: Show me.
DR REMNANT: Ballads by Robert Burns.
ANN: (*taking it*) I'll put it back.
MRS OPIE: (*taking it from her*) I've never heard of him.
DR REMNANT: Oh, ma'am, a very vulgar poet!
> (GEORGE LEETE *comes quickly down the steps.*)
GEORGE: (*to* REMNANT) How are you?
DR REMNANT: Yours, sir.
GEORGE: Ann.
ANN: Good morning George.
GEORGE: Did you sleep well?
ANN: I always do . . but I dreamt.
GEORGE: I must sit down for a minute. (*nodding*) Mrs Opie.

MRS OPIE: I wish you a good morning, sir.
GEORGE: (*to* ANN) Don't look so solemn.
        (LADY COTTESHAM *comes quickly to the top of the steps.*)
SARAH: Is Papa badly hurt?
ANN: (*jumping up*) Oh, what has happened?
GEORGE: Not badly.
SARAH: He won't see me.
        (*His three children look at each other.*)
DR REMNANT: (*tactfully*) May I go my ways to the library?
SARAH: Please do, Doctor Remnant.
DR REMNANT: I flatly contradicted all that was being said in the village.
SARAH: Thoughtful of you.
DR REMNANT: But tell me nothing.
        (DR REMNANT *bows formally and goes.* GEORGE *is about to*
        speak when SARAH *with a look at* MRS OPIE *says .. *)
SARAH: George, hold your tongue.
MRS OPIE: (*with much hauteur*) I am in the way.
        (*At this moment* DIMMUCK, *an old but unbenevolent-looking butler,*
        comes to the top of the steps.)
DIMMUCK: The master wants Mrs Opie.
MRS OPIE: Thank you.
GEORGE: Your triumph!
        (MRS OPIE *is departing radiant.*)
DIMMUCK: How was I to know you was in the garden?
MRS OPIE: I am sorry to have put you to the trouble of a search, Mr Dimmuck.
DIMMUCK: He's in his room.
        (*And he follows her towards the house.*)
GEORGE: Carp fought with him at twelve o'clock.
        (*The other two cannot speak from amazement.*)
SARAH: No!
GEORGE: Why, they didn't tell me and I didn't ask. Carp was laughing. Tatton
    chuckled .. afterwards.
SARAH: What had he to do?
GEORGE: Carp's second.
SARAH: Unaccountable children!
GEORGE: Feather parade .. throw in .. parry quarte: over the arm .. put by: feint
    .. flanconade and through his arm .. damned easy. The father didn't wince or
    say a word. I bound it up .. the sight of blood makes me sick.
        (*After a moment,* SARAH *turns to* ANN.)
SARAH: Yes, and you've been a silly child.
GEORGE: Ah, give me a woman's guess and the most unlikely reason to account
    for anything!
ANN: I hate that man. I'm glad Papa's not hurt. What about a surgeon?
GEORGE: No, you shall kiss the place well, and there'll be poetic justice done.
SARAH: How did you all part?

---

feather parade .. flanconade: fencing moves.

GEORGE: With bows and without a word.
SARAH: Coming home with him?
GEORGE: Not a word.
SARAH: Papa's very clever; but I'm puzzled.
GEORGE: Something will happen next, no doubt.
ANN: Isn't this done with?
SARAH: So it seems.
ANN: I should like to be told just what the game has been.
GEORGE: Bravo, Ann.
ANN: Tell me the rules .. for next time.
SARAH: It would have been most advantageous for us to have formed an alliance
    with Lord John Carp, who stood here for his father and his father's party ..
    now in opposition.
GEORGE: Look upon yourself – not too seriously – Ann, as the instrument of
    political destiny.
ANN: I'm afraid I take in fresh ideas very slowly. Why has Papa given up the Stamp
    Office?
SARAH: His colleagues wouldn't support him.
ANN: Why was that?
SARAH: They disapproved of what he did.
ANN: Did he do right .. giving it up?
SARAH: Yes.
GEORGE: We hope so. Time will tell. An irreverent quipster once named him
    Carnaby Leech.
SARAH: I know.
GEORGE: I wonder if his true enemies think him wise to have dropped off the
    Stamp Office?
ANN: Has he quarrelled with Sir Charles?
SARAH: Politically.
ANN: Isn't that awkward for you?
SARAH: Not a bit.
GEORGE: Hear a statement that includes our lives. Markswayde goes at his death
    .. see reversionary mortgage. The income's an annuity now. The cash in the
    house will be ours. The debts are paid .. at last.
ANN: And there remains me.
GEORGE: Bad grammar. Meanwhile our father is a tongue, which is worth buying;
    but I don't think he ought to go over to the enemy .. for the second time.
SARAH: One party is as good as another; each works for the same end, I should
    hope.
GEORGE: I won't argue about it.
ANN: I suppose that a woman's profession is marriage.
GEORGE: My lord has departed.
ANN: There'll be others to come. I'm not afraid of being married.

Stamp Office: presumably, the ministry collecting revenue from stamp duties.
reversionary mortgage: a reversion is normally the return of an estate to the grantor after the
grant has expired. Here it seems that Carnaby has mortgaged Markswayde and its income for
ready cash and an annuity; at his death the mortgage-holder will assume ownership.

SARAH: What did Papa want Mrs Opie for?

ANN: There'll be a great many things I shall want to know about men now.

GEORGE: Wisdom cometh with sorrow .. oh, my sister.

SARAH: I believe you two are both about as selfish as you can be.

GEORGE: I'm an egotist .. with attachments.

ANN: Make use of me.

GEORGE: Ann, you marry – when you marry – to please yourself.

ANN: There's much in life that I don't like, Sally.

SARAH: There's much more that you will.

GEORGE: I think we three have never talked together before.

> (ABUD, *who has been in sight on the terrace for a few moments, now comes down the steps.*)

ABUD: May I make so bold, sir, as to ask how is Mrs George Leete?

GEORGE: She was well when I last heard.

ABUD: Thank you, sir.

> (*And he returns to his work.*)

ANN: I wonder will it be a boy or a girl.

GEORGE: Poor weak woman.

SARAH: Be grateful to her.

ANN: A baby is a wonderful thing.

SARAH: Babyhood in the abstract .. beautiful.

ANN: Even kittens ..

> (*She stops, and then in rather childish embarrassment, moves away from them.*)

SARAH: Don't shudder, George.

GEORGE: I have no wish to be a father. Why?

SARAH: It's a vulgar responsibility.

GEORGE: My wayside flower!

SARAH: Why pick it?

GEORGE: Sarah, I love my wife.

SARAH: That's easily said.

GEORGE: She should be here.

SARAH: George, you married to please yourself.

GEORGE: By custom her rank is my own.

SARAH: Does she still drop her aitches?

GEORGE: Dolly ..

SARAH: Pretty name.

GEORGE: Dolly aspires to be one of us.

SARAH: Child-bearing makes these women blowzy.

GEORGE: Oh heaven!

ANN: (*calling to* ABUD *on the terrace*) Finish today, Abud. If it rains..

> (*She stops, seeing* MR TETGEEN *standing at the top of the steps leading from the house. This is an intensely respectable, self-contained-looking lawyer, but a man of the world too.*)

MR TETGEEN: Lady Cottesham.

SARAH: Sir?

MR TETGEEN: My name is Tetgeen.

SARAH: Mr Tetgeen. How do you do?

MR TETGEEN: The household appeared to be in some confusion and I took the liberty to be my own messenger. I am anxious to speak with you.

SARAH: Ann, dear, ask if Papa will see you now.

(DIMMUCK *appears.*)

DIMMUCK: The master wants you, Miss Ann.

SARAH: Ask Papa if he'll see me soon.

(ANN *goes towards the house.*)

SARAH: Dimmuck, Mr Tetgeen has been left to find his own way here.

DIMMUCK: I couldn't help it, my lady.

(*And he follows* ANN.)

SARAH: Our father is confined to his room.

GEORGE: By your leave.

(*Then* GEORGE *takes himself off up the steps, and out of sight. The old lawyer bows to* LADY COTTESHAM, *who regards him steadily.*)

MR TETGEEN: From Sir Charles . . a talking machine.

SARAH: Please sit.

(*He sits carefully upon the rim of the fountain, she upon the seat opposite.*)

SARAH: (*glancing over her shoulder*) Will you talk nonsense until the gardener is out of hearing? He is on his way away. You have had a tiring journey?

MR TETGEEN: Thank you, no . . by the night coach to Reading and thence I have walked.

SARAH: The country is pretty, is it not?

MR TETGEEN: It compares favourably with other parts.

SARAH: Do you travel much, Mr Tetgeen? He has gone.

MR TETGEEN: (*deliberately and sharpening his tone ever so little*) Sir Charles does not wish to petition for a divorce.

SARAH: (*controlling even her sense of humour*) I have no desire to jump over the moon.

MR TETGEEN: His scruples are religious. The case would be weak upon some important points, and there has been no public scandal . . at the worst, very little.

SARAH: My good manners are, I trust, irreproachable, and you may tell Sir Charles that my conscience is my own.

MR TETGEEN: Your husband's in the matter of . .

SARAH: Please say the word.

MR TETGEEN: Pardon me . . not upon mere suspicion.

SARAH: Now, is it good policy to suspect what is incapable of proof?

MR TETGEEN: I advise Sir Charles, that, should you come to an open fight, he can afford to lose.

SARAH: And have I no right to suspicions?

MR TETGEEN: Certainly. Are they of use to you?

SARAH: I have been a tolerant wife, expecting toleration.

MR TETGEEN: Sir Charles is anxious to take into consideration any complaints you may have to make against him.

SARAH: I complain if he complains of me.

MR TETGEEN: For the first time, I think . . formally.

SARAH: Why not have come to me?

MR TETGEEN: Sir Charles is busy.

SARAH: (*disguising a little spasm of pain*) Shall we get to business?

(MR TETGEEN *now takes a moment to find his phrase.*)

MR TETGEEN: I don't know the man's name.

SARAH: This, surely, is how you might address a seduced housemaid.

MR TETGEEN: But Sir Charles and he, I understand, have talked the matter over.

(*The shock of this brings* SARAH *to her feet, white with anger.*)

SARAH: Divorce me.

MR TETGEEN: (*sharply*) Is there ground for it?

SARAH: (*with a magnificent recovery of self control*) I won't tell you that.

MR TETGEEN: I have said that we have no case . . that is to say, we don't want one; but any information is a weapon in store.

SARAH: You did quite right to insult me.

MR TETGEEN: As a rule I despise such methods.

SARAH: It's a lie that they met . . those two men?

MR TETGEEN: It may be.

SARAH: It must be.

MR TETGEEN: I have Sir Charles's word.

(*Now he takes from his pocket some notes, putting on his spectacles to read them.*)

SARAH: What's this . . a written lecture?

MR TETGEEN: We propose . . first: that the present complete severance of conjugal relations shall continue. Secondly: that Lady Cottesham shall be at liberty to remove from South Audley Street and Ringham Castle all personal and private effects, excepting those family jewels which have merely been considered her property. Thirdly: Lady Cottesham shall undertake, formally and in writing not to molest – a legal term – Sir Charles Cottesham. (*Her handkerchief has dropped, here he picks it up and restores it to her.*) Allow me, my lady.

SARAH: I thank you.

MR TETGEEN: (*continuing*) Fourthly: Lady Cottesham shall undertake . . etc. . . not to inhabit or frequent the city and towns of London, Brighthelmstone, Bath, The Tunbridge Wells, and York. Fifthly: Sir Charles Cottesham will, in acknowledgement of the maintainance of this agreement, allow Lady C. the sum of two hundred and fifty pounds per annum, which sum he considers sufficient for the upkeep of a small genteel establishment; use of the house known as Pater House, situate some seventeen miles from the Manor of Barton-le-Street, Yorkshire; coals from the mine adjoining; and from the

---

South Audley Street: early eighteenth-century street off Grosvenor Square in London.
Ringham Castle: apparently fictitious, like Markswayde.
Brighthelmstone: usual eighteenth-century name for Brighton, which, because of the patronage of the Prince, was becoming a fashionable spa equal in importance to Bath and Tunbridge Wells. By prohibiting Sarah to visit them, London, and York, her husband is exiling her from society.

home farm, milk, butter and eggs. (*Then he finds a further note.*) Lady
   Cottesham is not to play cards.
SARAH: I am a little fond of play.
MR TETGEEN: There is no question of jointure.
SARAH: None. Mr Tetgeen . . I love my husband.
MR TETGEEN: My lady . . I will mention it.
SARAH: Such a humorous answer to this. No . . don't. What is important? Bread
   and butter . . and eggs. Do I take this?
MR TETGEEN: (*handing her the paper*) Please.
SARAH: (*with the ghost of a smile*) I take it badly.
MR TETGEEN: (*courteously capping her jest*) I take my leave.
SARAH: This doesn't call for serious notice? I've done nothing legal by accepting it?
MR TETGEEN: There's no law in the matter; it's one of policy.
SARAH: I might bargain for a bigger income. (MR TETGEEN *bows*) On the whole
   I'd rather be divorced.
MR TETGEEN: Sir Charles detests scandal.
SARAH: Besides there's no case . . is there?
MR TETGEEN: Sir Charles congratulates himself.
SARAH: Sir Charles had best not bully me so politely . . tell him.
MR TETGEEN: My lady!
SARAH: I will not discuss this impertinence. Did those two men meet and talk . .
   chat together? What d'you think of that?
MR TETGEEN: 'Twas very practical. I know that the woman is somehow the
   outcast.
SARAH: A bad woman . . an idle woman! But I've tried to do so much that lay to
   my hands without ever questioning . .! Thank you, I don't want this retailed to
   my husband. You'll take a glass of wine before you go?
MR TETGEEN: Port is grateful.
         (*She takes from her dress two sealed letters.*)
SARAH: Will you give that to Sir Charles . . a letter he wrote me which I did not
   open. This, my answer, which I did not send.
         (*He takes the one letter courteously, the other she puts back.*)
SARAH: I'm such a coward, Mr Tetgeen.
MR TETGEEN: May I say how sorry . .?
SARAH: Thank you.
MR TETGEEN: And let me apologise for having expressed one opinion of my own.
SARAH: He wants to get rid of me. He's a bit afraid of me, you know, because I
   fight . . and my weapons are all my own. This'll blow over.
MR TETGEEN: (*with a shake of his head*) You are to take this offer as final.
SARAH: Beyond this?
MR TETGEEN: As I hinted, I am prepared to advise legal measures.
SARAH: I could blow it over . . but I won't perhaps. I must smile at my husband's
   consideration in suppressing even to you . . the man's name. Butter and eggs . .
   and milk. I should grow fat.

---

jointure: practice of law whereby a husband sets aside property for his wife's use in case of his
death.

(ANN *appears suddenly.*)

ANN: We go to Brighton tomorrow! (*And she comes excitedly to her sister.*)

SARAH: Was that duel a stroke of genius?

ANN: All sorts of things are to happen.

SARAH: (*turning from her to* MR TETGEEN) And you'll walk as far as Reading?

MR TETGEEN: Dear me, yes.

SARAH: (*to* ANN) I'll come back.

>(SARAH *takes* MR TETGEEN *towards the house.* ANN *seats herself. After a moment* LORD JOHN CARP, *his clothes dusty with some riding, appears from the other quarter. She looks up to find him gazing at her.*)

LORD JOHN: Ann, I've ridden back to see you.

ANN: (*after a moment*) We're coming to Brighton tomorrow.

LORD JOHN: Good.

ANN: Papa's not dead.

LORD JOHN: (*with equal cheerfulness*) That's good.

ANN: And he said we should be seeing more of you.

LORD JOHN: Here I am. I love you, Ann. (*He goes on his knees.*)

ANN: D'you want to marry me?

LORD JOHN: Yes.

ANN: Thank you very much; it'll be very convenient for us all. Won't you get up?

LORD JOHN: At your feet.

ANN: I like it.

LORD JOHN: Give me your hand.

ANN: No.

LORD JOHN: You're beautiful.

ANN: I don't think so. You don't think so.

LORD JOHN: I do think so.

ANN: I should like to say I don't love you.

LORD JOHN: Last night you kissed me.

ANN: Do get up, please.

LORD JOHN: As you wish.

>(*Now he sits by her.*)

ANN: Last night you were nobody in particular .. to me.

LORD JOHN: I love you.

ANN: Please don't; I can't think clearly.

LORD JOHN: Look at me.

ANN: I'm sure I don't love you because you're making me feel very uncomfortable and that wouldn't be so.

LORD JOHN: Then we'll think.

ANN: Papa .. perhaps you'd rather not talk about Papa.

LORD JOHN: Give yourself to me.

ANN: (*drawing away from him*) Four words! There ought to be more in such a sentence .. it's ridiculous. I want a year to think about its meaning. Don't speak.

LORD JOHN: Papa joins our party.

ANN: That's what we're after .. thank you.

LORD JOHN: I loathe politics.

ANN: Tell me something against them.

LORD JOHN: In my opinion your father's not a much bigger blackguard – I beg your pardon – than the rest of us.

ANN: .. Miserable sinners.

LORD JOHN: Your father turns his coat. Well .. ?

ANN: I see nothing at all in that.

LORD JOHN: What's right and what's wrong?

ANN: Papa's right .. for the present. When shall we be married?

LORD JOHN: Tomorrow?

ANN: (*startled*) If you knew that it isn't easy for me to be practical you wouldn't make fun.

LORD JOHN: Why not tomorrow?

ANN: Papa –

LORD JOHN: Papa says yes .. suppose.

ANN: I'm very young .. not to speak of clothes. I must have lots of new dresses.

LORD JOHN: Ask me for them.

ANN: Why do you want to marry me?

LORD JOHN: I love you.

ANN: It suddenly occurs to me that sounds unpleasant.

LORD JOHN: I love you.

ANN: Out of place.

LORD JOHN: I love you.

ANN: What if Papa were to die?

LORD JOHN: I want *you.*

ANN: I'm nothing .. I'm nobody .. I'm part of my family.

LORD JOHN: I want you.

ANN: Won't you please forget last night?

LORD JOHN: I want you. Look straight at me.

   (*She looks, and stays fascinated.*)

LORD JOHN: If I say now that I love you –

ANN: I know it.

LORD JOHN: And love me?

ANN: I suppose so.

LORD JOHN: Make sure.

ANN: But I hate you too .. I know that.

LORD JOHN: Shall I kiss you?

ANN: (*helplessly*) Yes.

   (*He kisses her full on the lips.*)

ANN: I can't hate you enough.

LORD JOHN: (*triumphantly*) Speak the truth now.

ANN: I feel very degraded.

LORD JOHN: Nonsense.

ANN: (*wretchedly*) This is one of the things which don't matter.

LORD JOHN: Ain't you to be mine?

ANN: You want the right to behave like that as well as the power.

LORD JOHN: You shall command me.

ANN: (*with a poor laugh*) I rather like this in a way.

LORD JOHN: Little coquette!

ANN: It does tickle my vanity.

> (*For a moment he sits looking at her, then shakes himself to his feet.*)

LORD JOHN: Now I must go.

ANN: Yes .. I want to think.

LORD JOHN: For Heaven's sake .. no!

ANN: I came this morning straight to where we were last night.

LORD JOHN: As I hung about the garden my heart was beating.

ANN: I shall like you better when you're not here.

LORD JOHN: We're to meet in Brighton?

ANN: I'm afraid so.

LORD JOHN: Good-bye.

ANN: There's just a silly sort of attraction between certain people, I believe.

LORD JOHN: Can you look me in the eyes and say you don't love me?

ANN: If I looked you in the eyes you'd frighten me again. I can say anything.

LORD JOHN: You're a deep child.

> (GEORGE LEETE *appears on the terrace.*)

GEORGE: My lord!

LORD JOHN: (*cordially*) My dear Leete.

GEORGE: No .. I am not surprised to see you.

ANN: George, things are happening.

LORD JOHN: Shake hands.

GEORGE: I will not.

ANN: Lord John asks me to be married to him. Shake hands.

GEORGE: Why did you fight?

ANN: Why *did* you fight?

LORD JOHN: (*shrugging*) Your father struck me.

ANN: Now you've hurt him .. that's fair.

> (*Then the two men do shake hands, not heartily.*)

GEORGE: We've trapped you, my lord.

LORD JOHN: I know what I want. I love your sister.

ANN: I don't like you .. but if you're good and I'm good we shall get on.

GEORGE: Why shouldn't one marry politically?

LORD JOHN: (*in* ANN'S *ear*) I love you.

ANN: No .. no .. no .. no .. no .. (*Discovering in this an echo of her father, she stops short.*)

GEORGE: We're a cold-blooded family.

LORD JOHN: I don't think so.

GEORGE: I married for love.

LORD JOHN: Who doesn't? But, of course there should be other reasons.

GEORGE: You won't receive my wife.

LORD JOHN: Here's your sister.

> (LADY COTTESHAM *comes from the direction of the house.*)

SARAH: Back again?

LORD JOHN: You see.

> (*From the other side appears* MR TATTON.)

TATTON: As you all seem to be here I don't mind interrupting.

GEORGE: (*hailing him*) Well . . neighbour?

TATTON: Come . . come . . what's a little fighting more or less!

GEORGE: Bravo, English sentiment . . relieves a deal of awkwardness.
   (*The two shake hands.*)

SARAH: (*who by this has reached* LORD JOHN) . . And back so soon?

ANN: Lord John asks to marry me.

LORD JOHN: Yes.

TATTON: I guessed so . . give me a bit of romance!

SARAH: (*suavely*) This is perhaps a little sudden, my dear Lord John. Papa may
  naturally be a little shocked.

GEORGE: Not at all, Sarah.

TATTON: How's the wound?

GEORGE: Not serious . . nothing's serious.

SARAH: You are very masterful, wooing sword in hand.

ANN: George and I have explained to Lord John that we are all most anxious to
  marry me to him and he doesn't mind—

LORD JOHN: Being made a fool of. I love—

ANN: I will like you.

GEORGE: Charming cynicism, my dear Sarah.

TATTON: Oh, Lord!

ANN: (*to her affianced*) Good-bye now.

LORD JOHN: When do I see you?

ANN: Papa says soon.

LORD JOHN: Very soon, please. Tatton, my friend, Brighton's no nearer.

TATTON: Lady Cottesham . . Miss Leete . . I kiss your hands.

LORD JOHN: (*ebulliently clapping* GEORGE *on the back*) Look more pleased.
  (*Then he bends over* LADY COTTESHAM'S *hand.*) Lady Charlie . . my
  service to you . . all. Ann. (*He takes* ANN'S *hand to kiss.*)

ANN: If I can think better of all this, I shall. Good-bye.
   (*She turns away from him. He stands for a moment considering her,*
   but follows TATTON *away through the orchard.* GEORGE *and*
   SARAH *are watching their sister, who then comments on her little*
   affair with life.)

ANN: I'm growing up. (*then with a sudden tremor*) Sally, don't let me be forced to
  marry.

GEORGE: Force of circumstances, my dear Ann.

ANN: Outside things. Why couldn't I run away from this garden and over the hills . .
  I suppose there's something on the other side of the hills.

SARAH: You'd find yourself there . . and circumstances.

ANN: So I'm trapped as well as that Lord John.

SARAH: What's the injury?

ANN: I'm taken by surprise and I know I'm ignorant and I think I'm learning things
  backwards.

GEORGE: You must cheer up and say: John's not a bad sort.

SARAH: A man of his age is a young man.

ANN: I wish you wouldn't recommend him to me.

SARAH: Let's think of Brighton. What about your gowns?

ANN: I've nothing to wear.

SARAH: We'll talk to Papa.

GEORGE: The war-purse is always a long one.

SARAH: George .. be one of us for a minute.

GEORGE: But I want to look on too, and laugh.

SARAH: (*caustically*) Yes .. that's your privilege .. except occasionally. (*then to her sister*) I wish you all the happiness of courtship days.

GEORGE: Arcadian expression!

ANN: I believe it means being kissed .. often.

SARAH: Have you not a touch of romance in you, little girl?

ANN: Am I not like Mr Dan Tatton? He kisses dairy-maids and servants and all the farmer's daughters .. I beg your pardon, George.

GEORGE: (*nettled*) I'll say to you, Ann, that – in all essentials – one woman is as good as another.

SARAH: That is not so in the polite world.

GEORGE: When you consider it no one *lives* in the polite world.

ANN: Do they come outside for air sooner or later?

SARAH: (*briskly*) Three best dresses you must have and something very gay if you're to go near the Pavilion.

ANN: You're coming to Brighton, Sally?

SARAH: No.

ANN: Why not?

SARAH: I don't wish to meet my husband.

GEORGE: That man was his lawyer.

ANN: The political difference, Sally?

SARAH: Just that. (*then with a deft turn of the subject*) I don't say that yours is a pretty face, but I should think you would have charm.

GEORGE: For fashion's sake cultivate sweetness.

SARAH: You dance as well as they know how in Reading.

ANN: Yes .. I can twiddle my feet.

SARAH: Do you like dancing?

ANN: I'd sooner walk.

GEORGE: What .. and get somewhere!

ANN: Here's George laughing.

SARAH: He's out of it.

ANN: Are you happy, George?

GEORGE: Alas .. Dolly's disgraceful ignorance of etiquette damns us both from the beautiful drawing-room.

SARAH: That laugh is forced. But how can you .. look on?

  (*There is a slight pause in their talk. Then..*)

ANN: He'll bully me with love.

SARAH: Your husband will give you just what you ask for.

Pavilion: the grand pleasure palace in Brighton was first constructed for the Prince in 1787, and subsequently much altered and enlarged, especially by John Nash, into the romantic–oriental Xanadu it remains today. At the time of the play, however, it was a rather conventional classical building with a central rotunda and flanking wings.

ANN: I hate myself too. I want to take people mentally.

GEORGE: You want a new world . . you new woman.

ANN: And I'm a good bit frightened of myself.

SARAH: We have our places to fill in this. My dear child, leave futile questions
alone.

GEORGE: Neither have I any good advice to give you.

ANN: I think happiness is a thing one talks too much about.

> (DIMMUCK *appears. And by now* ABUD'S *work has brought him
> back to the terrace.*)

DIMMUCK: The master would like to see your Ladyship now.

SARAH: I'll say we've had a visitor . . Guess.

GEORGE: And you've had a visitor, Sarah.

ANN: Papa will know.

SARAH: Is he in a questioning mood?

ANN: I always tell everything.

SARAH: It saves time.

> (*She departs towards the house.*)

DIMMUCK: Mr George.

GEORGE: What is it?

DIMMUCK: He said No to a doctor when I haven't even mentioned the matter.
Had I better send . . ?

GEORGE: Do . . if you care to waste the doctor's time.

> (DIMMUCK *gives an offended sniff and follows* LADY
> COTTESHAM.)

ANN: I could sit here for days. George, I don't think I quite believe in anything I've
been told yet.

GEORGE: What's that man's name?

ANN: John – John is a common name – John Abud.

GEORGE: Abud!

ABUD: Sir?

GEORGE: Come here.

> (ABUD *obediently walks towards his young master and stands before
> him.*)

GEORGE: Why did you ask after the health of Mrs George Leete?

ABUD: We courted once.

GEORGE: (*after a moment*) Listen, Ann. Do you hate me, John Abud?

ABUD: No, sir.

GEORGE: You're a fine looking fellow. How old are you?

ABUD: Twenty-seven, sir.

GEORGE: Is Once long ago?

ABUD: Two years gone.

GEORGE: Did Mrs Leete quarrel with you?

ABUD: No, sir.

GEORGE: Pray tell me more.

ABUD: I was beneath her.

GEORGE: But you're a fine looking fellow.

ABUD: Farmer Crowe wouldn't risk his daughter being unhappy.

GEORGE: But she was beneath me.

ABUD: That was another matter, sir.

GEORGE: I don't think you intend to be sarcastic.

ABUD: And .. being near her time for the first time, sir .. I wanted to know if she is in danger of dying yet.

GEORGE: Every precaution has been taken .. a nurse .. there is a physician near. I need not tell you .. but I do tell you.

ABUD: Thank you, sir.

GEORGE: I take great interest in my wife.

ABUD: We all do, sir.

GEORGE: Was it ambition that you courted her?

ABUD: I thought to start housekeeping.

GEORGE: Did you aspire to rise socially?

ABUD: I wanted a wife to keep house, sir.

GEORGE: Are you content?

ABUD: I think so, sir.

GEORGE: With your humble position?

ABUD: I'm a gardener, and there'll always be gardens.

GEORGE: Frustrated affections .. I beg your pardon .. To have been crossed in love should make you bitter and ambitious.

ABUD: My father was a gardener and my son will be a gardener if he's no worse a man than I and no better.

GEORGE: Are you married?

ABUD: No, sir.

GEORGE: Are you going to be married?

ABUD: Not especially, sir.

GEORGE: Yes .. you must marry .. some decent woman; we want gardeners.

ABUD: Do you want me any more now, sir?

GEORGE: You have interested me. You can go back to your work.

    (ABUD *obeys.*)

GEORGE: (*almost to himself*) I am hardly human.

    (*He slowly moves away and out of sight.*)

ANN: John Abud.

    (*He comes back and stands before her too.*)

ANN: I am very sorry for you.

ABUD: I am very much obliged to you, Miss.

ANN: Both those sayings are quite meaningless. Say something true about yourself.

ABUD: I am not sorry for myself.

ANN: I won't tell. It's very clear you ought to be in a despairing state. Don't stand in the sun with your hat off.

ABUD: (*putting on his hat*) Thank you, Miss.

ANN: Have you nearly finished the rose-trees?

ABUD: I must work till late this evening.

ANN: Weren't you ambitious for Dolly's sake?

ABUD: She thought me good enough.

ANN: I'd have married her.

ABUD: She was ambitious for me.

ANN: And are you frightened of the big world?

ABUD: Fine things dazzle me sometimes.

ANN: But gardening is all that you're fit for?

ABUD: I'm afraid so, Miss.

ANN: But it's great to be a gardener .. to sow seeds and to watch flowers grow and to cut away dead things.

ABUD: Yes, Miss.

ANN: And you're in the fresh air all day.

ABUD: That's very healthy.

ANN: Are you very poor?

ABUD: I get my meals in the house.

ANN: Rough clothes last a long time.

ABUD: I've saved money.

ANN: Where do you sleep?

ABUD: At Mrs Hart's .. at a cottage .. it's a mile off.

ANN: And you want no more than food and clothes and a bed and you earn all that with your hands.

ABUD: The less a man wants, Miss, the better.

ANN: But you mean to marry?

ABUD: Yes .. I've saved money.

ANN: Whom will you marry? Would you rather not say? Perhaps you don't know yet?

ABUD: It's all luck what sort of a maid a man gets fond of. It won't be a widow.

ANN: Be careful, John Abud.

ABUD: No .. I shan't be careful.

ANN: You'll do very wrong to be made a fool of.

ABUD: I'm safe, Miss; I've no eye for a pretty face.

(DIMMUCK *arrives asthmatically at the top of the steps.*)

DIMMUCK: Where's Mr George? Here's a messenger come post.

ANN: Find him, Abud.

ABUD: (*to* DIMMUCK) From Dolly?

DIMMUCK: Speak respectful.

ABUD: Is it from his wife?

DIMMUCK: Go find him.

ANN: (*as* ABUD *is immovable*) Dimmuck .. tell me about Mrs George.

DIMMUCK: She's doing well, Miss.

ABUD: (*shouting joyfully now*) Mr George! Mr George!

ANN: A boy or a girl, Dimmuck?

DIMMUCK: Yes, Miss.

ABUD: Mr George! Mr George!

DIMMUCK: Ecod .. is he somewhere else?

(DIMMUCK, *somewhat excited himself, returns to the house.*)

ANN: George!

ABUD: Mr George! Mr George!

(GEORGE *comes slowly along the terrace, in his hand an open book, which some people might suppose he was reading. He speaks with studied calm.*)

GEORGE: You are very excited, my good man.
ABUD: She's brought you a child, sir.
ANN: Your child!
GEORGE: Certainly.
ABUD: Thank God, sir!
GEORGE: I will if I please.
ANN: And she's doing well.
ABUD: There's a messenger come post.
GEORGE: To be sure .. it might have been bad news.
>   (*And slowly he crosses the garden towards the house.*)
ABUD: (*suddenly, beyond all patience*) Run .. damn you!
>   (GEORGE *makes one supreme effort to maintain his dignity, but fails*
>   *utterly. He gasps out* ..)
GEORGE: Yes, I will. (*And runs off as hard as he can.*)
ABUD: (*in an ecstasy*) This is good. Oh, Dolly and God .. this is good!
ANN: (*round eyed*) I wonder that you can be pleased.
ABUD: (*apologising .. without apology*) It's life.
ANN: (*struck*) Yes, it is.
>   (*And she goes towards the house, thinking this over.*)

ACT III

It is near to sunset. The garden is shadier than before. ABUD *is still working.*
CARNABY *comes from the house followed by* DR REMNANT. *He wears his right*
arm in a sling. His face is flushed, his speech rapid.

CARNABY: Parson, you didn't drink enough wine .. damme, the wine was good.
DR REMNANT: I am very grateful for an excellent dinner.
CARNABY: A good dinner, sir, is the crown to a good day's work.
DR REMNANT: It may also be a comfort in affliction. Our philosophy does ill, Mr
>   Leete, when it despises the more simple means of contentment.
CARNABY: And which will be the better lover of a woman, a hungry or a well-fed
>   man?
DR REMNANT: A good meal digests love with it; for what is love but a food to live
>   by .. but a hungry love will ofttimes devour its owner.
CARNABY: Admirable! Give me a man in love to deal with. Vous l'avez vu?
DR REMNANT: Speak Latin, Greek or Hebrew to me, Mr Leete.
CARNABY: French is the language of little things. My poor France! Ours is a little
>   world, Parson .. a man may hold it here (*his open hand*). Lord John Carp's a
>   fine fellow.
DR REMNANT: Son of a Duke.
CARNABY: And I commend to you the originality of his return. At twelve we fight
>   .. at one-thirty he proposes marriage to my daughter. D'ye see him humbly on
>   his knees? Will there be rain, I wonder?
DR REMNANT: We need rain .. Abud?
ABUD: Badly, sir.
CARNABY: Do we want a wet journey tomorow! Where's Sarah?

DR REMNANT: Lady Cottesham's taking tea.

CARNABY: (*to* ABUD *with a sudden start*) And why the devil didn't you marry my daughter-in-law .. my own gardener?

(GEORGE *appears dressed for riding.*)

GEORGE: Good-bye, sir, for the present.

CARNABY: Boots and breeches!

GEORGE: You shouldn't be about in the evening air with a green wound in your arm. You drank wine at dinner. Be careful, sir.

CARNABY: Off to your wife and the expected?

GEORGE: Yes, sir.

CARNABY: Riding to Watford?

GEORGE: From there alongside the North Coach, if I'm in time.

CARNABY: Don't founder my horse. Will ye leave the glorious news with your grandfather at Wycombe?

GEORGE: I won't fail to. (*then to* ABUD) We've been speaking of you.

ABUD: It was never any secret, sir.

GEORGE: Don't apologise.

(*Soon after this* ABUD *passes out of sight.*)

CARNABY: Nature's an encumbrance to us, Parson.

DR REMNANT: One disapproves of flesh uninspired.

CARNABY: She allows you no amusing hobbies .. always takes you seriously.

GEORGE: Good-bye, Parson.

DR REMNANT: (*as he bows*) Your most obedient.

CARNABY: And you trifle with damnable democracy, with the pretty theories of the respect due to womanhood and now the result .. hark to it squalling.

DR REMNANT: Being fifty miles off might not one say: The cry of the newborn?

CARNABY: Ill-bred babies squall. There's no poetic glamour in the world will beautify an undesired infant .. George says so.

GEORGE: I did say so.

CARNABY: I feel the whole matter deeply.

(GEORGE *half laughs.*)

CARNABY: George, after days of irritability, brought to bed of a smile. That's a home thrust of a metaphor.

(GEORGE *laughs again.*)

CARNABY: Twins!

GEORGE: Yes, a boy and a girl .. I'm the father of a boy and a girl.

CARNABY: (*in dignified, indignant horror*) No one of you dared tell me that much!

(SARAH *and* ANN *come from the house.*)

GEORGE: You could have asked me for news of your grandchildren.

CARNABY: Twins is an insult.

SARAH: But you look very cheerful, George.

GEORGE: I am content.

SARAH: I'm surprised.

GEORGE: I am surprised.

SARAH: Now what names for them?

CARNABY: No family names, please.

GEORGE: We'll wait for a dozen years or so and let them choose their own.

DR REMNANT: But, sir, christening will demand –

CARNABY: Your son should have had my name, sir.

GEORGE: I know the rule .. as I have my grandfather's which I take no pride in.

SARAH: George!

GEORGE: Not to say that it sounds his, not mine.

CARNABY: Our hopes of you were high once.

GEORGE: Sarah, may I kiss you? (*He kisses her cheek.*) Let me hear what you decide to do.

CARNABY: The begetting you, sir, was a waste of time.

GEORGE: (*quite pleasantly*) Don't say that.

> (*At the top of the steps* ANN *is waiting for him.*)

ANN: I'll see you into the saddle.

GEORGE: Thank you, sister Ann.

ANN: Why didn't you leave us weeks ago?

GEORGE: Why!

> (*They pace away, arm-in-arm.*)

CARNABY: (*bitterly*) Glad to go! Brighton, Sarah.

SARAH: No, I shall not come, Papa.

CARNABY: Coward. (*then to* REMNANT) Good-night.

DR REMNANT: (*covering the insolent dismissal*) With your kind permission I will take my leave. (*Then he bows to* SARAH.) Lady Cottesham.

SARAH: (*curtseying*) Doctor Remnant, I am yours.

CARNABY: (*sitting by the fountain, stamping his foot*) Oh, this cracked earth! Will it rain .. will it rain?

DR REMNANT: I doubt now. That cloud has passed.

CARNABY: Soft, pellucid rain! There's a good word and I'm not at all sure what it means.

DR REMNANT: Per .. lucere.. letting light through.

> (REMNANT *leaves them.*)

CARNABY: Soft, pellucid rain! .. thank you. Brighton, Sarah.

SARAH: Ann needs new clothes.

CARNABY: See to it.

SARAH: I shall not be there.

> (*She turns from him.*)

CARNABY: Pretty climax to a quarrel!

SARAH: Not a quarrel.

CARNABY: A political difference.

SARAH: Don't look so ferocious.

CARNABY: My arm is in great pain and the wine's in my head.

SARAH: Won't you go to bed?

CARNABY: I'm well enough .. to travel. This marriage makes us safe, Sarah .. an anchor in each camp .. There's a mixed metaphor.

SARAH: If you'll have my advice, Papa, you'll keep those plans clear from Ann's mind.

CARNABY: John Carp is so much clay .. a man of forty ignorant of himself.

SARAH: But if the Duke will not ..

CARNABY: The Duke hates a scandal.

SARAH: Does he detest scandal!

CARNABY: The girl is well-bred and harmless .. why publicly quarrel with John and incense her old brute of a father? There's the Duke in a score of words. He'll take a little time to think it out so.

SARAH: And I say: Do you get on the right side of the Duke once again – that's what we've worked for – and leave these two alone.

CARNABY: Am I to lose my daughter?

SARAH: Papa .. your food's intrigue.

CARNABY: Scold at Society .. and what's the use?

SARAH: We're over-civilised.

(ANN *rejoins them now. The twilight is gathering.*)

CARNABY: My mother's very old .. your grandfather's younger and seventy-nine .. he swears I'll never come into the title. There's little else.

SARAH: You're feverish .. why are you saying this?

CARNABY: Ann .. George .. George via Wycombe .. Wycombe Court .. Sir George Leete baronet, Justice of the Peace, Deputy Lieutenant .. the thought's tumbled. Ann, I first saw your mother in this garden .. there.

ANN: Was she like me?

SARAH: My age when she married.

CARNABY: She was not beautiful .. then she died.

ANN: Mr Tatton thinks it a romantic garden.

CARNABY: (*pause*) D'ye hear the wind sighing through that tree?

ANN: The air's quite still.

CARNABY: I hear myself sighing .. when I first saw your mother in this garden .. that's how it was done.

SARAH: For a woman must marry.

CARNABY: (*rises*) You all take to it as ducks to water .. but apple sauce is quite correct .. I must not mix metaphors.

(MRS OPIE *comes from the house.*)

SARAH: Your supper done, Mrs Opie?

MRS OPIE: I eat little in the evening.

SARAH: I believe that saves digestion.

MRS OPIE: Ann, do you need me more tonight?

ANN: Not any more.

MRS OPIE: Ann, there is gossip among the servants about a wager ..

ANN: Mrs Opie, that was .. yesterday.

MRS OPIE: Ann, I should be glad to be able to contradict a reported .. embrace.

ANN: I was kissed.

MRS OPIE: I am shocked.

CARNABY: Mrs Opie, is it possible that all these years I have been nourishing a prude in my .. back drawing-room?

MRS OPIE: I presume I am discharged of Ann's education; but as the salaried mistress of your household, Mr Leete, I am grieved not to be able to deny such a rumour to your servants.

(*She sails back, righteously indignant.*)

CARNABY: Call out that you're marrying the wicked man .. comfort her.

SARAH: Mrs Opie!

CARNABY: Consider that existence. An old maid .. so far as we know. Brevet rank .. missis. Not pleasant.

ANN: She wants nothing better .. at her age.

SARAH: How forgetful!

CARNABY: (*the force of the phrase growing*) Brighton, Sarah.

SARAH: Now you've both read the love-letter which Tetgeen brought me.

CARNABY: Come to Brighton.

ANN: Come to Brighton, Sally.

SARAH: No. I have been thinking. I think I will accept the income, the house, coals, butter and eggs.

CARNABY: I give you a fortnight to bring your husband to his knees .. to your feet.

SARAH: I'm not sure that I could. My marriage has come naturally to an end.

CARNABY: Sarah, don't annoy me.

SARAH: Papa, you joined my bridegroom's political party .. now you see fit to leave it.

(*She glances at* ANN, *who gives no sign, however.*)

CARNABY: What have you been doing in ten years?

SARAH: Waiting for this to happen .. now I come to think.

CARNABY: Have ye the impudence to tell me that ye've never cared for your husband?

SARAH: I was caught by the first few kisses; but he ..

CARNABY: Has he ever been unkind to you?

SARAH: Never. He's a gentleman through and through .. quite charming to live with.

CARNABY: I see what more you expect. And he neither drinks nor .. nor .. no one ever could suppose your leaving him.

SARAH: No. I'm disgraced.

CARNABY: Fight for your honour.

SARAH: You surprise me sometimes by breaking out into cant phrases.

CARNABY: What is more useful in the world than honour?

SARAH: I think we never had any .. we!

CARNABY: Give me more details. Tell me, who is this man?

SARAH: I'm innocent .. if that were all.

ANN: Sally, what do they say you've done?

SARAH: I cry out like any poor girl.

CARNABY: There must be no doubt that you're innocent. Why not go for to force Charles into court?

SARAH: My innocence is not of the sort which shows up well.

CARNABY: Hold publicity in reserve. No fear of the two men arranging to meet, is there?

SARAH: They've met .. and they chatted about me.

CARNABY: (*after a moment*) There's sound humour in that.

SARAH: I shall feel able to laugh at them both from Yorkshire.

Brevet rank: honorary higher rank given to a military officer without increase of pay or authority; Carnaby means that Mrs Opie is addressed as a married woman but is not one.

CARNABY: God forbid! Come to Brighton .. we'll rally Charles no end.

SARAH: Papa, I know there's nothing to be done.

CARNABY: Coward!

SARAH: Besides I don't think I want to go back to my happiness.
> (*They are silent for a little.*)

CARNABY: How still! Look .. leaves falling already. Can that man hear what we're saying?

SARAH: (*to* ANN) Can Abud overhear?

ANN: I've never talked secrets in the garden before today. (*raising her voice but a very little*) Can you hear me, Abud?
> (*No reply comes.*)

CARNABY: Evidently not. There's brains shown in a trifle.

SARAH: Does your arm pain you so much?

ANN: Sarah, this man that you're fond of and that's not your husband is not by any chance Lord John Carp?

SARAH: No.

ANN: Nothing would surprise me.

SARAH: You are witty .. but a little young to be so hard.

CARNABY: Keep to your innocent thoughts.

ANN: I must study politics.

SARAH: We'll stop talking of this.

ANN: No .. let me listen .. quite quietly.

CARNABY: Let her listen .. she's going to be married.

SARAH: Good luck, Ann.

CARNABY: I have great hopes of Ann.

SARAH: I hope she may be heartless. To be heartless is to be quite safe.

CARNABY: Now we detect a taste of sour grapes in your mouth.

SARAH: Butter and eggs.

CARNABY: We must all start early in the morning. Sarah will take you, Ann, round the Brighton shops .. fine shops. You shall have the money..

SARAH: I will not come with you.

CARNABY: (*vexedly*) How absurd .. how ridiculous .. to persist in your silly sentiment.

SARAH: (*her voice rising*) I'm tired of that world .. which goes on and on, and there's no dying .. one grows into a ghost .. visible .. then invisible. I'm glad paint has gone out of fashion .. the painted ghosts were very ill to see.

CARNABY: D'ye scoff at civilisation?

SARAH: Look ahead for me.

CARNABY: Banished to a hole in the damned provinces! But you're young yet, you're charming .. you're the wife .. and the honest wife of one of the country's best men. My head aches. D'ye despise good fortune's gifts? Keep as straight in your place in the world as you can. A monthly packet of books to Yorkshire .. no .. you never were fond of reading. Ye'd play patience .. cultivate chess problems .. kill yourself!

SARAH: When one world fails take another.

CARNABY: You have no more right to commit suicide than to desert the society you were born into. My head aches.

SARAH: George is happy.

CARNABY: D'ye dare to think so?

SARAH: No .. it's a horrible marriage.

CARNABY: He's losing refinement .. mark me .. he no longer polishes his nails.

SARAH: But there are the children now.

CARNABY: You never have wanted children.

SARAH: I don't want a little child.

CARNABY: She to be Lady Leete .. some day .. soon! What has he done for his family?

SARAH: I'll come with you. You are clever, Papa. And I know just what to say to Charles.

CARNABY: (*with a curious change of tone*) If you study anatomy you'll find that the brain, as it works, pressing forward the eyes .. thought is painful. Never be defeated. Chapter the latest .. the tickling of the Carp. And my throat is dry .. shall I drink that water?

SARAH: No, I wouldn't.

CARNABY: Not out of my hand?

ANN: (*speaking in a strange quiet voice, after her long silence*) I will not come to Brighton with you.

CARNABY: Very dry!

ANN: You must go back, Sally.

CARNABY: (*as he looks at her, standing stiffly*) Now what is Ann's height .. five feet ..?

ANN: Sally must go back, for she belongs to it .. but I'll stay here where I belong.

CARNABY: You've spoken three times and the words are jumbling in at my ears meaninglessly. I certainly took too much wine at dinner .. or else .. Yes .. Sally goes back .. and you'll go forward. Who stays here? Don't burlesque your sister. What's in the air .. what disease is this?

ANN: I mean to disobey you .. to stay here .. never to be unhappy.

CARNABY: So pleased!

ANN: I want to be an ordinary woman .. not clever .. not fortunate.

CARNABY: I can't hear.

ANN: Not clever. I don't believe in you, Papa.

CARNABY: I exist .. I'm very sorry.

ANN: I won't be married to any man. I refuse to be tempted .. I won't see him again.

CARNABY: Yes. It's raining.

SARAH: Raining!

CARNABY: Don't you stop it raining.

ANN: (*in the same level tones, to her sister now, who otherwise would turn, alarmed, to their father*) And I curse you .. because, we being sisters, I suppose I am much what you were, about to be married; and I think, Sally, you'd have cursed your present self. I could become all that you are and more .. but I don't choose.

SARAH: Ann, what is to become of you?

CARNABY: Big drops .. big drops!

(*At this moment* ABUD *is passing towards the house, his work finished.*)

ANN: John Abud .. you mean to marry. When you marry .. will you marry me?

(*a blank silence, into which breaks* CARNABY'S *sick voice*)

CARNABY: Take me indoors. I heard you ask the gardener to marry you.

ANN: I asked him.

CARNABY: I heard you say that you asked him. Take me in .. but not out of the rain.

ANN: Look .. he's straight-limbed and clear eyed .. and I'm a woman.

SARAH: Ann, are you mad?

ANN: If we two were alone here in this garden and everyone else in the world were dead .. what would you answer?

ABUD: (*still amazed*) Why .. yes.

CARNABY: Then that's settled .. pellucid.

(*He attempts to rise, but staggers backwards and forwards.* SARAH *goes to him alarmed.*)

SARAH: Papa! .. there's no rain yet.

CARNABY: Hush, I'm dead.

ANN: (*her nerves failing her*) Oh .. oh .. oh ..!

SARAH: Abud, don't ever speak of this.

ABUD: No, my lady.

ANN: (*with a final effort*) I mean it all. Wait three months.

CARNABY: Help me up steps .. son-in-law.

(CARNABY *has started to grope his way indoors. But he reels and falls helpless.*)

ABUD: I'll carry him.

(*Throwing down his tools* ABUD *lifts the frail sick man and carries him towards the house.* SARAH *follows.*)

ANN: (*sobbing a little, and weary*) Such a long day it has been .. now ending.

(*She follows too.*)

ACT IV

SCENE 1. *The hall at Markswayde is square; in decoration strictly eighteenth century. The floor polished. Then comes six feet of soberly painted wainscot, and above, the greenish blue and yellowish green wall painted into panels. At intervals are low relief pilasters; the capitals of these are gilded. The ceiling is white and in the centre of it there is a frosted glass dome through which a dull light struggles. Two sides only of the hall are seen. In the corner is a hat stand and on it are many cloaks and hats and beneath it several pairs of very muddy boots.*

In the middle of the left hand wall are the double doors of the dining-room led up to by three or four stairs with balusters, and on either side standing against the wall long, formal, straight backed sofas. In the middle of the right hand wall is the front door; glass double doors can be seen and there is evidently a porch beyond. On the left of the front door a small window. On the right a large fireplace, in which a large fire is roaring. Over the front door, a clock (the hands pointing to half-past one). Over the fireplace a family portrait (temp. Queen Anne), below this a blunderbuss and several horse-pistols. Above the sofa full-length family portraits (temp. George I). Before the front door a wooden screen, of lighter wood than the wainscot, and in the middle of it a small glass panel. Before this a heavy square table on which are whips and sticks, a hat or two and brushes; by the table a wooden chair. On either side the fire stand tall closed-in armchairs, and between the fireplace and the door a smaller red-baize screen. When the dining-room doors are thrown open another wooden screen is to be seen. There are a few rugs on the floor, formally arranged.

MRS OPIE *stands in the middle of the hall, holding out a woman's brown cloak: she drops one side to fetch out her handkerchief and apply it to her eye.* DIMMUCK *comes in by the front door, which he carefully closes behind him. He is wrapped in a hooded cloak and carries a pair of boots and a newspaper. The boots he arranges to warm before the fire. Then he spreads the Chronicle newspaper upon the arm of a chair, then takes off his cloak and hangs it upon a peg close to the door.*

DIMMUCK: Mrs Opie .. will you look to its not scorching?

> (MRS OPIE *still mops her eyes.* DIMMUCK *goes towards the dining-room door, but turns.*)

DIMMUCK: Will you kindly see that the *Chronicle* newspaper does not burn?

MRS OPIE: I was crying.

DIMMUCK: I leave this tomorrow sennight .. thankful, ma'am, to have given notice in a dignified manner.

MRS OPIE: I understand .. Those persons at table..

DIMMUCK: You give notice.

MRS OPIE: Mr Dimmuck, this is my home.

> (LORD ARTHUR CARP *comes out of the dining-room. He is a thinner and more earnest-looking edition of his brother.* MRS OPIE *turns a chair and hangs the cloak to warm before the fire, and then goes into the dining-room.*)

LORD ARTHUR: My chaise round?

DIMMUCK: I've but just ordered it, my lord. Your lordship's man has give me your boots.

LORD ARTHUR: Does it snow?

DIMMUCK: Rather rain than snow.

> (LORD ARTHUR *takes up the newspaper.*)

DIMMUCK: Yesterday's, my lord.

LORD ARTHUR: I've seen it. The mails don't hurry hereabouts. Can I be in London by the morning?

DIMMUCK: I should say you might be, my lord.

> (LORD ARTHUR *sits by the fire, while* DIMMUCK *takes off his pumps and starts to put on his boots.*)

LORD ARTHUR: Is this a horse called 'Ronald'?

DIMMUCK: Which horse, my lord?

LORD ARTHUR: Which I'm to take back with me .. my brother left here. I brought the mare he borrowed.

---

temp.: Latin *tempore*, 'in the time of'.
sennight: a 'seven night' or a week; archaic expression, like much of Dimmuck's language.

DIMMUCK: I remember, my lord. I'll enquire.
LORD ARTHUR: Tell Parker ..
DIMMUCK: Your lordship's man?
LORD ARTHUR: .. he'd better ride the beast.
>   (SARAH *comes out of the dining-room. He stands up; one boot, one*
>   *shoe.*)
SARAH: Please put on the other.
LORD ARTHUR: Thank you .. I *am* in haste.
SARAH: To depart before the bride's departure.
LORD ARTHUR: Does the bride go with the bridegroom?
SARAH: She goes away.
LORD ARTHUR: I shall never see such a thing again.
SARAH: I think this entertainment is unique.
LORD ARTHUR: Any commissions in town?
SARAH: Why can't you stay to travel with us tomorrow and talk business to Papa
    by the way?
>   (DIMMUCK *carrying the pumps and after putting on his cloak goes*
>   *out through the front door. When it is closed, her voice changes.*)
SARAH: Why .. Arthur?
>   (*He does not answer. Then* MRS OPIE *comes out of the dining-room*
>   *to fetch the cloak. The two, with an effort, reconstruct their casual*
>   *disjointed conversation.*)
SARAH: .. Before the bride's departure?
LORD ARTHUR: Does the bride go away with the bridegroom?
SARAH: She goes.
LORD ARTHUR: I shall never see such an entertainment again.
SARAH: We are quite unique.
LORD ARTHUR: Any commissions in town?
SARAH: Is she to go soon too, Mrs Opie?
MRS OPIE: It is arranged they are to walk .. in this weather .. ten miles .. to the
    house.
SARAH: Cottage.
MRS OPIE: Hut.
>   (MRS OPIE *takes the cloak into the dining-room. Then* SARAH
>   *comes a little towards* LORD ARTHUR, *but waits for him to speak.*)
LORD ARTHUR: (*a little awkwardly*) You are not looking well.
SARAH: To our memory .. and beyond your little chat with my husband about me
    .. I want to speak an epitaph.
LORD ARTHUR: Charlie Cottesham behaved most honourably.
SARAH: And I think you did. Why have you not let me tell you so in your ear till
    now, today?
LORD ARTHUR: Sarah .. we had a narrow escape from ..
SARAH: How's your wife?
LORD ARTHUR: Well .. thank you.
SARAH: Nervous, surely, at your travelling in winter?
LORD ARTHUR: I was so glad to receive a casual invitation from you and to come
    .. casually.

SARAH: Fifty miles.

LORD ARTHUR: Your father has been ill?

SARAH: Very ill through the autumn.

LORD ARTHUR: Do you think he suspects us?

SARAH: I shouldn't care to peep into Papa's innermost mind. You are to be very useful to him.

LORD ARTHUR: No.

SARAH: Then he'll go back to the government.

LORD ARTHUR: If he pleases .. if they please .. if you please.

SARAH: I am not going back to my husband. Arthur .. be useful to him.

LORD ARTHUR: No .. you are not coming to me. Always your father! (*after a moment*) It was my little home in the country somehow said aloud you didn't care for me.

SARAH: I fooled you to small purpose.

LORD ARTHUR: I wish you had once made friends with my wife.

SARAH: If we .. this house I'm speaking of .. had made friends where we've only made tools and fools we shouldn't now be cursed as we are .. all. George, who is a cork, trying to sink socially. Ann is mad .. and a runaway.

LORD ARTHUR: Sarah, I've been devilish fond of you.

SARAH: Be useful to Papa. (*He shakes his head, obstinately.*) Praise me a little. Haven't I worked my best for my family?

LORD ARTHUR: Suppose I could be useful to him now, would you, in spite of all, come to me .. no half measures?

SARAH: Arthur .. (*He makes a little passionate movement towards her, but she is cold.*) It's time for me to vanish from this world, because I've nothing left to sell.

LORD ARTHUR: I can't help him. I don't want you.

(*He turns away.*)

SARAH: I feel I've done my best.

LORD ARTHUR: Keep your father quiet.

SARAH: I mean to leave him.

LORD ARTHUR: What does he say to that?

SARAH: I've not yet told him.

LORD ARTHUR: What happens?

SARAH: To sell my jewels .. spoils of a ten years' war. Three thousand pound .. how much a year?

LORD ARTHUR: I'll buy them.

SARAH: And return them? You have almost the right to make such a suggestion.

LORD ARTHUR: Stick to your father. He'll care for you?

SARAH: No .. we all pride ourselves on our lack of sentiment.

LORD ARTHUR: You must take money from your husband.

SARAH: I have earned that and spent it.

LORD ARTHUR: (*yielding once again to temptation*) I'm devilish fond of you ..

(*At that moment* ABUD *comes out of the dining-room. He is dressed in his best.* SARAH *responds readily to the interruption.*)

SARAH: And you must give my kindest compliments to Lady Arthur and my .. affectionately .. to the children and I'll let Papa know that you're going.

LORD ARTHUR: Letters under cover to your father?

SARAH: Papa will stay in town through the session of course .. but they all tell me that seventy-five pounds a year is a comfortable income in .. Timbuctoo.

> (*She goes into the dining-room.* ABUD *has selected his boots from the corner and now stands with them in his hand looking rather helpless. After a moment –*)

LORD ARTHUR: I congratulate you, Mr Abud.

ABUD: My lord .. I can't speak of myself.

> (CARNABY *comes out of the dining-room. He is evidently by no means recovered from his illness. He stands for a moment with an ironical eye on* JOHN ABUD.)

CARNABY: Son-in-law.

ABUD: I'm told to get on my boots, sir.

CARNABY: Allow me to assist you?

ABUD: I couldn't sir.

CARNABY: Désolé!

> (*Then he passes on.* ABUD *sits on the sofa, furtively puts on his boots and afterwards puts his shoes in his pockets.*)

LORD ARTHUR: You were so busy drinking health to the two fat farmers that I wouldn't interrupt you.

CARNABY: Good-bye. Describe all this to your brother John.

LORD ARTHUR: So confirmed a bachelor!

CARNABY: Please say that we missed him.

> (LORD ARTHUR *hands him the newspaper.*)

LORD ARTHUR: I've out-raced your *Chronicle* from London by some hours. There's a paragraph .. second column .. near the bottom.

CARNABY: (*looking at it blindly*) They print villainously nowadays.

LORD ARTHUR: Inspired.

CARNABY: I trust his grace is well?

LORD ARTHUR: Gouty.

CARNABY: Now doesn't the social aspect of this case interest you?

LORD ARTHUR: I object to feeding with the lower classes.

CARNABY: There's pride! How useful to note their simple manners! From the meeting of extremes new ideas spring .. new life.

LORD ARTHUR: Take that for a new social-political creed, Mr Leete.

CARNABY: Do I lack one?

LORD ARTHUR: Please make my adieux to the bride.

CARNABY: Appropriate .. 'à Dieu' .. she enters Nature's cloister. My epigram.

LORD ARTHUR: But .. good heavens .. are we to choose to be toiling animals?

CARNABY: To be such is my daughter's ambition.

LORD ARTHUR: You have not read that.

CARNABY: (*giving back the paper, vexedly*) I can't see.

LORD ARTHUR: 'The Right Honourable Carnaby Leete is, we are glad to hear, completely recovered and will return to town for the opening of Session.'

CARNABY: I mentioned it.

---

letters under cover to your father: shall I send you letters using your father's address.

LORD ARTHUR: 'We understand that although there has been no reconciliation with the Government it is quite untrue that this gentleman will in any way resume his connection with the Opposition.'

CARNABY: Inspired?

LORD ARTHUR: I am here from my father to answer any questions.

CARNABY: (*with some dignity and the touch of a threat*) Not now, my lord.

(DIMMUCK *comes in at the front door.*)

DIMMUCK: The chaise, my lord.

CARNABY: I will conduct you.

LORD ARTHUR: Please don't risk exposure.

CARNABY: Nay, I insist.

LORD ARTHUR: Health and happiness to you both, Mr Abud.

(LORD ARTHUR *goes out, followed by* CARNABY, *followed by* DIMMUCK. *At that moment* MR SMALLPEICE *skips excitedly out of the dining-room. A ferret-like little lawyer.*)

MR SMALLPEICE: Oh .. where is Mr Leete?

(*Not seeing him* MR SMALLPEICE *skips as excitedly back into the dining-room.* DIMMUCK *returns and hangs up his cloak then goes towards* ABUD, *whom he surveys.*)

DIMMUCK: Sir!

(*With which insult he starts for the dining-room reaching the door just in time to hold it open for* SIR GEORGE LEETE *who comes out. He surveys* ABUD *for a moment, then explodes.*)

SIR GEORGE LEETE: Damn you .. stand in the presence of your grandfather-in-law.

(ABUD *stands up.* CARNABY *returns coughing, and* SIR GEORGE *looks him up and down.*)

SIR GEORGE LEETE: I shall attend your funeral.

CARNABY: My daughter Sarah still needs me.

SIR GEORGE LEETE: I wonder at you, my son.

CARNABY: Have you any money to spare?

SIR GEORGE LEETE: No.

CARNABY: For Sarah, my housekeeper; I foresee a busy session.

(ABUD *is now gingerly walking up the stairs.*)

SIR GEORGE LEETE: Carnaby .. look at that.

CARNABY: Sound in wind and limb. Tread boldly, son-in-law.

(ABUD *turns, stands awkwardly for a moment and then goes into the dining-room.*)

SIR GEORGE LEETE: (*relapsing into a pinch of snuff*) I'm calm.

CARNABY: Regard this marriage with a wise eye .. as an amusing little episode.

SIR GEORGE LEETE: Do you?

CARNABY: And forget its oddity. Now that the humiliation is irrevocable, is it a personal grievance to you?

SIR GEORGE LEETE: Give me a dinner a day for the rest of my life and I'll be content.

CARNABY: Lately, one by one opinions and desires have been failing me .. a flicker and then extinction. I shall shortly attain to being a most able critic upon life.

SIR GEORGE LEETE: Shall I tell you again? You came into this world without a conscience. That explains you and it's all that does. That such a damnable coupling as this should be permitted by God Almighty .. or that the law shouldn't interfere! I've said my say.

(MR SMALLPEICE *again comes out of the dining-room.*)

MR SMALLPEICE: Mr Leete.

CARNABY: (*ironically polite*) Mr Smallpeice.

MR SMALLPEICE: Mr Crowe is proposing your health.

(MR CROWE *comes out. A crop-headed beefy-looking farmer of sixty.*)

MR CROWE: Was.

CARNABY: There's a good enemy!

MR CROWE: Get out of my road .. lawyer Smallpeice.

CARNABY: Leave enough of him living to attend to my business.

MR SMALLPEICE: (*wriggling a bow at* CARNABY) Oh .. dear sir!

SIR GEORGE LEETE: (*disgustedly to* MR SMALLPEICE) You!

MR SMALLPEICE: Employed in a small matter .. as yet.

CARNABY: (*to* CROWE) I hope you spoke your mind of me.

MR CROWE: Not behind your back, sir.

(MRS GEORGE LEETE *leads* LADY LEETE *from the dining-room.* LADY LEETE *is a very old, blind and decrepit woman.* DOLLY *is a buxom young mother; whose attire borders on the gaudy.*)

CARNABY: (*with some tenderness*) Well .. Mother .. dear?

MR CROWE: (*bumptiously to* SIR GEORGE LEETE) Did my speech offend you, my lord?

SIR GEORGE LEETE: (*sulkily*) I'm a baronet.

LADY LEETE: Who's this here?

CARNABY: Carnaby.

DOLLY: Step down .. grandmother.

LADY LEETE: Who did ye say you were?

DOLLY: Mrs George Leete.

LADY LEETE: Take me to the fire-side.

(*So* CARNABY *and* DOLLY *lead her slowly to a chair by the fire where they carefully bestow her.*)

MR SMALLPEICE: (*to* CROWE) He's leaving Markswayde, you know .. and me agent.

LADY LEETE: (*suddenly bethinking her*) Grace was not said. Fetch my chaplain .. at once.

MR SMALLPEICE: I will run.

(*He runs into the dining-room.*)

DOLLY: (*calling after with her country accent*) Not parson Remnant .. t'other one.

LADY LEETE: (*demanding*) Snuff.

CARNABY: (*to his father*) Sir .. my hand is a little unsteady.

(SIR GEORGE *and* CARNABY *between them give* LADY LEETE *her snuff.*)

---

baronet: titled hereditary order, but not noble and thus not to be addressed as 'lord'.

MR CROWE: Dolly .. ought those children to be left so long?

DOLLY: All right, father .. I have a maid.

> (LADY LEETE *sneezes*.)

SIR GEORGE LEETE: She'll do that once too often altogether.

LADY LEETE: I'm cold.

DOLLY: I'm cold .. I lack my shawl.

MR CROWE: Call out to your man for it.

DOLLY: (*going to the dining-room door*) Will a gentleman please ask Mr George Leete for my Cache-y-mire shawl?

MR CROWE: (*to* CARNABY) And I drank to the health of our grandson.

CARNABY: Now suppose George were to assume your name, Mr Crowe?

> (MR TOZER *comes out of the dining-room. Of the worst type of eighteenth century parson, for which one may see Hogarth's 'Harlot's Progress'. He is very drunk.*)

SIR GEORGE LEETE: (*in his wife's ear*) Tozer!

LADY LEETE: When .. why!

SIR GEORGE LEETE: To say grace.

> (LADY LEETE *folds her withered hands.*)

MR TOZER: (*through his hiccoughs*) Damn you all.

LADY LEETE: (*reverently, thinking it is said*) Amen.

MR TOZER: Only my joke.

CARNABY: (*rising to the height of the occasion*) Mr Tozer, I am indeed glad to see you, upon this occasion so delightfully drunk.

MR TOZER: Always a gen'elman .. by nature.

SIR GEORGE LEETE: Lie down .. you dog.

> (GEORGE *comes out carrying the cashmere shawl.*)

GEORGE: (*to his father*) Dolly wants her father to rent Markswayde, sir.

MR CROWE: Not me, my son. You're to be a farmer-baronet.

SIR GEORGE LEETE: Curse your impudence!

CARNABY: My one regret in dying would be to miss seeing him so.

> (GEORGE *goes back into the dining-room.*)

MR CROWE: I am tickled to think that the man marrying your daughter wasn't good enough for mine.

CARNABY: And yet at fisticuffs, I'd back John Abud against our son George.

> (DR REMNANT *has come out of the dining-room.* TOZER *has stumbled towards him and is wagging an argumentative finger.*)

MR TOZER: .. Marriage means enjoyment!

DR REMNANT: (*controlling his indignation*) I repeat that I have found in my own copy of the prayer book no insistence upon a romantic passion.

MR TOZER: My 'terpretation of God's word is 'bove criticism.

> (MR TOZER *reaches the door and falls into the dining-room.*)

CARNABY: (*weakly to* DR REMNANT) Give me your arm for a moment.

DR REMNANT: I think Lady Cottesham has Mrs John Abud prepared to start, sir.

CARNABY: I trust Ann will take no chill walking through the mud.

DR REMNANT: Won't you sit down, sir?

Cache-y-mire: Dolly's country pronunciation of cashmere.

CARNABY: No.
>(*For some moments* CROWE *has been staring indignantly at* SIR GEORGE. *Now he breaks out.*)

MR CROWE: The front door of this mansion is opened to a common gardener and only then to me and mine!

SIR GEORGE LEETE: (*virulently*) Damn you and yours and damn them .. and damn you again for the worse disgrace.

MR CROWE: Damn *you*, sir .. have you paid him to marry the girl?
>(*He turns away, purple faced, and* SIR GEORGE *chokes impotently.* ABUD *and* MR PRESTIGE *come out talking. He is younger and less assertive than* CROWE.)

MR PRESTIGE: (*pathetically*) All our family always has got drunk at weddings.

ABUD: (*in remonstrance*) Please, uncle.

CARNABY: Mr Crowe .. I have been much to blame for not seeking you sooner.

MR CROWE: (*mollified*) Shake hands.

CARNABY: (*offering his with some difficulty*) My arm is stiff .. from an accident. This is a maid's marriage, I assure you.

MR PRESTIGE: (*open mouthed to* DR REMNANT) One *could* hang bacon here!

DOLLY: (*very high and mighty*) The family don't.

CARNABY: (*to his father*) And won't you apologise for your remarks to Mr Crowe, sir?

LADY LEETE: (*demanding*) Snuff!

CARNABY: And your box to my mother, sir.
>(SIR GEORGE *attends to his wife.*)

DOLLY: (*anxiously to* DR REMNANT) Can a gentleman change his name?

MR CROWE: Parson .. once noble always noble, I take it.

DR REMNANT: Certainly .. but I hope you have money to leave them, Mr Crowe.

DOLLY: (*to* ABUD) John.

ABUD: Dorothy.

DOLLY: You've not seen my babies yet.
>(LADY LEETE *sneezes.*)

SIR GEORGE LEETE: Carnaby .. d'ye intend to murder that Crowe fellow .. or must I?
>(MR SMALLPEICE *skips from the dining-room.*)

MR SMALLPEICE: Mr John Abud ..

MR CROWE: (*to* DR REMNANT *as he nods towards* CARNABY) Don't tell me he's got over that fever yet.

MR SMALLPEICE: .. The ladies say .. are you ready or are you not?

MR PRESTIGE: I'll get thy cloak, John.
>(MR PRESTIGE *goes for the cloak.* CARNABY *has taken a pistol from the mantle-piece and now points it at* ABUD.)

CARNABY: He's fit for heaven!
>(GEORGE LEETE *comes from the dining-room and noticing his father's action says sharply ..*)

GEORGE: I suppose you know that pistol's loaded.
>(*Which calls everyone's attention.* DOLLY *shrieks.*)

CARNABY: What if there had been an accident!

(*And he puts back the pistol.* ABUD *takes his cloak from*
PRESTIGE.)

ABUD: Thank you, uncle.

MR PRESTIGE: I'm a proud man. Mr Crowe ..

CARNABY: Pride!

GEORGE: (*has a sudden inspiration and strides up to* ABUD) Here ends the joke,
my good fellow. Be off without your wife.

　　　　(ABUD *stares, as do the others. Only* CARNABY *suddenly catches*
　　　　REMNANT'S *arm.*)

MR PRESTIGE: (*solemnly*) But it's illegal to separate them.

GEORGE: (*giving up*) Mr Prestige .. you are the backbone of England.

CARNABY: (*to* REMNANT) Where are your miracles?

　　　　(MRS PRESTIGE *comes out. A motherly farmer's wife, a mountain*
　　　　of a woman.)

MRS PRESTIGE: John .. kiss your aunt.

　　　　(ABUD *goes to her, and she obliterates him in an embrace.*)

GEORGE: (*to his father*) Sense of humour .. Sense of humour!

LADY LEETE: Snuff.

　　　　(*But no one heeds her this time.*)

CARNABY: It doesn't matter.

GEORGE: Smile. Let's be helpless gracefully.

CARNABY: There are moments when I'm not sure –

GEORGE: It's her own life.

　　　　(TOZER *staggers from the dining-room drunker than ever. He falls*
　　　　against the baluster and waves his arms.)

MR TOZER: Silence there for the corpse!

MR CROWE: You beast!

MR TOZER: Respect my cloth .. Mr Prestige.

MR CROWE: That's not my name.

MR TOZER: I'll have you to know that I'm Sir George Leete's baronet's most boon
companion and her la'ship never goes nowhere without me. (*He subsides into a*
chair.)

LADY LEETE: (*tearfully*) Snuff.

　　　　(*From the dining-room comes* ANN; *her head bent. She is crossing the*
　　　　hall when SARAH *follows, calling her.*)

SARAH: Ann!

　　　　(ANN *turns back to kiss her. The rest of the company stand gazing.*
　　　　SIR GEORGE *gives snuff to* LADY LEETE.)

ANN: Good-bye, Sally.

SARAH: (*in a whisper*) Forget us.

GEORGE: (*relieving his feelings*) Good-bye, everybody .. good-bye, everything.

　　　　(ABUD *goes to the front door and opening it stands waiting for her.*
　　　　She goes coldly, but timidly to her father, to whom she puts her face up
　　　　to be kissed.)

ANN: Good-bye, Papa.

CARNABY: (*quietly, as he kisses her cheek*) I can do without you.

SIR GEORGE LEETE: (*raging at the draught*) Shut that door.

ANN: I'm gone.
> (*She goes with her husband.* MRS OPIE *comes hurriedly out of the dining-room, too late.*)

MRS OPIE: Oh!

DR REMNANT: Run .. Mrs Opie.

CARNABY: There has started the new century!
> (MRS OPIE *opens the front door to look after them.*)

SIR GEORGE LEETE: (*with double energy*) Shut that door.
> (LADY LEETE *sneezes and then chokes. There is much commotion in her neighbourhood.*)

SIR GEORGE LEETE: Now she's hurt again.

DOLLY: Water!

MR CROWE: Brandy!

SARAH: (*going*) I'll fetch both.

GEORGE: We must all die .. some day.

MR TOZER: (*who has struggled up to see what is the matter*) And go to –

DR REMNANT: Hell. You do believe in that, Mr Toper.

MRS OPIE: (*fanning the poor old lady*) She's better.

CARNABY: (*to his guests*) Gentlemen .. punch.
> (PRESTIGE *and* SMALLPEICE; MRS PRESTIGE, GEORGE *and* DOLLY *move towards the dining-room.*)

MR PRESTIGE: (*to* SMALLPEICE) You owe all this to me.

MR CROWE: Dolly .. I'm going.

MRS PRESTIGE: (*to her husband as she nods towards* CARNABY) Nathaniel ..
look at 'im.

GEORGE: (*to his father-in-law*) Must we come too?

MRS PRESTIGE: (*as before*) I can't help it .. a sneerin' carpin' cavillin' devil!

MRS OPIE: Markswayde is to let .. as I hear .. Mr Leete?

CARNABY: Markswayde is to let.
> (*He goes on his way to the dining-room, meeting* SARAH *who comes out carrying a glass of water and a decanter of brandy.* SIR GEORGE LEETE *is comfortably warming himself at the fire.*)

SCENE 2. *The living room of* JOHN ABUD'S *new cottage has bare plaster walls and its ceilings and floor are of red brick; all fresh looking but not new. In the middle of the middle wall there is a latticed window, dimity curtained; upon the plain shelf in front are several flower-pots. To the right of this, a door, cross beamed and with a large lock to it besides the latch. Against the right hand wall is a dresser, furnished with dishes and plates: below it is a common looking grandfather clock; below this a small door which when opened shows winding stairs leading to the room above. In the left hand wall there is a door which is almost hidden by the fireplace which juts out below it. In the fireplace a wood fire is laid but not lit. At right angles to this stands a heavy oak settle opposite a plain deal table; just beyond which is a little bench. On*

Toper: a drunkard.
dimity: strong and rough cotton fabric, woven with raised stripes or figures.
settle: long bench with high back, often with storage space below.
deal: cheap fir or pine.

either side of the window is a Windsor armchair. Between the window and the door hangs a framed sampler.

In the darkness the sound of the unlocking of a door and of ABUD *entering is heard. He walks to the table, strikes a light upon a tinder-box and lights a candle which he finds there.* ANN *is standing in the doorway.* ABUD *is in stocking feet.*

ABUD: Don't come further. Here are your slippers.

> (*He places one of the Windsor chairs for her on which she sits while he takes off her wet shoes and puts on her slippers which he found on the table. Then he takes her wet shoes to the fireplace. She sits still. Then he goes to the door and brings in his own boots from the little porch and puts them in the fireplace too. Then he locks the door and hangs up the key beside it. Then he stands looking at her; but she does not speak, so he takes the candle, lifts it above his head and walks to the dresser.*)

ABUD: (*encouragingly*) Our dresser .. Thomas Jupp made that. Plates and dishes. Here's Uncle Prestige's clock.

ANN: Past seven.

ABUD: That's upstairs. Table and bench, deal. Oak settle .. solid.

ANN: Charming.

ABUD: Windsor chairs .. Mother's sampler.

ANN: Home.

ABUD: Is it as you wish? I have been glad at your not seeing it until tonight.

ANN: I'm sinking into the strangeness of the place.

ABUD: Very weary? It's been a long nine miles.

> (*She does not answer. He goes and considers the flower-pots in the window.*)

ANN: I still have on my cloak.

ABUD: Hang it behind the door there .. no matter if the wet drips.

ANN: .. I can wipe up the puddle.

> (*She hangs up her cloak. He selects a flower-pot and brings it to her.*)

ABUD: Hyacinth bulbs for the spring.

ANN: (*after a glance*) I don't want to hold them.

> (*He puts back the pot, a little disappointed.*)

ABUD: Out there's the scullery.

ANN: It's very cold.

ABUD: If we light the fire now that means more trouble in the morning.

> (*She sits on the settle.*)

ANN: Yes, I am very weary.

ABUD: Go to bed.

ANN: Not yet. (*after a moment*) How much light one candle gives! Sit where I may see you.

> (*He sits on the bench. She studies him curiously.*)

ANN: Well .. this is an experiment.

ABUD: (*with reverence*) God help us both.

Windsor armchair: common eighteenth-century chair with high spoked back.

ANN: Amen. Some people are so careful of their lives. If we fail miserably we'll hold our tongues .. won't we?

ABUD: I don't know .. I can't speak of this.

ANN: These impossible things which are done mustn't be talked of .. that spoils them. We don't want to boast of this, do we?

ABUD: I fancy nobody quite believes that we are married.

ANN: Here's my ring .. real gold.

ABUD: (*with a sudden fierce throw up of his head*) Never you remind me of the difference between us.

ANN: Don't speak to me so.

ABUD: Now I'm your better.

ANN: My master .. The door's locked.

ABUD: (*nodding*) I know that I must be .. or be a fool.

ANN: (*after a moment*) Be kind to me.

ABUD: (*with remorse*) Always I will.

ANN: You are master here.

ABUD: And I've angered you?

ANN: And if I fail .. I'll never tell you .. to make a fool of you. And you're trembling. (*She sees his hand, which is on the table, shake.*)

ABUD: Look at that now.

ANN: (*lifting her own*) My white hands must redden. No more dainty appetite .. no more pretty books.

ABUD: Have you learned to scrub?

ANN: Not this floor.

ABUD: Mother always did bricks with a mop. Tomorrow I go to work. You'll be left for all day.

ANN: I must make friends with the other women around.

ABUD: My friends are very curious about you.

ANN: I'll wait to begin till I'm seasoned.

ABUD: Four o'clock's the hour for getting up.

ANN: Early rising always was a vice of mine.

ABUD: Breakfast quickly .. and I take my dinner with me.

ANN: In a handkerchief.

ABUD: Hot supper, please.

ANN: It shall be ready for you.

(*There is a silence between them for a little. Then he says timidly*)

ABUD: May I come near to you?

ANN: (*in a low voice*) Come.

(*He sits beside her, gazing.*)

ABUD: Wife .. I never have kissed you.

ANN: Shut your eyes.

ABUD: Are you afraid of me?

ANN: We're not to play such games at love.

ABUD: I can't help wanting to feel very tender towards you.

ANN: Think of me .. not as a wife .. but as a mother of your children .. if it's to be so. Treat me so.

ABUD: You are a part of me.

ANN: We must try and understand it .. as a simple thing.

ABUD: But shall I kiss you?

ANN: (*lowering her head*) Kiss me.

    (*But when he puts his arms round her she shrinks.*)

ANN: No.

ABUD: But I will. It's my right.

    (*Almost by force he kisses her. Afterwards she clenches her hands and seems to suffer.*)

ABUD: Have I hurt you?

    (*She gives him her hand with a strange little smile.*)

ANN: I forgive you.

ABUD: (*encouraged*) Ann .. we're beginning life together.

ANN: Remember .. work's enough .. no stopping to talk.

ABUD: I'll work for you.

ANN: I'll do my part .. something will come of it.

    (*For a moment they sit together hand in hand. Then she leaves him and paces across the room. There is a slight pause.*)

ANN: Papa .. I said .. we've all been in too great a hurry getting civilised. False dawn. I mean to go back.

ABUD: He laughed.

ANN: So he saw I was of no use to him and he's penniless and he let me go. When my father dies what will he take with him? .. for you do take your works with you into Heaven or Hell, I believe. Much wit. Sally is afraid to die. Don't you aspire like George's wife. I was afraid to live .. and now .. I am content.

    (*She walks slowly to the window and from there to the door against which she places her ear. Then she looks round at her husband.*)

ANN: I can hear them chattering.

    (*Then she goes to the little door and opens it. ABUD takes up the candle.*)

ABUD: I'll hold the light .. the stairs are steep.

    (*He lights her up the stairs.*)

THE VOYSEY INHERITANCE

Written 1903–5

First performed at the Court Theatre as a Vedrenne–Barker Matinee on 7 November 1905, with the following cast:

MR VOYSEY	A. E. George
MRS VOYSEY	Florence Haydon
TRENCHARD VOYSEY, K. C.	Eugene Mayeur
HONOR VOYSEY	Geraldine Oliffe
MAJOR BOOTH VOYSEY	Charles Fulton
EMILY (his wife)	Grace Edwin
CHRISTOPHER (their son)	Harry C. Duff
EDWARD VOYSEY	Thalberg Corbett
HUGH VOYSEY	Dennis Eadie
BEATRICE (his wife)	Henrietta Watson
ETHEL VOYSEY	Alexandra Carlisle
DENIS TREGONING (her fiancé)	Frederick Lloyd
ALICE MAITLAND	Mabel Hackney
MR GEORGE BOOTH	O. B. Clarence
REV. EVAN COLPUS	Edmund Gwenn
PEACEY	Trevor Lowe
PHOEBE	Gwynneth Galton
MARY	Mrs Fordyce

Directed by Granville Barker.

A slightly revised version (the basis of the present text) was presented at the Kingsway Theatre on 7 September 1912, directed by Granville Barker. A third, much revised version was presented at the Sadler's Wells Theatre on 3 May 1934, directed by Granville Barker and Harcourt Williams.

ACT I

The Office of Voysey and Son is in the best part of Lincoln's Inn. Its panelled rooms give out a sense of grandmotherly comfort and security, very grateful at first to the hesitating investor, the dubious litigant. MR VOYSEY'S *own room into which he walks about twenty past ten of a morning radiates enterprise besides. There is polish on everything; on the windows, on the mahogany of the tidily packed writing-table that stands between them, on the brasswork of the fireplace in the other wall, on the glass of the firescreen which preserves only the pleasantness of a sparkling fire, even on* MR VOYSEY'S *hat as he takes it off to place it on the little red curtained shelf behind the door.* MR VOYSEY *is sixty or more and masterful; would obviously be master anywhere from his own home outwards, or wreck the situation in his attempt. Indeed there is a buccaneering air sometimes in the twist of his glance, not altogether suitable to a family solicitor. On this bright October morning,* PEACEY, *the head clerk, follows just too late to help him off with his coat, but in time to take it and hang it up with a quite unnecessary subservience.* MR VOYSEY *is evidently not capable enough to like capable men about him.* PEACEY, *not quite removed from Nature, has made some attempts to acquire protective colouring. A very drunken client might mistake him for his master. His voice very easily became a toneless echo of* MR VOYSEY'S; *later his features caught a line or two from that mirror of all the necessary virtues into which he was so constantly gazing; but how his clothes even when new contrive to look like old ones of* MR VOYSEY'S *is a mystery, and to his tailor a most annoying one. And* PEACEY *is just a respectful number of years his master's junior. Relieved of his coat,* MR VOYSEY *carries to his table the bunch of beautiful roses he is accustomed to bring to the office three times a week and places them for a moment only near the bowl of water there ready to receive them while he takes up his letters. These lie ready too, opened mostly, one or two private ones left closed and discreetly separate. By this time the usual salutations have passed,* PEACEY'S '*Good morning, sir';* MR VOYSEY'S '*Morning, Peacy.' Then as he gets his letters* MR VOYSEY *starts his day's work.*

MR VOYSEY: Any news for me?
PEACEY: I hear bad accounts of Alguazils preferred, sir.
MR VOYSEY: Oh .. who from?
PEACEY: Merrit and James's head clerk in the train this morning.
MR VOYSEY: They looked all right on .. Give me the Times. (PEACEY *goes to the fireplace for the Times; it is warming there.* MR VOYSEY *waves a letter, then places it on the table.*) Here, that's for you .. Gerrard's Cross business. Anything else?
PEACEY: (*as he turns the Times to its Finance page*) I've made the usual notes.

Lincoln's Inn: one of the four Inns of Court, the legal societies in London with exclusive right of admission to the Bar, located between the City and Westminster.
Alguazils preferred: apparently a fictitious stock.
warming: the paper for *The Times* used to be dampened before printing in order to effect a sharper type, and arrived in the morning still wet. It was common practice to dry it before the fire, or even to iron it.
Gerrard's Cross: small town in Buckinghamshire.

MR VOYSEY: Thank'ee.

PEACEY: Young Benham isn't back yet.

MR VOYSEY: Mr Edward must do as he thinks fit about that. Alguazils, Alg – oh, yes.

> (*He is running his eye down the columns.* PEACEY *leans over the letters.*)

PEACEY: This is from Mr Leader about the codicil . . You'll answer that?

MR VOYSEY: Mr Leader. Yes. Alguazils. Mr Edward's here, I suppose.

PEACEY: No, sir.

MR VOYSEY: (*his eye twisting with some sharpness*) What!

PEACEY: (*almost alarmed*) I beg pardon, sir.

MR VOYSEY: Mr Edward.

PEACEY: Oh, yes, sir, been in his room some time. I thought you said Headley; he's not due back till Thursday.

> (MR VOYSEY *discards the Times and sits to his desk and his letters.*)

MR VOYSEY: Tell Mr Edward I've come.

PEACEY: Yes, sir. Anything else?

MR VOYSEY: Not for the moment. Cold morning, isn't it?

PEACEY: Quite surprising, sir.

MR VOYSEY: We had a touch of frost down at Chislehurst.

PEACEY: So early!

MR VOYSEY: I want it for the celery. All right, I'll call through about the rest of the letters.

> (PEACEY *goes, having secured a letter or two, and* MR VOYSEY *having sorted the rest [a proportion into the waste-paper basket] takes up the forgotten roses and starts setting them into a bowl with an artistic hand. Then his son* EDWARD *comes in.* MR VOYSEY *gives him one glance and goes on arranging the roses but says cheerily.*)

MR VOYSEY: Good morning, my dear boy.

> (EDWARD *has little of his father in him and that little is undermost. It is a refined face but self-consciousness takes the place in it of imagination, and in suppressing traits of brutality in his character it looks as if the young man had suppressed his sense of humour too. But whether or no, that would not be much in evidence now, for* EDWARD *is obviously going through some experience which is scaring him [there is no better word]. He looks not to have slept for a night or two, and his standing there, clutching and unclutching the bundle of papers he carries, his eyes on his father, half appealingly but half accusingly too, his whole being altogether so unstrung and desperate, makes* MR VOYSEY'S *uninterrupted arranging of the flowers seem very calculated indeed. At last the little tension of silence is broken.*)

EDWARD: Father . .

MR VOYSEY: Well?

EDWARD: I'm glad to see you.

Chislehurst: residential suburb eleven miles southeast of central London.

(*This is a statement of fact. He doesn't know that the commonplace phrase sounds ridiculous at such a moment.*)

MR VOYSEY: I see you've the papers there.

EDWARD: Yes.

MR VOYSEY: You've been through them?

EDWARD: As you wished me . .

MR VOYSEY: Well? (EDWARD *doesn't answer. Reference to the papers seems to overwhelm him with shame.* MR VOYSEY *goes on with cheerful impatience.*) Come, come, my dear boy, don't take it like this. You're puzzled and worried, of course. But why didn't you come down to me on Saturday night? I expected you . . I told you to come. Then your mother was wondering why you weren't with us for dinner yesterday.

EDWARD: I went through all the papers twice. I wanted to make quite sure.

MR VOYSEY: Sure of what? I told you to come to me.

EDWARD: (*He is very near crying.*) Oh, father.

MR VOYSEY: Now look here, Edward, I'm going to ring and dispose of these letters. Please pull yourself together. (*He pushes the little button on his table.*)

EDWARD: I didn't leave my rooms all day yesterday.

MR VOYSEY: A pleasant Sunday! You must learn, whatever the business may be, to leave it behind you at the Office. Why, life's not worth living else. (PEACEY *comes in to find* MR VOYSEY *before the fire ostentatiously warming and rubbing his hands.*) Oh, there isn't much else, Peacey. Tell Simmons that if he satisfies you about the details of this lease it'll be all right. Make a note for me of Mr Grainger's address at Menton. I shall have several things to dictate to Atkinson. I'll whistle for him.

PEACEY: Mr Burnett . . Burnett and Marks has just come in, Mr Edward.

EDWARD: (*without turning*) It's only fresh instructions. Will you take them?

PEACEY: All right.

(PEACEY *goes, lifting his eyebrows at the queerness of* EDWARD'S *manner. This* MR VOYSEY *sees, returning to his table with a little scowl.*)

MR VOYSEY: Now sit down. I've given you a bad forty-eight hours, have I? Well, I've been anxious about you. Never mind, we'll thresh the thing out now. Go through the two accounts. Mrs Murberry's first . . how do you find it stands?

EDWARD: (*his feelings choking him*) I hoped you were playing off some joke on me.

MR VOYSEY: Come now.

(EDWARD *separates the papers precisely and starts to detail them; his voice quite toneless. Now and then his father's sharp comments ring out in contrast.*)

EDWARD: We've got the lease of her present house, several agreements . . and here's her will. Here's also a power of attorney expired some time over her securities and her property generally . . it was made out for six months.

MR VOYSEY: She was in South Africa.

EDWARD: Here's the Sheffield mortgage and the Henry Smith mortgage with Banker's receipts . . her Banker's to us for the interest up to date . . four and a

half and five per cent. Then .. Fretworthy Bonds. There's a note scribbled in
your writing that they are at the Bank; but you don't say what Bank.

MR VOYSEY: My own .. Stukeley's.

EDWARD: (*just dwelling on the words*) Your own. I queried that. There's eight
thousand five hundred in three and a half India Stock. And there are her
Banker's receipts for cheques on account of those dividends. I presume for
those dividends.

MR VOYSEY: Why not?

EDWARD: (*gravely*) Because then, father, there are her Banker's half yearly
receipts for other sums amounting to an average of four hundred and twenty
pounds a year. But I find no record of any capital to produce this.

MR VOYSEY: Go on. What do you find?

EDWARD: Till about three years back there seems to have been eleven thousand in
Queenslands which would produce – did produce exactly the same sum. But
after January of that year I find no record of 'em.

MR VOYSEY: In fact the Queenslands are missing, vanished?

EDWARD: (*hardly uttering the word*) Yes.

MR VOYSEY: From which you conclude?

EDWARD: I supposed at first that you had not handed me all the papers.

MR VOYSEY: Since Mrs Murberry evidently still gets that four twenty a year,
somehow; lucky woman.

EDWARD: (*in agony*) Oh!

MR VOYSEY: Well, we'll return to the good lady later. Now let's take the other.

EDWARD: The Hatherley Trust.

MR VOYSEY: Quite so.

EDWARD: (*with one accusing glance*) Trust.

MR VOYSEY: Go on.

EDWARD: Father ..

> (*His grief comes uppermost again and* MR VOYSEY *meets it kindly.*)

MR VOYSEY: I know, my dear boy. I shall have lots to say to you. But let's get
quietly through with these details first.

EDWARD: (*bitterly now*) Oh, this is simple enough. We're young Hatherley's only
trustees till his coming of age in about five years' time. The property was
eighteen thousand invested in Consols. Certain sums were to be allowed for his
education; we seem to be paying them.

MR VOYSEY: Regularly.

EDWARD: Quite. But where's the capital?

MR VOYSEY: No record?

EDWARD: Yes .. A note by you on a half sheet .. Refer to the Bletchley Land
Scheme.

MR VOYSEY: That was ten years ago. Haven't I credited him with the interest on
his capital?

---

three and a half India stock: Colonial Government security, the funds invested in official Indian
enterprises, producing a return of 3.5 per cent.
Queenslands: another Colonial Government security, this one in Australian enterprises.
Consols: Consolidated Annuities, a government bond issue with a fixed but relatively low rate
of interest: a common safe investment in the period.

EDWARD: The balance ought to be re-invested. There's this (*a sheet of figures*) in your hand-writing. You credit him with the Consol interest.

MR VOYSEY: Quite so.

EDWARD: But I think I've heard you say that the Bletchley scheme paid seven and a half.

MR VOYSEY: At one time. Have you also taken the trouble to calculate what will be due from us to the lad?

EDWARD: Yes .. even on the Consol basis .. capital and compound interest .. about twenty six thousand pounds.

MR VOYSEY: A respectable sum. In five years' time?

EDWARD: When he comes of age.

MR VOYSEY: That gives us, say, four years and six months in which to think about it.

> (EDWARD *waits, hopelessly, for his father to speak again; then says ..*)

EDWARD: Thank you for showing me these, sir. Shall I put them back in your safe now?

MR VOYSEY: Yes, you'd better. There's the key. (EDWARD *reaches for the bunch, his face hidden.*) Put them down. Your hand shakes .. why, you might have been drinking .. I'll put them away later. It's no use having hysterics, Edward. Look your trouble in the face.

> (EDWARD'S *only answer is to go to the fire, as far from his father as the room allows. And there he leans on the mantelpiece, his shoulders heaving.*)

MR VOYSEY: I'm sorry, my dear boy. I wouldn't tell you if I could help it.

EDWARD: I can't believe it. And that you should be telling me .. such a thing.

MR VOYSEY: Let yourself go .. have your cry out, as the women say. It isn't pleasant, I know. It isn't pleasant to inflict it on you.

EDWARD: How I got through that outer office this morning, I don't know. I came early but some of them were here. Peacey came into my room; he must have seen that there was something up.

MR VOYSEY: That's no matter.

EDWARD: (*able to turn to his father again; won round by the kind voice*) How long has it been going on? Why didn't you tell me before? Oh, I know you thought you'd pull through; but I'm your partner .. I'm responsible too. Oh, I don't want to shirk that .. don't think I mean to shirk that, father. Perhaps I ought to have discovered, but those affairs were always in your hands. I trusted .. I beg your pardon. Oh, it's us .. not you. Everyone has trusted us.

MR VOYSEY: (*calmly and kindly still*) You don't seem to notice that I'm not breaking my heart like this.

EDWARD: What's the extent of the mischief? When did it begin? Father, what made you begin it?

MR VOYSEY: I didn't begin it.

EDWARD: You didn't. Who then?

MR VOYSEY: My father before me. (EDWARD *stares.*) That calms you a little.

EDWARD: I'm glad .. my dear father! (*And he puts out his hand. Then just a doubt enters his mind.*) But I .. it's amazing.

MR VOYSEY: (*shaking his head*) My inheritance, Edward.

EDWARD: My dear father!

MR VOYSEY: I had hoped it wasn't to be yours.

EDWARD: D'you mean to tell me that this sort of thing has been going on here for years? For more than thirty years!

MR VOYSEY: Yes.

EDWARD: That's a little hard to understand just at first, sir.

MR VOYSEY: (*sententiously*) We do what we must in this world, Edward; I have done what I had to do.

EDWARD: (*his emotion well cooled by now*) Perhaps I'd better just listen quietly while you explain.

MR VOYSEY: (*concentrating*) You know that I'm heavily into Northern Electrics.

EDWARD: Yes.

MR VOYSEY: But you don't know how heavily. When I got the tip the Municipalities were organising the purchase, I saw of course the stock must be up a hundred and forty five – a hundred and fifty in no time. Now Leeds will keep up her silly quarrel with the other place .. they won't apply for powers for another ten years. I bought at ninety five. What are they today?

EDWARD: Seventy two.

MR VOYSEY: Seventy one and a half. And in ten years I may be .. I'm getting on for seventy, Edward. That's mainly why you've had to be told.

EDWARD: With whose money are you so heavily into Northern Electrics?

MR VOYSEY: The firm's money.

EDWARD: Clients' money?

MR VOYSEY: Yes.

EDWARD: (*coldly*) Well .. I'm waiting for your explanation, sir.

MR VOYSEY: You seem to have recovered pretty much.

EDWARD: No, sir, I'm trying to understand, that's all.

MR VOYSEY: (*with a shrug*) Children always think the worst of their parents, I suppose. I did of mine. It's a pity.

EDWARD: Go on, sir, go on. Let me know the worst.

MR VOYSEY: There's no immediate danger. I should think anyone could see that from the figures there. There's no real risk at all.

EDWARD: Is that the worst?

MR VOYSEY: (*his anger rising*) Have you studied these two accounts or have you not?

EDWARD: Yes, sir.

MR VOYSEY: Well, where's the deficiency in Mrs Murberry's income .. has she ever gone without a shilling? What has young Hatherley lost?

EDWARD: He stands to lose –

MR VOYSEY: He stands to lose nothing if I'm spared for a little, and you will only bring a little common sense to bear and try to understand the difficulties of my position.

EDWARD: Father, I'm not thinking ill of you .. that is, I'm trying not to. But won't you explain how you're justified ..?

MR VOYSEY: In putting our affairs in order?

EDWARD: Are you doing that?

MR VOYSEY: What else?

EDWARD: (*starting patiently to examine the matter*) How bad were things when you first came to control them?

MR VOYSEY: Oh, I forget.

EDWARD: You can't forget.

MR VOYSEY: Well . . pretty bad.

EDWARD: Do you know how it was my grandfather began to –

MR VOYSEY: Muddlement, muddlement! Fooled away hundreds and thousands on safe things . . well, then, what was he to do? He'd no capital, no credit, and was in terror of his life. My dear Edward, if I hadn't found it out in time, he'd have confessed to the first man who came and asked for a balance sheet.

EDWARD: Well, what exact sum was he to the bad then?

MR VOYSEY: I forget. Several thousands.

EDWARD: But surely it has not taken all these years to pay off –

MR VOYSEY: Oh, hasn't it!

EDWARD: (*making his point*) Then how does it happen, sir, that such a comparatively recent trust as young Hatherley's has been broken into?

MR VOYSEY: Well, what could be safer than to use that money? There's a Consol investment and not a sight wanted of either capital or interest for five years.

EDWARD: (*utterly beaten*) Father, are you mad?

MR VOYSEY: On the contrary, when my clients' money is entirely under my control, I sometimes re-invest it. The difference between the income this money was bringing to them and the profits it then actually brings to me, I . . I utilise in my endeavour to fill up the deficit in the firm's accounts . . I use it to put things straight. Doesn't it follow that the more low-interest-bearing capital I can use the better . . the less risky things I have to put it into. Most of the young Hatherley's Consol capital . . the Trust gives me full discretion . . is now out on mortgage at four and a half and five . . safe as safe can be.

EDWARD: But he should have the benefit.

MR VOYSEY: He has the amount of his Consol interest.

EDWARD: Where are the mortgages? Are they in his name?

MR VOYSEY: Some of them . . some of them. That really doesn't matter. With regard to Mrs Murberry . . those Fretworthy Bonds at my bank . . I've raised five thousand on them. But I can release her Bonds tomorrow if she wants them.

EDWARD: Where's the five thousand?

MR VOYSEY: I'm not sure . . it was paid into my own account. Yes, I do remember. Some of it went to complete a purchase . . that and two thousand more out of the Skipworth fund.

EDWARD: But, my dear father –

MR VOYSEY: Well?

EDWARD: (*summing it all up very simply*) It's not right.

> (MR VOYSEY *considers his son for a moment with a pitying shake of the head.*)

MR VOYSEY: Why? . . why is it so hard for a man to see beyond the letter of the law! Will you consider, Edward, the position in which I found myself at that moment! Was I to see my father ruined and disgraced without lifting a finger to help him? . . quite apart from the interest of our clients. I paid back to the man who would have lost most by my father's mistakes every penny of his money. And he never knew the danger he'd been in . . never passed an uneasy moment about it. It was I that lay awake. I have now somewhere a letter from that man to my father thanking him effusively for the way in which he'd conducted some matter. It comforted my poor father. Well, Edward, I stepped outside the letter of the law to do that service. Was I right or wrong?

EDWARD: In the result, sir, right.

MR VOYSEY: Judge me by the result. I took the risk of failure . . I should have suffered. I could have kept clear of the danger if I'd liked.

EDWARD: But that's all past. The thing that concerns me is what you are doing now.

MR VOYSEY: (*gently reproachful now*) My boy, can't you trust me a little? It's all very well for you to come in at the end of the day and criticise. But I who have done the day's work know how that work had to be done. And here's our firm, prosperous, respected and without a stain on its honour. That's the main point, isn't it?

EDWARD: (*quite irresponsive to this pathetic appeal*) Very well, sir. Let's dismiss from our minds all prejudices about speaking the truth . . acting upon one's instructions, behaving as any honest firm of solicitors must behave . .

MR VOYSEY: Nonsense, I tell no unnecessary lies. If a man of any business ability gives me definite instructions about his property, I follow them.

EDWARD: Father, no unnecessary lies!

MR VOYSEY: Well, my friend, go and knock it into Mrs Murberry's head, if you can, that four hundred and twenty pounds of her income hasn't, for the last eight years, come from the place she thinks it's come from, and see how happy you'll make her.

EDWARD: But is that four hundred and twenty a year as safe to come to her as it was before you meddled with the capital?

MR VOYSEY: I see no reason why –

EDWARD: What's the security?

MR VOYSEY: (*putting his coping stone on the argument*) My financial ability.

EDWARD: (*really not knowing whether to laugh or cry*) Why, one'd think you were satisfied with this state of things.

MR VOYSEY: Edward, you really are most unsympathetic and unreasonable. I give all I have to the firm's work . . my brain . . my energies . . my whole life. I can't turn my abilities into hard cash at par . . I wish I could. Do you suppose that if I could establish every one of these people with a separate and consistent bank balance tomorrow that I shouldn't do it?

EDWARD: (*thankfully able to meet anger with anger*) Do you mean to tell me that you couldn't somehow have put things right by this?

MR VOYSEY: Somehow? How?

EDWARD: If thirty years of this sort of thing hasn't brought you hopelessly to grief . . during that time there must have been opportunities . .

MR VOYSEY: Must there! Well, I hope that when I'm under ground, you may find them.

EDWARD: I!

MR VOYSEY: Put everything right with the stroke of your pen, if it's so easy!

EDWARD: I!

MR VOYSEY: You're my partner and my son; you'll inherit the business.

EDWARD: (*realising at last that he has been led to the edge of this abyss*) Oh no, father.

MR VOYSEY: Why else have I had to tell you all this?

EDWARD: (*very simply*) Father, I can't. I can't possibly. I don't think you've any right to ask me.

MR VOYSEY: Why not, pray?

EDWARD: It's perpetuating the dishonesty.

(MR VOYSEY *hardens at the unpleasant word.*)

MR VOYSEY: You don't believe that I've told you the truth.

EDWARD: I want to believe it.

MR VOYSEY: It's no proof .. my earning these twenty or thirty people their rightful incomes for the last – how many years?

EDWARD: Whether what you have done and are doing is wrong or right .. I can't meddle in it.

(*For the moment* MR VOYSEY *looks a little dangerous.*)

MR VOYSEY: Very well. Forget all I've said. Go back to your room. Get back to your own mean drudgery. My life work – my splendid life work – ruined! What does that matter?

EDWARD: Whatever did you expect of me?

MR VOYSEY: (*making a feint at his papers*) Oh, nothing, nothing. (*Then he slams them down with great effect.*) Here's a great edifice built up by years of labour and devotion and self-sacrifice .. a great arch you may call it .. a bridge which is to carry our firm to safety with honour. (*This variation of Disraeli passes unnoticed.*) My work! And now, as I near the end of my life, it still lacks the key-stone. Perhaps I am to die with my work just incomplete. Then is there nothing that a son might do? Do you think I shouldn't be proud of you, Edward .. that I shouldn't bless you from – wherever I may be, when you completed my life's work .. with perhaps just one kindly thought of your father?

(*In spite of this oratory, the situation is gradually impressing* EDWARD.)

EDWARD: What will happen if I .. if I desert you?

MR VOYSEY: I'll protect you as best I can.

EDWARD: I wasn't thinking of myself, sir.

MR VOYSEY: (*with great nonchalance*) Well, I shan't mind the exposure, you know. It won't make me blush in my coffin .. and you're not so quixotic, I hope, as to be thinking of the feelings of your brothers and sisters. Considering how simple it would have been for me to have gone to my grave in peace and quiet and let you discover the whole thing afterwards, the fact that I *didn't*, that I have taken thought for the future of all of you might perhaps have convinced you that I ..! But there .. consult your own safety.

(EDWARD *has begun to pace the room; indecision growing upon him.*)

EDWARD: This is a queer thing to have to make up one's mind about, isn't it, father?

MR VOYSEY: (*watching him closely and modulating his voice*) My dear boy, I understand the shock to your feelings that this disclosure must have been.

EDWARD: Yes, I came this morning thinking that next week would see us in the dock together.

MR VOYSEY: And I suppose if I'd broken down and begged your pardon for my folly, you'd have done anything for me, gone to prison smiling, eh?

EDWARD: I suppose so.

MR VOYSEY: Yes, it's easy enough to forgive. I'm sorry I can't go in sack-cloth and ashes to oblige you. (*Now he begins to rally his son; easy in his strength.*) My dear Edward, you've lived a quiet humdrum life up to now, with your poetry and your sociology and your agnosticism and your ethics of this and your ethics of that .. dear me, these are the sort of garden oats which young men seem to sow nowadays! .. and you've never before been brought face to face with any really vital question. Now don't make a fool of yourself just through inexperience. Try and give your mind without prejudice to the consideration of a very serious matter. I'm not angry at what you've said to me. I'm quite willing to forget it. And it's for your own sake and not for mine, Edward, that I do beg you to – to – to be a man and take a practical common-sense view of the position you find yourself in. It's not a pleasant position, I know, but it's unavoidable.

EDWARD: You should have told me before you took me into partnership.

(*Oddly enough it is this last flicker of rebellion which breaks down* MR VOYSEY'S *caution. Now he lets fly with a vengeance.*)

MR VOYSEY: Should I be telling you at all if I could possibly help it? Don't I know that you're all about as fit for the job as a babe unborn? Haven't I been worrying over that for these last three years? But I'm in a corner .. and am I to see my firm come to smash simply because of your scruples? If you're a son of mine you'll do as I tell you. Hadn't I the same choice to make? .. and it's a safer game for you now than it was for me then. D'you suppose I didn't have scruples? If you run away from this, Edward, you're a coward. My father was a coward and he suffered for it to the end of his days. I was sick-nurse to him here more than partner. Good lord! .. of course it's pleasant and comfortable to keep within the law .. then the law will look after you. Otherwise you have to look pretty sharp after yourself. You have to cultivate your own sense of right and wrong; deal your own justice. But that makes a bigger man of you, let me tell you. How easily .. how easily could I have walked out of my father's office and left him to his fate; no one would have blamed me! But I didn't. I thought it my better duty to stay and .. yes, I say it with all reverence .. to take up my cross. Well, I've carried that cross pretty successfully. And what's more, it's made a happy man of me .. a better, stronger man than skulking about in shame and in fear of his life ever made of my poor dear father. (*Relieved at having let out the truth, but doubtful of his wisdom in doing so, he changes his tone.*) I don't want what I've been saying to influence you, Edward. You are a free agent .. and you must decide upon your own course of action. Now don't let's discuss the matter any more for the moment.

(EDWARD *looks at his father with clear eyes.*)

EDWARD: Don't forget to put these papers away.

    (*He restores them to their bundles and hands them back: it is his only comment.* MR VOYSEY *takes them and his meaning in silence.*)

MR VOYSEY: Are you coming down to Chislehurst soon? We've got Hugh and his wife, and Booth and Emily, and Christopher for two or three days, till he goes back to school.

EDWARD: How is Chris?

MR VOYSEY: All right again now . . grows more like his father. Booth's very proud of him. So am I.

EDWARD: I think I can't face them all just at present.

MR VOYSEY: Nonsense.

EDWARD: (*a little wave of emotion going through him*) I feel as if this thing were written on my face. How I shall get through business I don't know!

MR VOYSEY: You're weaker than I thought, Edward.

EDWARD: (*a little ironically*) A disappointment to you, father?

MR VOYSEY: No, no.

EDWARD: You should have brought one of the others into the firm . . Trenchard or Booth.

MR VOYSEY: (*hardening*) Trenchard! (*He dismisses that.*) Well, you're a better man than Booth. Edward, you mustn't imagine that the whole world is standing on its head merely because you've had an unpleasant piece of news. Come down to Chislehurst tonight . . well, say tomorrow night. It'll be good for you . . stop your brooding . . that's your worst vice, Edward. You'll find the household as if nothing had happened. Then you'll remember that nothing really has happened. And presently you'll get to see that nothing need happen, if you keep your head. I remember times, when things have seemed at their worst, what a relief it's been to me . . my romp with you all in the nursery just before your bedtime. Do you remember?

EDWARD: Yes. And cutting your head open once with that gun.

MR VOYSEY: (*in a full glow of fine feeling*) And, my dear boy, if I knew that you were going to inform the next client you met of what I've just told you . .

EDWARD: (*with a shudder*) Oh, father!

MR VOYSEY: . . And that I should find myself in prison tomorrow, I wouldn't wish a single thing I've ever done undone. I have never wilfully harmed man or woman. My life's been a happy one. Your dear mother has been spared to me. You're most of you good children and a credit to what I've done for you.

EDWARD: (*the deadly humour of this too much for him*) Father!

MR VOYSEY: Run along now, run along. I must finish my letters and get into the City.

    (*He might be scolding a schoolboy for some trifling fault.* EDWARD *turns to have a look at the keen unembarrassed face.* MR VOYSEY *smiles at him and proceeds to select from the bowl a rose for his buttonhole.*)

EDWARD: I'll think it over, sir.

MR VOYSEY: Of course, you will. And don't brood, Edward, don't brood.

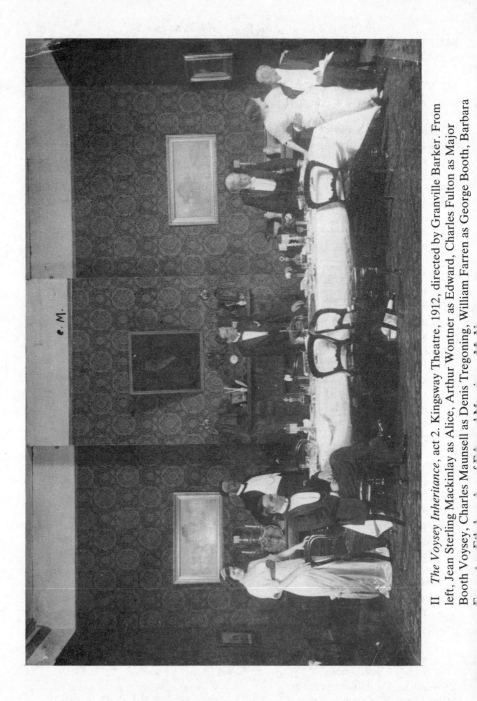

II *The Voysey Inheritance*, act 2. Kingsway Theatre, 1912, directed by Granville Barker. From left, Jean Sterling Mackinlay as Alice, Arthur Wontner as Edward, Charles Fulton as Major Booth Voysey, Charles Maunsell as Denis Tregoning, William Farren as George Booth, Barbara

(*So* EDWARD *leaves him; and having fixed the rose to his
satisfaction, he rings his table telephone and calls through it to
the listening clerk.*)
Send Atkinson to me, please. (*Then he gets up, keys in hand, to lock away Mrs
Murberry's and the Hatherley Trust papers.*)

ACT II

The VOYSEY *dining-room at Chislehurst, when children and grandchildren are
visiting, is dining-table and very little else. And at this moment in the evening when
five or six men are sprawling back in their chairs, and the air is clouded with smoke, it
is a very typical specimen of the middle-class English domestic temple; the daily
sacrifice consummated, the acolytes dismissed, the women safely in the drawing-room,
and the chief priests of it taking their surfeited ease round the dessert-piled altar. It has
the usual red-papered walls (like a reflection, they are, of the underdone beef so much
consumed within them), the usual varnished woodwork which is known as grained
oak; there is the usual, hot, mahogany furniture; and, commanding point of the whole
room, there is the usual black-marble sarcophagus of a fireplace. Above this hangs
one of the two or three oil paintings, which are all that break the red pattern of the
walls, the portrait painted in 1880 of an undistinguished looking gentleman aged sixty;
he is shown sitting in a more graceful attitude than it could ever have been comfortable
for him to assume.* MR VOYSEY'S *father it is, and the brass plate at the bottom of
the frame tells us that the portrait was a presentation one. On the mantlepiece stands,
of course, a clock; at either end a china vase filled with paper spills. And in front of
the fire – since that is the post of vantage, stands at this moment* MAJOR BOOTH
VOYSEY. *He is the second son, of the age that it is necessary for a Major to be, and
of an appearance that many ordinary Majors in ordinary regiments are. He went into
the army because he thought it would be like a schoolboy's idea of it; and, being there,
he does his little all to keep it so. He stands astride, hands in pockets, coat-tails
through his arms, cigar in mouth, moustache bristling. On either side of him sits at the
table an old gentleman; the one is* MR EVAN COLPUS, *the vicar of their parish, the
other* MR GEORGE BOOTH, *a friend of long standing, and the Major's godfather.*
MR COLPUS *is a harmless enough anachronism, except for the waste of £400 a year
in which his stipend involves the community. Leaving most of his parochial work to
an energetic curate, he devotes his serious attention to the composition of two sermons
a week. They deal with the difficulties of living the Christian life as experienced by
people who have nothing else to do. Published in series from time to time, these form
suitable presents for bedridden parishioners.* MR GEORGE BOOTH, *on the
contrary, is as gay an old gentleman as can be found in Chislehurst. An only son, his
father left him at the age of twenty-five a fortune of a hundred thousand pounds (a
plum, as he called it). At the same time he had the good sense to dispose of his father's
business, into which he had been most unwillingly introduced five years earlier, for a
like sum before he was able to depreciate its value. It was* MR VOYSEY'S *invaluable*

---

dessert: not the sweet course but fresh fruit and nuts at the end of dinner, usually taken with
port and cigars after the women had withdrawn from the table.

assistance in this transaction which first bound the two together in great friendship. Since that time MR BOOTH *has been bent on nothing but enjoying himself. He has even remained a bachelor with that object. Money has given him all he wants, therefore he loves and reverences money; while his imagination may be estimated by the fact that he has now reached the age of sixty-five, still possessing more of it than he knows what to do with. At the head of the table, meditatively cracking walnuts, sits* MR VOYSEY. *He has his back there to the conservatory door – you know it is the conservatory door because there is a curtain to pull over it, and because half of it is frosted glass with a purple key pattern round the edge. On* MR VOYSEY'S *left is* DENIS TREGONING, *a nice enough young man. And at the other end of the table sits* EDWARD, *not smoking, not talking, hardly listening, very depressed. Behind him is the ordinary door of the room, which leads out into the dismal draughty hall. The* MAJOR'S *voice is like the sound of a cannon through the tobacco smoke.*

MAJOR: Of course I'm hot and strong for conscription . .

MR BOOTH: My dear boy, the country'd never stand it. No Englishman –

MAJOR: (*dropping the phrase heavily upon the poor old gentleman*) I beg your pardon. If we . . the Army . . say to the country . . upon our honour conscription is necessary for your safety . . what answer has the country? What? (*He pauses defiantly.*) There you are . . none!

TREGONING: Booth will imagine because one doesn't argue that one has nothing to say. You ask the country.

MAJOR: Perhaps I will. Perhaps I'll chuck the Service and go into the House. (*then falling into the sing-song of a favourite phrase*) I'm not a conceited man . . but I believe that if I speak out upon a subject I understand and only upon that subject the House will listen . . and if others followed my example we should be a far more business-like and go-ahead community.

(*He pauses for breath and* MR BOOTH *seizes the opportunity.*)

MR BOOTH: If you think the gentlemen of England will allow themselves to be herded with a lot of low fellers and made to carry guns –!

MAJOR: (*obliterating him once more*) Just one moment. Have you thought of the physical improvement which conscription would bring about in the manhood of the country? What England wants is Chest! (*He generously inflates his own.*) Chest and Discipline. Never mind how it's obtained. Don't we suffer from a lack of it in our homes? The servant question now . .

MR VOYSEY: (*with a crack of a nut*) Your godson talks a deal, don't he? You know, when our Major gets into a club, he gets on the committee . . gets on any committee to enquire into anything . . and then goes on at 'em just like this. Don't you, Booth?

(MAJOR *knuckles under easily enough to his father's sarcasm.*)

MAJOR: Well, sir, people tell me I'm a useful man on committees.

MR VOYSEY: I don't doubt it . . your voice must drown all discussion.

MAJOR: You can't say I don't listen to you, sir.

MR VOYSEY: I don't . . and I'm not blaming you. But I must say I often think what a devil of a time the family will have with you when I'm gone. Fortunately for your poor mother, she's deaf.

MAJOR: And wouldn't you wish me, sir, as eldest son . . Trenchard not counting . .

MR VOYSEY: (*with a crack of another nut*) Trenchard not counting. By all means, bully them. Never mind whether you're right or wrong .. bully them. I don't manage things that way myself, but I think it's your best chance .. if there weren't other people present I might say your only chance, Booth.

MAJOR: (*with some discomfort*) Ha! If I were a conceited man, sir, I could trust you to take it out of me.

MR VOYSEY: (*as he taps* MR BOOTH *with the nut crackers*) Help yourself, George, and drink to your godson's health. Long may he keep his chest notes! Never heard him on parade, have you?

TREGONING: I notice military men must display themselves .. that's why Booth acts as a firescreen. I believe that after mess that position is positively rushed.

MAJOR: (*cheering to find an opponent he can tackle*) If you want a bit of fire, say so, you sucking Lord Chancellor. Because I mean to allow you to be my brother-in-law, you think you can be impertinent.

> (*So* TREGONING *moves to the fire and that changes the conversation.*)

MR VOYSEY: By the bye, Vicar, you were at Lady Mary's yesterday. Is she giving us anything towards that window?

COLPUS: Five pounds more; she has promised me five pounds.

MR VOYSEY: Then how will the debt stand?

COLPUS: Thirty-three .. no, thirty-two pounds.

VOYSEY: We're a long time clearing it off.

COLPUS: (*gently querulous*) Yes, now that the window is up, people don't seem so ready to contribute as they were.

TREGONING: We must mention that to Hugh!

COLPUS: (*tactful at once*) Not that the work is not universally admired. I have heard Hugh's design praised by quite competent judges. But certainly I feel now it might have been wiser to have delayed the unveiling until the money was forthcoming.

TREGONING: Never deliver goods to the Church on credit.

COLPUS: Eh? (TREGONING *knows that he is a little hard of hearing.*)

VOYSEY: Well, as it was my wish that my son should do the design, I suppose in the end I shall have to send you a cheque.

MAJOR: Anonymously.

COLPUS: Oh, that would be –

VOYSEY: No, why should I? Here, George Booth, you shall halve it with me.

MR BOOTH: I'm damned if I do.

COLPUS: (*proceeding, conveniently deaf*) You remember that at the meeting we had of the parents and friends to decide on the positions of the names of the poor fellows and the regiments and coats of arms and so on .. when Hugh said so violently that he disapproved of the war and made all those remarks about land-lords and Bibles and said he thought of putting in a figure of Britannia blushing for shame or something .. I'm beginning to fear that may have created a bad impression.

---

sucking: budding or infantile. The Lord Chancellor is the Speaker of the House of Lords and the highest judicial officer of England.

MAJOR: Why should they mind .. what on earth does Hugh know about war? He couldn't tell a battery horse from a bandsman. I don't pretend to criticise art. I think the window'd be very pretty if it wasn't so broken up into bits.

MR BOOTH: (*fortified by his 'damned' and his last glass of port*) These young men are so ready with their disapproval. When I was young, people weren't always questioning this and questioning that.

MAJOR: Lack of discipline.

MR BOOTH: (*hurrying on*) The way a man now even stops to think what he's eating and drinking. And in religious matters .. Vicar, I put it to you .. there's no uniformity at all.

COLPUS: Ah .. I try to keep myself free from the disturbing influences of modern thought.

MR BOOTH: You know, Edward, you're worse even than Hugh is.

EDWARD: (*glancing up mildly at this sudden attack*) What have I done, Mr Booth?

MR BOOTH: (*not the readiest of men*) Well .. aren't you another of those young men who go about the world making difficulties?

EDWARD: What sort of difficulties?

MR BOOTH: (*triumphantly*) Just so .. I never can make out .. Surely when you're young you can ask the advice of your elders and when you grow up you find Laws .. lots of laws divine and human laid down for our guidance. (*Well in possession of the conversation he spreads his little self.*) I look back over a fairly long life and .. perhaps I should say by Heaven's help .. I find nothing that I can honestly reproach myself with. And yet I don't think I ever took more than five minutes to come to a decision upon any important point. One's private life is, I think, one's own affair .. I should allow no one to pry into that. But as to worldly things .. well, I have come into several sums of money and my capital is still intact .. ask your father. (MR VOYSEY *nods gravely.*) I've never robbed any man. I've never lied over anything that mattered. As a citizen I pay my taxes without grumbling very much. Yes, and I sent conscience money too upon one occasion. I consider that any man who takes the trouble can live the life of a gentleman. (*And he finds that his cigar is out.*)

MAJOR: (*not to be outdone by this display of virtue*) Well, I'm not a conceited man, but –

TREGONING: Are you sure, Booth?

MAJOR: Shut up. I was going to say when my young cub of a brother-in-law-to-be interrupted me, that *Training*, for which we all have to be thankful to you, Sir, has much to do with it. (*Suddenly he pulls his trousers against his legs.*) I say, I'm scorching! D'you want another cigar, Denis?

TREGONING: No, thank you.

MAJOR: I do.

> (*And he glances round, but* TREGONING *sees a box on the table and reaches it. The Vicar gets up.*)

COLPUS: M-m-m-must be taking my departure.

MR VOYSEY: Already!

MAJOR: (*frowning upon the cigar box*) No, not those. Where are the Ramon Allones? What on earth has Honor done with them?

MR VOYSEY: Spare time for a chat with Mrs Voysey before you go. She has ideas about a children's tea fight.

COLPUS: Certainly I will.

MAJOR: (*scowling helplessly around*) My goodness! .. one can never find anything in this house.

COLPUS: I won't say good-bye then.

> (*He is sliding through the half opened door when* ETHEL *meets him flinging it wide. She is the younger daughter, the baby of the family, but twenty-three now.*)

MR VOYSEY: I say, it's cold again tonight! An ass of an architect who built this place .. such a draught between these two doors.

> (*He gets up to draw the curtain. When he turns* COLPUS *has disappeared, while* ETHEL *has been followed into the room by* ALICE MAITLAND, *who shuts the door after her.* MISS ALICE MAITLAND *is a young lady of any age to thirty. Nor need her appearance alter for the next fifteen years; since her nature is healthy and well-balanced. She possesses indeed the sort of athletic chastity which is a characteristic charm of Northern spinsterhood. It mayn't be a pretty face, but it has alertness and humour; and the resolute eyes and eyebrows are a more innocent edition of* MR VOYSEY'S, *who is her uncle.* ETHEL *goes straight to her father [though her glance is on* DENIS *and his on her] and chirps, birdlike, in her spoiled-child way.*)

ETHEL: We think you've stayed in here quite long enough.

MR VOYSEY: That's to say, Ethel thinks Denis has been kept out of her pocket much too long.

ETHEL: Ethel wants billiards .. not proper billiards .. snooker or something. Oh, Papa, what a dessert you've eaten. Greedy pig!

> (ALICE *is standing behind* EDWARD, *considering his hair-parting apparently.*)

ALICE: Crack me a filbert, please, Edward .. I had none.

EDWARD: (*jumping up, rather formally, well-mannered*) I beg your pardon, Alice. Won't you sit down?

ALICE: No.

MR VOYSEY: (*taking* ETHEL *on his knee*) Come here, puss. Have you made up your mind yet what you want for a wedding present?

ETHEL: (*rectifying a stray hair in his beard*) After mature consideration, I decide on a cheque.

MR VOYSEY: Do you!

ETHEL: Yes, I think that a cheque will give most scope to your generosity. If you desire to add any trimmings in the shape of a piano or a Turkey carpet you may .. and Denis and I will be very grateful. But I think I'd let yourself go over a cheque.

MR VOYSEY: You're a minx.

ETHEL: What's the use of having money if you don't spend it on me?

MAJOR: (*giving up the cigar search*) Here, who's going to play?

MR BOOTH: (*pathetically as he gets up*) Well, if my wrist will hold out ..

MAJOR: (*to* TREGONING) No, don't you bother to look for them. (*He strides*

from the room, his voice echoing through the hall.) Honor, where are those
Ramon Allones?
ALICE: (*calling after*) She's in the drawing-room with Auntie and Mr Colpus.
MR VOYSEY: Now I should suggest that you and Denis go and take off the billiard
table cover. You'll find folding it up a very excellent amusement.
(*He illustrates his meaning with his table napkin and by putting
together the tips of his forefingers, roguishly.*)
ETHEL: I am not going to blush. I do kiss Denis . . occasionally . . when he asks me.
MR BOOTH: (*teasing her*) You are blushing.
ETHEL: I am not. If you think we're ashamed of being in love, we're not, we're
very proud of it. We will go and take off the billiard table cover and fold it up
. . and then you can come in and play. Denis, my dear, come along solemnly
and if you flinch I'll never forgive you. (*She marches off and reaches the door
before her defiant dignity breaks down; then suddenly –*) Denis, I'll race you.
(*And she flashes out. TREGONING loyal, but with no histrionic
instincts, follows her rather sheepishly.*)
TREGONING: Ethel, I can't after dinner.
MR VOYSEY: Women play that game better than men. A man shuffles through
courtship with one eye on her relations.
(*The MAJOR comes stalking back, followed in a fearful flurry by his
elder sister, HONOR. Poor HONOR [her female friends are apt to
refer to her as Poor HONOR] is a phenomenon common to most large
families. From her earliest years she has been bottle-washer to her
brothers. While they were expensively educated she was grudged
schooling; her highest accomplishment was meant to be mending their
clothes. Her fate is a curious survival of the intolerance of parents
towards her sex until the vanity of their hunger for sons had been
satisfied. In a less humane society she would have been exposed at
birth. But if a very general though patronising affection, accompanied
by no consideration at all, can bestow happiness, HONOR is not
unhappy in her survival. At this moment, however, her life is a
burden.*)
MAJOR: Honor, they are not in the dining-room.
HONOR: But they must be! – Where else can they be?
(*She has the habit of accentuating one word in each sentence and often
the wrong one.*)
MAJOR: That's what you ought to know.
MR VOYSEY: (*as he moves towards the door*) Well . . will you have a game?
MR BOOTH: I'll play you fifty up, not more. I'm getting old.
MR VOYSEY: (*stopping at a dessert dish*) Yes, these are good apples of Bearman's.
I think six of my trees are spoilt this year.
HONOR: Here you are, Booth.
(*She triumphantly discovers the discarded box, at which the MAJOR
becomes pathetic with indignation.*)
MAJOR: Oh, Honor, don't be such a fool. These are what we've been smoking. I
want the Ramon Allones.
HONOR: I don't know the difference.

MAJOR: No, you don't, but you might learn.

MR VOYSEY: (*in a voice like the crack of a very fine whip*) Booth.

MAJOR: (*subduedly*) What is it, sir?

MR VOYSEY: Look for your cigars yourself. Honor, go back to your reading or sewing or whatever you were fiddling at, and fiddle in peace.

> (MR VOYSEY *departs, leaving the room rather hushed.* MR BOOTH *has not waited for this parental display. Then* ALICE *insinuates a remark very softly.*)

ALICE: Have you looked in the Library?

MAJOR: (*relapsing to an injured mutter*) Where's Emily?

HONOR: Upstairs with little Henry, he woke up and cried.

MAJOR: Letting her wear herself to rags over the child ..!

HONOR: Well, she won't let me go.

MAJOR: Why don't you stop looking for those cigars?

HONOR: If you don't mind, I want a reel of blue silk now I'm here.

MAJOR: I daresay they are in the Library. What a house!

> (*He departs.*)

HONOR: Booth is so trying.

ALICE: Honor, why do you put up with it?

HONOR: Someone has to.

ALICE: (*discreetly nibbling a nut, which* EDWARD *has cracked for her*) I'm afraid that I think Master Major Booth ought to have been taken in hand early .. with a cane.

HONOR: (*as she vaguely burrows into corners*) Papa did. But it's never prevented him booming at us .. oh, ever since he was a baby. Now he's flustered me so I simply can't think where this blue silk is.

ALICE: All the Pettifers desired to be remembered to you, Edward.

HONOR: I must do without it. (*But she goes on looking.*) I sometimes think, Alice, that we're a very difficult family .. except perhaps Edward.

EDWARD: Why except me?

HONOR: (*who has only excepted out of politeness to present company*) And you were always difficult .. to yourself. (*Then she starts to go, threading her way through the disarranged chairs.*) Mr Colpus will shout so loud at Mother and she hates people to think she's so very deaf. I thought Mary Pettifer looking old .. (*and she talks herself out of the room*)

ALICE: (*after her*) She's getting old.

> (*Now* ALICE *does sit down; as if she'd be glad of her tête-a-tête.*)

ALICE: I was glad not to spend August abroad for once. We drove into Cheltenham to a dance .. carpet. I golfed a lot.

EDWARD: How long were you with them?

ALICE: Not a fortnight. It doesn't seem three months since I was here, does it?

EDWARD: I'm down so very little.

ALICE: I'm here a disgraceful deal.

EDWARD: You know they're always pleased.

ALICE: Well, being a homeless person! But what a cart-load to descend all at once .. yesterday and today. The Major and Emily .. Emily's not at all well. Hugh and Mrs Hugh. And me. Are you staying?

EDWARD: No. I must get a word with my father ..

ALICE: Edward, a business life is not healthy for you. You look more like half-baked pie-crust than usual.

EDWARD: (*a little enviously*) You're very well.

ALICE: I'm always well and nearly always happy.

> (MAJOR *returns. He has the right sort of cigar in his mouth and is considerably mollified.*)

ALICE: You found them?

MAJOR: Of course, they were there. Thank you very much, Alice. Now I want a knife.

ALICE: I must get you a cigar-cutter for Christmas, Booth.

MAJOR: Beastly things, I hate 'em, thank you. (*He eyes the dessert disparagingly.*) Nothing but silver ones.

> (EDWARD *hands him a carefully opened pocket knife.*)

MAJOR: Thank you, Edward. And I must take one of the candles. Something's gone wrong with the library ventilator and you never can see a thing in that room.

ALICE: Is Mrs Hugh there?

MAJOR: Writing letters. Things are neglected, Edward, unless one is constantly on the look out. The Pater only cares for his garden. I must speak seriously to Honor.

> (*He has returned the knife, still open, and now having lit his cigar at the candle he carries this off.*)

ALICE: Honor has the patience of a .. of an old maid.

EDWARD: Yes, I suppose her mission in life isn't a very pleasant one. (*He gives her a nut, about the fifteenth.*) Here; 'scuse fingers.

ALICE: Thank you. (*looking at him, with her head on one side and her face more humorous than ever*) Edward, why have you given up proposing to me?

> (*He starts, flushes; then won't be outdone in humour.*)

EDWARD: One can't go on proposing for ever.

ALICE: (*reasonably*) Why not? Have you seen anyone you like better?

EDWARD: No.

ALICE: Well .. I miss it.

EDWARD: What satisfaction did you find in refusing me?

ALICE: (*as she weighs the matter*) I find satisfaction in feeling that I'm wanted.

EDWARD: Without any intention of giving yourself .. throwing yourself away.

ALICE: (*teasing his sudden earnestness*) Ah, now you come from mere vanity to serious questions.

EDWARD: Mine was a very serious question to you.

ALICE: But, Edward, all questions are serious to you. I call you a perfect little pocket-guide to life .. all questions and answers; what to eat, drink, and avoid, what to believe and what to say ..

EDWARD: (*sententiously*) Well .. everything matters.

ALICE: (*making a face*) D'you plan out every detail of your life .. every step you take .. every mouthful?

EDWARD: That would be waste of thought. One must lay down principles.

ALICE: I prefer my plan, I always do what I know I want to
  nut.
EDWARD: Haven't you had enough?
ALICE: I *know* I want one more.
     (*He cracks another, with a sigh which sounds ridi*
     connection.)
ALICE: I know it just as I knew I didn't want to marry you .. ea
EDWARD: Oh, you didn't make a rule of saying no.
ALICE: As you proposed .. on principle? No, I always gave you a fair chance. I'll
  give you one now if you like. Courage, I might say yes .. all in a flash. Oh,
  you'd never get over it.
EDWARD: I think we won't run the risk.
ALICE: Edward, how rude you are. (*She eats her nut contentedly.*) There's nothing
  wrong, is there?
EDWARD: Nothing at all.
     (*They are interrupted by the sudden appearance of* MRS HUGH
     VOYSEY, *a brisk, bright little woman, in an evening gown, which she*
     has bullied a cheap dressmaker into making look exceedingly smart.
     BEATRICE *is as hard as nails and as clever as paint. But if she keeps*
     her feelings buried pretty deep it is because they are precious to her;
     and if she is impatient with fools it is because her own brains have had
     to win her everything in the world, so perhaps she does overvalue them
     a little. She speaks always with great decision and little effort.)
BEATRICE: I believe I could write important business letters upon an island in the
  middle of Fleet Street. But while Booth is poking at a ventilator with a billiard
  cue .. no, I can't.
     (*She goes to the fireplace, waving her half finished letter.*)
ALICE: (*soothingly*) Didn't you expect Hugh back to dinner?
BEATRICE: Not specially .. He went to rout out some things from his studio. He'll
  come back in a filthy mess.
ALICE: Ssh! Now if you listen .. Booth doesn't enjoy making a fuss by himself ..
  you'll hear him put up Honor.
     (*They listen. But what happens is that The* MAJOR *appears at the*
     door, billiard cue in hand, and says solemnly ..)
MAJOR: Edward, I wish you'd come and have a look at this ventilator, like a good
  fellow.
     (*Then he turns and goes again, obviously with the weight of an*
     important matter on his shoulders. With the ghost of a smile
     EDWARD *gets up and follows him.*)
ALICE: If I belonged to this family I should hate Booth. (*With which comment she*
  joins BEATRICE *at the fireplace.*)
BEATRICE: A good day's shopping?
ALICE: 'M. The baby bride and I bought clothes all the morning. Then we had
  lunch with Denis and bought furniture.
BEATRICE: Nice furniture?
ALICE: Very good and very new. They neither of them know what they want.
     (*Then suddenly throwing up her chin and exclaiming.*) When it's a question of

money I can understand it .. but if one can provide for oneself or is independent why get married! Especially having been brought up on the sheltered life principle .. one may as well make the most of its advantages .. one doesn't go falling in love all over the place as men seem to .. most of them. Of course with Ethel and Denis it's different. They've both been caught young. They're two little birds building their nest and it's all ideal. They'll soon forget they've ever been apart.

(*Now* HONOR *flutters into the room, patient but wild-eyed.*)

HONOR: Mother wants last week's Notes and Queries. Have you seen it?

BEATRICE: (*exasperated at the interruption*) No.

HONOR: It ought not to be in here. (*So she proceeds to look for it.*) She's having a long argument with Mr Colpus over Oliver Cromwell's relations.

ALICE: (*her eyes twinkling*) I thought Auntie didn't approve of Oliver Cromwell.

HONOR: She doesn't, and she's trying to prove that he was a brewer or something. I suppose someone has taken it away.

(*So she gives up the search and flutters out again.*)

ALICE: This is a most unrestful house.

BEATRICE: I once thought of putting the Voyseys into a book of mine. Then I concluded they'd be as dull there as they are anywhere else.

ALICE: They're not duller than most people.

BEATRICE: But how very dull that is!

ALICE: They're a little nosier and perhaps not quite so well mannered. But I love them.

BEATRICE: I don't. I should have thought love was just what they couldn't inspire.

ALICE: Of course, Hugh is unlike any of the others.

BEATRICE: He has most of their bad points. But I don't love Hugh.

ALICE: (*her eyebrows up, though she smiles*) Beatrice, you shouldn't say so.

BEATRICE: Sounds affected, doesn't it? Never mind; when he dies I'll wear mourning .. but not weeds; I bargained against that when we were engaged.

ALICE: (*her face growing a little thoughtful*) Beatrice, I'm going to ask questions. You were in love with Hugh when you married him?

BEATRICE: Well .. I married him for his money ..

ALICE: He hadn't much.

BEATRICE: I had none .. and I wanted to write books. Yes, I loved him.

ALICE: And you thought you'd be happy?

BEATRICE: (*considering carefully*) No, I didn't. I hoped he'd be happy.

ALICE: (*a little ironical*) Did you think your writing books would make him so?

BEATRICE: My dear Alice, shouldn't a man .. or a woman feel it a very degrading thing to have their happiness depend upon somebody else?

ALICE: (*after pausing to find her phrase*) There's a joy of service. Is that very womanly of me?

BEATRICE: (*ironically herself now*) Ah, but you've four hundred a year.

ALICE: What has that to do with it?

BEATRICE: (*putting her case very precisely*) Fine feelings, my dear, are as much a luxury as clean gloves. Now, I've had to earn my own living; consequently

---

Notes and Queries: a long-lived weekly journal consisting of brief notes on literary, historical, and intellectual matters.

there isn't one thing in my life that I have ever done quite genuinely for its own sake .. but always with an eye towards bread-and-butter, pandering to the people who were to give me that. I warned Hugh .. he took the risk.

ALICE: What risk?

BEATRICE: That one day I'd be able to get on without him.

ALICE: By the time he'd learnt how not to without you?

BEATRICE: Well, women must have the courage to be brutal.

> (*The conservatory door opens and through it come* MR VOYSEY *and* MR BOOTH *in the midst of a discussion.*)

MR VOYSEY: My dear man, stick to the shares and risk it.

MR BOOTH: No, of course, if you seriously advise me –

MR VOYSEY: I never advise greedy children; I let 'em overeat 'emselves and take the consequences –

ALICE: (*shaking a finger*) Uncle Trench, you've been in the garden without a hat after playing billiards in that hot room.

MR BOOTH: We had to give up .. my wrist was bad. They've started pool.

BEATRICE: Is Booth going to play?

MR VOYSEY: We left him instructing Ethel how to hold a cue.

BEATRICE: Ah! I can finish my letter.

> (*Off she goes.* ALICE *is idly following with a little paper her hand has fallen on behind the clock.*)

MR VOYSEY: Don't run away, my dear.

ALICE: I'm taking this to Auntie .. Notes and Queries .. she wants it.

MR BOOTH: Damn .. this gravel's stuck to my shoe.

MR VOYSEY: That's a new made path.

MR BOOTH: Now don't you think it's too early to have put in those plants?

MR VOYSEY: No, we've had a frost or two already.

MR BOOTH: I should have kept the bed a good ten feet further from that tree.

MR VOYSEY: Nonsense, the tree's to the north of it. This room's cold. Why don't they keep the fire up! (*He proceeds to put coals on it.*)

MR BOOTH: You were too hot in that billiard room. You know, Voysey .. about those Alguazils?

MR VOYSEY: (*through the rattling of the coals*) What?

MR BOOTH: (*trying to pierce the din*) Those Alguazils.

> (MR VOYSEY *with surprising inconsequence points a finger at the silk handkerchief across* MR BOOTH'S *shirt front.*)

MR VOYSEY: What d'you put your handkerchief there for?

MR BOOTH: Measure of precau – (*at that moment he sneezes*) Damn it .. if you've given me a chill dragging me through your infernal garden ..

MR VOYSEY: (*slapping him on the back*) You're an old crock.

MR BOOTH: Well, I'll be glad of this winter in Egypt. (*He returns to his subject.*) And if you think seriously, that I ought to sell out of the Alguazils before I go ..? (*He looks with childlike enquiry at his friend, who is apparently yawning slightly.*) Why can't you take them in charge? .. and I'll give you a power of attorney .. or whatever it is .. and you can sell out if things look bad.

> (*At this moment* PHOEBE, *the middle aged parlour maid, comes in, tray in hand. Like an expert fisherman* MR VOYSEY *once more lets loose the thread of the conversation.*)

MR VOYSEY: D'you want to clear?

PHOEBE: It doesn't matter, sir.

MR VOYSEY: No, go on .. go on.

> (*So* MARY, *the young housemaid, comes in as well, and the two start to clear the table. All of which fidgets poor* MR BOOTH *considerably. He sits shrivelled up in the armchair by the fire; and now* MR VOYSEY *attends to him.*)

MR VOYSEY: What d'you want with high interest at all .. you never spend half your income?

MR BOOTH: I like to feel that my money is doing some good in the world. Mines are very useful things and forty-two per cent is pleasing.

MR VOYSEY: You're an old gambler.

MR BOOTH: (*propitiatingly*) Ah, but then I've you to advise me. I always do as you tell me in the end, now you can't deny that ..

MR VOYSEY: The man who don't know must trust in the man who do! (*He yawns again.*)

MR BOOTH: (*modestly insisting*) There's five thousand in Alguazils – what else could we put it into?

MR VOYSEY: I can get you something at four and a half.

MR BOOTH: Oh, Lord .. that's nothing.

MR VOYSEY: (*with a sudden serious friendliness*) I wish, my dear George, you'd invest more on your own account. You know – what with one thing and the other – I've got control of practically all you have in the world. I might be playing old Harry with it for all you know.

MR BOOTH: (*overflowing with confidence*) My dear feller .. if I'm satisfied! Ah, my friend, what'll happen to your firm when you depart this life! .. not before my time, I hope, though.

MR VOYSEY: (*with a little frown*) What d'ye mean?

MR BOOTH: Edward's no use.

MR VOYSEY: I beg your pardon .. very sound in business.

MR BOOTH: May be .. but I tell you he's no use. Too many principles, as I told him just now. Men have confidence in a personality, not in principles. Where would you be without the confidence of your clients?

MR VOYSEY: (*candidly*) True!

MR BOOTH: He'll never gain that.

MR VOYSEY: I fear you dislike Edward.

MR BOOTH: (*with pleasant frankness*) Yes, I do.

MR VOYSEY: That's a pity. That's a very great pity.

MR BOOTH: (*with a flattering smile*) He's not his father and never will be. What's the time?

MR VOYSEY: (*with inappropriate thoughtfulness*) Twenty to ten.

MR BOOTH: I must be trotting.

MR VOYSEY: It's early.

MR BOOTH: Oh, and I've not said a word to Mrs Voysey .. (*As he goes to the door he meets* EDWARD, *who comes in apparently looking for his father; at any rate catches his eye immediately, while* MR BOOTH *obliviously continues.*)

MR BOOTH: Will you stroll round home with me?

MR VOYSEY: I can't.

MR BOOTH: (*mildly surprised at the short reply*) Well, good-night. Good-night, Edward.

> (*He trots away.*)

MR VOYSEY: Leave the rest of the table, Phoebe.

PHOEBE: Yes, sir.

MR VOYSEY: You can come back in ten minutes.

> (PHOEBE *and* MARY *depart and the door is closed. Alone with his son* MR VOYSEY *does not move; his face grows a little keener, that's all.*)

MR VOYSEY: Well, Edward?

> (EDWARD *starts to move restlessly about, like a cowed animal in a cage; silently for a moment or two. Then when he speaks, his voice is toneless and he doesn't look at his father.*)

EDWARD: Would you mind, sir, dropping with me for the future all these protestations about putting the firm's affairs straight . . about all your anxieties and sacrifices. I see now, of course . . a cleverer man than I could have seen it yesterday . . that for some time, ever since, I suppose, you recovered from the first shock and got used to the double dealing, this hasn't been your object at all. You've used your clients' capital to produce your own income . . to bring us up and endow us with. Booth's ten thousand pounds; what you are giving Ethel on her marriage . . It's odd it never struck me yesterday that my own pocket money as a boy must have been quite simply withdrawn from some client's account. You've been very generous to us all, Father. I suppose about half the sum you've spent on us first and last would have put things right.

MR VOYSEY: No, it would not.

EDWARD: (*appealing for the truth*) Yes, yes . . at some time or other!

MR VOYSEY: Well, if there have been good times there have been bad times. At present the three hundred a year I'm to allow your sister is going to be rather a pull.

EDWARD: Three hundred a year . . while you don't attempt to make a single client safe. Since it isn't lunacy, sir . . I can only conclude that you enjoy such a position.

MR VOYSEY: Safe? Three trusts – two of them big ones – have been wound up within this last eighteen months, and the accounts have been above suspicion. What's the object of all this rodomontade, Edward?

EDWARD: If I'm to remain in the firm, it had better be with a very clear understanding of things as they are.

MR VOYSEY: (*firmly, not too anxiously*) Then you do remain?

EDWARD: (*in a very low voice*) I must remain.

MR VOYSEY: (*quite gravely*) That's wise of you . . I'm very glad. (*And he is silent for a moment.*) And now we needn't discuss the unpractical side of it any more.

EDWARD: But I want to make one condition. And I want some information.

MR VOYSEY: (*his sudden cheerfulness relapsing again*) Well?

---

rodomontade: boasting or bragging.

EDWARD: Of course no one has ever discovered .. and no one suspects this state
of things?

MR VOYSEY: Peacey knows.

EDWARD: Peacey!

MR VOYSEY: His father found out.

EDWARD: Oh. Does he draw hush money?

MR VOYSEY: (*curling a little at the word*) It is my custom to make him a little
present every Christmas. (*He becomes benevolent.*) I don't grudge the money
.. Peacey's a devoted fellow.

EDWARD: Certainly this should be a heavily taxed industry. (*Then he smiles at his
vision of the mild old clerk.*) Peacey! There's another thing I want to ask, sir.
Have you ever under stress of circumstances done worse than just make this
temporary use of a client's capital? You boasted to me yesterday that no one
had ever suffered in pocket in the end because of you. Is that absolutely true?

(MR VOYSEY *draws himself up, dignified and magniloquent.*)

MR VOYSEY: My dear Edward, for the future my mind is open to you; you can
discover for yourself how matters stand today. But I decline to gratify your
curiosity as to what is over and done with.

EDWARD: (*with entire comprehension*) Thank you, sir. The condition of my
remaining is that we should really try as unobtrusively as you like and put
things straight.

MR VOYSEY: (*with a little polite shrug*) I've no doubt you'll prove an abler man of
business than I.

EDWARD: We can begin by halving the salary I draw from the firm; that leaves me
enough.

MR VOYSEY: I see .. Retrenchment and Reform.

EDWARD: And it seems to me that you can't give Ethel this five thousand pounds
dowry.

MR VOYSEY: (*shortly, with one of the quick twists of his eye*) I have given my word
to Denis ..

EDWARD: Because the money isn't yours to give.

MR VOYSEY: (*in an indignant crescendo*) I should not dream of depriving Ethel of
what, as my daughter, she has every right to expect. I am surprised at your
suggesting such a thing.

EDWARD: (*pale and firm*) I'm set on this, Father.

MR VOYSEY: Don't be such a fool, Edward. What would it look like .. suddenly
to refuse without rhyme or reason? What would old Tregoning think?

EDWARD: Oh, can't you see it's my duty to prevent this?

MR VOYSEY: You can prevent it by telling the nearest policeman. It is my duty to
pay no more attention to these scruples of yours than a nurse pays to her
child's tantrums. Understand, Edward, I don't want to force you to continue
my partner. Come with me gladly or don't come at all.

EDWARD: (*dully*) It is my duty to be of what use I can to you, sir. Father, I want to
save you if I can.

(*He flashes into this exclamation of almost broken-hearted affection.*
MR VOYSEY *looks at his son for a moment and his lip quivers. Then
he steels himself.*)

MR VOYSEY: Thank you! I have saved myself quite satisfactorily for the last thirty years, and you must please believe that by this time I know my own business best.

EDWARD: (*hopelessly*) Can't we find the money some other way? How do you manage now about your own income?

MR VOYSEY: I have a bank balance and a cheque book, haven't I? I spend what I think well to spend. What's the use of earmarking this or that as my own? You say none of it is my own. I might say it's all my own. I think I've earned it.

EDWARD: (*anger coming on him*) That's what I can't forgive. If you'd lived poor .. if you'd really done all you could for your clients and not thought only of your own aggrandisement .. then, even though things were no better than they are now, I could have been proud of you. But, Father, own the truth to me, at least .. that's my due from you, considering how I'm placed by all you've done. Didn't you simply seize this opportunity as a means to your own ends, to your own enriching?

MR VOYSEY: (*with a sledge hammer irony*) Certainly. I sat that morning in my father's office, studying the helmet of the policeman in the street below, and thinking what a glorious path I had happened on to wealth and honour and renown. (*Then he begins to bully* EDWARD *in the kindliest way.*) My dear boy, you evidently haven't begun to grasp the A.B.C. of my position. What has carried me to victory? The confidence of my clients. What has earned that confidence? A decent life, my integrity, my brains? No, my reputation for wealth .. that, and nothing else. Business nowadays is run on the lines of the confidence trick. What makes old George Booth so glad to trust me with every penny he possesses? Not affection .. he's never cared for anything in his life but his collection of prints.

EDWARD: (*stupefied, helpless*) Is he involved?

MR VOYSEY: Of course he's involved, and he's always after high interest too .. it's little one makes out of him. But there's a further question here, Edward. Should I have had confidence in myself, if I'd remained a poor man? No, I should not. You must either be the master of money or its servant. And if one is not opulent in one's daily life one loses that wonderful .. financier's touch. One must be confident oneself .. and I saw from the first that I must at any cost inspire confidence. My whole public and private life has tended to that. All my surroundings .. you and your brothers and sisters that I have brought into, and up, and put out in the world so worthily .. you in your turn inspire confidence.

EDWARD: Not our worth, not our abilities, nor our virtues, but the fact that we travel first class and take cabs when we want to.

MR VOYSEY: (*impatiently*) Well, I haven't organised Society upon a basis of wealth.

EDWARD: I sat down yesterday to make a list of the people who are good enough to trust their money to us. It'll be a pretty long one .. and it's an interesting one, from George Booth with his big income to old Nursie with her savings which she brought you so proudly to invest. But you've let those be, at least.

MR VOYSEY: I just .. took the money ..

EDWARD: Father!

MR VOYSEY: Five hundred pounds. Not worth worrying about.

EDWARD: That's damnable.

MR VOYSEY: Indeed. I give her seventy-five pounds a year for it. Would you like to take charge of that account, Edward? I'll give you five hundred to invest tomorrow.

> (EDWARD, *hopelessly beaten, falls into an almost comic state of despair.*)

EDWARD: My dear Father, putting every moral question aside .. it's all very well your playing Robin Hood in this magnificent manner; but have you given a moment's thought to the sort of inheritance you'll be leaving me?

MR VOYSEY: (*pleased for the first time*) Ah! That is a question you have every right to ask.

EDWARD: If you died tomorrow could we pay eight shillings in the pound .. or seventeen .. or five? Do you know?

MR VOYSEY: And the answer is, that by your help I have every intention, when I die, of leaving a will behind me of property to you all running into six figures. D'you think I've given my life and my talents for a less result than that? I'm fond of you all .. and I want you to be proud of me .. and I mean that the name of Voysey shall be carried high in the world by my children and grandchildren. Don't you be afraid, Edward. Ah, you lack experience, my boy .. you're not full grown yet .. your impulses are a bit chaotic. You emotionalise over your work, and you reason about your emotions. You must sort yourself. You must realise that money making is one thing, and religion another, and family life a third .. and that if we apply our energies whole-heartedly to each of these in turn, and realise that different laws govern each, that there is a different end to be served, a different ideal to be striven for in each ..

> (*His coherence is saved by the sudden appearance of his wife, who comes round the door smiling benignly. Not in the least put out, in fact a little relieved, he greets her with an affectionate shout, for she is very deaf.*)

MR VOYSEY: Hullo, Mother!

MRS VOYSEY: Oh, there you are, Trench. I've been deserted.

MR VOYSEY: George Booth gone?

MRS VOYSEY: Are you talking business? Perhaps you don't want me.

MR VOYSEY: No, no .. no business.

MRS VOYSEY: (*who has not looked for his answer*) I suppose the others are in the billiard room.

MR VOYSEY: (*vociferously*) We're not talking business, old lady.

EDWARD: I'll be off, sir.

MR VOYSEY: (*genial as usual*) Why don't you stay? I'll come up with you in the morning.

EDWARD: No, thank you, sir.

MR VOYSEY: Then I shall be up about noon tomorrow.

EDWARD: Good-night, Mother.

> (MRS VOYSEY *places a plump kindly hand on his arm and looks up affectionately.*)

MRS VOYSEY: You look tired.
EDWARD: No, I'm not.
MRS VOYSEY: What did you say?
EDWARD: (*too weary to repeat himself*) Nothing, Mother dear.
> (*He kisses her cheek, while she kisses the air.*)
MR VOYSEY: Good night, my boy.
> (*Then he goes. MRS VOYSEY is carrying her Notes and Queries.*
> *This is a dear old lady, looking older too than probably she is. Placid*
> *describes her. She has had a life of little joys and cares, has never*
> *measured herself against the world, never even questioned the shape*
> *and size of the little corner of it in which she lives. She has loved an*
> *indulgent husband and borne eight children, six of them surviving,*
> *healthy. That is her history.*)
MRS VOYSEY: George Booth went some time ago. He said he thought you'd taken
> a chill walking round the garden.
MR VOYSEY: I'm all right.
MRS VOYSEY: D'you think you have?
MR VOYSEY: (*in her ear*) No.
MRS VOYSEY: You should be careful, Trench. What did you put on?
MR VOYSEY: Nothing.
MRS VOYSEY: How very foolish! Let me feel your hand. You are quite feverish.
MR VOYSEY: (*affectionately*) You're a fuss-box, old lady.
MRS VOYSEY: (*coquetting with him*) Don't be rude, Trench.
> (*HONOR descends upon them. She is well into that nightly turmoil of*
> *putting everything and everybody to rights which always precedes her*
> *bedtime. She carries a shawl which she clasps round her mother's*
> *shoulders, her mind and gaze already on the next thing to be done.*)
HONOR: Mother, you left your shawl in the drawing-room. Can they finish
> clearing?
MR VOYSEY: (*arranging the folds of the shawl with real tenderness*) Now who's
> careless!
> (*PHOEBE comes into the room.*)
HONOR: Phoebe, finish here and then you must bring in the tray for Mr Hugh.
MRS VOYSEY: (*having looked at the shawl, and HONOR, and connected the*
> *matter in her mind*) Thank you, Honor. You'd better look after your father;
> he's been walking round the garden without his cape.
HONOR: Papa!
MR VOYSEY: Phoebe, you get that little kettle and boil it, and brew me some
> whiskey and water. I shall be all right.
HONOR: (*fluttering more than ever*) I'll get it. Where's the whiskey? And Hugh
> coming back at ten o'clock with no dinner. No wonder his work goes wrong.
> Here it is! Papa, you do deserve to be ill.
> (*Clasping the whiskey decanter, she is off again. MRS VOYSEY sits*
> *at the dinner table and adjusts her spectacles. She returns to Notes and*
> *Queries, one elbow firmly planted and her plump hand against her*
> *plump cheek. This is her favourite attitude; and she is apt, when*
> *reading, to soliloquise in her deaf woman's voice. At least, whether she*

considers it soliloquy or conversation is not easy to discover. MR
VOYSEY *stands with his back to the fire, grumbling and pulling
faces.*)

MRS VOYSEY: This is a very perplexing correspondence about the Cromwell
family. One can't deny the man had good blood in him .. his grandfather Sir
Henry, his uncle Sir Oliver ..

MR VOYSEY: There's a pain in my back.

MRS VOYSEY: .. and it's difficult to discover where the taint crept in.

MR VOYSEY: I believe I strained myself putting in all those strawberry plants.

(MARY, *the house parlour maid, carries in a tray of warmed-up
dinner for* HUGH *and plants it on the table.*)

MRS VOYSEY: Yes, but then how was it he came to disgrace himself so? I believe
the family disappeared. Regicide is a root and branch curse. You must read
this letter signed C. W. A. .. it's quite interesting. There's a misprint in mine
about the first umbrella maker .. now where was it .. (*and so the dear lady will
ramble on indefinitely*)

ACT III

*The dining-room looks very different in the white light of a July noon. Moreover on
this particular day, it isn't even its normal self. There is a peculiar luncheon spread on
the table. The embroidered cloth is placed cornerwise and on it are decanters of port
and sherry; sandwiches, biscuits and an uncut cake; two little piles of plates and one
little pile of napkins. There are no table decorations, and indeed the whole room has
been made as bare and as tidy as possible. Such preparations denote one of the
recognised English festivities, and the appearance of* PHOEBE, *the maid, who has
just completed them, the set solemnity of her face and the added touches of black to
her dress and cap, suggest that this is probably a funeral. When* MARY *comes in, the
fact that she has evidently been crying and that she decorously does not raise her voice
above an unpleasant whisper makes it quite certain.*

MARY: Phoebe, they're coming back .. and I forgot one of the blinds in the
drawing-room.

PHOEBE: Well, pull it up quick and make yourself scarce. I'll open the door.

(MARY *got rid of,* PHOEBE *composes her face still more rigorously
into the aspect of formal grief and with a touch to her apron as well
goes to admit the funeral party. The first to enter are* MRS VOYSEY
and MR BOOTH, *she on his arm; and the fact that she is in widow's
weeds makes the occasion clear. The little old man leads his old friend
very tenderly.*)

MR BOOTH: Will you come in here?

MRS VOYSEY: Thank you.

(*With great solicitude he puts her in a chair; then takes her hand.*)

MR BOOTH: Now I'll intrude no longer.

MRS VOYSEY: You'll take some lunch?

MR BOOTH: No.

MRS VOYSEY: Not a glass of wine?

MR BOOTH: If there's anything I can do just send round.

MRS VOYSEY: Thank you.

> (*He reaches the door, only to be met by the* MAJOR *and his wife. He shakes hands with them both.*)

MR BOOTH: My dear Emily! My dear Booth!

> (EMILY *is a homely, patient, pale little woman of about thirty-five. She looks smaller than usual in her heavy black dress and is meeker than usual on an occasion of this kind. The* MAJOR, *on the other hand, though his grief is most sincere, has an irresistible air of being responsible for, and indeed rather proud of, the whole affair.*)

MAJOR: I think it all went off as he would have wished.

MR BOOTH: (*feeling that he is called on for praise*) Great credit .. great credit.

> (*He makes another attempt to escape and is stopped this time by* TRENCHARD VOYSEY, *to whom he is extending a hand and beginning his formula. But* TRENCHARD *speaks first.*)

TRENCHARD: Have you the right time?

MR BOOTH: (*taken aback and fumbling for his watch*) I think so .. I make it fourteen minutes to one. (*He seizes the occasion.*) Trenchard, as a very old and dear friend of your father's, you won't mind me saying how glad I was that you were present today. Death closes all. Indeed .. it must be a great regret to you that you did not see him before .. before ..

TRENCHARD: (*his cold eye freezing this little gush*) I don't think he asked for me.

MR BOOTH: (*stoppered*) No? No! Well .. well .. (*At this third attempt to depart he actually collides with someone in the doorway. It is* HUGH VOYSEY.)

MR BOOTH: My dear Hugh .. I won't intrude.

> (*Quite determined to escape he grasps his hand, gasps out his formula and is off.* TRENCHARD *and* HUGH, *eldest and youngest son, are as unlike each other as it is possible for* VOYSEYS *to be, but that isn't very unlike.* TRENCHARD *has in excelsis the cocksure manner of the successful barrister;* HUGH *the rather sweet though querulous air of diffidence and scepticism belonging to the unsuccessful man of letters or artist. The self-respect of* TRENCHARD'S *appearance is immense, and he cultivates that air of concentration upon any trivial matter, or even upon nothing at all, which will some day make him an impressive figure upon the Bench.* HUGH *is always vague, searching Heaven or the corners of the room for inspiration, and even on this occasion his tie is abominably crooked. The inspissated gloom of this assembly, to which each member of the family as he arrives adds his share, is unbelievable. Instinct apparently leads them to reproduce as nearly as possible the appearance and conduct of the corpse on which their minds are fixed.* HUGH *is depressed partly at the inadequacy of his grief:* TRENCHARD *conscientiously preserves an air of the indifference which he feels; the* MAJOR *stands statuesque at the mantelpiece; while* EMILY *is by* MRS VOYSEY, *whose face in its quiet grief is nevertheless a mirror of many happy memories of her husband.*)

MAJOR: I wouldn't hang over her, Emily.

EMILY: No, of course not.

> (*Apologetically, she sits by the table.*)

TRENCHARD: I hope your wife is well, Hugh?

HUGH: Thank you, Trench: I think so. Beatrice is in America .. doing some work there.

TRENCHARD: Really!

> (*There comes in a small, well-groomed, bullet-headed boy in Etons.
> This is the* MAJOR'S *eldest son. Looking scared and solemn he goes
> straight to his mother.*)

EMILY: Now be very quiet, Christopher ..

> (*Then* DENIS TREGONING *appears.*)

TRENCHARD: Oh, Tregoning, did you bring Honor back?

TREGONING: Yes.

MAJOR: (*at the table*) A glass of wine, Mother.

MRS VOYSEY: What?

> (*The* MAJOR *hardly knows how to turn his whisper decorously into
> enough of a shout for his mother to hear. But he manages it.*)

MAJOR: Have a glass of wine?

MRS VOYSEY: Sherry, please.

> (*While he pours it out with an air of its being medicine on this occasion
> and not wine at all,* EDWARD *comes quickly into the room, his face
> very set, his mind obviously on other matters than the funeral. No one
> speaks to him for the moment and he has time to observe them all.*
> TRENCHARD *is continuing his talk to* TREGONING.)

TRENCHARD: Give my love to Ethel. Is she ill that –

TREGONING: Not exactly, but she couldn't very well be with us. I thought perhaps you might have heard. We're expecting ..

> (*He hesitates with the bashfulness of a young husband.*
> TRENCHARD *helps him out with a citizen's bow of respect for a
> citizen's duty.*)

TRENCHARD: Indeed. I congratulate you. I hope all will be well. Please give my best love to Ethel.

MAJOR: (*in an awful voice*) Lunch, Emily?

EMILY: (*scared*) I suppose so, Booth, thank you.

MAJOR: I think the boy had better run away and play .. (*He checks himself on the word.*) Well, take a book and keep quiet; d'ye hear me, Christopher?

> (CHRISTOPHER, *who looks incapable of a sound, gazes at his
> father with round eyes.* EMILY *whispers 'Library' to him and adds a
> kiss in acknowledgement of his good behaviour. After a moment he
> slips out, thankfully.*)

EDWARD: How's Ethel, Denis?

TREGONING: A little smashed, of course, but no harm done .. I hope.

Etons: uniform of a student at Eton College, one of the oldest and most established of public schools, consisting of a black waist-length jacket with wide lapels and a stiff white collar that overlaps them.

(ALICE MAITLAND *comes in, brisk and businesslike; a little impatient of this universal cloud of mourning.*)

ALICE: Edward, Honor has gone to her room; I must take her some food and make her eat it. She's very upset.

EDWARD: Make her drink a glass of wine, and say it is necessary she should come down here. And d'you mind not coming back yourself, Alice?

ALICE: (*her eyebrows up*) Certainly, if you wish.

MAJOR: (*overhearing*) What's this? What's this?

(ALICE *gets her glass of wine and goes. The* MAJOR *is suddenly full of importance.*)

MAJOR: What is this, Edward?

EDWARD: I have something to say to you all.

MAJOR: What?

EDWARD: Well, Booth, you'll hear when I say it.

MAJOR: Is it business? . . because I think this is scarcely the time for business.

EDWARD: Why?

MAJOR: Do you find it easy and reverent to descend from your natural grief to the consideration of money? . . I do not. (*He finds* TRENCHARD *at his elbow.*) I hope you are getting some lunch, Trenchard.

EDWARD: This is business and rather more than business, Booth. I choose now, because it is something I wish to say to the family, not write to each individually . . and it will be difficult to get us all together again.

MAJOR: (*determined at any rate to give his sanction*) Well, Trenchard, as Edward is in the position of trustee – executor . . I don't know your terms . . I suppose . .

TRENCHARD: I don't see what your objection is.

MAJOR: (*with some superiority*) Don't you? I should not have called myself a sentimental man, but . .

EDWARD: You had better stay, Denis; you represent Ethel.

TREGONING: (*who has not heard the beginning of this*) Why?

(HONOR *has obediently come down from her room. She is pale and thin, shaken with grief and worn out besides; for needless to say the brunt of her father's illness, the brunt of everything has been on her. Six weeks' nursing, part of it hopeless, will exhaust anyone. Her handkerchief is to her eyes and every minute or two she cascades tears.* EDWARD *goes and affectionately puts his arm round her.*)

EDWARD: My dear Honor, I am sorry to be so . . so merciless. There! . . there!
(*He hands her into the room; then turns and once more surveys the family, who at this time mostly return the compliment. Then he says shortly*) I think you might all sit down. (*and then*) Shut the door, Booth.

MAJOR: Shut the door!

(EDWARD *goes close to his mother and speaks very distinctly, very kindly.*)

EDWARD: Mother, we're all going to have a little necessary talk over matters . . now, because it's most convenient. I hope it won't . . I hope you don't mind. Will you come to the table?

(MRS VOYSEY *looks up as if understanding more than he says.*)

MRS VOYSEY: Edward . .

EDWARD: Yes, Mother dear?

MAJOR: (*commandingly*) You'll sit here, Mother, of course.

>   (*He places her in her accustomed chair at the foot of the table. One by one the others sit down,* EDWARD *apparently last. But then he discovers that* HUGH *has lost himself in a corner of the room and is gazing into vacancy.*)

EDWARD: Hugh, would you mind attending?

HUGH: What is it?

EDWARD: There's a chair.

>   (HUGH *takes it. Then for a minute – while* EDWARD *is trying to frame in coherent sentences what he must say to them – for a minute there is silence, broken only by* HONOR'S *sniffs, which culminate at last in a noisy little cascade of tears.*)

MAJOR: Honor, control yourself.

>   (*And to emphasise his own perfect control he helps himself majestically to a glass of sherry. Then says* ..)

MAJOR: Well, Edward?

EDWARD: I'll come straight to the point which concerns you. Our father's will gives certain sums to you all .. the gross amount would be something over a hundred thousand pounds. There will be no money.

>   (*He can get no further than the bare statement, which is received only with varying looks of bewilderment, until* MRS VOYSEY, *discovering nothing from their faces, breaks this second silence.*)

MRS VOYSEY: I didn't hear.

HUGH: (*in his mother's ear*) Edward says there's no money.

TRENCHARD: (*precisely*) I think you said .. 'will be.'

MAJOR: (*in a tone of mitigated thunder*) Why will there be no money?

EDWARD: (*letting himself go*) Because every penny by right belongs to the clients father spent his life in defrauding. I mean that in its worst sense .. swindling .. thieving. I have been in the swim of it, for the past year .. oh, you don't know the sink of iniquity. And now I must collect every penny, any money that you can give me; put the firm into bankruptcy; pay back all we can. I'll stand my trial .. it'll come to that with me .. and as soon as possible. (*He pauses, partly for breath, and glares at them all.*) Are none of you going to speak? Quite right, what is there to be said? (*then with a gentle afterthought*) I'm sorry to hurt you, Mother.

>   (*The* VOYSEY *family is simply buried deep by this avalanche of horror.* MRS VOYSEY, *though, who has been watching* EDWARD *closely, says very calmly* ..)

MRS VOYSEY: I can't hear quite all you say, but I guess what it is. You don't hurt me, Edward .. I have known of this for a long time.

EDWARD: (*with almost a cry*) Oh, Mother, did he know you knew?

MRS VOYSEY: What do you say?

TRENCHARD: (*collected and dry*) I may as well tell you, Edward, I suspected everything wasn't right about the time of the last quarrel with my father. I took care not to pursue my suspicions. Was father aware that you knew, Mother?

MRS VOYSEY: We never discussed it. There was once a great danger, I believe ..

when you were all younger .. of his being found out. But we never discussed it.

EDWARD: (*swallowing a fresh bitterness*) I'm glad it isn't such a shock to all of you.

HUGH: (*alive to a dramatic aspect of the matter*) My God .. before the earth has settled on his grave!

EDWARD: I thought it wrong to put off telling you.

> (HONOR, *the word swindling having spelt itself out in her mind, at last gives way to a burst of piteous grief.*)

HONOR: Oh, poor papa! .. poor papa!

EDWARD: (*comforting her kindly*) Honor, we shall want your help and advice.

> (*The* MAJOR *has recovered from the shock, to swell with importance. It being necessary to make an impression he instinctively turns first to his wife.*)

MAJOR: I think, Emily, there was no need for you to have been present at this exposure, and that now you had better retire.

EMILY: Very well, Booth.

> (*She gets up to go, conscious of her misdemeanour. But as she reaches the door, an awful thought strikes the* MAJOR.)

MAJOR: Good Heavens .. I hope the servants haven't been listening! See where they are, Emily .. and keep them away .. distract them. Open the door suddenly. (*She does so, more or less, and there is no one behind it.*) That's all right.

> (*Having watched his wife's departure, he turns with gravity to his brother.*)

MAJOR: I have said nothing as yet, Edward. I am thinking.

TRENCHARD: (*a little impatient at this exhibition*) That's the worst of these family practices .. a lot of money knocking around and no audit ever required. The wonder to me is to find an honest solicitor at all.

MAJOR: Really, Trenchard!

TRENCHARD: Well, do think of the temptation.

EDWARD: Why are one's clients such fools?

TRENCHARD: The world's getting more and more into the hands of its experts, and it certainly does require a particular sort of honesty.

EDWARD: Here were all these funds simply a lucky bag into which he dipped.

TRENCHARD: Did he keep no accounts of *any* sort?

EDWARD: Scraps of paper. Most of the original investments I can't even trace. The money doesn't exist.

MAJOR: Where't it gone?

EDWARD: (*very directly*) You've been living on it.

MAJOR: Good God!

TRENCHARD: What can you pay in the pound?

EDWARD: As we stand? .. six or seven shillings, I daresay. But we must do better than that.

> (*To which there is no response.*)

---

six or seven shillings: since twenty shillings made a pound, the firm is capable of paying only 30 or 35 per cent of its obligations to clients.

MAJOR: All this is very dreadful. Does it mean beggary for the whole family?

EDWARD: Yes, it should.

TRENCHARD: (*sharply*) Nonsense.

EDWARD: (*joining issue at once*) What right have we to a thing we possess?

TRENCHARD: He didn't make you an allowance, Booth .. your capital's your own, isn't it?

MAJOR: (*awkwardly placed between the two of them*) Really .. I – I suppose so.

TRENCHARD: Then that's all right.

EDWARD: (*vehemently*) It was stolen money, most likely.

TRENCHARD: Ah, most likely. But Booth took it in good faith.

MAJOR: I should hope so.

EDWARD: (*dwelling on the words*) It's stolen money.

MAJOR: (*bubbling with distress*) I say, what ought I to do?

TRENCHARD: Do .. my dear Booth? Nothing.

EDWARD: (*with great indignation*) Trenchard, we owe reparation –

TRENCHARD: (*readily*) Quite so, but to whom? From which client or client's account was Booth's money taken? You say yourself you don't know. Very well then!

EDWARD: (*grieved*) Trenchard!

TRENCHARD: No, my dear Edward. The law will take anything it has a right to and all it can get; you needn't be afraid. There's no obligation, legal or moral, for any of us to throw our pounds into the wreck that they may become pence.

EDWARD: That's just what he would have said.

TRENCHARD: It's what *I* say. But what about your own position .. can we get you clear?

EDWARD: That doesn't matter.

> (*The* MAJOR'S *head has been turning incessantly from one to another and by this he is just a bristle of alarm.*)

MAJOR: But I say, you know, this is awful! Will this have to be made public?

TRENCHARD: No help for it.

> (*The* MAJOR'S *jaw drops; he is speechless.* MRS VOYSEY'S *dead voice steals in.*)

MRS VOYSEY: What is all this?

TRENCHARD: Edward suggests that the family should beggar itself in order to pay back to every client to whom father owed a pound perhaps ten shillings instead of seven.

MRS VOYSEY: He will find that my estate has been kept quite separate.

> (EDWARD *hides his face in his hands.*)

TRENCHARD: I'm very glad to hear it, Mother.

MRS VOYSEY: When Mr Barnes died, your father agreed to appointing another trustee.

TREGONING: (*diffidently*) I suppose, Edward, I'm involved?

EDWARD: (*lifting his head quickly*) Denis, I hope not. I didn't know that anything of yours –

TREGONING: Yes .. all I got under my aunt's will.

EDWARD: See how things are .. I've not found a trace of that yet. We'll hope for the best.

TREGONING: (*setting his teeth*) It can't be helped.

> (MAJOR BOOTH *leans over the table and speaks in the loudest of whispers.*)

MAJOR: Let me advise you to say nothing of this to Ethel at such a critical time.

TREGONING: Thank you, Booth, naturally I shan't.

> (HUGH, *by a series of contortions, has lately been giving evidence of a desire or intention to say something.*)

EDWARD: Well, what is it, Hugh?

HUGH: I have been wondering . . if he can hear this conversation.

> (*Up to now it has all been meaningless to* HONOR, *in her nervous dilapidation, but this remark brings a fresh burst of tears.*)

HONOR: Oh, poor papa . . poor papa!

MRS VOYSEY: I think I'll go to my room. I can't hear what any of you are saying. Edward can tell me afterwards.

EDWARD: Would you like to go too, Honor?

HONOR: (*through her sobs*) Yes, please, I would.

TREGONING: I'll get out, Edward. Whatever you think fit to do . . Oh, well, I suppose there's only one thing to be done.

EDWARD: Only that.

TREGONING: I wish I were in a better position as to work, for Ethel's sake and – and the child's.

EDWARD: Shall I speak to Trenchard?

TREGONING: No . . he knows I exist in a wig and gown. If I can be useful to him, he'll be useful to me, I daresay. Good-bye, Hugh. Good-bye, Booth.

> (*By this time* MRS VOYSEY *and* HONOR *have been got out of the room:* TREGONING *follows them. So the four brothers are left together.* HUGH *is vacant,* EDWARD *does not speak, the* MAJOR *looks at* TRENCHARD, *who settles himself to acquire information.*)

TRENCHARD: How long have things been wrong?

EDWARD: He told me the trouble began in his father's time and that he'd been battling with it ever since.

TRENCHARD: (*smiling*) Oh, come now . . that's impossible.

EDWARD: I believed him! Now I look through the papers, such as they are, I can only find one irregularity that's more than ten years old, and that's only to do with old George Booth's business.

MAJOR: But the Pater never touched his money . . why, he was a personal friend.

EDWARD: Did you hear what Denis said?

TRENCHARD: Very curious his evolving that fiction about his father . . I wonder why. I remember the old man. He was honest as the day.

EDWARD: To get my sympathy, I suppose.

TRENCHARD: I think one can trace the psychology of it deeper than that. It would give a finish to the situation . . his handing on to you an inheritance he had received. You know every criminal has a touch of the artist in him.

HUGH: (*suddenly roused*) That's true.

TRENCHARD: What position did you take up when he told you?

I exist in a wig and gown: I am a barrister.

EDWARD: (*shrugging*) You know what the Pater was.

TRENCHARD: Well .. what did you attempt to do?

EDWARD: I urged him at least to put some of the smaller people right. He said ..
he said that would be penny wise and pound foolish. So I've done what I could
myself .. since he's been ill .. Nothing to count ..

TRENCHARD: With your own money?

EDWARD: The little I had. He kept tight hold to the end.

TRENCHARD: Can you prove that you did that?

EDWARD: I suppose I could.

TRENCHARD: It's a good point.

MAJOR: (*not to be quite left out*) Yes, I must say –

TRENCHARD: You ought to have written him a letter, and left the firm the
moment you found out. Even then, legally ..! But as he was your father ..
What was his object in telling you? He didn't think you'd take a hand?

EDWARD: I've thought of every reason .. and now I really believe it was that he
might have someone to boast to of his financial exploits.

TRENCHARD: (*appreciatively*) I daresay.

MAJOR: Scarcely a thing to boast of!

TRENCHARD: Depends on the point of view.

EDWARD: Then, of course, he always protested that things would come right ..
that he'd clear the firm and have a hundred thousand to the good. Or that if he
were not spared I might do it. But he must have known that was impossible.

TRENCHARD: But there's the gambler all over.

EDWARD: Drawing up his will!

TRENCHARD: Childish!

EDWARD: I'm the sole executor.

TRENCHARD: So I should think! Was I down for anything?

EDWARD: No.

TRENCHARD: (*without resentment*) How he did hate me!

EDWARD: You're safe from the results of his affection anyway.

TRENCHARD: What on earth made you stay in the firm once you knew?

> (EDWARD *does not answer for a moment.*)

EDWARD: I thought I might prevent things from getting any worse. I think I did ..

TRENCHARD: You knew the personal risk you were running?

EDWARD: (*bowing his head*) Yes.

> (TRENCHARD, *the only one of the three who comprehends, looks at
> his brother for a moment with something that might almost be
> admiration. Then he stirs himself.*)

TRENCHARD: I must be off. Work waiting .. end of term, you know.

MAJOR: Shall I walk to the station with you?

TRENCHARD: I'll spend a few minutes with mother. (*he says, at the door, very
respectfully*) You'll count on my professional assistance, please, Edward.

EDWARD: (*simply*) Thank you, Trenchard.

> (*So* TRENCHARD *goes. And the* MAJOR, *who has been
> endeavouring to fathom his final attitude, then comments –*)

MAJOR: No heart, y'know! Great brain! If it hadn't been for that distressing quarrel
he might have saved our poor father. Don't you think so, Edward?

EDWARD: Perhaps.

HUGH: (*giving vent to his thoughts at last with something of a relish*) The more I think this out, the more devilishly humorous it gets. Old Booth breaking down by the grave .. Colpus reading the service ..

EDWARD: Yes, the Vicar's badly hit.

HUGH: Oh, the Pater had managed his business for years.

MAJOR: Good God .. how shall we ever look old Booth in the face again?

EDWARD: I don't worry about him; he can die quite comfortably enough on our six shillings in the pound. It's only one or two of the smaller fry who will suffer.

MAJOR: Now, just explain to me .. I didn't interrupt while Trenchard was talking .. of what exactly did this defrauding consist?

EDWARD: Speculating with a client's capital .. pocketing the gains .. you cut the losses; and you keep paying the client his ordinary income.

MAJOR: So that he doesn't find it out?

EDWARD: Quite so.

MAJOR: In point of fact, he doesn't suffer?

EDWARD: He doesn't suffer till he finds it out.

MAJOR: And all that's wrong now is that some of their capital is missing.

EDWARD: (*half amused, half amazed at this process of reasoning*) Yes, that's all that's wrong.

MAJOR: What is the – ah – deficit? (*The word rolls from his tongue.*)

EDWARD: Anything between two and three hundred thousand pounds.

MAJOR: (*very impressed and not unfavourably*) Dear me .. this is a big affair!

HUGH: (*following his own line of thought*) Quite apart from the rights and wrongs of this, only a very able man could have kept a straight face to the world all these years, as the Pater did.

MAJOR: I suppose he sometimes made money by these speculations.

EDWARD: Very often. His own expenditure was heavy, as *you* know.

MAJOR: (*with gratitude for favours received*) He was a very generous man.

HUGH: Did nobody ever suspect?

EDWARD: You see, Hugh, when there was any pressing danger .. if a big trust had to be wound up .. he'd make a great effort and put the accounts straight.

MAJOR: Then he did put some accounts straight?

EDWARD: Yes, when he couldn't help himself.

> (*The* MAJOR *looks very enquiring and then squares himself up to the subject.*)

MAJOR: Now look here, Edward. You told us that he told you that it was the object of his life to put these accounts straight. Then you laughed at that. Now you tell me that he did put some accounts straight.

EDWARD: (*wearily*) My dear Booth, you don't understand.

MAJOR: Well, let me understand .. I am anxious to understand.

EDWARD: We can't pay ten shillings in the pound.

MAJOR: That's very dreadful. But do you know that there wasn't a time when we couldn't have paid five?

EDWARD: (*acquiescent*) Perhaps.

MAJOR: Very well then! If it was true about his father and all that .. and why shouldn't we believe him if we can? .. and he did effect an improvement, that's to his credit, isn't it? Let us at least be just, Edward.

EDWARD: (*patiently polite*) I am sorry if I seem unjust. But he has left me in a rather unfortunate position.

MAJOR: Yes, his death was a tragedy. It seems to me that if he had been spared he might have succeeded at length in this tremendous task and restored to us our family honour.

EDWARD: Yes, Booth, he spoke very feelingly of that.

MAJOR: (*Irony lost upon him.*) I can well believe it. And I can tell you that now .. I may be right or I may be wrong .. I am feeling far less concerned about the clients' money than I am at the terrible blow to the Family which this exposure will strike. Money, after all, can to a certain extent be done without .. but Honour –

(*This is too much for* EDWARD.)

EDWARD: Our honour! Does any one of you mean to give me a single penny towards undoing all the wrong that has been done?

MAJOR: I take Trenchard's word for it that that would be illegal.

EDWARD: Well .. don't talk to me of honour.

MAJOR: (*somewhat nettled at this outburst*) I am speaking of the public exposure. Edward, can't that be prevented?

EDWARD: (*with quick suspicion*) How?

MAJOR: Well .. how was it being prevented before he died – before we knew anything about it?

EDWARD: (*appealing to the spirits that watch over him*) Oh, listen to this! First Trenchard .. and now you! You've the poison in your blood, every one of you. Who am I to talk? I daresay so have I.

MAJOR: (*reprovingly*) I am beginning to think that you have worked yourself into rather an hysterical state over this unhappy business.

EDWARD: (*rating him*) Perhaps you'd have been glad .. glad if I'd held my tongue and gone on lying and cheating .. and married and begotten a son to go on lying and cheating after me .. and to pay you your interest in the lie and the cheat.

MAJOR: (*with statesman-like calm*) Look here, Edward, this rhetoric is exceedingly out of place. The simple question before us is .. What is the best course to pursue?

EDWARD: There is no question before us. There's only one course to pursue.

MAJOR: (*crushingly*) You will let me speak, please. In so far as our poor father was dishonest to his clients, I pray that he may be forgiven. In so far as he spent his life honestly endeavouring to right a wrong which he had found already committed .. I forgive him. I admire him, Edward. And I feel it my duty to – er – reprobate most strongly the – er – gusto with which you have been holding him up in memory to us .. ten minutes after we have stood round his grave .. as a monster of wickedness. I think I may say I knew him as well as you .. better. And .. thank God! .. there was not between him and me this – this unhappy business to warp my judgement of him. (*He warms to his subject.*) Did you ever know a more charitable man .. a larger-hearted? He was a faithful husband .. and what a father to all of us, putting us out into the world and fully intending to leave us comfortably settled there. Further .. as I see this matter, Edward .. when as a young man he was told this terrible secret and entrusted with such a frightful task .. did he turn his back on it like a coward? No. He went through it heroically to the end of his life. And as he died I imagine there was no more torturing thought than that he had left his work unfinished. (*He is very satisfied with this peroration.*) And now if all these clients can be kept receiving their natural incomes and if father's plan could be carried out of gradually replacing the capital –

> (EDWARD *at this raises his head and stares with horror.*)

EDWARD: You're asking me to carry on this .. Oh, you don't know what you're talking about!

> (*The* MAJOR, *having talked himself back to a proper eminence, remains good-tempered.*)

MAJOR: Well, I'm not a conceited man .. but I do think that I can understand a simple financial problem when it has been explained to me.

EDWARD: You don't know the nerve .. the unscrupulous daring it requires to –

MAJOR: Of course, if you're going to argue round your own incompetence –

EDWARD: (*very straight*) D'you want your legacy?

MAJOR: (*with dignity*) In one moment I shall get very angry. Here am I doing my best to help you and your clients .. and there you sit imputing to me the most sordid motives. Do you suppose I should touch, or allow to be touched, the money which father has left us till every client's claim was satisfied?

EDWARD: My dear Booth, I know you mean well –

MAJOR: I'll come down to your office and work with you.

> (*At this cheerful prospect even poor* EDWARD *can't help smiling.*)

EDWARD: I'm sure you would.

MAJOR: (*feeling that it is a chance lost*) If the Pater had ever consulted me ..

> (*At this point* TRENCHARD *looks round the door to say ..*)

TRENCHARD: Are you coming, Booth?

MAJOR: Yes, certainly. I'll talk this over with Trenchard. (*As he gets up and automatically stiffens, he is reminded of the occasion and his voice drops.*) I say .. we've been speaking very loud. You must do nothing rash. I've no doubt he and I can devise something which will obviate .. and then I'm sure I shall convince you .. (*glancing into the hall he apparently catches* TRENCHARD'S *impatient eye, for he departs abruptly saying ..*) All right, Trenchard, you've eight minutes.

> (*The* MAJOR'S *departure leaves* HUGH, *at any rate, really at his ease.*)

HUGH: This is an experience for you, Edward!

EDWARD: (*bitterly*) And I feared what the shock might be to you all! Booth has made a good recovery.

HUGH: You wouldn't have him miss such a chance of booming at us.

EDWARD: It's strange that people will believe you can do right by means which they know to be wrong.

HUGH: (*taking great interest in this*) Come, what do we know about right and wrong? Let's say legal and illegal. You're so down on the governor because he has trespassed against the etiquette of your own profession. But now he's dead

.. and if there weren't the scandal to think of .. it's no use the rest of us
pretending to feel him a criminal, because we don't. Which just shows that
money .. and property –

> (*At this point he becomes conscious that* ALICE MAITLAND *is
> standing behind him; her eyes fixed on his brother. So he interrupts
> himself to ask* ..)

HUGH: D'you want to speak to Edward?

ALICE: Please, Hugh.

HUGH: I'll go.

> (*He goes, a little martyrlike, to conclude the evolution of his theory in
> soliloquy; his usual fate.* ALICE *still looks at* EDWARD *with soft
> eyes, and he at her rather appealingly.*)

ALICE: Auntie has told me.

EDWARD: He was fond of you. Don't think worse of him than you can help.

ALICE: I'm thinking of you.

EDWARD: I may just escape.

ALICE: So Trenchard says.

EDWARD: My hands are clean, Alice.

ALICE: (*her voice falling lovingly*) I know that.

EDWARD: Mother's not very upset.

ALICE: She had expected a smash in his lifetime.

EDWARD: I'm glad that didn't happen.

ALICE: Yes. I've put Honor to bed. It was a mercy to tell her just at this moment.
She can grieve for his death and his disgrace at the same time .. and the one
grief will soften the other perhaps.

EDWARD: Oh, they're all shocked enough at the disgrace .. but will they open
their purses to lessen the disgrace?

ALICE: Will it seem less disgraceful to have stolen ten thousand pounds than
twenty?

EDWARD: I should think so.

ALICE: I should think so, but I wonder if that's the Law. If it isn't, Trenchard
wouldn't consider the point. I'm sure Public Opinion doesn't say so .. and
that's what Booth is considering.

EDWARD: (*with contempt*) Yes.

ALICE: (*ever so gently ironical*) Well, he's in the Army .. he's almost in Society ..
and he has to get on in both; one mustn't blame him. Of course if the money
could have been given back with a flourish of trumpets ..! But even then I
doubt whether the advertisement would bring in what it cost.

EDWARD: (*very serious*) But when one thinks how the money was obtained!

ALICE: When one thinks how most money is obtained!

EDWARD: They've not *earned* it!

ALICE: (*her eyes humorous*) If they had they might have given it you and earned
more. Did I ever tell you what my guardian said to me when I came of age?

EDWARD: I'm thankful that your money's out of the mess.

ALICE: It wouldn't have been, but I was made to look after it myself .. much
against my will. My guardian was a person of great character and no principles,
the best and most loveable man I've ever met .. I'm sorry you never knew

him, Edward .. and he said once to me .. You've no particular right to your
money. You've not earned it or deserved it in any way. And don't be either
surprised or annoyed when any enterprising person tries to get it from you. He
has at least as much right to it as you have .. if he can use it better perhaps he
has more right. Shocking sentiments, aren't they? But perhaps that's why I've
less patience with some of these clients than you have, Edward.

> (EDWARD *shakes his head, treating these paradoxes as they deserve.*)

EDWARD: Alice .. one or two of them will be beggared.

ALICE: (*sincerely*) Yes, that is bad. What's to be done?

EDWARD: There's old nurse .. with her poor little savings gone!

ALICE: Surely that can be helped?

EDWARD: The Law's no respecter of persons .. that's its boast. Old Booth with
more than he wants will keep enough and to spare. My old nurse, with just
enough, may starve. But it'll be a relief to clear out this nest of lies, even
though one suffers one's self. I've been ashamed to walk into that office, Alice
.. I'll hold my head high in prison though.

> (*He shakes himself stiffly erect, his chin high.* ALICE *quizzes him.*)

ALICE: Edward, I'm afraid you're feeling heroic.

EDWARD: I!

ALICE: You looked quite like Booth for the moment. (*This effectually removes the
starch.*) Please don't glory in your martyrdom. It would be very stupid to send
you to prison and you must do your best to keep out. (*She goes on very
practically.*) We were thinking if anything could be done for these people
who'll be beggared.

EDWARD: It isn't that I'm not sorry for them all ..

ALICE: Of course not.

EDWARD: I suppose I was feeling heroic. I didn't mean to.

> (*He has become a little like a child with her.*)

ALICE: It's the worst of acting on principle .. one is so apt to think more of one's
attitude than of the use of what one is doing.

EDWARD: Fraud must be exposed.

ALICE: And people must be ruined ..!

EDWARD: What else is there to be done?

ALICE: Well .. have you thought?

EDWARD: There's nothing else to be done.

ALICE: No. When on principle there's nothing to be done I'm afraid I've no use for
that principle.

> (*He looks at her; she is smiling, it is true, but smiling quite gravely.*
> EDWARD *is puzzled. Then the yeast of her suggestion begins to work
> in his mind slowly, perversely at first.*)

EDWARD: Unless you expect me to take Booth's advice .. go on with the game ..
as an honest cheat .. plunge, I suppose, just twice as wildly as my father did on
the chance that things might come right .. which he never bothered his head
about. Booth offers to come to the office and assist me.

ALICE: There's something attractive about Booth at the right distance.

EDWARD: Oh .. give him the money .. send him to the City or Monte Carlo .. he
might bring it off. He's like my father .. believes in himself.

ALICE: These credulous men!

EDWARD: (*ignoring her little joke*) But don't think I've any talents that way, principles or no. What have I done so far? Sat in the shame of it for a year. I did take a hand .. if you knew what it felt like .. I managed to stop one affair going from bad to worse.

ALICE: If that was the best you could do wasn't it worth doing? Never mind your feelings.

EDWARD: And that may cost me .. at the best I'll be struck off .. one's livelihood gone.

ALICE: The cost is your own affair.

    (*She is watching him, stilly and closely. Suddenly his face lights a little and he turns to her.*)

EDWARD: I'll tell you what I could do.

ALICE: Yes.

EDWARD: It's just as irregular.

ALICE: That doesn't shock me .. I'm lawless by birthright, being a woman.

EDWARD: There are four or five accounts I believe I could get quite square. Mrs. Travers .. well, she'd never starve, but I'd like to see those two young Lyndhursts safe. There's money to play with, Heaven knows. It'd take a year or more to get it right and cover the tracks. Cover the tracks .. sounds well doesn't it?

ALICE: Then you'd give yourself up as you'd meant to do now?

EDWARD: Go bankrupt.

ALICE: It'd be worse for you then at the trial?

EDWARD: (*with a touch of another sort of pride*) You said that it was my affair.

ALICE: (*pain in her voice and eyes*) Oh, Edward!

EDWARD: Shall I do it?

ALICE: (*turning away*) Why must you ask me?

EDWARD: If you've taken my principles from me, give me advice in exchange.

ALICE: (*after a moment*) No .. you must decide for yourself.

    (*He jumps up and begins to pace about, doubtful, distressed.*)

EDWARD: Ah, but .. it means still lying and shuffling! And I'd sworn to be free of that. And .. it wouldn't be easy. I'm no good at that sort of devilment. I should muddle it and fail.

ALICE: Would you?

    (*He catches a look from her.*)

EDWARD: I might not.

ALICE: And do you need success for a lure .. like a common man?

EDWARD: You want me to try?

    (*For answer she dares only put out her hand, and he takes it.*)

ALICE: Oh, my dear .. cousin!

EDWARD: (*excitedly*) My people must hold their tongues. I needn't have told them.

ALICE: Don't tell them this! *They* won't understand. *I* shall be jealous if you tell them.

---

struck off: removed from the roll of licensed solicitors.

EDWARD: (*looking at her as she at him*) You'll have the right to be. If I bring it off the glory shall be yours.
ALICE: Thank you. I've always wanted to have something useful to my credit . . and I'd almost given up hoping.
> (*Then suddenly his face changes, his voice changes and he grips the hand he is holding so tightly as to hurt her.*)
EDWARD: Ah, no, no, no, no, if my father's story were true . . perhaps he began like this. Doing the right thing in the wrong way . . then doing the wrong thing . . then bringing himself to what he was . . and so me to this. (*He flings away from her.*) No, Alice, I won't . . I won't do it. I daren't take that first step down. There's a worse risk than failure . . I might succeed.
> (*ALICE stands very still, looking at him.*)
ALICE: Yes, that's the big risk. Well . . I'll take it.
> (*He turns to her, in wonder.*)
EDWARD: You?
ALICE: I'll risk your becoming a bad man. That's a big risk for me.
> (*He understands, and is calmed and made happy.*)
EDWARD: Then there's no more to be said, is there?
ALICE: Not now. (*As she drops this gentle hint she hears something – the hall door opening.*) Here's Booth back again.
EDWARD: (*with a really mischievous grin*) He'll be so glad he's convinced me.
ALICE: I must go back to Honor, poor girl. I wonder she has a tear left.
> (*She leaves him, briskly, brightly; leaves her cousin with his mouth set and a light in his eyes.*)

ACT IV

MR VOYSEY'S *room at the office is* EDWARD'S *now. It has somehow lost that brilliancy which the old man's occupation seemed to give it. Perhaps it is only because this December morning is dull and depressing, but the fire isn't bright and the panels and windows don't shine as they did. There are no roses on the table either.*
EDWARD, *walking in as his father did, hanging his hat and coat where his father's used to hang, is certainly the palest shadow of that other masterful presence. A depressed, drooping shadow too. This may be what* PEACEY *feels, if no more, for he looks very surly as he obeys the old routine of following his chief to this room on his arrival. Nor has* EDWARD *so much as a glance for his clerk. They exchange the formalest of greetings.* EDWARD *sits joylessly to his desk, on which the morning's pile of letters lies, unopened now.*

PEACEY: Good morning, sir.
EDWARD: Good morning, Peacey. Any notes for me?
PEACEY: Well, I've hardly been through the letters yet, sir.
EDWARD: (*his eyebrows meeting*) Oh . . and I'm half an hour late myself this morning.
PEACEY: I'm very sorry, sir.
EDWARD: If Mr Bullen calls you had better show him those papers I gave you.

III *The Voysey Inheritance*, act 4. Kingsway Theatre, 1912. Edward (Arthur Wontner) tells George Booth (William Farren) that he has been robbed of his money. The original picture editor inserted the old thief at the bottom (Edmund Maurice as Mr Voysey), brooding over the scene.

Write to Metcalfe as soon as possible; say I've seen Mr Vickery myself this
morning and the houses will not be proceeded with. Better show me the letter.
PEACEY: Very good, sir.
EDWARD: That's all, thank you.
       (PEACEY *gets to the door, where he stops, looking not only surly but*
       nervous now.)
PEACEY: May I speak to you a moment, sir?
EDWARD: Certainly.
       (PEACEY, *after a moment, makes an effort, purses his mouth and*
       begins.)
PEACEY: Bills are beginning to come in upon me as is usual at this season, sir. My
    son's allowance at Cambridge is now rather a heavy item of my expenditure. I
    hope that the custom of the firm isn't to be neglected now that you are the
    head of it, Mr Edward .. Two hundred your father always made it at
    Christmas .. in notes if you please.
       (*Towards the end of this* EDWARD *begins to pay great attention.*
       When he answers his voice is harsh.)
EDWARD: Oh, to be sure .. your hush money.
PEACEY: (*bridling*) That's not a very pleasant word.
EDWARD: This is an unpleasant subject.
PEACEY: Well, it's not one I wish to discuss. Your father always gave me the notes
    in an envelope when he shook hands with me at Christmas.
EDWARD: Why notes now? Why not a rise in salary?
PEACEY: Mr Voysey's custom, sir, from before my time .. my father ..
EDWARD: Yes. It's an hereditary pull you have over the firm, isn't it?
PEACEY: I remember my father only saying to me when he retired .. been dead
    twenty-six years, Mr Edward .. I have told the governor you know what I
    know; then Mr Voysey saying .. I treat you as I did your father, Peacey. We'd
    never another word with him on the subject.
EDWARD: A decent arrangement .. and the cheapest, no doubt. Of the raising of
    salaries there might have been no end.
PEACEY: Mr Edward, that's uncalled for. We have served you and yours most
    faithfully. I know my father would sooner have cut off his hand than do
    anything to embarrass the firm.
EDWARD: But business is business, Peacey. Surely he could have had a partnership
    for the asking.
PEACEY: Ah, that's another matter, sir.
EDWARD: Well ..
PEACEY: A matter of principle, if you'll excuse me. I must not be taken to approve
    of the firm's conduct. Nor did my dear father approve. And at anything like
    partnership he would have drawn the line.
EDWARD: I beg your pardon.
PEACEY: Well, that's all right, sir. Always a bit of friction in coming to an
    understanding about anything, isn't there, sir?
       (*He is going when* EDWARD'S *question stops him.*)
EDWARD: Why didn't you speak about this last Christmas?
PEACEY: You were so upset at your father's death.

EDWARD: My father died the August before that.

PEACEY: Well .. truthfully, Mr Edward?

EDWARD: As truthfully as you think suitable.

> (*The irony of this is wasted on* PEACEY, *who becomes pleasantly candid.*)

PEACEY: Well, I'd always thought there must be a smash when your father died .. but it didn't come. I couldn't make you out. But then again by Christmas you seemed all on edge and I thought anything might happen. So I kept quiet and said nothing.

EDWARD: I see. Your son's at Cambridge?

PEACEY: Yes.

EDWARD: I wonder you didn't bring him into the firm.

PEACEY: (*taking this very kind*) Thank you. But I hope James may go to the bar. Our only son .. I didn't grudge him my small savings to help him wait for his chance .. ten years if need be.

EDWARD: I hope he'll make his mark before then. I'm glad to have had this talk with you, Peacey. I'm sorry you can't have the money you want.

> (*He returns to his letters, a little steely-eyed.* PEACEY, *quite at his ease, makes for the door yet again, saying ..*)

PEACEY: Oh, any time will do, sir.

EDWARD: You can't have it at all.

PEACEY: (*brought up short*) Can't I?

EDWARD: (*very decidedly indeed*) No .. I made up my mind about this eighteen months ago. My father had warned me, but since his death the trust business of the firm is not conducted as it used to be. We no longer make illicit profits out of our clients. There are none for you to share.

> (*Having thus given the explanation he considers due, he goes on with his work. But* PEACEY *has flushed up.*)

PEACEY: Look here, Mr Edward, I'm sorry we began this discussion. You'll give me my two hundred as usual, please, and we'll drop the subject.

EDWARD: You can drop the subject.

PEACEY: (*his voice rising sharply*) I want the money. I think it's not gentlemanly in you, Mr Edward, to try like this and get out of paying it me. Your father would never have made such an excuse.

EDWARD: (*flabbergasted*) Do you think I'm lying to you?

PEACEY: (*with a deprecating swallow*) I've no wish to criticise your statements or your actions at all, sir. It was no concern of mine how your father treated his clients.

EDWARD: And now it's not to concern you how honest I am. You want your money just the same.

PEACEY: Well, don't be sarcastic .. a man does get used to a state of affairs whatever it may be.

EDWARD: (*with considerable force*) My friend, if I drop sarcasm I shall have to tell you very candidly what I think of you.

PEACEY: That I'm a thief because I've taken money from a thief?

EDWARD: Worse than a thief. You're content that others should steal for you.

PEACEY: And who isn't?

(EDWARD *is really pleased with the aptness of this. He at once changes his tone, which indeed had become rather bullying.*)

EDWARD: What, my dear Peacey, you study sociology? Well, it's too big a question to discuss now. But I'm afraid the application of this bit of it is that I have for the moment, at some inconvenience to myself, ceased to receive stolen goods, so I am in a position to throw a stone at you. I have thrown it.

(PEACEY, *who would far sooner be bullied than talked to like this, turns very sulky.*)

PEACEY: Then I resign my position here.

EDWARD: Very well.

PEACEY: And I happen to think the secret's worth its price.

EDWARD: Perhaps someone will pay it you.

PEACEY: (*feebly threatening*) Don't presume upon it's not being worth my while to make use of what I know.

EDWARD: (*not unkindly*) My good Peacey, it happens to be the truth I told you just now. Well, how on earth do you suppose you can successfully blackmail a man who has so much to gain by exposure and so little to lose as I?

PEACEY: (*peeving*) I don't want to ruin you, sir, and I have a great regard for the firm .. but you must see that I can't have my income reduced in this way without a struggle.

EDWARD: (*with great cheerfulness*) Very well, my friend, struggle away.

PEACEY: (*his voice rising high and thin*) Well, is it fair dealing on your part to dock the money suddenly like this? I have been counting on it most of the year, and I have been led into heavy expenses. Why couldn't you have warned me?

EDWARD: Yes, that's true, Peacey, it was stupid of me. I'm sorry.

(PEACEY *is a little comforted by this quite candid acknowledgement.*)

PEACEY: Things may get easier for you by and bye.

EDWARD: I hope so.

PEACEY: Will you reconsider the matter then?

(*At this gentle insinuation* EDWARD *looks up exasperated.*)

EDWARD: Then you don't believe what I told you?

PEACEY: Yes, I do.

EDWARD: But you think that the fascination of swindling one's clients will ultimately prove irresistible?

PEACEY: That's what your father found, I suppose you know.

(*This gives* EDWARD *such pause that he drops his masterful tone.*)

EDWARD: I didn't.

PEACEY: He got things as right as rain once.

EDWARD: Did he?

PEACEY: So my father told me. But he started again.

EDWARD: Are you sure of this?

PEACEY: (*expanding pleasantly*) Well, sir, I knew your father pretty well. When I first came into the firm, now, I simply hated him. He was that sour; so snappy with everyone .. as if he had a grievance against the whole world.

EDWARD: (*pensively*) It seems he had in those days.

PEACEY: His dealings with his clients were no business of mine. I speak as I find.

After a bit he was very kind to me, thoughtful and considerate. He got to be so pleasant and generous to everyone –

EDWARD: That you have great hopes of me yet?

PEACEY: (*who has a simple mind*) No, Mr Edward, no. You're different from your father .. one must make up one's mind to that. And you may believe me or not, but I should be very glad to know that the firm was solvent and going straight. I'm getting on in years myself now. I'm not much longer for the business, and there have been times when I have sincerely regretted my connection with it. If you'll let me say so, I think it's very noble of you to have undertaken the work you have. (*then, as everything seems smooth again*) And, Mr Edward, if you'll give me enough to cover this year's extra expense I think I may promise you that I shan't expect money again.

EDWARD: (*good-tempered, as he would speak to an importunate child*) No, Peacey, no!

PEACEY: (*fretful again*) Well, sir, you make things very difficult for me.

EDWARD: Here's a letter from Mr Cartwright which you might attend to. If he wants an appointment with me, don't make one till the New Year. His case can't come on before February.

PEACEY: (*taking the letter*) I show myself anxious to meet you in every way – (*He is handed another.*)

EDWARD: 'Percival Building Estate' .. that's yours too.

PEACEY: (*putting them both down resolutely*) But I refuse to be ignored. I must consider my whole position. I hope I may not be tempted to make use of the power I possess. But if I am driven to proceed to extremities ..

EDWARD: (*breaking in upon this bunch of tags*) My dear Peacey, don't talk nonsense .. you couldn't proceed to an extremity to save your life. You've taken this money irresponsibly for all these years. You'll find you're no longer capable even of such a responsible act as tripping up your neighbour.

> (*This does completely upset the gentle blackmailer. He loses one grievance in another.*)

PEACEY: Really, Mr Edward, I am a considerably older man than you, and I think that whatever our positions –

EDWARD: Don't let us argue, Peacey. You're quite at liberty to do whatever you think worth your while.

PEACEY: It's not the money, I can do without that, but these personalities –

EDWARD: I apologise for them. Don't forget the letters.

PEACEY: I will not, sir.

> (*He takes them with great dignity and is leaving the room.*)

PEACEY: Here's Mr Hugh waiting.

EDWARD: To see me? Ask him in.

PEACEY: Come in, Mr Hugh, please.

> (*HUGH comes in, PEACEY holding the door for him with a frigid politeness of which he is quite oblivious. At this final slight PEACEY goes out in dudgeon.*)

EDWARD: How are you, Hugh?

HUGH: Good Lord!

> (*And he throws himself into the chair by the fire. EDWARD, quite*

*used to this sort of thing, goes quietly on with his work, adding
encouragingly after a moment . .)*

EDWARD: How's Beatrice?

HUGH: She's very busy.

*(He studies his boots with the gloomiest expression. And indeed, they
are very dirty and his turned-up trousers are muddy at the edge. They
are dark trousers and well cut, but he wears with them a loose coat and
waistcoat of a peculiar light brown check. Add to this the roughest of
overcoats and a very soft hat. Add also the fact that he doesn't shave
well or regularly and that his hair wants cutting, and HUGH'S
appearance this morning is described. As he is quite capable of sitting
silently by the fire for a whole morning EDWARD asks him at last . .)*

EDWARD: What d'you want?

HUGH: *(with vehemence)* I want a machine gun planted in Regent Street . . and one
in the Haymarket . . and one in Leicester Squre and one in the Strand . . and a
dozen in the City. An earthquake would be simpler. Or why not a nice clean
tidal wave? It's no good preaching and patching up any longer, Edward. We
must begin afresh. Don't you feel, even in your calmer moments, that this
whole country is simply hideous? The other nations must look after
themselves. I'm patriotic . . I only ask that we should be destroyed.

EDWARD: It has been promised.

HUGH: I'm sick of waiting. *(then as EDWARD says nothing)* You say this is the cry
of the weak man in despair! I wouldn't be anything but a weak man in this
world. I wouldn't be a king, I wouldn't be rich . . I wouldn't be a Borough
Councillor . . I should be so ashamed. I've walked here this morning from
Hampstead. I started to curse because the streets were dirty. You'd think that
an Empire could keep its streets clean! But then I saw that the children were
dirty too.

EDWARD: That's because of the streets.

HUGH: Yes, it's holiday time. Those that can cross a road safely are doing some
work now . . earning some money. You'd think a governing race, grabbing
responsibilities, might care for its children.

EDWARD: Come, we educate them now. And I don't think many work in holiday
time.

HUGH: *(encouraged by contradiction)* Education! What's that? Joining the great
conspiracy which we call our civilization. But one mustn't. One must stand
aside and give the show away. By the bye, that's what I've come for.

EDWARD: *(pleasantly)* What? I thought you'd only come to talk.

HUGH: Take that money of mine for your clients. You ought to have had it when
you asked for it. It has never belonged to me, in any real . . in any spiritual
sense, so it has been just a clog to my life.

EDWARD: *(surprised)* My dear Hugh . . this is very generous of you.

HUGH: Not a bit. I only want to start fresh and free.

EDWARD: *(sitting back from his work)* Hugh, do you really think our money
carries a curse with it?

HUGH: *(with great violence)* Think! I'm the proof of it! Look at me! I felt I must
create or die. I said I'd be an artist. The governor gave me a hundred and fifty

a year .. the rent of a studio and the price of a velvet coat he thought it; that was all he knew about art. But my respectable training got me engaged and married. Marriage in a studio puzzled the governor, so he guessed it at two hundred and fifty a year .. and looked for lay-figure babies, I suppose. Ha, ha! Well, I've learnt my job. I work in a sort of way, Edward, though you mightn't think it. Well, what have I really learnt .. about myself .. that's the only learning .. that there's nothing I can do or be but reflects our drawing-room at Chislehurst.

EDWARD: (*considering*) What do you earn in a year? I doubt if you can afford to give this up.

HUGH: Oh, Edward .. you clank the chain with the best of them. Afford! If I can't get free from these crippling advantages .. Unless I find out what I'm worth in myself .. whether I even exist or not? Am I only a pretence of a man animated by an income?

EDWARD: But you can't return to nature on the London pavements.

HUGH: No. Nor in England at all .. it's nothing but a big back garden. (*Now he collects himself for a final outburst.*) Is there no place on this earth where a man can prove his right to live by some other means than robbing his neighbour? Put me there naked and penniless. Put me to that test. If I can't answer it, then turn down your thumb .. Oh God .. and I won't complain.

(EDWARD *waits till the effects of this explosion are over.*)

EDWARD: And what does Beatrice say to your emigrating to the backwoods .. if that is exactly what you mean?

HUGH: Now that we're separating –

EDWARD: (*taken aback*) What?

HUGH: We mean to separate.

EDWARD: The first I've heard of it.

HUGH: Beatrice is making some money by her books, so it has become possible.

EDWARD: (*humorously*) Have you told anyone yet?

HUGH: We must now, I suppose.

EDWARD: Say nothing at home until after Christmas.

HUGH: They'll insist on discussing it solemnly. Ar-r-r. (*then he whistles*) Emily knows!

EDWARD: (*having considered*) I shan't take your money .. there's no need. All the good has been done that I wanted to do. No one will be quite beggared now. So why should you be?

HUGH: (*with clumsy affection*) We've taken a fine lot of interest in your labours, haven't we, Hercules?

EDWARD: You hold your tongue about the office affairs, don't you? It's not through one of us it should come out, and I've told you more than Booth and the others.

HUGH: When will you be quit of the beastly business?

EDWARD: (*becoming reserved and cold at once*) Some day.

HUGH: What do you gain by hanging on now?

EDWARD: Occupation.

---

lay-figure: jointed model of the human body used by artists.

HUGH: But, Edward, it must be an awfully wearying state of things. I suppose any moment a policeman may knock at the door .. so to speak?

EDWARD: (*appreciating the figure of speech*) Any moment. I take no precautions. I made up my mind that at least I wouldn't lower myself to that. And perhaps it's why the policeman doesn't come. At first I listened for him, day by day. Then I said to myself .. next week. But a year has gone by and more. I've ceased expecting to hear the knock at all.

HUGH: But look here .. is all this worth while, and have you the right to make a mean thing of your life like this?

EDWARD: Does my life matter?

HUGH: Well .. of course!

EDWARD: It's so much easier to believe not. The world that you kick against is using me up. A little wantonly .. a little needlessly, I do think. But let her. As I sit here now drudging honestly, I declare I begin to understand my father. But no doubt, it's all I'm fit for .. to nurse fools' money.

HUGH: (*responding at once to this vein*) Nonsense. We all want a lesson in values. We're never taught what is worth having and what isn't. Why should your real happiness be sacrificed to the sham happiness which people have invested in the firm? I've never believed that money was valuable. I remember once giving a crossing-sweeper a sovereign. The sovereign was nothing. But the sensation I gave him was an intrinsically valuable thing.

(*He is fearfully pleased with his essay in philosophy.*)

EDWARD: And he could buy other sensations with the sovereign.

HUGH: But none like the first. You mean to stay here till something happens?

EDWARD: I do. This is what I'm brought to. No more good to be done. And I haven't the faith in myself to do wrong. And it's only your incurable optimist who has enterprise enough for suicide .. even business suicide.

HUGH: Ah .. I'm that. But I can't boast. Heaven knows when I shall really get out of it either. (*Then the realities of life overwhelm him again.*) Beatrice won't let me go until we're each certain of two hundred a year. And she's quite right .. I should only get into debt. You know that two fifty a year of mine is a hundred and eighty now.

EDWARD: (*mischievous*) Why would you invest sensationally?

HUGH: (*with great seriousness*) I put money into things which I knew ought to succeed ..

(*The telephone rings.* EDWARD *speaks through it.*)

EDWARD: Certainly .. bring him in. (*Then to his brother who sits on the table idly disarranging everything.*) You'll have to go now, Hugh.

HUGH: (*shaking his head gloomily*) You're one of the few people I can talk to, Edward.

EDWARD: I like listening.

HUGH: (*as much cheered as surprised*) Do you? I believe talking does stir up the world's atoms a bit.

(*In comes old* MR GEORGE BOOTH, *older too in looks than he*

---

sovereign: gold coin worth a pound.

was eighteen months back. Very dandyishly dressed, he still seems by no means so happy as his clothes might be making him.)

MR BOOTH: 'Ullo, Hugh! I thought I should find you, Edward.

EDWARD: (*formally*) Good morning, Mr Booth.

HUGH: (*as he collects his hat, his coat, his various properties*) Well .. Beatrice and I go down to Chislehurst tomorrow. I say .. d'you know that old Nursie is furious with you about something?

EDWARD: (*shortly*) Yes, I know. Good-bye.

HUGH: How are you?

> (*He launches this enquiry at* MR BOOTH *with great suddenness just as he leaves the room. The old gentleman jumps; then jumps again at the slam of the door. And then he frowns at* EDWARD *in a frightened sort of way.*)

EDWARD: Will you come here .. or will you sit by the fire?

MR BOOTH: This'll do. I shan't detain you long.

> (*He takes the chair by the table and occupies the next minute or two carefully disposing of his hat and gloves.*)

EDWARD: Are you feeling all right again?

MR BOOTH: A bit dyspeptic. How are you?

EDWARD: Quite well, thanks.

MR BOOTH: I'm glad .. I'm glad. (*He now proceeds to cough a little, hesitating painfully.*) I'm afraid this isn't very pleasant business I've come upon.

EDWARD: D'you want to go to Law with anyone?

MR BOOTH: No .. oh, no. I'm getting too old to quarrel.

EDWARD: A pleasant symptom.

MR BOOTH: (*with a final effort*) I mean to withdraw my securities from the custody of your firm .. (*and he adds apologetically*) with the usual notice, of course.

> (*It would be difficult to describe what* EDWARD *feels at this moment. Perhaps something of the shock that the relief of death may be as an end to pain so long endured that it has been half forgotten. He answers very quietly, without a sign of emotion.*)

EDWARD: Thank you .. May one ask why?

MR BOOTH: (*relieved that the worst is over*) Certainly .. certainly. I think you must know, Edward, I have never been able to feel that implicit confidence in your ability which I had in your father's. Well, it is hardly to be expected, is it?

EDWARD: (*with a grim smile*) No.

MR BOOTH: I can say that without unduly depreciating you. Men like your father are few and far between. No doubt things go on here as they have always done, but .. since his death I have not been happy about my affairs.

EDWARD: (*speaking as it is his duty to*) I think you need be under no apprehension ..

MR BOOTH: I daresay not. But for the first time in my long life to be worried about money affairs .. I don't like the feeling. The possession of money has always been a pleasure to me .. and for what are perhaps my last years I don't wish it to be otherwise. Remember you have practically my entire property unreservedly in your control.

EDWARD: Perhaps we can arrange to hand you over the reins to an extent which will ease your mind, and at the same time not ..

MR BOOTH: I thought of that. I am very sorry to seem to be slighting your father's son. I have not moved in the matter for eighteen months. Really, one feels a little helpless .. and the transaction of business requires more energy than .. But I saw my doctor yesterday, Edward, and he told me .. well, it was a warning. And so I felt it my duty .. especially as I made up my mind to it some time ago. (*He comes to the end of this havering at last and adds ..*) In point of fact, Edward, more than a year before your father died I had quite decided that I could never trust my affairs to you as I had to him.

> (EDWARD *starts almost out of his chair; his face pale, his eyes black.*)

EDWARD: Did he know that?

MR BOOTH: (*resenting this new attitude*) I think I never said it in so many words. But I fancy he guessed.

EDWARD: (*as he relaxes and turns, almost shuddering, from the possibility of dreadful knowledge*) Don't say so .. he never guessed. (*then, with a sudden fresh impulse*) I hope you won't do this, Mr Booth.

MR BOOTH: I have quite made up my mind.

EDWARD: Let me persuade you –

MR BOOTH: (*conciliatory*) I shall make a point of telling the family that you are in no way to blame. And in the event of any personal legal difficulties I shall always be delighted to come to you. My idea is for the future to employ merely a financial agent –

EDWARD: (*still quite unstrung really, and his nerves betraying him*) Why didn't you tell my father .. why didn't you?

MR BOOTH: I did not choose to distress him by –

EDWARD: (*pulling himself together; speaking half to himself*) Well .. well .. this is one way out. And it's not my fault.

MR BOOTH: You're making a fearful fuss about a very simple matter, Edward. The loss of one client, however important he may be .. Why, this is one of the best family practices in London. I am surprised at your lack of dignity.

> (EDWARD *yields smilingly to this assertiveness.*)

EDWARD: Yes .. I have no dignity. Will you walk off with your papers now?

MR BOOTH: What notice is usual?

EDWARD: To a good solicitor, five minutes. Ten to a poor one.

MR BOOTH: You'll have to explain matters a bit to me.

> (*Now* EDWARD *settles to his desk again; really with a certain grim enjoyment of the prospect.*)

EDWARD: I will. Mr Booth, how much do you think you're worth?

MR BOOTH: (*easily*) Do you know, I actually couldn't say off-hand.

EDWARD: But you've a rough idea?

MR BOOTH: To be sure.

EDWARD: You'll get not quite half that out of us.

MR BOOTH: (*precisely*) I think I said I had made up my mind to withdraw the whole amount.

EDWARD: You should have made up your mind sooner.

MR BOOTH: I don't in the least understand you, Edward.

EDWARD: The greater part of your capital doesn't exist.

MR BOOTH: (*with some irritation*) Nonsense, it must exist. (*He scans* EDWARD'S *set face in vain.*) You mean that it won't be prudent to realise? You can hand over the securities. I don't want to reinvest simply because –

EDWARD: I can't hand over what I haven't got.

> (*This sentence falls on the old man's ears like a knell.*)

MR BOOTH: Is anything . . *wrong*?

EDWARD: (*grim and patient*) How many more times am I to say that we have robbed you of half your property?

MR BOOTH: (*his senses failing him*) Say that again.

EDWARD: It's quite true.

MR BOOTH: My money . . *gone*?

EDWARD: Yes.

MR BOOTH: (*clutching at a straw of anger*) You've been the thief . . you . . you . .?

EDWARD: I wouldn't tell you if I could help it . . my father.

> (*That actually calls the old man back to something like dignity and self-possession. He thumps on* EDWARD'S *table furiously.*)

MR BOOTH: I'll make you prove that.

> (*And now* EDWARD *buries his face in his arms and just goes off into hysterics.*)

EDWARD: Oh, you've fired a mine!

MR BOOTH: (*scolding him well*) Slandering your dead father . . and lying to me, revenging yourself by frightening me . . because I detest you.

EDWARD: Why . . haven't I thanked you for putting an end to my troubles? I do . . I promise you I do.

MR BOOTH: (*shouting, and his sudden courage failing as he shouts*) Prove it . . prove it to me! You don't frighten me so easily. One can't lose half of all one has and then be told of it in two minutes . . sitting at a table. (*His voice tails off to a piteous whimper.*)

EDWARD: (*quietly now and kindly*) If my father had told you in plain words you'd have believed him.

MR BOOTH: (*bowing his head*) Yes.

> (EDWARD *looks at the poor old thing with great pity.*)

EDWARD: What on earth did you want to do this for? You need never have known . . you could have died happy. Settling with all those charities in your will would certainly have smashed us up. But proving your will is many years off yet, we'll hope.

MR BOOTH: (*pathetic and bewildered*) I don't understand. No, I don't understand . . because your father . . But I *must* understand, Edward.

EDWARD: Don't shock yourself trying to understand my father, for you never will. Pull yourself together, Mr Booth. After all, this isn't a vital matter to you. It's not even as if you had a family to consider . . like some of the others.

MR BOOTH: (*vaguely*) What others?

---

realise: sell the shares and holdings for cash.

EDWARD: Don't imagine your money has been specially selected for pilfering.

MR BOOTH: (*with solemn incredulity*) One has read of this sort of thing but . . I thought people always got found out.

EDWARD: (*brutally humorous*) Well . . you've found us out.

MR BOOTH: (*rising to the full appreciation of his wrongs*) Oh . . I've been foully cheated!

EDWARD: (*patiently*) I've told you so.

MR BOOTH: (*his voice breaks, he appeals pitifully*) But by you, Edward . . say it's by you.

EDWARD: (*unable to resist his quiet revenge*) I've not the ability or the personality for such work, Mr Booth . . nothing but principles, which forbid me even to lie to you.

      (*The old gentleman draws a long breath and then speaks with great awe, blending into grief.*)

MR BOOTH: I think your father is in Hell . . I'd have gone there myself to save him from it. I loved him very truly. How he could have had the heart! We were friends for nearly fifty years. Am I to think now he only cared for me to cheat me?

EDWARD: (*venturing the comfort of an explanation*) No . . he didn't value money quite as you do.

MR BOOTH: (*with sudden shrill logic*) But he took it. What d'you mean by that?

      (EDWARD *leans back in his chair and changes the tenor of their talk.*)

EDWARD: Well, you're master of the situation now. What are you going to do?

MR BOOTH: To get my money back?

EDWARD: No, that's gone.

MR BOOTH: Then give me what's left and –

EDWARD: Are you going to prosecute?

MR BOOTH: (*shifting uneasily in his chair*) Oh, dear . . is that necessary? Can't somebody else do that? I thought the Law . . What'll happen if I don't?

EDWARD: What do you suppose I'm doing here still?

MR BOOTH: (*as if he were being asked a riddle*) I don't know.

EDWARD: (*earnestly*) As soon as my father died, I began of course to try and put things straight . . doing as I thought best . . that is . . as best I could. Then I made up my accounts showing who has lost and who hasn't . . they can criticise those as they please and that's all done with. And now I've set myself to a duller sort of work. I throw penny after penny hardly earned into the half-filled pit of our deficit. But I've been doing that for what it's worth in the time that was left to me . . till this should happen. If you choose to let things alone – which won't hurt you, will it? – and hold your tongue, I can go on with the job till the next smash comes, and I'll beg that off too if I can. This is my duty, and it's my duty to ask you to let me go on with it. (*He searches* MR BOOTH'S *face and finds there only disbelief and fear. He bursts out.*) Oh, you might at least believe me. It can't hurt you to believe me.

MR BOOTH: You must admit, Edward, it isn't easy to believe anything in this office . . just for the moment.

EDWARD: (*bowing to the extreme reasonableness of this*) I suppose not . . I can

prove it to you. I'll take you through the books .. you won't understand them
.. but I can boast of this much.

MR BOOTH: I think I'd rather not. D'you think I ought to hold any further
communication with you at all? (*And at this he takes his hat.*)

EDWARD: (*with a little explosion of contemptuous anger*) Certainly not. Prosecute
.. prosecute!

MR BOOTH: (*with dignity*) Don't lose your temper. You know it's my place to be
angry with you.

EDWARD: But .. (*then he is elaborately explanatory*) I shall be *grateful* if you'll
prosecute.

MR BOOTH: (*more puzzled than ever*) There's something in this which I don't
understand.

EDWARD: (*with deliberate unconcern*) Think it over.

MR BOOTH: (*hesitatingly, fidgeting*) Surely I oughtn't to have to make up my mind!
There must be a right or a wrong thing to do. Edward, can't *you* tell me?

EDWARD: I'm prejudiced, you see.

MR BOOTH: (*angrily*) I believe you're simply trying to practise upon my goodness
of heart. Certainly I ought to prosecute at once .. Oughtn't I? (*then at the
nadir of helplessness*) Can't I consult another solicitor?

EDWARD: (*his chin in the air*) You can write to the Times about it!

MR BOOTH: (*shocked and grieved at his attitude*) Edward, how can you be so cool
and heartless?

EDWARD: (*changing his tone*) D'you think I shan't be glad to sleep at nights?

MR BOOTH: Perhaps you'll be put in prison?

EDWARD: I *am* in prison .. a less pleasant one than Wormwood Scrubbs. But
we're all prisoners, Mr Booth.

MR BOOTH: (*wagging his head*) Yes, this is what comes of your philosophy. Why
aren't you on your knees?

EDWARD: To *you*?

> (*This was not what* MR BOOTH *meant, but as he gets up from his
> chair he feels all but mighty.*)

MR BOOTH: And why should you expect me to shrink from vindicating the Law?

EDWARD: (*shortly*) I don't. I've explained you'll be doing me a kindness. When
I'm wanted you'll find me here at my desk. (*then as an afterthought*) If you
take long to decide .. don't alter your behaviour to my family in the
meantime. They know the main points of the business and –

MR BOOTH: (*knocked right off his balance*) Do they! Good God! .. I'm invited to
dinner the day after tomorrow .. that's Christmas Eve. The hypocrites!

EDWARD: (*unmoved*) I shall be there .. that will have given you two days. Will
you tell me then?

MR BOOTH: (*protesting violently*) I can't go .. I can't have dinner with them. I
must be ill.

EDWARD: (*with a half smile*) I remember I went to dine at Chislehurst to tell my
father of my decision.

MR BOOTH: (*testily*) What decision?

Wormwood Scrubbs: the chief London prison (now spelled with a single *b*).

EDWARD: To remain in the firm when I first knew what was happening.

MR BOOTH: (*interested*) Was I there?

EDWARD: I daresay.

> (MR BOOTH *stands there, hat, stick and gloves in hand, shaken by this experience, helpless, at his wits' end. He falls into a sort of fretful reverie, speaking half to himself but yet as if he hoped that* EDWARD, *who is wrapped in his own thoughts, would have the decency to answer, or at least listen, to what he is saying.*)

MR BOOTH: Yes, how often I dined with him. Oh, it was monstrous! (*His eyes fall on the clock.*) It's nearly lunch time now. Do you know I still can hardly believe it all? I wish I hadn't found it out. If he hadn't died I should never have found it out. I hate to have to be vindictive .. it's not my nature. Indeed I'm sure I'm more grieved than angry. But it isn't as if it were a small sum. And I don't see that one is called upon to forgive crimes .. or why does the Law exist? I feel that this will go near to killing me. I'm too old to have such troubles .. it isn't right. And now if I have to prosecute –

EDWARD: (*at last throwing in a word*) Well .. you need not.

MR BOOTH: (*thankful for the provocation*) Don't you attempt to influence me, sir. (*He turns to go.*)

EDWARD: And what's more, with the money you have left ..

> (EDWARD *follows him politely.* MR BOOTH *flings the door open.*)

MR BOOTH: You'll make out a cheque for that at once, sir, and send it me.

EDWARD: You might ..

MR BOOTH: (*clapping his hat on, stamping his stick*) I shall do the right thing, sir, never fear.

> (*So he marches off in fine style, having, he thinks, had the last word and all. But* EDWARD, *closing the door after him, mutters ..*)

EDWARD:.. Save your soul! .. I'm afraid I was going to say.

ACT V

Naturally it is the dining-room – consecrated as it is to the distinguishing orgy of the season – which bears the brunt of what an English household knows as Christmas decorations. They consist chiefly of the branches of holly (that unyielding tree), stuck cock-eyed behind the top edges of the pictures. The one picture conspicuously not decorated is that which now hangs over the fireplace, a portrait of MR VOYSEY, *with its new gilt frame and its brassplate marking it also as a presentation.* HONOR, *hastily and at some bodily peril, pulled down the large bunch of mistletoe, which a callous housemaid had suspended above it, in time to obviate the shock to family feelings which such impropriety would cause. Otherwise the only difference between the dining-room's appearance at half-past nine on Christmas Eve and on any other evening in the year is that little piles of queer shaped envelopes seem to be lying about, while there is quite a lot of tissue paper and string to be seen peeping from odd corners. The electric light is reduced to one bulb, but when the maid opens the door showing in* MR GEORGE BOOTH *she switches on the rest.*

PHOEBE: This room is empty, sir. I'll tell Mr Edward.

(*She leaves him to fidget towards the fireplace and back, not removing his comforter or his coat, scarcely turning down the collar, screwing his cap in his hands. In a very short time* EDWARD *comes in, shutting the door and taking stock of the visitor before he speaks.*)

EDWARD: Well?

MR BOOTH: (*feebly*) I hope my excuse for not coming to dinner was acceptable. I did have .. I have a very bad headache.

EDWARD: I daresay they believed it.

MR BOOTH: I have come immediately to tell you my decision .. perhaps this trouble will then be a little more off my mind.

EDWARD: What is it?

MR BOOTH: I couldn't think the matter out alone. I went this afternoon to talk it over with my old friend Colpus. (*At this news* EDWARD'S *eyebrows contract and then rise.*) What a terrible shock to him!

EDWARD: Oh, nearly three of his four thousand pounds are quite safe.

MR BOOTH: That you and your father .. you, whom he baptised .. should have robbed him! I never saw a man so utterly prostrate with grief. That it should have been your father! And his poor wife! .. though she never got on with your father.

EDWARD: (*with a cheerful irony*) Oh, Mrs Colpus knows too, does she?

MR BOOTH: Of course he told Mrs Colpus. This is an unfortunate time for the storm to break on him. What with Christmas Day and Sunday following so close they're as busy as can be. He has resolved that during this season of peace and goodwill he must put the matter from him if he can. But once Christmas is over ..! (*He envisages the Christian old vicar giving* EDWARD *a hell of a time then.*)

EDWARD: (*coolly*) So you mean to prosecute. If you don't, you've inflicted on the Colpuses a lot of unnecessary pain and a certain amount of loss by telling them.

MR BOOTH: (*naïvely*) I never thought of that. No, Edward, I have decided not to prosecute.

(EDWARD *hides his face for a moment.*)

EDWARD: And I've been hoping to escape! Well .. it can't be helped (*and he sets his teeth*).

MR BOOTH: (*with touching solemnity*) I think I could not bear to see the family I have loved brought to such disgrace. And I want to ask your pardon, Edward, for some of the hard thoughts I have had of you. I consider this effort of yours to restore to the firm the credit which your father lost a very striking one. You sacrifice your profits, I understand, to replacing the capital that has been misappropriated. Very proper .. more than proper.

EDWARD: No. No. To pay interest on the money that doesn't exist but ought to .. and the profits don't cover that or anything like it.

MR BOOTH: Patience .. I shouldn't be surprised if you worked up the business very well.

EDWARD: (*again laying the case before* MR BOOTH, *leaning forward to him*) Mr Booth, you were fond of my father. You see the help you could give us, don't you?

MR BOOTH: By not prosecuting?

EDWARD: (*earnestly*) Beyond that. If you'd cut your losses .. for the moment, and take only what's yours by right .. why, that would relieve me of four thousand three hundred a year .. and I could do so much with it. There are one or two bad cases still. One woman – I believe you know her – it's not that she's so poor .. and perhaps I'm not justified now in doing anything special .. but she's got children .. and if you'd help ..

MR BOOTH: Stop, Edward .. stop at once. If you attempt to confuse me I must take professional advice. Colpus and I have discussed this and quite made up our minds. And I've made a note or two. (*He produces a bit of paper and a pencil. EDWARD stiffens.*) May we understand that in straightening affairs you can show a proper preference for one client over another?

EDWARD: (*pulled up, draws back in his chair*) No .. you had better not understand that.

MR BOOTH: Why can't you?

EDWARD: Well .. suppose if I want to, I can?

MR BOOTH: Edward, do please be straightforward.

EDWARD: Why should I?

MR BOOTH: You certainly should. Do you mean to compare your father's ordinary business transactions – the hundreds of them – with his black treachery to .. to the Vicar?

EDWARD: Or to you?

MR BOOTH: Or to me.

EDWARD: Besides that, holding your tongue should be worth something extra now, shouldn't it?

MR BOOTH: I don't want to argue. My own position morally – and otherwise – is a strong one .. so Colpus impresses on me .. and he has some head for business.

EDWARD: Well, what are your terms?

MR BOOTH: This is my note of them. (*He takes refuge in his slip of paper.*) I make these conditions, if you please, Edward, on the Vicar's behalf and my own. They are .. (*Now the pencil comes into play, ticking off each item.*) that you return to us the balance of any capital there is left ..

EDWARD: (*cold again*) I am providing for that.

MR BOOTH: Good. That you should continue, of course, to pay us the usual interest upon the rest of our capital, which ought to exist and does not. And that you should, year by year, pay us back by degrees out of the earnings of the firm as much of that capital as you can afford. We will agree upon the sum .. say a thousand a year. I doubt if you can ever restore us all we have lost, but do your best and I shan't complain. There, I think that is fair dealing!

(EDWARD *does not take his eyes off* MR BOOTH *until the whole meaning of this proposition has settled in his brain. Then, without warning, he goes off into peals of laughter, much to the alarm of* MR BOOTH, *who has never thought him over-sane.*)

EDWARD: How funny! How very funny!

MR BOOTH: Edward, don't laugh.

EDWARD: I never heard anything quite so funny!

MR BOOTH: Edward, stop laughing.

EDWARD: Oh, you Christian gentlemen!

MR BOOTH: Don't be hysterical. The money's ours.

> (EDWARD'S *laughter gives way to the deepest anger of which he is capable.*)

EDWARD: I'm giving my soul and body to restoring you and the rest of you to your precious money bags .. and you'll wring me dry. Won't you? Won't you?

MR BOOTH: Now be reasonable. Argue the point quietly.

EDWARD: Go to the devil, sir.

> (*And with that he turns away from the flabbergasted old gentleman.*)

MR BOOTH: Don't be rude.

EDWARD: (*his anger vanishing*) I beg your pardon.

MR BOOTH: You're just excited. If you take time to think of it, I'm reasonable.

EDWARD: (*his sense of humour returning*) Most! Most! (*There is a knock at the door.*) Come in. Come in.

> (HONOR *intrudes an apologetic head.*)

HONOR: Am I interrupting business? I'm so sorry.

EDWARD: (*crowing in a mirthless enjoyment of his own joke*) No! Business is over .. quite over. Come in, Honor.

> (HONOR *puts on the table a market basket bulging with little paper parcels, and, oblivious of* MR BOOTH'S *distracted face, tries to fix his attention.*)

HONOR: I thought, dear Mr Booth, perhaps you wouldn't mind carrying round this basket of things yourself. It's so very damp underfoot that I don't want to send one of the maids out tonight if I can possibly avoid it .. and if one doesn't get Christmas presents the very first thing on Christmas morning quite half the pleasure in them is lost, don't you think?

MR BOOTH: Yes .. yes.

HONOR: (*fishing out the parcels one by one*) This is a bell for Mrs Williams .. something she said she wanted so that you can ring for her, which saves the maids: cap and apron for Mary: cap and apron for Ellen: shawl for Davis when she goes out to the larder – all useful presents – and that's something for you, but you're not to look at it till the morning.

> (*Having shaken each of these at the old gentleman, she proceeds to re-pack them. He is now trembling with anxiety to escape before any more of the family find him there.*)

MR BOOTH: Thank you .. thank you! I hope my lot has arrived. I left instructions ..

HONOR: Quite safely .. and I have hidden them. Presents are put on the breakfast table tomorrow.

EDWARD: (*with an inconsequence that still further alarms* MR BOOTH) When we were all children our Christmas breakfast was mostly made off chocolates.

> (*Before the basket is packed,* MRS VOYSEY *sails slowly into the room, as smiling and as deaf as ever.* MR BOOTH *does his best not to scowl at her.*)

MRS VOYSEY: Are you feeling better, George Booth?

MR BOOTH: No. (*Then he elevates his voice with a show of politeness.*) No, thank you .. I can't say I am.

MRS VOYSEY: You don't look better.

MR BOOTH: I still have my headache. (*with a distracted shout*) Headache.

MRS VOYSEY: Bilious, perhaps! I quite understood you didn't care to dine. But why not have taken your coat off? How foolish in this warm room!

MR BOOTH: Thank you. I'm – er – just off.

> (*He seizes the market basket. At that moment* BEATRICE *appears.*)

BEATRICE: Your shawl, mother. (*And she clasps it round* MRS VOYSEY'S *shoulders.*)

MRS VOYSEY: Thank you, Beatrice. I thought I had it on. (*then to* MR BOOTH *who is now entangled in his comforter*) A merry Christmas to you.

BEATRICE: Good evening, Mr Booth.

MR BOOTH: I beg your pardon. Good evening, Mrs Hugh.

HONOR: (*with sudden inspiration, to the company in general*) Why shouldn't I write in here .. now the table's cleared!

MR BOOTH: (*sternly, now he is safe by the door*) Will you see me out, Edward?

EDWARD: Yes.

> (*He follows the old man and his basket, leaving the others to distribute themselves about the room. It is a custom of the female members of the* VOYSEY *family, especially about Christmas time, to return to the dining room, when the table has been cleared, and occupy themselves in various ways which require space and untidiness. Sometimes as the evening wears on they partake of cocoa, sometimes they abstain.* BEATRICE *has a little work-basket, containing a buttonless glove and such things, which she is rectifying.* HONOR'S *writing is done with the aid of an enormous blotting book, which bulges with apparently a year's correspondence. She sheds its contents upon the end of the dining table and spreads them abroad.* MRS VOYSEY *settles to the fire, opens the Nineteenth Century and is instantly absorbed in it.*)

BEATRICE: Where's Emily?

HONOR: (*mysteriously*) Well, Beatrice, she's in the library talking to Booth.

BEATRICE: Talking to her husband; good Heavens! I know she has taken my scissors.

HONOR: I think she's telling him about you.

BEATRICE: What about me?

HONOR: You and Hugh.

BEATRICE: (*with a little movement of annoyance*) I suppose this is Hugh's fault. It was carefully arranged no one was to be told till after Christmas.

HONOR: Emily told me .. and Edward knows .. and Mother knows ..

BEATRICE: I warned Mother a year ago.

HONOR: Everyone seems to know but Booth .. so I thought he'd better be told. I suggested one night so that he might have time to think it over .. but Emily said that'd wake Alfred. Besides she's nearly always asleep herself when he comes to bed.

BEATRICE: Why do they still have that baby in their room?

The Nineteenth Century: a monthly political and intellectual journal. After 1901 its full title was actually *The Nineteenth Century and After.*

HONOR: Emily thinks it her duty.

> (*At this moment* EMILY *comes in, looking rather trodden upon.* HONOR *concludes in the most audible of whispers* . .)

HONOR: Don't say anything . . it's my fault.

BEATRICE: (*fixing her with a severe forefinger*) Emily . . have you taken my best scissors?

EMILY: (*timidly*) No, Beatrice.

HONOR: (*who is diving into the recesses of the blotting book*) Oh, here they are! I must have taken them. I do apologise!

EMILY: (*more timidly still*) I'm afraid Booth's rather cross . . he's gone to look for Hugh.

BEATRICE: (*with a shake of her head*) Honor . . I've a good mind to make you do this sewing for me.

> (*In comes the* MAJOR, *strepitant. He takes, so to speak, just time enough to train himself on* BEATRICE *and then fires.*)

MAJOR: Beatrice, what on earth is this Emily has been telling me?

BEATRICE: (*with elaborate calm*) Emily, what have you been telling Booth?

MAJOR: Please . . please do not prevaricate. Where is Hugh?

MRS VOYSEY: (*looking over her spectacles*) What did you say, Booth?

MAJOR: I want Hugh, Mother.

MRS VOYSEY: I thought you were playing billiards together.

> (EDWARD *strolls back from despatching* MR BOOTH, *his face thoughtful.*)

MAJOR: (*insistently*) Edward, where is Hugh?

EDWARD: (*with complete indifference*) I don't know.

MAJOR: (*in trumpet tones*) Honor, will you oblige me by finding Hugh and saying I wish to speak to him, here, immediately?

> (HONOR, *who has leapt at the sound of her name, flies from the room without a word.*)

BEATRICE: I know quite well what you want to talk about, Booth. Discuss the matter by all means if it amuses you . . but don't shout.

MAJOR: I use the voice Nature has gifted me with, Beatrice.

BEATRICE: (*as she searches for a glove button*) Certainly Nature did let herself go over your lungs.

MAJOR: (*glaring round with indignation*) This is a family matter, otherwise I should not feel it my duty to interfere . . as I do. Any member of the family has a right to express an opinion. I want Mother's. Mother, what do you think?

MRS VOYSEY: (*amicably*) What about?

MAJOR: Hugh and Beatrice separating.

MRS VOYSEY: They haven't separated.

MAJOR: But they mean to.

MRS VOYSEY: Fiddle-de-dee!

MAJOR: I quite agree with you.

BEATRICE: (*with a charming smile*) Such reasoning would convert a stone.

MAJOR: Why have I not been told?

BEATRICE: You have just been told.

MAJOR: (*thunderously*) Before.

BEATRICE: The truth is, dear Booth, we're all so afraid of you.

MAJOR: (*a little mollified*) Ha .. I should be glad to think that.

BEATRICE: (*sweetly*) Don't you?

MAJOR: (*intensely serious*) Beatrice, your callousness shocks me! That you can dream of deserting Hugh .. a man of all others who requires constant care and attention.

BEATRICE: May I remark that the separation is as much Hugh's wish as mine?

MAJOR: I don't believe that.

BEATRICE: (*her eyebrows up*) Really!

MAJOR: I don't imply that you're lying. But you must know that it's Hugh's nature to wish to do anything that he thinks anybody wishes him to do. All my life I've had to stand up for him .. and by Jove, I'll continue to do so.

EDWARD: (*from the depths of his armchair*) If you'd taught him to stand up for himself –

> (*The door is flung almost off its hinges by* HUGH *who then stands stamping and pale green with rage.*)

HUGH: Look here, Booth .. I will not have you interfering with my private affairs. Is one never to be free from your bullying?

MAJOR: You ought to be grateful.

HUGH: Well, I'm not.

MAJOR: This is a family affair.

HUGH: It is not!

MAJOR: (*at the top of his voice*) If all you can do is contradict me, you'd better listen to what I've got to say .. quietly.

> (HUGH, *quite shouted down, flings himself petulantly into a chair. A hush falls.*)

EMILY: (*in a still small voice*) Would you like me to go, Booth?

MAJOR: (*severely*) No, Emily. Unless anything has been going on which cannot be discussed before you .. (*then more severely still*) and I hope that is not so.

HUGH: (*muttering rebelliously*) Oh, you have the mind of a .. an official flunkey!

MAJOR: Why do you wish to separate?

HUGH: What's the use of telling you? You won't understand.

BEATRICE: (*who sews on undisturbed*) We don't get on well together.

MAJOR: (*amazedly*) Is that all?

HUGH: (*snapping at him*) Yes, that's all. Can you find a better reason?

MAJOR: (*with brotherly contempt*) I have given up expecting common sense from you. But Beatrice –! (*His tone implores her to be reasonable.*)

BEATRICE: It doesn't seem to me any sort of sense that people should live together for purposes of mutual irritation.

MAJOR: (*protesting*) My dear girl! .. that sounds like a quotation from your last book.

BEATRICE: It isn't. I do think, Booth, you might read that book .. for the honour of the Family.

MAJOR: (*successfully side-tracked ..*) I have bought it, Beatrice, and –

BEATRICE: That's the principal thing, of course –

MAJOR: (.. *and discovering it*) But do let us keep to the subject.

BEATRICE: (*with flattering sincerity*) Certainly, Booth. And there is hardly any subject that I wouldn't ask your advice about. But upon this .. please let me know better. Hugh and I will be happier apart.

MAJOR: (*obstinately*) Why?

BEATRICE: (*with resolute patience, having vented a little sigh*) Hugh finds that my opinions distress him. And I have at last lost patience with Hugh.

MRS VOYSEY: (*who has been trying to follow this through her spectacles*) What does Beatrice say?

MAJOR: (*translating into a loud sing-song*) That she wishes to leave her husband because she has lost patience!

MRS VOYSEY: (*with considerable acrimony*) Then you must be a very ill-tempered woman. Hugh has a sweet nature.

HUGH: (*shouting self-consciously*) Nonsense, Mother.

BEATRICE: (*shouting good-humouredly*) I quite agree with you, Mother. (*She continues to her husband in an even just tone.*) You have a sweet nature, Hugh, and it is most difficult to get angry with you. I have been seven years working up to it. But now that I'm angry, I shall never get pleased again.

    (*The* MAJOR *returns to his subject, refreshed by a moment's repose.*)

MAJOR: How has he failed in his duty? Tell us. I'm not bigoted in his favour. I know your faults, Hugh.

    (*He wags his head at* HUGH, *who writhes with irritation.*)

HUGH: Why can't you leave them alone .. leave us alone?

BEATRICE: I'd state my case against Hugh, if I thought he'd retaliate.

HUGH: (*desperately rounding on his brother*) If I tell you, you won't understand. You understand nothing! Beatrice is angry with me because I won't prostitute my art to make money.

MAJOR: (*glancing at his wife*) Please don't use metaphors of that sort.

BEATRICE: (*reasonably*) Yes, I think Hugh ought to earn more money.

MAJOR: (*quite pleased to be getting along at last*) Well, why doesn't he?

HUGH: I don't want money.

MAJOR: You can't say that you don't want money any more than you can say you don't want bread.

BEATRICE: (*as she breaks off her cotton*) It's when one has known what it is to be a little short of both ..

    (*Now the* MAJOR *spreads himself and begins to be very wise, while* HUGH, *to whom this is more intolerable than all, can only clutch his hair.*)

MAJOR: You know I never considered Art a very good profession for you, Hugh. And you won't even stick to one department of it. It's a profession that gets people into very bad habits, I consider. Couldn't you take up something else? You could still do those wood-cuts in your spare time to amuse yourself.

HUGH: (*commenting on this with two deliberate shouts of simulated mirth*) Ha! Ha!

MAJOR: (*sublimely superior*) Well, it wouldn't much matter if you didn't do them at all!

BEATRICE: (*subtly*) Booth, there speaks the true critic.

MAJOR: (*deprecating any title to omniscience*) Well, I don't pretend to know much about Art but –

HUGH: It would matter to me. There speaks the artist.

BEATRICE: The arrogance of the artist!
HUGH: We have a right to be arrogant.
BEATRICE: Good workmen are humble.
HUGH: And look to their wages.
BEATRICE: Well, I'm only a workman.
> (*With that she breaks the contact of this quiet deadly hopeless little quarrel by turning her head away. The* MAJOR, *who has given it most friendly attention, comments* ..)

MAJOR: Of course! Quite so! I'm sure all that is a very interesting difference of opinion. But it's nothing to separate about.
> (MRS VOYSEY *leaves her armchair for her favourite station at the dining-table.*)

MRS VOYSEY: Booth is the only one of you that I can hear at all distinctly. But if you two foolish young people think you want to separate .. try it. You'll soon come back to each other and be glad to. People can't fight against Nature for long. And marriage is a natural state .. once you're married.
MAJOR: (*with intense approval*) Quite right, Mother.
MRS VOYSEY: I know.
> (*She resumes the Nineteenth Century. The* MAJOR, *to the despair of everybody, makes yet another start; trying oratory this time.*)

MAJOR: My own opinion is, Beatrice and Hugh, that you don't realise the meaning of the word marriage. I don't call myself a religious man .. but dash it all, you were married in Church! .. And you then entered upon an awful compact! .. Surely .. as a woman, Beatrice .. the religious point of it ought to appeal to you. Good Lord, suppose everybody were to carry on like this! And have you considered, Beatrice, that .. whether you're right or whether you're wrong .. if you desert Hugh, you cut yourself off from the Family.
BEATRICE: (*with the sweetest of smiles*) That will distress me terribly.
MAJOR: (*not doubting her for a moment*) Of course.
> (HUGH *flings up his head and finds relief at last in many words.*)

HUGH: I wish to Heaven I'd ever been able to cut myself off from the family! Look at Trenchard.
MAJOR: (*gobbling a little at this unexpected attack*) I do not forgive Trenchard for quarrelling with and deserting our father.
HUGH: Trenchard quarrelled because that was his only way of escape.
MAJOR: Escape from what?
HUGH: From tyranny! .. from hypocrisy! .. from boredom! .. from his Happy English Home!
BEATRICE: (*kindly*) Hugh .. Hugh .. it's no use.
MAJOR: (*attempting sarcasm*) Speak so that Mother can hear you!
> (*But* HUGH *isn't to be stopped now.*)

HUGH: Why are we all dull, cubbish, uneducated .. that is hopelessly middle-class.
MAJOR: (*taking this as very personal*) Cubbish!
HUGH: .. Because it's the middle-class ideal that you should respect your parents .. live with them .. think with them .. grow like them. Natural affection and gratitude! That's what's expected, isn't it?
MAJOR: (*not to be obliterated*) Certainly.

HUGH: Keep your children ignorant of all that you don't know, penniless except for your good pleasure, dependent on you for permission to breathe freely . . and be sure that their gratitude will be most disinterested, and their affection very natural. If your father's a drunkard or poor, then perhaps you get free and can form an opinion of your own . . and can love him or hate him as he deserves. But our father and mother were models. They did their duty by us . . and taught us ours. Trenchard escaped, as I say. You took to the Army . . so of course you've never discovered how behind the times *you* are. (*The* MAJOR *is stupent.*) I tried to express myself in art . . and found there was nothing to express . . I'd been so well brought up. D'you blame me if I wander about in search of a soul of some sort? And Honor –

MAJOR: (*disputing savagely*) Honor is very happy at home. Everyone loves her.

HUGH: (*with fierce sarcasm*) Yes . . what do we call her? Mother's right hand! I wonder they bothered to give her a name. By the time little Ethel came they were tired of training children . . (*His voice loses its sting; he doesn't complete this sentence.*)

BEATRICE: Poor little Ethel . .

MAJOR: Poor Ethel!

    (*They speak as one speaks of the dead, and so the wrangling stops. Then* EDWARD *interposes quietly.*)

EDWARD: Ah, my dear Hugh . .

HUGH: I haven't spoken of your fate, Edward. That's too shameful.

EDWARD: Not at all. I sit at my desk daily as the servant of men whose ideal of life is to have a thousand a year . . or two thousand . . or three . .

MAJOR: Well?

EDWARD: That's all.

MAJOR: What's the point? One must live.

HUGH: And if Booth can be said to think, he honestly thinks that's living.

MAJOR: We will return, if you please, to the original subject of discussion. Hugh, this question of a separation –

    (*Past all patience,* HUGH *jumps up and flings his chair back to its place.*)

HUGH: Beatrice and I mean to separate. And nothing you may say will prevent us. The only difficulty in the way is money. Can we command enough to live apart comfortably?

MAJOR: Well?

HUGH: Well . . we can't.

MAJOR: Well?

HUGH: So we can't separate.

MAJOR: (*speaking with bewilderment*) Then what in Heaven's name have we been discussing it for?

HUGH: I haven't discussed it! I don't want to discuss it! Mind – can't you mind your own business? Now I'll go back to the billiard room and my book.

    (*He is gone before the poor* MAJOR *can recover his lost breath.*)

MAJOR: (*as he does recover it*) I am not an impatient man . . but really . . (*and then words fail him*).

BEATRICE: (*commenting calmly*) Hugh, I am told, was a spoilt child. They grow to hate their parents sooner than others. You taught him to cry for what he wanted. Now that he's older and doesn't get it, that makes him a wearisome companion.

MAJOR: (*very sulky now*) You married him with your eyes open, I suppose?

BEATRICE: How few women marry with their eyes open!

MAJOR: You have never made the best of Hugh.

BEATRICE: I have spared him that indignity.

MAJOR: (*vindictively*) I am very glad that you can't separate.

BEATRICE: As soon as I'm reasonably sure of earning an income I shall walk off from him.

(*The MAJOR revives.*)

MAJOR: You will do nothing of the sort. Beatrice.

BEATRICE: (*unruffled*) How will you stop me, Booth?

MAJOR: I shall tell Hugh he must command you to stay.

BEATRICE: (*with a little smile*) I wonder would that still make a difference. It was one of the illusions of my girlhood that I should love a man who would master me.

MAJOR: Hugh must assert himself.

(*He begins to walk about, giving some indication of how it should be done. BEATRICE'S smile has vanished.*)

BEATRICE: Don't think I've enjoyed taking the lead in everything throughout my married life. But someone had to plan and scheme and be foreseeing .. we weren't sparrows or lilies of the field .. someone had to get up and do something, if not for money, at least for the honour of it. (*She becomes conscious of his strutting and smiles rather mischievously.*) Ah .. if I'd married you, Booth!

(*The MAJOR'S face grows beatific.*)

MAJOR: Well, I must own to thinking that I am a masterful man .. that it's the duty of every man to be so. (*he adds forgivingly*) Poor old Hugh!

BEATRICE: (*unable to resist temptation*) If I'd tried to leave you, Booth, you'd have whipped me .. wouldn't you?

MAJOR: (*ecstatically complacent*) Ha .. well ..!

BEATRICE: Do say yes. Think how it'll frighten Emily.

(*The MAJOR strokes his moustache and is most friendly.*)

MAJOR: Hugh's been a worry to me all my life. And now as Head of the Family .. Well, I suppose I'd better go and give the dear chap another talking to. I quite see your point of view, Beatrice.

BEATRICE: Why disturb him at his book?

(*MAJOR BOOTH leaves them, squaring his shoulders as becomes a lord of creation. The two sisters-in-law go on with their work silently for a moment; then BEATRICE adds .. *)

BEATRICE: Do you find Booth difficult to manage, Emily?

EMILY: (*putting down her knitting to consider the matter*) No. It's best to allow him to talk himself out. When he's done that he'll often come to me for advice. I let him get his own way as much as possible .. or think he's getting it. Otherwise he becomes so depressed.

BEATRICE: (*quietly amused*) Edward shouldn't hear this. What has he to do with women's secrets?

EDWARD: I won't tell .. and I'm a bachelor.

EMILY: (*solemnly as she takes up her knitting again*) Do you really mean to leave Hugh?

BEATRICE: (*slightly impatient*) Emily, I've said so.

(*They are joined by* ALICE MAITLAND, *who comes in gaily.*)

ALICE: What's Booth shouting about in the billiard room?

EMILY: (*pained*) Oh .. on Christmas Eve, too!

BEATRICE: Don't you take any interest in my matrimonial affairs?

(MRS VOYSEY *shuts up the Nineteenth Century and removes her spectacles.*)

MRS VOYSEY: That's a very interesting article. The Chinese Empire must be in a shocking state! Is it ten o'clock yet?

EDWARD: Past.

MRS VOYSEY: (*as* EDWARD *is behind her*) Can anyone see the clock?

ALICE: It's past ten, Auntie.

MRS VOYSEY: Then I think I'll go to my room.

EMILY: Shall I come and look after you, Mother?

MRS VOYSEY: If you'd find Honor for me, Emily.

(EMILY *goes in search of the harmless necessary* HONOR *and* MRS VOYSEY *begins her nightly chant of departure.*)

MRS VOYSEY: Good-night, Alice. Good-night, Edward.

EDWARD: Good-night, Mother.

MRS VOYSEY: (*with sudden severity*) I'm not pleased with you, Beatrice.

BEATRICE: I'm sorry, Mother.

(*But without waiting to be answered the old lady has sailed out of the room.* BEATRICE, EDWARD, *and* ALICE *are attuned to each other enough to be able to talk with ease.*)

BEATRICE: Hugh is right about his family. It'll never make any new life for itself.

EDWARD: There are Booth's children.

BEATRICE: Poor little devils!

ALICE: (*judicially*) Emily is an excellent mother.

BEATRICE: Yes .. they'll grow up good men and women. And one will go into the Army and one into the Navy and one into the Church .. and perhaps one to the Devil and the Colonies. They'll serve their country and govern it and help to keep it like themselves .. dull and respectable .. hopelessly middle-class. (*She puts down her work now and elevates an oratorical fist.*) Genius and Poverty may exist in England, if they'll hide their heads. For show days we've our aristocracy. But never let us forget, gentlemen, that it is the plain solid middle-class man who has made us .. what we are.

EDWARD: (*in sympathetic derision*) Hear hear ..! and cries of bravo!

BEATRICE: Now, that *is* out of my book .. the next one. (*She takes up her work again.*) You know, Edward .. however scandalous it was, your father left you a man's work to do.

EDWARD: (*his face cloudy*) An outlaw's!

BEATRICE: (*whimsical after a moment*) I mean that. At all events you've not had

to be your father's right arm .. or the instrument of justice .. or a
representative of the people .. or anything second-hand of that sort, have you?
EDWARD: (*with sudden excitement*) Do you know what I found out the other day
about (*he nods at the portrait*) .. him?
BEATRICE: (*enquiring calmly*) What?
EDWARD: He saved his firm once. That was true. A pretty capable piece of
heroism. Then, fifteen years afterwards .. he started again.
BEATRICE: (*greatly interested*) Did he now?
EDWARD: It can't have been merely through weakness ..
BEATRICE: (*with artistic enthusiasm*) Of course not. He was a man of imagination
and a great financier. He had to find scope for his abilities or die. He despised
these fat little clients living so snugly on their fattening little incomes .. and
put them and their money to the best use he could.
EDWARD: (*shaking his head solemnly*) Fine phrases for robbery.
(BEATRICE *turns her clever face to him and begins to follow up her
subject keenly.*)
BEATRICE: But didn't Hugh tell me that your golden deed has been robbing your
rich clients for the benefit of the poor ones?
ALICE: (*who hasn't missed a word*) That's true.
EDWARD: (*gently*) Well .. we're all a bit in debt to the poor, aren't we?
BEATRICE: Quite so. And you don't possess and your father didn't possess that
innate sense of the sacredness of property .. (*she enjoys that phrase*) which
mostly makes your merely honest man. Nor did the man possess it who picked
my pocket last Friday week .. nor does the tax-gatherer .. nor do I. And
whether we can boast of our opinions depends on such a silly lot of prejudices
and cowardices that –
EDWARD: (*a little pained by as much of this as he takes to be serious*) Why
wouldn't he own the truth to me about himself?
BEATRICE: He was a bit of a genius. Perhaps he took care not to know it. Would
you have understood?
EDWARD: Perhaps not. But I loved him.
(BEATRICE *looks again at the gentle, earnest face.*)
BEATRICE: Through it all?
EDWARD: Yes. And not from mere force of habit either.
BEATRICE: (*with reverence in her voice now*) That might silence a bench of judges.
Well .. well ..
(*Her sewing finished, she stuffs the things into her basket, gets up in
her abrupt unconventional way and goes without another word. Her
brain is busy with the Voysey Inheritance. EDWARD and ALICE are
left in chairs by the fire, facing each other like an old domestic couple.*)
EDWARD: Stay and talk to me.
ALICE: I want to. Something has happened .. since dinner.
EDWARD: Can you see that?
ALICE: What is it?
EDWARD: (*with sudden exultation*) The smash has come .. and not by my fault.
Old George Booth –
ALICE: Has he been here?

EDWARD: Can you imagine it? He got at the truth. I told him to take his money . .
what there was of it . . and prosecute. He won't prosecute, but he bargains to
take the money . . and then to bleed us, sovereign by sovereign, as I earn
sovereign by sovereign with the sweat of my soul. I'll see him in his Christian
Heaven first . . the Jew!

ALICE: (*keeping her head*) You can't reason with him?

EDWARD: No. He thinks he has the whip hand, and the Vicar has been told . . who
has told his wife. She knows how not to keep a secret. It has come at last.

ALICE: So you're glad?

EDWARD: So thankful – my conscience is clear. I've done my best. (*Then as usual
with him, his fervour collapses.*) And oh, Alice . . has it been worth doing?

ALICE: (*encouragingly*) Half a dozen poor devils pulled safe out of the fire.

EDWARD: But I'm wondering now if that won't be found out, or if I shan't just
confess to the pious fraud when the time comes. Somehow I don't seem to
have the conviction to carry any job through. A weak nature, my father said.
He knew.

ALICE: You have a religious nature.

EDWARD: (*surprised*) Oh, no!

ALICE: (*proceeding to explain*) Which means, of course, that you don't cling to
creeds and ceremonies. And the good things and the well-done jobs of this
worldly world don't satisfy you . . so you shirk contact with it all you can.

EDWARD: (*his eyes far away*) Yes. Do you never feel that there aren't enough
windows in a house?

ALICE: (*prosaically*) In this weather . . too many.

EDWARD: In my office then – I feel it when I'm at work – one is out of all hearing
of all the music of the world. And when one does get back to Nature, instead
of being curves to her roundness, one is all corners.

ALICE: (*smiling at him*) And you love to think prettily, don't you . . just as Hugh
does. You do it quite well, too. (*then briskly*) But, Edward, may I scold you?

EDWARD: For that?

ALICE: Why have you grown to be more of a sloven than ever lately? Yes, a
spiritual sloven, I call it – deliberately letting yourself be unhappy.

EDWARD: Is happiness under one's control?

ALICE: My friend, you shouldn't neglect your happiness any more than you neglect
to wash your face. I was desperate about you . . so I came down to your office.

EDWARD: Yes, you did.

ALICE: But I found you master there, and I thanked God. Because with us,
Edward, for these last eighteen months you've been more like a moral portent
than a man – without a smile to throw to a friend . . or an opinion upon any
subject. Why did you throw up your boys' club? Why didn't you vote last
November? – too out of keeping with your unhappy fate?

EDWARD: (*contrite at this*) I was wrong not to vote.

ALICE: You don't even eat properly.

(*With that she completes the accusation and* EDWARD *searches
round for a defence.*)

EDWARD: But, Alice, it was always an effort to do all these things . . and lately
every effort has had to go to my work, hasn't it?

ALICE: Oh .. if you only did them on principle .. I retract .. far better not to do them at all.

EDWARD: Don't laugh at me.

ALICE: Edward, is there nothing you want from life .. want for its own sake? That's the only test.

EDWARD: I daren't ask.

ALICE: Yes, you dare. It's all so long past that awful time when you were .. more than a bit of a prig.

EDWARD: (*with enough sense of humour to whisper back*) Was I?

ALICE: I'm afraid so! He still stalks through my dreams sometimes .. and I wake in a sweat. But I think he's nearly done with. (*Then her voice rises stirringly.*) Oh, don't you see what a blessing this cursed burden of disgrace and work was meant to be to you?

EDWARD: (*without a smile now*) But lately, Alice, I've hardly known myself. Sometimes I've lost my temper .. I've been brutal.

ALICE: I knew it. I knew that would happen. It's your own wicked nature coming out at last. That's what we've been waiting for .. that's what we want. That's you.

EDWARD: (*still serious*) I'm sorry for it.

ALICE: Oh, Edward, be a little proud of poor humanity .. take your own share in it gladly. It so discourages the rest of us if you don't.
(*Suddenly he breaks down completely.*)

EDWARD: I can't let myself be glad and live. There's the future to think of, and I'm so afraid of that. I must pretend I don't care .. even to myself .. even to you.

ALICE: (*her mocking at an end*) What is it you fear most about the future .. not just the obviously unpleasant things?

EDWARD: They'll put me in prison.

ALICE: Even then?

EDWARD: Who'll be the man who comes out?

ALICE: Yourself, and more than ever yourself.

EDWARD: No, no! I'm a coward. I can't stand alone, and after that I shall have to. I need affection .. I need friends. I cling to people that I don't care for deeply .. just for the comfort of it. I've no real home of my own. Every house that welcomes me now I like to think of as something of a home. And this disgrace in store will leave me .. homeless.
(*There he sits shaken. ALICE waits a moment, not taking her eyes from him; then speaks.*)

ALICE: Edward, there's something else I want to scold you for. You've still given up proposing to me. Certainly that shows a lack of courage .. and of perseverance. Or is it the loss of what I always considered a very laudable ambition?
(*EDWARD is hardly able to trust his ears. Then he looks into her face and his thankfulness frames itself into a single sentence.*)

EDWARD: Will you marry me?

ALICE: Yes, Edward.
(*For a minute he just holds his breath with happiness. But he shakes himself free of it, almost savagely.*)

EDWARD: No, no, no, we mustn't be stupid. I'm sorry I asked you that.

ALICE: (*with serene strength*) I'm glad that you want me. While I live .. where I am will be Home.

EDWARD: (*struggling with himself*) No, it's too late. And if you'd said Yes before I came into my inheritance .. perhaps I shouldn't have given myself to the work. So be glad that it's too late. I am.

ALICE: (*happily*) Marry you when you were only a well-principled prig .. Thanks! I didn't want you .. and I don't believe you really wanted me. But now you do, and you must always take what you want.

EDWARD: (*turning to her again*) My dear, what have we to start life upon .. to build our house upon? Poverty .. and prison.

ALICE: (*mischievous*) Edward, you seem to think that all the money in the world was invested in your precious firm. I have four hundred a year of my own. At least let that tempt you.

> (EDWARD *catches her in his arms with a momentary little burst of passion.*)

EDWARD: You're tempting me.

> (*She did not resist, but nevertheless he breaks away from her, disappointed with himself. She goes on, quietly, serenely.*)

ALICE: Am I? Unworthily? Oh, my dear, don't be afraid of wanting me. Shall we be less than friends by being more? If I thought that, should I ever have let it come to this? But now you must .. look at me and make your choice .. to refuse me my work and happiness in life and to cripple your own nature .. or to take my hand.

> (*She puts out her hand frankly, as a friend should. With only a second's thought he, happy too now, takes it as frankly. Then she sits beside him and quite cheerfully changes the subject.*)

ALICE: Now, about old Mr George Booth. What will he do?

EDWARD: (*responsive though impatient*) Nothing. I shall be before him.

ALICE: Can we bargain with him to keep the firm going somehow? .. for if we can, I'm afraid we must.

> (*At this* EDWARD *makes a last attempt to abandon himself to his troubles.*)

EDWARD: No, no .. let it end here, it'll be so useless. They'll all be round in a day or two after their money like wasps after honey. And now they know I won't lift a finger in my own defence .. what sort of mercy will they have?

ALICE: (*triumphantly completing her case*) Edward, I have a faith by which I hope to live, not humbly, but defying the world to be my master. Dare to surrender yourself entirely, and you'll find them powerless against you. You see, you had something to hope or fear from Mr Booth, for you hoped in your heart he'd end your trouble. But conquer that last little atom of fear which we call selfishness, and you'll find you are doing what you wish with selfish men. (*and she adds fervently*) Yes, the man who is able, and cares deeply, and yet has nothing to hope or fear is all powerful .. even in little things.

EDWARD: But will nothing ever happen to set me free? Shall I never be able to rest for a moment .. turn round and say I've succeeded or I've failed?

ALICE: That's asking too much, and it isn't what matters .. one must have faith to go on.

EDWARD: Suppose they all meet and agree and syndicate themselves and keep me at it for life.

ALICE: Yes, I daresay they will, but what else could you wish for?

EDWARD: Than that dreary round!

ALICE: But the world must be put tidy. And it's the work which splendid criminals leave for poor commonplace people to do.

EDWARD: (*with a little laugh*) And I don't believe in Heaven either.

ALICE: (*close to him*) But there's to be our life. What's wrong with that?

EDWARD: My dear, when they put me in prison for swindling – (*He makes the word sound its worst.*)

ALICE: I think they won't, for it wouldn't pay them. But if they are so stupid .. I must be very careful.

EDWARD: Of what?

ALICE: To avoid false pride. I shall be foolishly proud of you.

EDWARD: It's good to be praised sometimes .. by you.

ALICE: My heart praises you. Good-night.

EDWARD: Good-night.

> (*She kisses his forehead. But he puts up his face like a child, so she bends down and for the first time their lips meet. Then she steps back from him, adding happily, with perhaps just a touch of shyness.*)

ALICE: Till tomorrow.

EDWARD: (*echoing in gratitude the hope and promise in her voice*) Till tomorrow.

> (*She leaves him to sit there by the table for a few moments longer, looking into his future, streaked as it is to be with trouble and joy. As whose is not? From above .. from above the mantelpiece, that is to say .. the face of the late* MR VOYSEY *seems to look down upon his son not unkindly, though with that curious buccaneering twist of the eyebrows which distinguished his countenance in life.*)

WASTE

Written 1906–7

Refused a license by the Lord Chamberlain. First produced by the Stage Society in a private performance at the Imperial Theatre on 24 November 1907, with the following cast:

LADY DAVENPORT	Amy Coleman
WALTER KENT	Vernon Steel
MRS JULIA FARRANT	Beryl Faber
MISS FRANCES TREBELL	Henrietta Watson
MRS AMY O'CONNELL	Aimée de Burgh
LUCY DAVENPORT	Dorothy Thomas
GEORGE FARRANT	Frederick Lloyd
RUSSELL BLACKBOROUGH	A. Holmes-Gore
FOOTMAN	Allan Wade
HENRY TREBELL	Granville Barker
SIMPSON (his maid)	Mary Barton
GILBERT WEDGECROFT	Berte Thomas
LORD CHARLES CANTELUPE	Dennis Eadie
THE EARL OF HORSHAM	Henry Vibart
EDMUNDS (his servant)	Trevor Lowe
JUSTIN O'CONNELL	J. Fisher White

Directed by Granville Barker.

A completely re-written version was published in 1927, and presented at the Westminster Theatre on 1 December 1936, directed by Granville Barker and Michael MacOwan.

In Defiance of Mr. Redford

IV The seduction in *Waste*: a cartoon by Norman Morrow of the end of act 1. Henry Trebell (Granville Barker) carries off Amy O'Connell (Aimée de Burgh), as the real-life censor, G. A. Redford, rushes on to stop the play. Imperial Theatre, 1907, directed by Granville Barker.

ACT I

SCENE 1. *At Shapters*, GEORGE FARRANT'S *house in Hertfordshire. Ten o'clock on a Sunday evening in summer. Facing you at her piano by the window, from which she is protected by a little screen, sits* MRS [JULIA] FARRANT; *a woman of the interesting age, clear-eyed and all her face serene, except for a little pucker of the brows which shows a puzzled mind upon some important matters. To become almost an ideal hostess has been her achievement; and in her own home, as now, this grace is written upon every movement. Her eyes pass over the head of a girl, sitting in a low chair by a little table, with the shaded lamplight falling on her face. This is* LUCY DAVENPORT; *twenty-three, undefeated in anything as yet and so unsoftened. The book on her lap is closed, for she has been listening to the music. It is possibly some German philosopher, whom she reads with a critical appreciation of his shortcomings. On the sofa near her lounges* MRS [AMY] O'CONNELL; *a charming woman, if by charming you understand a woman who converts every quality she possesses into a means of attraction, and has no use for any others. On the sofa opposite sits* MISS [FRANCES] TREBELL. *In a few years, when her hair is quite grey, she will assume as by right the dignity of an old maid. Between these two in a low armchair is* LADY DAVENPORT. *She has attained to many dignities. Mother and grandmother, she has brought into the world and nourished not merely life but character. A wonderful face she has, full of proud memories and fearless of the future. Behind her, on a sofa between the windows, is* WALTER KENT. *He is just what the average English father would like his son to be. You can see the light shooting out through the windows and mixing with moonshine upon a smooth lawn. On your left is a door. There are many books in the room, hardly any pictures, a statuette perhaps. The owner evidently sets beauty of form before beauty of colour. It is a woman's room and it has a certain delicate austerity. By the time you have observed everything* MRS FARRANT *has played Chopin's Prelude opus 28, number 20, from beginning to end.*

LADY DAVENPORT: Thank you, my dear Julia.
KENT: (*protesting*) No more?
JULIA: I won't play for a moment longer than I feel musical.
FRANCES: Do you think it right, Julia, to finish with that after an hour's Bach?
JULIA: I suddenly came over Chopinesque, Fanny; . . what's your objection? (*as she sits by her*)
FRANCES: What . . when Bach has raised me to the heights of unselfishness!
AMY: (*grimacing sweetly, her eyes only half lifted*) Does he? I'm glad that I don't understand him.
FRANCES: (*putting mere prettiness in its place*) One may prefer Chopin when one is young.
AMY: And is that a reproach or a compliment?
KENT: (*boldly*) I do.
FRANCES: Or a man may . . unless he's a philosopher.

Chopin's Prelude: in C minor, a slow, stately piece of mostly bass chords, lasting about a minute and a half.

163

LADY DAVENPORT: (*to the rescue*) Miss Trebell, you're very hard on mere humanity.

FRANCES: (*completing the reproof*) That's my wretched training as a schoolmistress, Lady Davenport .. one grew to fear it above all things.

LUCY: (*throwing in the monosyllable with sharp youthful enquiry*) Why?

FRANCES: There were no textbooks on the subject.

JULIA: (*smiling at her friend*) Yes, Fanny .. I think you escaped to look after your brother only just in time.

FRANCES: In another year I might have been head-mistress, which commits you to approve of the system for ever.

LADY DAVENPORT: (*shaking her wise head*) I've watched the Education fever take England ..

FRANCES: If I hadn't stopped teaching things I didn't understand ..!

AMY: (*not without mischief*) And what was the effect on the pupils?

LUCY: I can tell you that.

AMY: Frances never taught you.

LUCY: No, I wish she had. But I was at her sort of a school before I went to Newnham. I know.

FRANCES: (*very distastefully*) Up-to-date, it was described as.

LUCY: Well, it was like a merry-go-round at top speed. You felt things wouldn't look a bit like that when you came to a standstill.

AMY: And they don't?

LUCY: (*with great decision*) Not a bit.

AMY: (*in her velvet tone*) I was taught the whole duty of woman by a parson-uncle who disbelieved in his Church.

KENT: When a man at Jude's was going to take orders ..

AMY: Jude's?

KENT: At Oxford. The dons went very gingerly with him over bits of science and history.

(*This wakes a fruitful thought in* JULIA FARRANT'S *brain.*)

JULIA: Mamma, have you ever discussed so-called anti-Christian science with Lord Charles?

FRANCES: .. Cantelupe?

JULIA: Yes. It was over appointing a teacher for the schools down here .. he was staying with us. The Vicar's his fervent disciple. However, we were consulted.

LUCY: Didn't Lord Charles want you to send the boys there till they were ready for Harrow?

JULIA: Yes.

FRANCES: Quite the last thing in Toryism!

JULIA: Mamma made George say we were too *nouveau riche* to risk it.

Education fever: in the latter third of the nineteenth century a series of reforms greatly extended state support for education, especially for poor children; by 1902 schooling was made compulsory until age ten, and secondary education had been encouraged.

Newnham: the second women's college at Cambridge, founded 1871, and known from the start for its unconventional pedagogy.

Jude's: fictitious. See Introduction, p. 18, on the mixture of factual and invented details.

Harrow: one of the preeminent public schools, located just outside London.

LADY DAVENPORT: (*as she laughs*) I couldn't resist that.

JULIA: (*catching something of her subject's dry driving manner*) Lord Charles takes the superior line and says .. that with his consent the Church may teach the unalterable Truth in scientific language or legendary, whichever is easier understood of the people.

LADY DAVENPORT: Is it the prospect of Disestablishment suddenly makes him so accommodating?

FRANCES: (*with large contempt*) He needn't be. The majority of people believe the world was made in an English week.

LUCY: Oh, no!

FRANCES: No Bishop dare deny it.

JULIA: (*from the heights of experience*) Dear Lucy, do you seriously think that the English spirit – the nerve that runs down the backbone – is disturbed by new theology .. or new anything?

LADY DAVENPORT: (*enjoying her epigram*) What a waste of persecution history shows us!

> (WALTER KENT *now captures the conversation with a very young politician's fervour.*)

KENT: Once they're disestablished they must make up their minds what they do believe.

LADY DAVENPORT: I presume Lord Charles thinks it'll hand the Church over to him and his .. dare I say 'Sect'?

KENT: Won't it? He knows what he wants.

JULIA: (*subtly*) There's the election to come yet.

KENT: But now both parties are pledged to a bill of some sort.

JULIA: Political prophesies have a knack of not coming true; but, d'you know, Cyril Horsham warned me to watch this position developing .. nearly four years ago.

FRANCES: Sitting on the opposition bench sharpens the eye-sight.

KENT: (*ironically*) Has he been pleased with the prospect?

JULIA: (*with perfect diplomacy*) If the Church must be disestablished .. better done by its friends than its enemies.

FRANCES: Still I don't gather he's pleased with his dear cousin Charles's conduct.

JULIA: (*shrugging*) Oh, lately, Lord Charles has never concealed his tactics.

FRANCES: And that speech at Leeds was the crowning move I suppose; just asking the Nonconformists to bring things to a head?

JULIA: (*judicially*) I think that was precipitate.

KENT: (*giving them* LORD CHARLES'S *oratory*) Gentlemen, in these latter days of Radical opportunism! – You know, I was there .. sitting next to an old gentleman who shouted 'Jesuit'.

---

understood: acceptable usage in the period, though slightly affected.

Disestablishment: see Introduction, pp. 18–19.

Nonconformists: Protestants who do not conform to the customs and doctrines of the Church of England, principally Methodists, Quakers, Baptists, and Unitarians. They had great influence on the Liberal Party in the nineteenth century.

FRANCES: But supposing Mallaby and the Nonconformists hadn't been able to
force the Liberals' hand?

JULIA: (*speaking as of inferior beings*) Why, they were glad of any cry going to the
Country!

FRANCES: (*as she considers this*) Yes .. and Lord Charles would still have had as
good a chance of forcing Lord Horsham's. It has been clever tactics.

LUCY: (*who has been listening, sharp-eyed*) Contrariwise, he wouldn't have liked a
Radical Bill though, would he?

KENT: (*with aplomb*) He knew he was safe from that. The government must have
dissolved before Christmas anyway .. and the swing of the pendulum's a sure
thing.

JULIA: (*with her smile*) It's never a sure thing.

KENT: Oh, Mrs Farrant, look how unpopular the Liberals are.

FRANCES: What made them bring in Resolutions?

KENT: (*overflowing with knowledge of the subject*) I was told Mallaby insisted on
their showing they meant business. I thought he was being too clever .. and it
turns out he was. Tommy Luxmore told me there was a fearful row in the
cabinet about it. But on their last legs, you know, it didn't seem to matter, I
suppose. Even then, if Prothero had mustered up an ounce of tact .. I believe
they could have pulled them through..

FRANCES: Not the Spoliation one.

KENT: Well, Mr Trebell dished that!

FRANCES: Henry says his speech didn't turn a vote.

JULIA: (*with charming irony*) How disinterested of him!

KENT: (*enthusiastic*) That speech did if ever a speech did.

FRANCES: Is there any record of a speech that ever did? He just carried his own
little following with him.

JULIA: But the crux of the whole matter is and has always been .. what's to be done
with the Church's money.

LUCY: (*visualising sovereigns*) A hundred millions or so .. think of it!

FRANCES: There has been from the start a good deal of anti-Nonconformist feeling
against applying the money to secular uses.

JULIA: (*deprecating false modesty, on anyone's behalf*) Oh, of course the speech
turned votes .. twenty of them at least.

LUCY: (*determined on information*) Then I was told Lord Horsham had tried to
come to an understanding himself with the Nonconformists about
Disestablishment – oh – a long time ago .. over the Education Bill.

FRANCES: Is that true, Julia?

Liberals: political party created by Gladstone out of the Whigs, standing for free trade and
laissez-faire economics, the principal opposition to the Conservative Party in the second half of
the nineteenth century.

going to the Country: calling a general parliamentary election.

Spoliation one/Spoliation question: difficult references. *Spoliation* is both a legal and an
ecclesiastical term, but neither meaning applies specifically here. In general, however, the
passage alludes to how the Radicals ruined their chances for a Disestablishment Bill and, with
Trebell's help, discredited the Liberal government.

Education Bill: a comprehensive Conservative measure of 1902 ('Balfour's Act') in which new
local education authorities were empowered to oversee both church and state schools, to build

JULIA: How should I know?

FRANCES: (*with some mischief*) You might.

JULIA: (*weighing her words*) I don't think it would have been altogether wise to make advances. They'd have asked more than a Conservative government could possibly persuade the Church to give up.

KENT: I don't see that Horsham's much better off now. He only turned the Radicals out on the Spoliation question by the help of Trebell. And so far .. I mean, till this election is over Trebell counts still as one of them, doesn't he, Miss Trebell? Oh .. perhaps he doesn't.

FRANCES: He'll tell you he never has counted as one of them.

JULIA: No doubt Lord Charles would sooner have done without his help. And that's why I didn't ask the gentle Jesuit this week-end if anyone wants to know.

KENT: (*stupent at this lack of party spirit*) What .. he'd rather have had the Liberals go to the Country undefeated!

JULIA: (*with finesse*) The election may bring us back independent of Mr Trebell and anything he stands for.

KENT: (*sharply*) But you asked Lord Horsham to meet him.

JULIA: (*with still more finesse*) I had my reasons. Votes aren't everything.

> (LADY DAVENPORT *has been listening with rather a doubtful smile; she now caps the discussion.*)

LADY DAVENPORT: I'm relieved to hear you say so, my dear Julia. On the other hand democracy seems to have brought itself to a pretty pass. Here's a measure, which the country as a whole neither demands nor approves of, will certainly be carried, you tell me, because a minority on each side is determined it shall be .. for totally different reasons.

JULIA: (*shrugging again*) It isn't our business to prevent popular government looking foolish, Mamma.

LADY DAVENPORT: Is that Tory cynicism or feminine?

> (*At this moment* GEORGE FARRANT *comes through the window; a good natured man of forty-five. He would tell you that he was educated at Eton and Oxford. But the knowledge which saves his life comes from the thrusting upon him of authority and experience; ranging from the management of an estate which he inherited at twenty-four, through the chairmanship of a newspaper syndicate, through a successful marriage, to a minor post in the last Tory cabinet and the prospect of one in the near-coming next. Thanks to his agents, editors, permanent officials, and his own common sense, he always acquits himself creditably. He comes to his wife's side and waits for a pause in the conversation.*)

LADY DAVENPORT: I remember Mr Disraeli once said to me .. Clever women are as dangerous to the State as dynamite.

---

secondary schools, and to give grants to existing grammar schools. The bill offended many Nonconformists and Liberals because it allowed public funds to be directed to Church of England and Roman Catholic schools.

Radicals: the left wing of the Liberal Party.

Disraeli: revitalized the Conservative Party in the nineteenth century. His major term as Prime Minister (1874–80) serves to date Lady Davenport.

FRANCES: (*not to be impressed by Disraeli*) Well, Lady Davenport, if men will leave our intellects lying loose about..

FARRANT: Blackborough's going, Julia.

JULIA: Yes, George.

LADY DAVENPORT: (*concluding her little apologue to* MISS TREBELL) Yes, my dear, but power without responsibility isn't good for the character that wields it either.

> (*There follows* FARRANT *through the window a man of fifty. He has about him that unmistakable air of acquired wealth and power which distinguishes many Jews and has therefore come to be regarded as a solely Jewish characteristic. He speaks always with that swift decision which betokens a narrowed view. This is* RUSSELL BLACKBOROUGH; *manufacturer, politician .. statesman, his own side calls him.*)

BLACKBOROUGH: (*to his hostess*) If I start now, they tell me, I shall get home before the moon goes down. I'm sorry I must get back tonight. It's been a most delightful week-end.

JULIA: (*gracefully giving him a good-bye hand*) And a successful one, I hope.

FARRANT: We talked Education for half an hour.

JULIA: (*her eyebrows lifting a shade*) Education!

FARRANT: Then Trebell went away to work.

BLACKBOROUGH: I've missed the music, I fear.

JULIA: But it's been Bach.

BLACKBOROUGH: No Chopin?

JULIA: For a minute only.

BLACKBOROUGH: Why don't these new Italian men write things for the piano! Good-night, Lady Davenport.

LADY DAVENPORT: (*as he bows over her hand*) And what has Education to do with it?

BLACKBOROUGH: (*non-committal himself*) Perhaps it was a subject that compromised nobody.

LADY DAVENPORT: Do you think my daughter has been wasting her time and her tact?

FARRANT: (*clapping him on the shoulder*) Blackborough's frankly flabbergasted at the publicity of this intrigue.

JULIA: Intrigue! Mr Trebell walked across the House .. actually into your arms.

BLACKBOROUGH: (*with a certain dubious grimness*) Well .. we've had some very interesting talks since. And his views upon Education are quite .. Utopian. Good-bye, Miss Trebell.

FRANCES: Good-bye.

JULIA: I wouldn't be so haughty till after the election, if I were you, Mr Blackborough.

BLACKBOROUGH: (*indifferently*) Oh, I'm glad he's with us on the Church question .. so far.

---

new Italian men: probably opera composers like Mascagni and Puccini.
walked across the House: changed political affiliation.

JULIA: So far as you've made up your minds? The electoral cat will jump soon.
BLACKBOROUGH: (*a little beaten by such polite cynicism*) Well .. our
conservative principles! After all we know what they are. Good-night, Mrs
O'Connell.
AMY: Good-night.
FARRANT: Your neuralgia better?
AMY: By fits and starts.
FARRANT: (*robustly*) Come and play billiards. Horsham and Maconochie started a
game. They can neither of them play. We left them working out a theory of
angles on bits of paper.
KENT: Professor Maconochie lured me on to golf yesterday. He doesn't suffer from
theories about that.
BLACKBOROUGH: (*with approval*) Started life as a caddie.
KENT: (*pulling a wry face*) So he told me after the first hole.
BLACKBOROUGH: What's this, Kent, about Trebell's making you his
secretary?
KENT: He thinks he'll have me.
BLACKBOROUGH: (*almost reprovingly*) No question of politics?
FARRANT: More intrigue, Blackborough.
KENT: (*with disarming candour*) The truth is, you see, I haven't any as yet. I was
Socialist at Oxford .. but of course that doesn't count. I think I'd better learn
my job under the best man I can find .. and who'll have me.
BLACKBOROUGH: (*gravely*) What does your father say?
KENT: Oh, as long as Jack will inherit the property in a Tory spirit! My father
thinks it my wild oats.
(*A FOOTMAN has come in.*)
FOOTMAN: Your car is round, sir.
BLACKBOROUGH: Ah! Good-night, Miss Davenport. Good-bye again, Mrs
Farrant .. a charming weekend.
(*He makes a business-like departure, FARRANT follows him.*)
FOOTMAN: A telephone message from Dr Wedgecroft, ma'am. His thanks; they
stopped the express for him at Hitchin and he has reached London quite
safely.
JULIA: Thank you.
(*The FOOTMAN goes out. MRS FARRANT exhales delicately as if
the air were a little refined by BLACKBOROUGH'S removal.*)
JULIA: Mr Blackborough and his patent turbines and his gas engines and what not
are the motive power of our party nowadays, Fanny.
FRANCES: Yes, you claim to be steering plutocracy. Do you never wonder if it isn't
steering you?
(*AMY O'CONNELL, growing restless, has wandered round the room
picking at the books in their cases.*)
AMY: I always like your books, Julia. It's an intellectual distinction to know
someone who has read them.
JULIA: That's the Communion I choose.
FRANCES: Aristocrat .. fastidious aristocrat.
JULIA: No, now. Learning's a great leveller.

FRANCES: But Julia .. books are quite unreal. D'you think life is a bit like
   them?

JULIA: They bring me into touch with .. Oh, there's nothing more deadening than
   to be boxed into a set in Society! Speak to a woman outside it .. she doesn't
   understand your language.

FRANCES: And do you think by prattling Hegel with Gilbert Wedgecroft when he
   comes to physic you –

JULIA: (*joyously*) Excellent physic that is. He never leaves a prescription.

LADY DAVENPORT: Don't you think an aristocracy of brains is the best
   aristocracy, Miss Trebell?

FRANCES: (*with a little more bitterness than the abstraction of the subject demands*)
   I'm sure it is just as out of touch with humanity as any other .. more so,
   perhaps. If I were a country I wouldn't be governed by arid intellects.

JULIA: Manners, Frances.

FRANCES: I'm one myself and I know. They're either dead or dangerous.

   (GEORGE FARRANT *comes back and goes straight to* AMY.)

FARRANT: (*still robustly*) Billiards, Mrs O'Connell.

AMY: (*declining sweetly*) I think not.

FARRANT: Billiards, Lucy?

LUCY: (*as robust as he*) Yes, Uncle George. You shall mark while Walter gives me
   twenty-five and I beat him.

KENT: (*with a none-of-your-impudence air*) I'll give you ten yards start and race you
   to the billiard room.

LUCY: Will you wear my skirt? Oh .. Grandmamma's thinking me vulgar.

LADY DAVENPORT: (*without prejudice*) Why, my dear, freedom of limb is worth
   having .. and perhaps it fits better with freedom of tongue.

FARRANT: (*in the proper avuncular tone*) I'll play you both .. and I'd race you
   both if you weren't so disgracefully young.

   (AMY O'CONNELL *has reached an open window.*)

AMY: I shall go for a walk with my neuralgia.

JULIA: Poor thing!

AMY: The moon's good for it.

LUCY: Shall you come, Aunt Julia?

JULIA: (*in flat protest*) No, I will not sit up while you play billiards.

   (AMY *goes out through the one window, stands for a moment,*
   wistfully romantic, gazing at the moon, then disappears. FARRANT
   and WALTER KENT *are standing at the other, looking across the*
   lawn.)

FARRANT: Horsham still arguing with Maconochie. They're got to Botany
   now.

KENT: Demonstrating something with a .. what's that thing?

   (KENT *goes out.*)

FARRANT: (*with a throw of his head towards the distant* HORSHAM) He was so
   bored with our politics .. having to give his opinion too. We could just hear
   your piano.

   (*And he follows* KENT.)

JULIA: Take Amy O'Connell that lace thing, will you, Lucy?

LUCY: (*her tone expressing quite wonderfully her sentiments towards the owner*)
Don't you think she'd sooner catch cold?
> (*She catches it up and follows the two men; then after looking round
> impatiently, swings off in the direction* MRS O'CONNELL *took. The
> three women now left together are at their ease.*)

FRANCES: Did you expect Mr Blackborough to get on well with Henry?

JULIA: He has become a millionaire by appreciating clever men when he met them.

LADY DAVENPORT: Yes, Julia, but his political conscience is comparatively
new-born.

JULIA: Well, Mamma, can we do without Mr Trebell?

LADY DAVENPORT: Everyone seems to think you'll come back with something
of a majority.

JULIA: (*a little impatient*) What's the good of that? The Bill can't be brought into
the Lords .. and who's going to take Disestablishment through the Commons
for us? Not Eustace Fowler .. not Mr Blackborough .. not Lord Charles .. not
George!

LADY DAVENPORT: (*warningly*) Not all your brilliance as a hostess will keep Mr
Trebell in a Tory cabinet.

JULIA: (*with wilful avoidance of the point*) Cyril Horsham is only too glad.

LADY DAVENPORT: Because you tell him he ought to be.

FRANCES: (*coming to the rescue*) There is this. Henry has never exactly called
himself a Liberal. He really is elected independently.

JULIA: I wonder will all the garden-cities become pocket-boroughs.

FRANCES: I think he has made a mistake.

JULIA: It makes things easier now .. his having kept his freedom.

FRANCES: I think it's a mistake to stand outside a system. There's an inhumanity in
that amount of detachment ..

JULIA: (*brilliantly*) I think a statesman may be a little inhuman.

LADY DAVENPORT: (*with keenness*) Do you mean superhuman? It's not the
same thing, you know.

JULIA: I know.

LADY DAVENPORT: Most people don't know.

JULIA: (*proceeding with her cynicism*) Humanity achieves .. what? Housekeeping
and children.

FRANCES: As far as a woman's concerned.

JULIA: (*a little mockingly*) Now, Mamma, say that is as far as a woman's concerned.

LADY DAVENPORT: My dear, you know I don't think so.

JULIA: We may none of us think so. But there's our position .. bread and butter
and a certain satisfaction until .. Oh, Mamma, I wish I were like you ..
beyond all the passions of life.

LADY DAVENPORT: (*with great vitality*) I'm nothing of the sort. It's my egoism's
dead .. that's an intimation of mortality.

---

garden-cities: planned new towns, owned by the residents, combining urban life with the beauty
of the country; the first was started at Letchworth in Hertfordshire in 1903.
pocket-boroughs: safe parliamentary seats. Prior to the reform of 1832, it was common for small
boroughs to be in the political control of the local nobleman or chief landowner, who could
dictate the votes of his tenants – the seat was 'in his pocket'.

JULIA: I accept the snub. But I wonder what I'm to do with myself for the next thirty years.

FRANCES: Help Lord Horsham to govern the country.

> (JULIA FARRANT *gives a little laugh and takes up the subject this time.*)

JULIA: Mamma .. how many people, do you think, believe that Cyril's *grande passion* for me takes that form?

LADY DAVENPORT: Everyone who knows Cyril and most people who know you.

JULIA: Otherwise I seem to have fulfilled my mission in life. The boys are old enough to go to school. George and I have become happily unconscious of each other.

FRANCES: (*with sudden energy of mind*) Till I was forty I never realised the fact that most women must express themselves through men.

JULIA: (*looking at* FRANCES *a little curiously*) Didn't your instinct lead you to marry .. or did you fight against it?

FRANCES: I don't know. Perhaps I had no vitality to spare.

LADY DAVENPORT: That boy is a long time proposing to Lucy.

> (*This effectually startles the other two from their conversational reverie.*)

JULIA: Walter? I'm not sure that he means to. She means to marry him if he does.

FRANCES: Has she told you so?

JULIA: No. I judge by her business-like interest in his welfare.

FRANCES: He's beginning to feel the responsibility of manhood .. doesn't know whether to be frightened or proud of it.

LADY DAVENPORT: It's a pretty thing to watch young people mating. When they're older and marry from disappointment or deliberate choice, thinking themselves so worldly-wise ..

JULIA: (*back to her politely cynical mood*) Well .. then at least they don't develop their differences at the same fire-side, regretting the happy time when neither possessed any character at all.

LADY DAVENPORT: (*giving a final douche of common sense*) My dear, any two reasonable people ought to be able to live together.

FRANCES: Granted three sitting rooms. That'll be the next middle-class political cry .. when women are heard.

JULIA: (*suddenly as practical as her mother*) Walter's lucky .. Lucy won't stand any nonsense. She'll have him in the cabinet by the time he's fifty.

LADY DAVENPORT: And are you the power behind your brother, Miss Trebell?

FRANCES: (*gravely*) He ignores women. I've forced enough good manners on him to disguise the fact decently. His affections are two generations ahead.

JULIA: People like him in an odd sort of way.

FRANCES: That's just respect for work done .. one can't escape from it.

> (*There is a slight pause in their talk. By some not very devious route* MRS FARRANT'S *mind travels to the next subject.*)

JULIA: Fanny .. how fond are you of Amy O'Connell?

FRANCES: She says we're great friends.

JULIA: She says that of me.

FRANCES: It's a pity about her husband.

JULIA: (*almost provokingly*) What about him?
FRANCES: It seems to be understood that he treats her badly.
LADY DAVENPORT: (*a little malicious*) Is there any particular reason he should
    treat her well?
FRANCES: Don't you like her, Lady Davenport?
LADY DAVENPORT: (*dealing out justice*) I find her quite charming to look at and
    talk to .. but why shouldn't Justin O'Connell live in Ireland for all that? I'm
    going to bed, Julia.
                (*She collects her belongings and gets up.*)
JULIA: I must look in at the billiard room.
FRANCES: I won't come, Julia.
JULIA: What's your brother working at?
FRANCES: I don't know. Something we shan't hear of for a year, perhaps.
JULIA: On the Church business, I daresay.
FRANCES: Did you hear Lord Horsham at dinner on the lack of dignity in an
    irreligious state?
JULIA: Poor Cyril .. he'll have to find a way round that opinion of his now.
FRANCES: Does he like leading his party?
JULIA: (*after due consideration*) It's an intellectual exercise. He's the right man,
    Fanny. You see it isn't a party in the active sense at all, except now and then
    when it's captured by someone with an axe to grind.
FRANCES: (*humorously*) Such as my brother.
JULIA: (*as humorous*) Such as your brother. It expresses the thought of the men
    who aren't taken in by the claptrap of progress.
FRANCES: Sometimes they've a queer way of expressing their love for the people
    of England.
JULIA: But one must use democracy. Wellington wouldn't .. Disraeli did.
LADY DAVENPORT: (*at the door*) Good-night, Miss Trebell.
FRANCES: I'm coming .. it's past eleven.
JULIA: (*at the window*) What a gorgeous night! I'll come in and kiss you, Mamma.
                (FRANCES *follows* LADY DAVENPORT *and* JULIA *starts across
                the lawn to the billiard room* ..)

SCENE 2. *An hour later you can see no change in the room except that only one lamp
is alight on the table in the middle.* AMY O'CONNELL *and* HENRY TREBELL
*walk past one window and stay for a moment in the light of the other. Her wrap is
about her shoulders. He stands looking down at her.*

AMY: There goes the moon .. it's quieter than ever now. (*She comes in.*) Is it very
    late?
TREBELL: (*as he follows*) Half-past twelve.
                (TREBELL *is hard-bitten, brainy, forty-five and very sure of himself.
                He has a cold keen eye, which rather belies a sensitive mouth; hands
                which can grip, and a figure that is austere.*)
AMY: I ought to be in bed. I suppose everyone has gone.
TREBELL: Early trains tomorrow. The billiard room lights are out.
AMY: The walk has just tired me comfortably.

TREBELL: Sit down. (*She sits by the table. He sits by her and says with the air of a certain buyer at a market.*) You're very pretty.

AMY: As well here as by moonlight? Can't you see any wrinkles?

TREBELL: One or two .. under the eyes. But they give character and bring you nearer my age. Yes, Nature hit on the right curve in making you.
> (*She stretches herself, cat-like.*)

AMY: Praise is the greatest of luxuries, isn't it, Henry? .. Henry .. (*She caresses the name.*)

TREBELL: Quite right .. Henry.

AMY: Henry .. Trebell.

TREBELL: Having formally taken possession of my name ..

AMY: I'll go to bed.
> (*His eyes have never moved from her. Now she breaks the contact and goes towards the door.*)

TREBELL: I wouldn't .. my spare time for love-making is so limited.
> (*She turns back, quite at ease, her eyes challenging him.*)

AMY: That's the first offensive thing you've said.

TREBELL: Why offensive?

AMY: I may flirt. Making love's another matter.

TREBELL: Sit down and explain the difference .. Mrs O'Connell.
> (*She sits down.*)

AMY: Quite so. 'Mrs O'Connell'. That's the difference.

TREBELL: (*provokingly*) But I doubt if I'm interested in the fact that your husband doesn't understand you and that your marriage was a mistake .. and how hard you find it to be strong.

AMY: (*kindly*) I'm not quite a fool though you think so on a three months' acquaintance. But tell me this .. what education besides marriage does a woman get?

TREBELL: (*his head lifting quickly*) Education ..

AMY: Don't be business-like.

TREBELL: I beg your pardon.

AMY: Do you think the things you like to have taught in schools are any use to one when one comes to deal with you?

TREBELL: (*after a little scrutiny of her face*) Well, if marriage is only the means to an end .. what's the end? Not flirtation.

AMY: (*with an air of self-revelation*) I don't know. To keep one's place in the world, I suppose, one's self-respect and a sense of humour.

TREBELL: Is that difficult?

AMY: To get what I want, without paying more than it's worth to me ..?

TREBELL: Never to be reckless.

AMY: (*with a side-glance*) One isn't so often tempted.

TREBELL: In fact .. to flirt with life generally. Now, what made your husband marry you?

---

love-making: though ambiguous here, generally in the period the phrase referred to courting and love-talk rather than the sexual act.

AMY: (*dealing with the impertinence in her own fashion*) What would make you marry me? Don't say: Nothing on earth.

TREBELL: (*speaking apparently of someone else*) A prolonged fit of idleness might make me marry .. a clever woman. But I've never been idle for more than a week. And I've never met a clever woman .. worth calling a woman.

AMY: (*bringing their talk back to herself, and fastidiously*) Justin has all the natural instincts.

TREBELL: He's a Roman Catholic, isn't he?

AMY: So am I .. by profession.

TREBELL: It's a poor religion unless you really believe in it.

AMY: (*appealing to him*) If I were to live at Linaskea and have as many children as God sent, I should manage to make Justin pretty miserable! And what would be left of me at all I should like to know?

TREBELL: So Justin lives at Linaskea alone?

AMY: I'm told now there's a pretty housemaid .. (*she shrugs*)

TREBELL: Does he drink too?

AMY: Oh, no. You'd like Justin, I daresay. He's clever. The thirteenth century's what he knows about. He has done a book on its statutes .. has been doing another.

TREBELL: And after an evening's hard work I find you here ready to flirt with.

AMY: What have you been working at?

TREBELL: A twentieth century statute perhaps. That's not any concern of yours either.

(*She does not follow his thought.*)

AMY: No, I prefer you in your unprofessional moments.

TREBELL: Real flattery. I didn't know I had any.

AMY: That's why you should flirt with me .. Henry .. to cultivate them. I'm afraid you lack imagination.

TREBELL: One must choose something to lack in this life.

AMY: Not develop your nature to its utmost capacity.

TREBELL: And then?

AMY: Well, if that's not an end in itself .. (*with a touch of romantic piety*) I suppose there's the hereafter.

TREBELL: (*grimly material*) What, more developing! I watch people wasting time on themselves with amazement .. I refuse to look forward to wasting eternity.

AMY: (*shaking her head*) You are very self-satisfied.

TREBELL: Not more so than any machine that runs smoothly. And I hope not self-conscious.

AMY: (*rather attractively treating him as a child*) It would do you good to fall really desperately in love with me .. to give me the power to make you unhappy.

(*He suddenly becomes very definite.*)

TREBELL: At twenty-three I engaged myself to be married to a charming and virtuous fool. I broke it off.

AMY: Did she mind much?

TREBELL: We both minded. But I had ideals of womanhood that I wouldn't sacrifice to any human being. Then I fell in with a woman who seduced me, and for a whole year led me the life of a French novel .. played about with my

emotion as I had tortured that other poor girl's brains. Education you'd call it
in the one case as I called it in the other. What a waste of time!

AMY: And what has become of your ideal?

TREBELL: (*relapsing to his former mood*) It's no longer a personal matter.

AMY: (*with coquetry*) You're not interested in my character?

TREBELL: Oh, yes, I am .. up to kissing point.

> (*She does not shrink, but speaks with just a shade of contempt.*)

AMY: You get that far more easily than a woman. That's one of my grudges against
men. Why can't women take love-affairs so lightly?

TREBELL: There are reasons. But make a good beginning with this one. Kiss me at
once.

> (*He leans towards her. She considers him quite calmly.*)

AMY: No.

TREBELL: When will you, then?

AMY: When I can't help myself .. if that time ever comes.

TREBELL: (*accepting the postponement in a business-like spirit*) Well .. I'm an
impatient man.

AMY: (*confessing engagingly*) I made up my mind to bring you within arms' length
of me when we'd met at Lady Percival's. Do you remember? (*His face shows
no sign of it.*) It was the day after your speech on the Budget.

TREBELL: Then I remember. But I haven't observed the process.

AMY: (*subtly*) Your sister grew to like me very soon. That's all the cunning there
has been.

TREBELL: The rest is just mutual attraction?

AMY: And opportunities.

TREBELL: Such as this.

> (*At the drop of their voices they become conscious of the silent house.*)

AMY: Do you really think everyone has gone to bed?

TREBELL: (*disregardful*) And what is it makes my pressing attentions endurable ..
if one may ask?

AMY: Some spiritual need or other, I suppose, which makes me risk unhappiness ..
in fact, welcome it.

TREBELL: (*with great briskness*) Your present need is a good shaking .. I seriously
mean that. You get to attach importance to these shades of emotion. A slight
physical shock would settle them all. That's why I asked you to kiss me just
now.

AMY: You haven't very nice ideas, have you?

TREBELL: There are three facts in life that call up emotion .. Birth, Death, and
the Desire for Children. The niceties are shams.

AMY: Then why do you want to kiss me?

TREBELL: I don't .. seriously. But I shall in a minute just to finish the argument.
Too much diplomacy always ends in a fight.

AMY: And if I don't fight .. it'd be no fun for you, I suppose?

TREBELL: You would get that much good out of me. For it's my point of honour ..
to leave nothing I touch as I find it.

---

nice: not in the modern sense, but 'proper' or 'scrupulous'.

(*He is very close to her.*)
AMY: You're frightening me a little..
TREBELL: Come and look at the stars again. Come along.
AMY: Give me my wrap. (*He takes it up, but holds it.*) Well, put it on me. (*He puts it round her, but does not withdraw his arms.*) Be careful, the stars are looking at you.
TREBELL: No, they can't see so far as we can. That's the proper creed.
AMY: (*softly, almost shyly*) Henry.
TREBELL: (*bending closer to her*) Yes, pretty thing.
AMY: Is this what you call being in love?
             (*He looks up and listens.*)
TREBELL: Here's somebody coming.
AMY: Oh!..
TREBELL: What does it matter?
AMY: I'm untidy or something..
             (*She slips out, for they are close to the window. The* FOOTMAN *enters, stops suddenly.*)
FOOTMAN: I beg your pardon, sir. I thought everyone had gone.
TREBELL: I've just been for a walk. I'll lock up if you like.
FOOTMAN: I can easily wait up, sir.
TREBELL: (*at the window*) I wouldn't. What do you do.. just slide the bolt?
FOOTMAN: That's all, sir.
TREBELL: I see. Good-night.
FOOTMAN: Good-night, sir.
             (*He goes.* TREBELL'S *demeanour suddenly changes, becomes alert, with the alertness of a man doing something in secret. He leans out of the window and whispers.*)
TREBELL: Amy!
             (*There is no answer, so he gently steps out. For a moment the room is empty and there is silence. Then* AMY *has flown from him into the safety of lights. She is flushed, trembling, but rather ecstatic, and her voice has lost all affectation now.*)
AMY: Oh.. oh.. you shouldn't have kissed me like that!
             (TREBELL *stands in the window-way; a light in his eyes, and speaks low but commandingly.*)
TREBELL: Come here.
             (*Instinctively she moves towards him. They speak in whispers.*)
AMY: He was locking up.
TREBELL: I've sent him to bed.
AMY: He won't go.
TREBELL: Never mind him.
AMY: We're standing full in the light.. anyone could see us.
TREBELL: (*with fierce egotism*) Think of me.. not of anyone else. (*He draws her from the window; then does not let her go.*) May I kiss you again?
AMY: (*her eyes closed*) Yes.
             (*He kisses her. She stiffens in his arms; then laughs almost joyously, and is commonplace.*)

AMY: Well . . let me get my breath.
TREBELL: (*letting her stand free*) Now . . go along.
            (*Obediently she turns to the door, but sinks on the nearest chair.*)
AMY: In a minute, I'm a little faint. (*He goes to her quickly.*) No, it's nothing.
TREBELL: Come into the air again. (*then half seriously*) I'll race you across the
      lawn.
AMY: (*still breathless and a little hysterical*) Thank you!
TREBELL: Shall I carry you?
AMY: Don't be silly. (*She recovers her self-possession, gets up and goes to the
      window, then looks back at him and says very beautifully.*) But the night's
      beautiful, isn't it?
            (*He has her in his arms again, more firmly this time.*)
TREBELL: Make it so.
AMY: (*struggling . . with herself*) Oh, why do you rouse me like this?
TREBELL: Because I want you.
AMY: Want me to . . ?
TREBELL: Want you to . . kiss me just once.
AMY: (*yielding*) If I do . . don't let me go mad, will you?
TREBELL: Perhaps. (*He bends over her, her head drops back.*) Now.
AMY: Yes!
            (*She kisses him on the mouth. Then he would release her, but suddenly
            she clings again.*)
AMY: Oh . . don't let me go.
TREBELL: (*with fierce pride of possession*) Not yet.
            (*She is fragile beside him. He lifts her in his arms and carries her out
            into the darkness.*)

ACT II

TREBELL'S *house in Queen Anne Street, London. Eleven o'clock on an October
morning.* TREBELL'S *working room is remarkable chiefly for the love of sunlight it
evidences in its owner. The walls are white; the window which faces you is bare of all
but the necessary curtains. Indeed, lack of draperies testifies also to his horror of dust.
There faces you besides a double door; when it is opened another door is seen. When
that is opened you discover a writing table, and beyond can discern a book-case filled
with heavy volumes – law reports perhaps. The little room beyond is, so to speak, an
under-study. Between the two rooms a window, again barely curtained, throws light
down the staircase. But in the big room, while the books are many the choice of them
is catholic; and the book-cases are low, running along the wall. There is an armchair
before the bright fire, which is on your right. There is a sofa. And in the middle of the
room is an enormous double writing table piled tidily with much appropriate
impedimenta, blue books and pamphlets and with an especial heap of unopened letters
and parcels. At the table sits* TREBELL *himself, in good health and spirits, but eyeing*

Queen Anne Street: between Regent's Park and Hyde Park; it crosses Harley Street, where the
offices of many exclusive physicians are still located, which explains why Dr Wedgecroft can call
so frequently on Trebell.
blue books: official Parliamentary reports, in dark blue paper covers.

askance the work to which he has evidently just returned. His sister looks in on him.
She is dressed to go out and has a housekeeping air.

FRANCES: Are you busy, Henry?

TREBELL: More or less. Come in.

FRANCES: You'll dine at home?

TREBELL: Anyone coming?

FRANCES: Julia Farrant and Lucy have run up to town, I think. I thought of going
round and asking them to come in .. but perhaps your young man will be
going there. Amy O'Connell said something vague about our going to Charles
Street .. but she may be out of town by now.

TREBELL: Well .. I'll be in anyhow.

FRANCES: (*going to the window as she buttons her gloves*) Were you on deck early
this morning? It must have been lovely.

TREBELL: No, I turned in before we got out of le Havre. I left Kent on deck and
found him there at six.

FRANCES: I don't think autumn means to come at all this year .. it'll be winter one
morning. September has been like a hive of bees, busy and drowsy. By the
way, Cousin Mary has another baby .. a girl.

TREBELL: (*indifferent to the information*) That's the fourth.

FRANCES: Fifth. They asked me down for the christening .. but I really couldn't.

TREBELL: September's the month for Tuscany. The car chose to break down one
morning just as we were starting North again; so we climbed one of the little
hills and sat for a couple of hours, while I composed a fifteenth century
electioneering speech to the citizens of Siena.

FRANCES: (*with a half smile*) Have you a vein of romance for holiday time?

TREBELL: (*dispersing the suggestion*) Not at all romantic .. nothing but figures and
fiscal questions. That was the hardest commercial civilization there has been,
though you only think of its art and its murders now.

FRANCES: The papers on both sides have been very full of you .. saying you hold
the moral balance .. or denying it.

TREBELL: An interviewer caught me at Basle. I offered to discuss the state of the
Swiss navy.

FRANCES: Was that before Lord Horsham wrote to you?

TREBELL: Yes, his letter came to Innsbruck. He 'expressed' it somehow. Why .. it
isn't known that he will definitely ask me to join?

FRANCES: The Whitehall had a leader before the Elections were well over to say
that he must .. but, of course, that was Mr Farrant.

TREBELL: (*knowingly*) Mrs Farrant. I saw it in Paris .. it just caught me up.

FRANCES: The Times is very shy over the whole question .. has a letter from a
fresh bishop every day .. doesn't talk of you very kindly yet.

TREBELL: Tampering with the Establishment, even Cantelupe's way, will be a pill
to the real old Tory right to the bitter end.

> (WALTER KENT *comes in, very fresh and happy-looking. A young*
> *man started in life.* TREBELL *hails him.*)

TREBELL: Hullo .. you've not been long getting shaved.

KENT: How do you do, Miss Trebell? Lucy turned me out.

FRANCES: My congratulations. I've not seen you since I heard the news.

KENT: (*glad and unembarrassed*) Thank you. I do deserve them, don't I? Mrs Farrant didn't come down .. she left us to breakfast together. But I've a message for you .. her love and she is in town. I went and saw Lord Charles, sir. He will come to you and be here at half past eleven.

TREBELL: Look at these.

(*He smacks on the back, so to speak, the pile of parcels and letters.*)

KENT: Oh, lord! .. I'd better start on them.

FRANCES: (*continuing in her smooth oldmaidish manner*) Thank you for getting engaged just before you went off with Henry .. it has given me my only news of him, through Lucy and your postcards.

TREBELL: Oh, what about Wedgecroft?

KENT: I think it was he spun up just as I'd been let in.

TREBELL: Oh, well .. (*and he rings at the telephone which is on his table*)

KENT: (*confiding in* MISS TREBELL) We're a common sense couple, aren't we? I offered to ask to stay behind but she ..

(SIMPSON, *the maid, comes in.*)

SIMPSON: Dr Wedgecroft, sir.

(WEDGECROFT *is on her heels. If you have an eye for essentials you may tell at once that he is a doctor, but if you only notice externals you will take him for anything else. He is over forty and in perfect health of body and spirit. His enthusiasms are his vitality and he has too many of them ever to lose one. He squeezes* MISS TREBELL'S *hand with an air of fearless affection which is another one of his characteristics and not the least loveable.*)

WEDGECROFT: How are you?

FRANCES: I'm very well thanks.

WEDGECROFT: (*to* TREBELL, *as they shake hands*) You're looking fit.

TREBELL: (*with tremendous emphasis*) I am!

WEDGECROFT: You've got the motor eye though.

TREBELL: Full of dust?

WEDGECROFT: Look at Kent's. (*He takes* KENT'S *arm.*) It's a slight but serious contraction of the pupil .. which I charge fifty guineas to cure.

FRANCES: It's the eye of faith in you and your homeopathic doses. Don't you interfere with it.

(FRANCES TREBELL, *housekeeper, goes out.* KENT *has seized on the letters and is carrying them to his room.*)

KENT: This looks like popularity and the great heart of the people, doesn't it?

WEDGECROFT: Trebell, you're not ill, and I've work to do.

TREBELL: I want ten minutes. Keep anybody out, Kent.

KENT: I'll switch that speaking tube arrangement to my room.

(TREBELL, *overflowing with vitality, starts to pace the floor.*)

TREBELL: I've seen the last of Pump Court, Gilbert.

WEDGECROFT: The Bar ought to give you a testimonial .. to the man who not only could retire on twenty years' briefs, but *has*.

Pump Court: street off Middle Temple Lane in the legal district of London.

TREBELL: Fifteen. But I bled the City sharks with a good conscience .. quite freely.

WEDGECROFT: (*with a pretence at grumbling*) I wish I could retire.

TREBELL: No you don't. Doctoring's a priestcraft .. you've taken vows.

WEDGECROFT: Then why don't you establish *our* Church instead of ..

TREBELL: Yes, my friend .. but you're a heretic. I'd have to give the Medical Council power to burn you at the stake.

KENT: (*with the book packages*) Parcel from the S.P.C.K., sir.

TREBELL: I know .. Disestablishment a crime against God; sermon preached by the Vicar of something Parva in eighteen seventy three. I hope you're aware it's your duty to read all those.

KENT: Suppose they convert me? Lucy wanted to know if she could see you.

TREBELL: (*his eyebrows up*) Yes, I'll call at Mrs Farrant's. Oh, wait. Aren't they coming to dinner?

KENT: Tonight? No, I think they go back to Shapters by the five o'clock. I told her she might come round about twelve on the chance.

TREBELL: Yes .. if Cantelupe's punctual .. I'd sooner not have too long with him.

KENT: All right, then.

> (*He goes, shutting the door; then you hear the door of his room shut too. The two friends face each other, glad of a talk.*)

TREBELL: Well?

WEDGECROFT: Well .. you'll never do it.

TREBELL: Yes, I shall.

WEDGECROFT: You can't carry any bill to be a credit to you with the coming Tory cabinet on your back. You know the government is cursing you with its dying breath.

TREBELL: (*rubbing his hands*) Of course. They've been beaten out of the House and in now. I suppose they will meet Parliament.

WEDGECROFT: They must, I think. It's over a month since –

TREBELL: (*his thoughts running quickly*) There'll only be a nominal majority of sixteen against them. The Labour lot are committed on their side .. and now that the Irish have gone –

WEDGECROFT: But they'll be beaten on the Address first go.

TREBELL: Yes .. Horsham hasn't any doubt of it.

WEDGECROFT: He'll be in office within a week of the King's speech.

Medical Council: empowered to oversee medical training and certification.

S.P.C.K.: Society for Promoting Christian Knowledge, a Church of England organization that publishes religious books and pamphlets.

Labour . . . Irish: the fledgling Labour Party and the Irish Nationalists would normally be allied to the Liberals in the Edwardian age.

Address . . . King's speech: Parliament opens with a speech read by the monarch but written by the Prime Minister, in which the governing party outlines its program for the session. In the fiction of *Waste*, the Liberals have just lost their majority in a general election and the opposition Tory Party expects them to be defeated on the speech in the House, forcing the cabinet to resign. The King would then command the Tories to form a new government. Another general election would not technically be necessary, but the Tories lean to calling one, and expect to receive a mandate from the country. In fact, something similar did happen in 1905–6, but the condition of the parties was reversed.

TREBELL: (*with another access of energy*) I'll pull the bill that's in my head through a Horsham cabinet and the House. Then I'll leave them, . . they'll go to the Country –

WEDGECROFT: You know Percival's pledge about that at Bristol wasn't very definite.

TREBELL: Horsham means to.

WEDGECROFT: (*with friendly contempt*) Oh, Horsham!

TREBELL: Anyway, it's about Percival I want you. How ill is he?

WEDGECROFT: Not very.

TREBELL: Is he going to die?

WEDGECROFT: Well, I'm attending him.

TREBELL: (*pinked*) Yes . . that's a good answer. How does he stomach me in prospect as a colleague, so far?

WEDGECROFT: Sir, professional etiquette forbids me to disclose what a patient may confess in the sweat of his agony.

TREBELL: He'll be Chancellor again and lead the House.

WEDGECROFT: Why not? He only grumbles that he's getting old.

TREBELL: (*thinking busily again*) The difficulty is I shall have to stay through one budget with them. He'll have a surplus . . well, it looks like it . . and my only way of agreeing with him will be to collar it.

WEDGECROFT: But . . good Heavens! . . you'll have a hundred million or so to give away when you've disendowed.

TREBELL: Not to give away. I'll sell every penny.

WEDGECROFT: (*with an incredulous grin*) You're not going back to extending old-age pensions after turning the unfortunate Liberals out on it, are you?

TREBELL: No, no . . none of your half crown measures. They can wait to round off their solution of that till they've the courage to make one big bite of it.

WEDGECROFT: We shan't see the day.

TREBELL: (*lifting the subject off its feet*) Not if I come out of the cabinet and preach revolution?

WEDGECROFT: Or will they make a Tory of you?

TREBELL: (*acknowledging that stroke with a return grin*) It'll be said they have when the bill is out.

WEDGECROFT: It's said so already.

TREBELL: Who knows a radical bill when he sees it!

WEDGECROFT: I'm not pleased you have to be running a tilt against the party system. (*He becomes a little dubious.*) My friend . . it's a nasty windmill. Oh, you've not seen that article in the Nation on Politics and Society . . it's written at Mrs Farrant and Lady Lurgashall and that set. They hint that the Tories would never have had you if it hadn't been for this bad habit of opposite party men meeting each other.

Chancellor: of the Exchequer, the chief finance minister of the government.

lead the House: the leader of the House of Commons is the member of the government with official initiative in its proceedings. Since Horsham is in the House of Lords, Percival would be the ranking cabinet minister in the Commons.

opposite party men meeting each other: it was common in Edwardian times for opposing leaders to meet socially, since they were normally members of the same class – part of the ruling oligarchy.

TREBELL: (*unimpressed*) Excellent habit! What we really want in this
country is a coalition of all the shibboleths with the rest of us in opposition . .
for five years only.

WEDGECROFT: (*smiling generously*) Well, it's a sensation to see you become
arbiter. The Tories are owning they can't do without you. Percival likes you
personally . . Townsend doesn't matter . . Cantelupe you buy with a price, I
suppose . . Farrant you can put in your pocket. I tell you I think the man you
may run up against is Blackborough.

TREBELL: No, all he wants is to be let look big . . and to have an idea given him
when he's going to make a speech, which isn't often.

WEDGECROFT: Otherwise . . I suppose . . now I may go down to history as having
been in your confidence. I'm very glad you've arrived.

TREBELL: (*with great seriousness*) I've sharpened myself as a weapon to this
purpose.

WEDGECROFT: (*kindly*) And you're sure of yourself, aren't you?

TREBELL: (*turning his wrist*) Try.

WEDGECROFT: (*slipping his doctor's fingers over the pulse*) Seventy, I should say.

TREBELL: I promise you it hasn't varied a beat these three big months.

WEDGECROFT: Well, I wish it had. Perfect balance is most easily lost. How do
you know you've the power of recovery? . . and it's that gets one up in the
morning day by day.

TREBELL: Is it? My brain works steadily on . . hasn't failed me yet. I keep it well
fed. (*He breathes deeply.*) But I'm not sure one shouldn't have been away from
England for five years instead of five weeks . . to come back to a job like this
with a fresh mind. D'you know why really I went back on the Liberals over
this question? Not because they wanted the Church money for their pensions
. . but because all they can see in Disestablishment is destruction. Any fool can
destroy! I'm not going to let a power like the Church get loose from the State.
A thirteen hundred years' tradition of service . . and all they can think of is to
cut it adrift!

WEDGECROFT: I think the Church is moribund.

TREBELL: Oh, yes, of course you do . . you sentimental agnostic anarchist.
Nonsense! The supernatural's a bit blown upon . . till we re-discover what it
means. But it's not essential. Nor is the Christian doctrine. Put a Jesuit in a
corner and shut the door and he'll own that. No . . the tradition of self-sacrifice
and fellowship in service for its own sake . . that's the spirit we've to capture
and keep.

WEDGECROFT: (*really struck*) A secular Church!

TREBELL: (*with reasoning in his tone*) Well . . why not? Listen here. In drafting an
act of Parliament one must alternately imagine oneself God Almighty and the
most ignorant prejudiced little blighter who will be affected by what's passed.
God says: Let's have done with Heaven and Hell . . it's the Earth that shan't
pass away. Why not turn all those theology mongers into doctors or
schoolmasters?

WEDGECROFT: As to doctors –

TREBELL: Quite so, you naturally prejudiced blighter. That priestcraft don't need
re-inforcing.

WEDGECROFT: It needs recognition.

TREBELL: What! It's the only thing most people believe in. Talk about
superstition! However, there's more life in you. Therefore it's to be
schoolmasters.

WEDGECROFT: How?

TREBELL: Listen again, young man. In the youth of the world, when priests were
the teachers of men . .

WEDGECROFT: (*not to be preached at*) And physicians of men.

TREBELL: Shut up.

WEDGECROFT: If there's any real reform going, I want my profession made into a
State department. I won't shut up for less.

TREBELL: (*putting this aside with one finger*) I'll deal with you later. There's still
Youth in the world in another sense; but the priests haven't found out the
difference yet, so they're wasting most of their time.

WEDGECROFT: Religious education won't do nowadays.

TREBELL: What's Nowadays? You're very dull, Gilbert.

WEDGECROFT: I'm not duller than the people who will have to understand your
scheme.

TREBELL: They won't understand it. I shan't explain to them that education *is*
religion, and that those who deal in it are priests without any laying on of
hands.

WEDGECROFT: No matter what they teach?

TREBELL: No . . the matter is how they teach it. I see schools in the future,
Gilbert, not built next to the Church, but on the site of the Church.

WEDGECROFT: Do you think the world is grown up enough to do without dogma?

TREBELL: Yes, I do.

WEDGECROFT: What! . . and am I to write my prescriptions in English?

TREBELL: Yes, you are.

WEDGECROFT: Lord save us! I never thought to find you a visionary.

TREBELL: Isn't it absurd to think that in a hundred years we shall be giving our
best brains and the price of them not to training grown men into the discipline
of destruction . . not even to curing the ills which we might be preventing . .
but to teaching our children. There's nothing else to be done . . nothing else
matters. But it's work for a priesthood.

WEDGECROFT: (*affected; not quite convinced*) Do you think you can buy a
tradition and transmute it?

TREBELL: Don't mock at money.

WEDGECROFT: I never have.

TREBELL: But you speak of it as an end not as a means. That's unfair.

WEDGECROFT: I speaks as I finds.

TREBELL: I'll buy the Church, not with money, but with the promise of new life.
(*A certain rather gleeful cunning comes over him.*) It'll only look like a dose of
reaction at first . . Sectarian Training Colleges endowed to the hilt.

WEDGECROFT: What'll the Nonconformists say?

TREBELL: Bribe them with the means of equal efficiency. The crux of the whole
matter will be in the statutes. I'll force on those colleges.

WEDGECROFT: They'll want dogma.

TREBELL: Dogma's not a bad thing if you've power to adapt it occasionally.

WEDGECROFT: Instead of spending your brains in explaining it. Yes, I agree.

TREBELL: (*with full voice*) But in the creed I'll lay down as unalterable there shall be neither Jew nor Greek .. What do you think of St Paul, Gilbert?

WEDGECROFT: I'd make him the head of a college.

TREBELL: I'll make the Devil himself head of a college, if he'll undertake to teach honestly all he knows.

WEDGECROFT: And he'll conjure up Comte and Robespierre for you to assist in this little *rechauffée* of their schemes.

TREBELL: Hullo! Comte I knew about. Have I stolen from Robespierre too?

WEDGECROFT: (*giving out the epigram with an air*) Property to him who can make the best use of it.

TREBELL: And then what we must do is to give the children power over their teachers?

        (*Now he is comically enigmatic.* WEDGECROFT *echoes him.*)

WEDGECROFT: And what exactly do you mean by that?

TREBELL: (*serious again*) How positive a pedagogue would you be if you had to prove your cases and justify your creed every century or so to the pupils who had learnt just a little more than you could teach them? Give power to the future, my friend .. not to the past. Give responsibility .. even if you give it for your own discredit. What's beneath trust deeds and last wills and testaments, and even acts of Parliament and official creeds? Fear of the verdict of the next generation .. fear of looking foolish in their eyes. Ah, we .. doing our best now .. must be ready for every sort of death. And to provide the means of change and disregard of the past is a secret of statesmanship. Presume that the world will come to an end every thirty years if it is not reconstructed. Therefore give responsibility .. give responsibility .. give the children power.

WEDGECROFT: (*disposed to whistle*) Those statutes will want some framing.

TREBELL: (*relapsing to a chuckle*) There's an incidental change to foresee. Disappearance of the parson into the schoolmaster .. and the Archdeacon into the Inspector .. and the Bishop into – I rather hope he'll stick to his mitre, Gilbert.

WEDGECROFT: Some Ruskin will arise and make him.

TREBELL: (*as he paces the room and the walls of it fade away to him*) What a Church could be made of the best brains in England, sworn only to learn all they could, teach what they knew, without fear of the future or favour to the past .. sworn upon their honour as seekers after truth, knowingly to tell no child a lie. It will come.

WEDGECROFT: A priesthood of women too? There's the tradition of service with them.

Jew nor Greek: in Galatians 3:28 St Paul proclaims that all people, Jew and Gentile, slave and free, male and female, are 'one in Christ Jesus'; so Trebell will proclaim universal equality of education.

rechauffée: warming up or rehashing.

Some Ruskin: John Ruskin (1819–1900), art critic and social reformer, is called upon as a generalized prophetic voice likely to demand responsible leadership for the disestablished Church.

TREBELL: (*with the sourest look yet on his face*) Slavery .. not quite the same thing. And the paradox of such slavery is that they're your only tyrants.
>   (*At this moment the bell of the telephone upon the table rings. He goes to it talking the while.*)
> One has to be very optimistic not to advocate the harem. That's simple and wholesome .. Yes?
>   (KENT *comes in.*)

KENT: Does it work?

TREBELL: (*slamming down the receiver*) You and your new toy! What is it?

KENT: I'm not sure about the plugs of it .. I thought I'd got them wrong. Mrs O'Connell has come to see Miss Trebell, who is out, and she says will *we* ask *you* if any message has been left for her.

TREBELL: No. Oh, about dinner? Well, she's round at Mrs Farrant's.

KENT: I'll ring them up.
>   (*He goes back into his room to do so leaving* TREBELL'S *door open. The two continue their talk.*)

TREBELL: My difficulties will be with Percival.

WEDGECROFT: Not over the Church.

TREBELL: You see I must discover how keen he'd be on settling the Education quarrel, once and for all .. what there is left of it.

WEDGECROFT: He's not sectarian.

TREBELL: It'll cost him his surplus. When'll he be up and about?

WEDGECROFT: Not for a week or more.

TREBELL: (*knitting his brow*) And I've to deal with Cantelupe. Curious beggar, Gilbert.

WEDGECROFT: Not my sort. He'll want some dealing with over your bill as introduced to me.

TREBELL: I've not cross-examined company promoters for ten years without learning how to do business with a professional high churchman.

WEDGECROFT: Providence limited .. eh?
>   (*The are interrupted by* MRS O'CONNELL'S *appearance in the doorway. She is rather pale, very calm; but there is pain in her eyes and her voice is unnaturally steady.*)

AMY: Your maid told me to come up and I'm interrupting business .. I thought she was wrong.

TREBELL: (*with no trace of self-consciousness*) Well .. how are you after this long time?

AMY: How do you do? (*Then she sees* WEDGECROFT *and has to control a shrinking from him.*) Oh!

WEDGECROFT: How are you, Mrs O'Connell?

TREBELL: Kent is telephoning to Frances. He knows where she is.

Cantelupe: his name probably refers to the Italian village of Cantalupo, once the country seat of the Pope, thus suggesting that the character is close to Rome.
high churchman: The high church wing of the Church of England places emphasis on ancient ritual and traditional belief, and is often close to Roman Catholicism in doctrine and practice.

AMY: How are you, Dr Wedgecroft? (*then to* TREBELL) Did you have a good holiday? London pulls one to pieces wretchedly. I shall give up living here at all.

WEDGECROFT: You look very well.

AMY: Do I!

TREBELL: A very good holiday. Sit down .. he won't be a minute.

> (*She sits on the nearest chair.*)

AMY: You're not ill .. interviewing a doctor?

TREBELL: The one thing Wedgecroft's no good at is doctoring. He keeps me well by sheer moral suasion.

> (KENT *comes out of his room and is off downstairs.* TREBELL *calls to him.*)

TREBELL: Mrs O'Connell's here.

KENT: Oh! (*He comes back and into the room.*) Miss Trebell hasn't got there yet.

> (WEDGECROFT *has suddenly looked at his watch.*)

WEDGECROFT: I must fly. Good-bye, Mrs O'Connell.

AMY: (*putting her hand, constrained by its glove, into his open hand*) I am always a little afraid of you.

WEDGECROFT: That isn't the feeling a doctor wants to inspire.

KENT: (*to* TREBELL) David Evans –

TREBELL: Evans?

KENT: The reverend one .. is downstairs and wants to see you.

WEDGECROFT: (*as he comes to them*) Hampstead Road Tabernacle .. Oh, the mammon of righteousness!

TREBELL: Shut up! How long have I before Lord Charles – ?

KENT: Only ten minutes.

> (MRS O'CONNELL *goes to sit at the big table, and apparently idly takes a sheet of paper to scribble on.*)

TREBELL: (*half thinking, half questioning*) He's a man I can say nothing to politely.

WEDGECROFT: I'm off to Percival's now. Then I've another case and I'm due back at twelve. If there's anything helpful to say I'll look in again for two minutes .. not more.

TREBELL: You're a good man.

WEDGECROFT: (*as he goes*) Congratulations, Kent.

KENT: (*taking him to the stairs*) Thank you very much.

AMY: (*beckoning with her eyes*) What's this, Mr Trebell?

TREBELL: Eh? I beg your pardon.

> (*He goes behind her and reads over her shoulder what she has written.* KENT *comes back.*)

KENT: Shall I bring him up here?

> (TREBELL *looks up and for a moment stares at his secretary rather sharply, then speaks in a matter-of-fact voice.*)

TREBELL: See him yourself, downstairs. Talk to him for five minutes .. find out what he wants. Tell him it will be as well for the next week or two if he can say he hasn't seen me.

KENT: Yes.

(*He goes.* TREBELL *follows him to the door which he shuts. Then he turns to face* AMY, *who is tearing up the paper she wrote on.*)

TREBELL: What is it?

AMY: (*her steady voice breaking, her carefully calculated control giving way*) Oh Henry .. Henry!

TREBELL: Are you in trouble?

AMY: You'll hate me, but .. oh, it's brutal of you to have been away so long.

TREBELL: Is it with your husband?

AMY: Perhaps. Oh, come nearer to me .. do.

TREBELL: (*coming nearer without haste or excitement*) Well? (*Her eyes are closed.*) My dear girl, I'm too busy for love-making now. If there are any facts to be faced, let me have them .. quite quickly.

(*She looks up at him for a moment; then speaks swiftly and sharply as one speaks of disaster.*)

AMY: There's a danger of my having a child .. your child .. some time in April. That's all.

TREBELL: (*a sceptic who has seen a vision*) Oh .. it's impossible.

AMY: (*flashing at him, revengefully*) Why?

TREBELL: (*brought to his mundane self*) Well .. are you sure?

AMY: (*in sudden agony*) D'you think I want it to be true? D'you think I – ? You don't know what it is to have a thing happening in spite of you.

TREBELL: (*his face set in thought*) Where have you been since we met?

AMY: Not to Ireland .. I haven't seen Justin for a year.

TREBELL: All the easier for you not to see him for another year.

AMY: That wasn't what you meant.

TREBELL: It wasn't .. but never mind.

(*They are silent for a moment .. miles apart. Then she speaks dully.*)

AMY: We do hate each other .. don't we!

TREBELL: Nonsense. Let's think of what matters.

AMY: (*aimlessly*) I went to a man at Dover .. picked him out of the directory .. didn't give my own name .. pretended I was off abroad. He was a kind old thing .. said it was all most satisfactory. Oh, my God!

TREBELL: (*He goes to bend over her kindly.*) Yes, you've had a torturing month or two. That's been wrong, I'm sorry.

AMY: Even now I have to keep telling myself that it's so .. otherwise I couldn't understand it. Any more than one really believes one will ever die .. one doesn't believe that, you know.

TREBELL: (*on the edge of a sensation that is new to him*) I am told that a man begins to feel unimportant from this moment forward. Perhaps it's true.

AMY: What has it to do with you anyhow? We don't belong to each other. How long were we together that night? Half an hour! You didn't seem to care a bit until after you'd kissed me and .. this is an absurd consequence.

TREBELL: Nature's a tyrant.

AMY: Oh, it's my punishment .. I see that well enough .. for thinking myself so clever .. forgetting my duty and religion .. not going to confession, I mean. (*then hysterically*) God can make you believe in Him when He likes, can't He?

TREBELL: (*with comfortable strength*) My dear girl, this needs your pluck. (*and he sits by her*) All we have to do is to prevent it being found out.

AMY: Yes .. the scandal would smash you, wouldn't it?

TREBELL: There isn't going to be any scandal.

AMY: No .. if we're careful. You'll tell me what to do, won't you? Oh, it's a relief to be able to talk about it.

TREBELL: For one thing, you must take care of yourself and stop worrying.

> (*It soothes her to feel that he is concerned; but it is not enough to be soothed.*)

AMY: Yes, I wouldn't like to have been the means of smashing you, Henry .. especially as you don't care for me.

TREBELL: I intend to care for you.

AMY: Love me, I mean. I wish you did .. a little; then perhaps I shouldn't feel so degraded.

TREBELL: (*a shade impatiently, a shade contemptuously*) I can say I love you if that'll make things easier.

AMY: (*more helpless than ever*) If you'd said it at first I should be taking it for granted .. though it wouldn't be anymore true, I daresay, than now .. when I should know you weren't telling the truth.

TREBELL: Then I'd do without so much confusion.

AMY: Don't be so heartless.

TREBELL: (*as he leaves her*) We seem to be attaching importance to such different things.

AMY: (*shrill even at a momentary desertion*) What do you mean? I want affection now just as I want food. I can't do without it .. I can't reason things out as you can. D'you think I haven't tried? (*then in sudden rebellion*) Oh, the physical curse of being a woman .. no better than any savage in this condition .. worse off than an animal. It's unfair.

TREBELL: Never mind .. you're here now to hand me half the responsibility, aren't you?

AMY: As if I could! If I have to lie through the night simply shaking with bodily fear much longer .. I believe I shall go mad.

> (*This aspect of the matter is meaningless to him. He returns to the practical issue.*)

TREBELL: There's nobody that need be suspecting, is there?

AMY: My maid sees I'm ill and worried and makes remarks .. only to me so far. Don't I look a wreck? I nearly ran away when I saw Dr Wedgecroft .. some of these men are so clever.

TREBELL: (*calculating*) Someone will have to be trusted.

AMY: (*burrowing into her little tortured self again*) And I ought to feel as if I had done Justin a great wrong .. but I don't. I hate you now; now and then. I was being myself. You've brought me down. I feel worthless.

> (*The last word strikes him. He stares at her.*)

TREBELL: Do you?

AMY: (*pleadingly*) There's only one thing I'd like you to tell me, Henry .. it isn't much. That night we were together .. it was for a moment different to everything that has ever been in your life before, wasn't it?

TREBELL: (*collecting himself as if to explain to a child*) I must make you understand .. I must get you to realise that for a little time to come you're above the law .. above even the shortcomings and contradictions of a man's affection.

AMY: But let us have one beautiful memory to share.

TREBELL: (*determined she shall face the cold logic of her position*) Listen. I look back on that night as one looks back on a fit of drunkenness.

AMY: (*neither understanding nor wishing to; only shocked and hurt*) You beast.

TREBELL: (*with bitter sarcasm*) No, don't say that. Won't it comfort you to think of drunkenness as a beautiful thing? There are precedents enough .. classic ones.

AMY: You mean I might have been any other woman.

TREBELL: (*quite inexorable*) Wouldn't any other woman have served the purpose .. and is it less of a purpose because we didn't know we had it? Does my unworthiness then .. if you like to call it so .. make you unworthy now? I must make you see that it doesn't.

AMY: (*petulantly hammering at her idée fixe*) But you didn't love me .. and you don't love me.

TREBELL: (*keeping his patience*) No .. only within the last five minutes have I really taken the smallest interest in you. And now I believe I'm half jealous. Can you understand that? You've been talking a lot of nonsense about your emotions and your immortal soul. Don't you see it's only now that you've become a person of some importance to the world .. and why?

AMY: (*losing her patience, childishly*) What do you mean by the World? You don't seem to have any personal feelings at all. It's horrible you should have thought of me like that. There has been no other man than you that I would have let come anywhere near me .. not for more than a year.

(*He realises that she will never understand.*)

TREBELL: My dear girl, I'm sorry to be brutal. Does it matter so much to you that I should have *wished* to be the father of your child?

AMY: (*ungracious but pacified by his change of tone*) It doesn't matter now.

TREBELL: (*friendly still*) On principle I don't make promises. But I think I can promise you that if you keep your head and will keep your health, this shall all be made as easy for you as if everyone could know. And let's think what the child may mean to you .. just the fact of his birth. Nothing to me, of course! Perhaps that accounts for the touch of jealousy. I've forfeited my rights because I hadn't honourable intentions. You can't forfeit yours. Even if you never see him and he has to grow up among strangers .. just to have had a child must make a difference to you. Of course, it may be a girl. I wonder.

(*As he wanders on so optimistically she stares at him and her face changes. She realises ..*)

AMY: Do you expect me to go through with this? Henry! .. I'd sooner kill myself.

(*There is silence between them. He looks at her as one looks at some unnatural thing. Then after a moment he speaks, very coldly.*)

TREBELL: Oh .. indeed. Don't get foolish ideas into your head. You've no choice now .. no reasonable choice.

AMY: (*driven to bay; her last friend an enemy*) I won't go through with it.

TREBELL: It hasn't been so much the fear of scandal then –

AMY: That wouldn't break my heart. You'd marry me, wouldn't you? We could go away somewhere. I could be very fond of you, Henry.

TREBELL: (*marvelling at these tangents*) Marry you! I should murder you in a week.

(*This sounds only brutal to her; she lets herself be shamed.*)

AMY: You've no more use for me than the use you've made of me.

TREBELL: (*logical again*) Won't you realise that there's a third party to our discussion .. that I'm of no importance beside him and you of very little. Think of the child.

(AMY *blazes into desperate rebellion.*)

AMY: There's no child because I haven't chosen there shall be and there shan't be because I don't choose. You'd have me first your plaything and then Nature's, would you?

TREBELL: (*a little abashed*) Come now, you knew what you were about.

AMY: (*thinking of those moments*) Did I? I found myself wanting you, belonging to you suddenly. I didn't stop to think and explain. But are we never to be happy and irresponsible .. never for a moment?

TREBELL: Well .. one can't pick and choose consequences.

AMY: Your choices in life have made you what you want to be haven't they? Leave me mine.

TREBELL: But it's too late to argue like that.

AMY: If it is, I'd better jump into the Thames. I've thought of it.

(*He considers how best to make a last effort to bring her to her senses. He sits by her.*)

TREBELL: Amy .. if you were my wife –

AMY: (*unresponsive to him now*) I was Justin's wife, and I went away from him sooner than bear him children. Had I the right to choose or had I not?

TREBELL: (*taking another path*) Shall I tell you something I believe? If we were left to choose, we should stand for ever deciding whether to start with the right foot or the left. We blunder into the best things in life. Then comes the test .. have we faith enough to go on .. to go through with the unknown thing?

AMY: (*so bored by these metaphysics*) Faith in what?

TREBELL: Our vitality. I don't give a fig for beauty, happiness, or brains. All I ask of myself is .. can I pay Fate on demand?

AMY: Yes .. in imagination. But I've got physical facts to face.

(*But he has her attention now and pursues the advantage.*)

TREBELL: Very well then .. let the meaning of them go. Look forward simply to a troublesome illness. In a little while you can go abroad quietly and wait patiently. We're not fools and we needn't find fools to trust in. Then come back to England ..

AMY: And forget. That seems simple enough, doesn't it?

TREBELL: If you don't want the child let it be mine .. not yours.

AMY: (*wondering suddenly at this bond between them*) Yours! What would you do with it?

TREBELL: (*matter-of-fact*) Provide for it, of course.

AMY: Never see it, perhaps.

TREBELL: Perhaps not. If there were anything to be gained .. for the child. I'll see that he has his chance as a human being.

AMY: How hopeful! (*Now her voice drops. She is looking back, perhaps at a past self.*) If you loved me .. perhaps I might learn to love the thought of your child.

TREBELL: (*as if half his life depended on her answer*) Is that true?

AMY: (*irritably*) Why are you picking me to pieces? I think that is true. If you had been loving me for a long, long time – (*The agony rushes back on her.*) But now I'm only afraid. You might have some pity for me .. I'm so afraid.

TREBELL: (*touched*) Indeed .. indeed, I'll take what share of this I can.

>   (*She shrinks from him unforgivingly.*)

AMY: No, let me alone. I'm nothing to you. I'm a sick beast in danger of my life, that's all .. cancerous!

>   (*He is roused for the first time, roused to horror and protest.*)

TREBELL: Oh, you unhappy woman! .. if life is like death to you ..

AMY: (*turning on him*) Don't lecture me! If you're so clever put a stop to this horror. Or you might at least say you're sorry.

TREBELL: Sorry! (*The bell on the table rings jarringly.*) Cantelupe!

>   (*He goes to the telephone. She gets up cold and collected, steadied merely by the unexpected sound.*)

AMY: I mustn't keep you from governing the country. I'm sure you'll do it very well.

TREBELL: (*at the telephone*) Yes, bring him up, of course .. isn't Mr Kent there? (*then to her*) I may be ten minutes with him or half an hour. Wait and we'll come to a conclusion.

>   (KENT *comes in, an open letter in his hand.*)

KENT: This note, sir. Had I better go round myself and see him?

TREBELL: (*as he takes the note*) Cantelupe's come.

KENT: (*glancing at the telephone*) Oh, has he!

TREBELL: (*as he reads*) Yes I think you had.

KENT: Evans was very serious.

>   (*He goes back into his room.* AMY *moves swiftly to where* TREBELL *is standing and whispers.*)

AMY: *Won't* you tell me whom to go to?

TREBELL: No.

AMY: Oh, really .. what unpractical sentimental children you men are! You and your consciences .. you and your laws. You drive us to distraction and sometimes to death by your stupidities. Poor women – !

>   (SIMPSON, *the maid, comes in to announce* LORD CHARLES CANTELUPE, *who follows her.* CANTELUPE *is forty, unathletic, and a gentleman in the best and worst sense of the word. He moves always with a caution which may betray his belief in the personality of the Devil. He speaks cautiously too, and as if not he but something inside him were speaking. One feels that before strangers he would not if he could help it move or speak at all. A pale face: the mouth would be hardened by fanaticism were it not for the elements of Christianity in his religion: and he has the limpid eye of the enthusiast.*)

TREBELL: Glad to see you. You know Mrs O'Connell.

>   (CANTELUPE *bows in silence.*)

AMY: We have met.

>   (*She offers her hand. He silently takes it and drops it.*)

TREBELL: Then you'll wait for Frances.

AMY: Is it worth while?
>   (KENT *with his hat on leaves his room and goes downstairs.*)

TREBELL: Have you anything better to do?

AMY: There's somewhere I can go. But I mustn't keep you chatting of my affairs. Lord Charles is impatient to disestablish the Church.

CANTELUPE: (*unable to escape a remark*) Forgive me, since that is also your affair.

AMY: Oh . . but I was received at the Oratory when I was married.

CANTELUPE: (*with contrition*) I beg your pardon.
>   (*Then he makes for the other side of the room.* TREBELL *and* MRS O'CONNELL *stroll to the door, their eyes full of meaning.*)

AMY: I think I'll go on to this place that I've heard of. If I wait . . for your sister . . she may disappoint me again.

TREBELL: Wait.
>   (KENT'S *room is vacant.*)

AMY: Well . . in here?

TREBELL: If you like law-books.

AMY: I haven't been much of an interruption now, have I?

TREBELL: Please wait.

AMY: Thank you.
>   (TREBELL *shuts her in, for a moment seems inclined to lock her in, but he comes back into his own room and faces* CANTELUPE, *who having primed and trained himself on his subject like a gun, fires off a speech, without haste, but also apparently without taking breath.*)

CANTELUPE: I was extremely thankful, Mr Trebell, to hear last week from Horsham that you will see your way to join his cabinet and undertake the Disestablishment Bill in the House of Commons. Any measure of mine, I have always been convinced, would be too much under the suspicion of blindly favouring Church interests to command the allegiance of that heterogeneous mass of thought . . in some cases, alas, of free thought . . which nowadays composes the Conservative party. I am more than content to exercise what influence I may from a seat in the cabinet which will authorise the bill.

TREBELL: Yes. That chair's comfortable.
>   (CANTELUPE *takes another.*)

CANTELUPE: Horsham forwarded to me your memorandum upon the conditions you held necessary and I incline to think I may accept them in principle on behalf of those who honour me with their confidences.
>   (*He fishes some papers from his pocket.* TREBELL *sits squarely at his table to grapple with the matter.*)

TREBELL: Horsham told me you did accept them . . it's on that I'm joining.

CANTELUPE: Yes . . in principle.

TREBELL: Well . . we couldn't carry a bill you disapproved of, could we?

CANTELUPE: (*with finesse*) I hope not.

TREBELL: (*a little dangerously*) And I have no intention of being made the scapegoat of a wrecked Tory compromise with the Nonconformists.

Oratory: Brompton Oratory, an important Roman Catholic church in Knightsbridge in London.

CANTELUPE: (*calmly ignoring the suggestion*) So far as I am concerned I meet the Nonconformists on their own ground .. that Religion had better be free from all compromise with the State.

TREBELL: Quite so .. if you're set free you'll look after yourselves. My discovery must be what to do with the men who think more of the State than their Church .. the majority of parsons, don't you think? .. if the question's really put and they can be made to understand it.

CANTELUPE: (*with sincere disdain*) There are more profitable professions.

TREBELL: And less. Will you allow me that it is statecraft to make a profession profitable?

(CANTELUPE *picks up his papers, avoiding theoretical discussion.*)

CANTELUPE: Well now .. will you explain to me this project for endowing Education with your surplus?

TREBELL: Putting Appropriation, the Buildings and the Representation question on one side for the moment?

CANTELUPE: Candidly, I have yet to master your figures..

TREBELL: The roughest figures so far.

CANTELUPE: Still I have yet to master them on the first two points.

TREBELL: (*firmly premising*) We agree that this is not diverting Church money to actually secular uses.

CANTELUPE: (*as he peeps from under his eyelids*) I can conceive that it might not be. You know that we hold Education to be a Church function. But..

TREBELL: Can you accept thoroughly now the secular solution for all Primary Schools?

CANTELUPE: Haven't we always preferred it to the undenominational? Are there to be facilities for *any* of the teachers giving dogmatic instruction?

TREBELL: I note your emphasis on any. I think we can put the burden of that decision on local authorities. Let us come to the question of Training Colleges for your teachers. It's on that I want to make my bargain.

CANTELUPE: (*alert and cautious*) You want to endow colleges?

TREBELL: Heavily.

CANTELUPE: Under public control?

TREBELL: Church colleges under Church control.

CANTELUPE: There'd be others?

TREBELL: To preserve the necessary balance in the schools.

CANTELUPE: Not founded with Church money?

TREBELL: Think of the grants in aid that will be released. I must ask the Treasury for a further lump sum and with that there may be sufficient for secular colleges .. if you can agree with me upon the statutes of those over which you'd otherwise have free control.

(TREBELL *is weighing his words.*)

CANTELUPE: 'You' meaning, for instance .. what authorities in the Church?

TREBELL: Bishops, I suppose .. and others. (CANTELUPE *permits himself to smile.*) On that point I shall be weakness itself and .. may I suggest .. your seat in the cabinet will give you some control.

CANTELUPE: Statutes?

TREBELL: To be framed in the best interests of educational efficiency.

CANTELUPE: (*finding an opening*) I doubt if we agree upon the meaning to be attached to that term.

TREBELL: (*forcing the issue*) What meaning do you attach to it?

CANTELUPE: (*smiling again*) I have hardly a sympathetic listener.

TREBELL: You have an unprejudiced one . . the best you can hope for. I was not educated myself. I learnt certain things that I desired to know . . from reading my first book – Don Quixote it was – to mastering Company Law. You see, as a man without formulas either for education or religion, I am perhaps peculiarly fitted to settle the double question. I have no grudges . . no revenge to take.

CANTELUPE: (*suddenly congenial*) Shelton's translation of Don Quixote I hope . . the modern ones have no flavour. And you took all the adventures as seriously as the Don did?

TREBELL: (*not expecting this*) I forget.

CANTELUPE: It's the finer attitude . . the child's attitude. And it would enable you immediately to comprehend mine towards an education consisting merely of practical knowledge. The life of Faith is still the happy one. What is more crushingly finite than knowledge? Moral discipline is a nation's only safety. How much of your science tends in support of the great spiritual doctrine of sacrifice!

      (TREBELL *returns to his subject as forceful as ever.*)

TREBELL: The Church has assimilated much in her time. Do you think it wise to leave agnostic science at the side of the plate? I think, you know, that this craving for common knowledge is a new birth in the mind of man; and if your Church won't recognise that soon, by so much will she be losing her grip for ever over men's minds. What's the test of godliness, but your power to receive the new idea in whatever form it comes and give it life? It is blasphemy to pick and choose your good. (*For a moment his thoughts seem to be elsewhere.*) That's an unhappy man or woman or nation . . I know it if it has only come to me this minute . . and I don't care what their brains or their riches or their beauty or any of their triumph may be . . they're unhappy and useless if they can't tell life from death.

CANTELUPE: (*interested in the digression*) Remember that the Church's claim has ever been to know that difference.

TREBELL: (*fastening to his subject again*) My point is this: A man's demand to know the exact structure of a fly's wing, and his assertion that it degrades any child in the street not to know such a thing, is a religious revival . . a token of spiritual hunger. What else can it be? And we commercialise our teaching!

CANTELUPE: I wouldn't have it so.

TREBELL: Then I'm offering you the foundation of a new Order of men and women who'll serve God by teaching His children. Now shall we finish the conversation in prose?

CANTELUPE: (*not to be put down*) What is the prose for God?

TREBELL: (*not to be put down either*) That's what we irreligious people are giving our lives to discover. (*He plunges into detail.*) I'm proposing to found about seventy-two new colleges, and of course, to bring the ones there are up to the new standard. Then we must gradually revise all teaching salaries in

government schools .. to a scale I have in mind. Then the course must be
compulsory and the training time doubled –
CANTELUPE: Doubled! Four years?
TREBELL: Well, a minimum of three .. a university course. Remember we're
turning a trade into a calling.
CANTELUPE: There's more to that than taking a degree.
TREBELL: I think so. You've fought for years for your tests and your atmosphere
with plain business men not able to understand such lunacy. Quite right ..
atmosphere's all that matters. If one and one don't make two by God's grace ..
CANTELUPE: Poetry again!
TREBELL: I beg your pardon. Well .. you've no further proof. If you can't plant
your thumb on the earth and your little finger on the pole star you know
nothing of distances. We must do away with text-book teachers.
    (CANTELUPE *is opening out a little in spite of himself.*)
CANTELUPE: I'm waiting for our opinions to differ
TREBELL: (*business-like again*) I'll send you a draft of the statutes I propose within
a week. Meanwhile shall I put the offer this way. If I accept your tests will you
accept mine?
CANTELUPE: What are yours?
TREBELL: I believe if one provides for efficiency one provides for the best part of
truth .. honesty of statement. I shall hope for a little more elasticity in your
dogmas than Becket or Cranmer or Laud would have allowed. When you've a
chance to re-formulate the reasons of your faith for the benefit of men teaching
mathematics and science and history and political economy, you won't neglect
to answer or allow for criticisms and doubts. I don't see why .. in spite of all
the evidence to the contrary .. such a thing as progress in a definite religious
faith is impossible.
CANTELUPE: Progress is a soiled word. (*And now he weighs his words.*) I shall be
very glad to accept on the Church's behalf control of the teaching of teachers
in these colleges.
TREBELL: Good. I want the best men.
CANTELUPE: You are surprisingly inexperienced if you think that creeds can ever
become mere forms except to those who have none.
TREBELL: But teaching – true teaching – is learning, and the wish to know is going
to prevail against any creed .. so I think. I wish you cared as little for the form
in which a truth is told as I do. On the whole, you see, I think I shall manage
to plant your theology in such soil this spring that the garden will be fruitful.
On the whole I'm a believer in Churches of all sorts and their usefulness to the
State. Your present use is out-worn. Have I found you in this the beginnings of
a new one?
CANTELUPE: The Church says: Thank you, it is a very old one.
TREBELL: (*winding up the interview*) To be sure, for practical politics our talk can

---

Becket or Cranmer or Laud: Archbishops of Canterbury, widely separated in period and in
creed, all put to death for treason or heresy; the difficulty in each case stemmed from
unshakable belief or doctrine which affronted the monarch (or the Parliament in the example of
Laud).

be whittled down to your accepting the secular solution for Primary Schools, if you're given these colleges under such statutes as you and I shall agree upon.

CANTELUPE: And the country will accept.

TREBELL: The country will accept any measure if there's enough money in it to bribe all parties fairly.

CANTELUPE: You expect very little of the constancy of my Church to her Faith, Mr Trebell.

TREBELL: I have only one belief myself. That is in human progress – yes, progress – over many obstacles and by many means. I have no ideals. I believe it is statesmanlike to use all the energy you find . . turning it into the nearest channel that points forward.

CANTELUPE: Forward to what?

TREBELL: I don't know . . and my caring doesn't matter. We do know . . and if we deny it it's only to be encouraged by contradiction . . that the movement is forward and with some gathering purpose. I'm friends with any fellow traveller.

> (CANTELUPE *has been considering him very curiously. Now he gets up to go.*)

CANTELUPE: I should like to continue our talk when I've studied your draft of the statutes. Of course the political position is favourable to a far more comprehensive bill than we had ever looked for . . and you've the advantage now of having held yourself very free from party ties. In fact not only will you give us the bill we shall most care to accept, but I don't know what other man would give us a bill we and the other side could accept at all.

TREBELL: I can let you have more Appropriation figures by Friday. The details of the Fabrics scheme will take a little longer.

CANTELUPE: In a way there's no such hurry. We're not in office yet.

TREBELL: When I'm building with figures I like to give the foundations time to settle. Otherwise they are the inexactest things.

CANTELUPE: (*smiling to him for the first time*) We shall have you finding Faith the only solvent of all problems some day.

TREBELL: I hope my mind is not afraid . . even of the Christian religion.

CANTELUPE: I am sure that the needs of the human soul . . be it dressed up in whatever knowledge . . do not alter from age to age . .

> (*He opens the door to find* WEDGECROFT *standing outside, watch in hand.*)

TREBELL: Hullo . . waiting?

WEDGECROFT: I was giving you two minutes by my watch. How are you, Cantelupe?

> (CANTELUPE, *with a gesture which might be mistaken for a bow, folds himself up.*)

TREBELL: Shall I bring you the figures on Friday . . that might save time.

> (CANTELUPE, *by taking a deeper fold in himself, seems to assent.*)

TREBELL: Will the afternoon do? Kent shall fix the hour.

CANTELUPE: (*with an effort*) Kent?

TREBELL: My secretary.

CANTELUPE: Friday. Any hour before five. I know my way.

(*The three phrases having meant three separate efforts,* CANTELUPE *escapes.* WEDGECROFT *has walked to the table, his brows a little puckered. Now* TREBELL *notices that* KENT'S *door is open; he goes quickly into the room and finds it empty. Then he stands for a moment irritable and undecided before returning.*)

TREBELL: Been here long?

WEDGECROFT: Five minutes . . more, I suppose.

TREBELL: Mrs O'Connell gone?

WEDGECROFT: To her dressmaker's.

TREBELL: Frances forgot she was coming and went out.

WEDGECROFT: Pretty little fool of a woman! D'you know her husband?

TREBELL: No.

WEDGECROFT: Says she's been in Ireland with him since we met at Shapters. He has trouble with his tenantry.

TREBELL: Won't he sell or won't they purchase?

WEDGECROFT: Curious chap. A Don at Balliol when I first knew him. Warped of late years . . perhaps by his marriage.

TREBELL: (*dismissing that subject*) Well . . how's Percival?

WEDGECROFT: Better this morning. I told him I'd seen you . . and in a little calculated burst of confidence what I'd reason to think you were after. He said you and he could get on though you differed on every point; but he didn't see how you'd pull with such a blasted weak-kneed lot as the rest of the Horsham's cabinet would be. He'll be up in a week or ten days.

TREBELL: Can I see him?

WEDGECROFT: You might. I admire the old man . . the way he sticks to his party, though they misrepresent now most things he believes in!

TREBELL: What a damnable state to arrive at . . doubly damned by the fact you admire it.

WEDGECROFT: And to think that at this time of day you should need instructing in the ethics of party government. But I'll have to do it.

TREBELL: Not now. I've been at ethics with Cantelupe.

WEDGECROFT: Certainly not now. What about my man with the stomach-ache at twelve o'clock sharp! Good-bye.

(*He is gone.* TREBELL *battles with uneasiness and at last mutters.* 'Oh . . why didn't she wait?' *Then the telephone bell rings. He goes quickly as if it were an answer to his anxiety.* 'Yes?' *Of course, it isn't* . . 'Yes.' *He paces the room, impatient, wondering what to do. The Maid comes in to announce* MISS DAVENPORT. LUCY *follows her. She has gained lately perhaps a little of the joy which was lacking and at least she brings now into this room a breath of very wholesome womanhood.*)

LUCY: It's very good of you to let me come; I'm not going to keep you more than three minutes.

TREBELL: Sit down.

Don: a tutor or fellow.
Balliol: one of the oldest colleges at Oxford.

(*Only women unused to busy men would call him rude.*)

LUCY: What I want to say is .. don't mind my being engaged to Walter. It shan't interfere with his work for you. If you want a proof that it shan't .. it was I got Aunt Julia to ask you to take him .. Though he didn't know .. so don't tell him that.

TREBELL: You weren't engaged then.

LUCY: I .. thought that we might be.

TREBELL: (*with cynical humour*) Which I'm not to tell him either?

LUCY: Oh, that wouldn't matter.

TREBELL: (*with decision*) I'll make sure you don't interfere.

LUCY: (*deliberately .. not to be treated as a child*) You couldn't, you know, if I wanted to.

TREBELL: Why, is Walter a fool?

LUCY: He's very fond of me, if that's what you mean?

(TREBELL *looks at her for the first time and changes his tone a little.*)

TREBELL: If it was what I meant .. I'm disposed to withdraw the suggestion.

LUCY: And, because I'm fond of his work as well, I shan't therefore ask him to tell me things .. secrets.

TREBELL: (*reverting to his humour*) It'll be when you're a year or two married that danger may occur .. in his desperate effort to make conversation.

(LUCY *considers this and him quite seriously.*)

LUCY: You're rather hard on women, aren't you .. just because they don't have the chances men do.

TREBELL: Do you want the chances?

LUCY: I think I'm as clever as most men I meet, though I know less, of course.

TREBELL: Perhaps I should have offered you the secretaryship instead.

LUCY: (*readily*) Don't you think I'm taking it in a way .. by marrying Walter? That's fanciful of course. But marriage is a very general and complete sort of partnership, isn't it? At least I'd like to make mine so.

TREBELL: He'll be more under your thumb in some things if you leave him free in others.

(*She receives the sarcasm in all seriousness and then speaks to him as she would to a child.*)

LUCY: Oh .. I'm not explaining what I mean quite well perhaps. Walter has been everywhere and done everything. He speaks three languages .. which all makes him an ideal private secretary.

TREBELL: Quite.

LUCY: Do you think he'd develop into anything else .. but for me?

TREBELL: So I have provided just a first step, have I?

LUCY: (*with real enthusiasm*) Oh, Mr Trebell, it's a great thing for us. There isn't anyone worth working under but you. You'll make him think and give him ideas instead of expecting them from him. But just for that reason he'd get so attached to you and be quite content to grow old in your shadow .. if it wasn't for me.

TREBELL: True .. I should encourage him in nothingness. What's more, I want extra brains and hands. It's not altogether a pleasant thing, is it .. the selfishness of the hard worked man?

LUCY: If you don't grudge your own strength, why should you be tender of other people's?

> (*He looks at her curiously.*)

TREBELL: *Your* ambition is making for only second-hand satisfaction though.

LUCY: What's a woman to do? She must work through men, mustn't she?

TREBELL: I'm told that's degrading .. the influencing of husbands and brothers and sons.

LUCY: (*only half humorously*) But what else is one to do with them? Of course, I've enough money to live on .. so I could take up some woman's profession .. What are you smiling at?

TREBELL: (*who has smiled very broadly*) As you don't mean to .. don't stop while I tell you.

LUCY: But I'd sooner get married. I want to have children. (*The words catch him and hold him. He looks at her reverently this time. She remembers she has transgressed convention; then, remembering that it is only convention, proceeds quite simply.*) I hope we shall have children.

TREBELL: I hope so.

LUCY: Thank you. That's the first kind thing you've said.

TREBELL: Oh .. you can do without compliments, can't you?

> (*She considers for a moment.*)

LUCY: Why have you been talking to me as if I were someone else?

TREBELL: (*startled*) Who else?

LUCY: No one particular. But you've shaken a moral fist so to speak. I don't think I provoked it.

TREBELL: It's a bad parliamentary habit. I apologise.

> (*She gets up to go.*)

LUCY: Now I shan't keep you longer .. you're always busy. You've been so easy to talk to. Thank you very much.

TREBELL: Why .. I wonder?

LUCY: I knew you would be or I shouldn't have come. You think Life's an important thing, don't you? That's priggish, isn't it? Good-bye. We're coming to dinner .. Aunt Julia and I. Miss Trebell arrived to ask us just as I left.

TREBELL: I'll see you down.

LUCY: What a waste of time for you. I know how the door opens.

> (*As she goes out* WALTER KENT *is on the way to his room. The two nod to each other like old friends.* TREBELL *turns away with something of a sigh.*)

KENT: Just come?

LUCY: Just going.

KENT: I'll see you at dinner.

LUCY: Oh, are you to be here? .. that's nice.

> (LUCY *departs as purposefully as she came.* KENT *hurries to* TREBELL, *whose thoughts are away again by now.*)

KENT: I haven't been long there and back, have I? The Bishop gave me these letters for you. He hasn't answered the last .. but I've his notes of what he means to say. He'd like them back tonight. He was just going out. I've one or two notes of what Evans said. Bit of a charlatan, don't you think?

TREBELL: Evans?

KENT: Well, he talked of his Flock. There are quite fifteen letters you'll have to deal with yourself, I'm afraid.

(TREBELL *stares at him: then, apparently, making up his mind . .*)

TREBELL: Ring up a messenger, will you . . I must write a note and send it.

KENT: Will you dictate?

TREBELL: I shall have done it while you're ringing . . it's only a personal matter. Then we'll start work.

(KENT *goes into his room and tackles the telephone there.* TREBELL *sits down to write the note, his face very set and anxious.*)

ACT III

At LORD HORSHAM'S *house in Queen Anne's Gate, in the evening, a week later. If rooms express their owners' character, the grey and black of* LORD HORSHAM'S *drawing room, the faded brocade of its furniture, reveal him as a man of delicate taste and somewhat thin intellectuality. He stands now before a noiseless fire, contemplating with a troubled eye either the pattern of the Old French carpet, or the black double doors of the library opposite, or the moulding on the Adams ceiling, which the flicker of all the candles casts into deeper relief. His grey hair and black clothes would melt into the decoration of his room, were the figure not rescued from such oblivion by the British white glaze of his shirt front and – to a sympathetic eye – by the loveable perceptive face of the man. Sometimes he looks at the sofa in front of him, on which sits* WEDGECROFT, *still in the frock coat of a busy day, depressed and irritable. With his back to them, on a sofa with its back to them, is* GEORGE FARRANT, *planted with his knees apart, his hands clasped, his head bent; very glum. And sometimes* HORSHAM *glances at the door, as if waiting for it to open. Then his gaze will travel back, up the long shiny black piano, with a volume of the Well Tempered Clavichord open on its desk, to where* CANTELUPE *is perched uncomfortably on the bench; paler than ever; more self-contained than ever, looking, to one who knows him as well as* HORSHAM *does, a little dangerous. So he returns to contemplation of the ceiling or the carpet. They wait there as men wait who have said all they want to say upon an unpleasant subject and yet cannot dismiss it. At last* FARRANT *breaks the silence.*

FARRANT: What time did you ask him to come, Horsham?

HORSHAM: Eh . . O'Connell? I didn't ask him directly. What time did you say, Wedgecroft?

WEDGECROFT: Any time after half past ten, I told him.

FARRANT: (*grumbling*) It's a quarter to eleven. Doesn't Blackborough mean to turn up at all?

Lord Horsham: the Earl of Horsham is a fictitious title (Horsham is a market town in Sussex).
Queen Anne's Gate: early eighteenth-century street bordering St James's Park and close to the Houses of Parliament. Despite the similarity of names, a considerable distance from Queen Anne Street, where Trebell lives.
Adams ceiling: the Adam brothers were eighteenth-century architects who designed many important public buildings and noble houses in London.

V *Waste*, act 3: the meeting of Justin O'Connell (J. Fisher White) and Trebell (Granville Barker). Others in this cartoon by Morrow are (from left) Frederick Lloyd as Farrant, Henry Vibart as Horsham, Dennis Eadie as Cantelupe (at piano), Trevor Lowe as Edmunds the butler (hands raised), and A. Holmes-Gore as Blackborough. Imperial Theatre, 1907.

HORSHAM: He was out of town .. my note had to be sent after him. I couldn't wire, you see.

FARRANT: No.

CANTELUPE: It was by the merest chance your man caught me, Cyril. I was taking the ten fifteen to Tonbridge and happened to go to James Street first for some papers.

(*The conversation flags again.*)

CANTELUPE: But since Mrs O'Connell is dead what is the excuse for a scandal?

(*At this unpleasant dig into the subject of their thoughts the three other men stir uncomfortably.*)

HORSHAM: Because the inquest is unavoidable .. apparently.

WEDGECROFT: (*suddenly letting fly*) I declare I'd have risked penal servitude and given a certificate, but just before the end O'Connell would call in old Fielding Andrews, who has moral scruples about everything – it's his trademark – and of course about this ..!

FARRANT: Was he told of the whole business?

WEDGECROFT: No .. O'Connell kept things up before him. Well .. the woman was dying.

HORSHAM: Couldn't you have kept the true state of the case from Sir Fielding?

WEDGECROFT: And been suspected of the malpractice myself if he'd found it out? .. which he would have done .. he's no fool. Well .. I thought of trying that ..

FARRANT: My dear Wedgecroft .. how grossly quixotic! You have a duty to yourself.

HORSHAM: (*rescuing the conversation from unpleasantness*) I'm afraid I feel that our position tonight is most irregular, Wedgecroft.

WEDGECROFT: Still if you can make O'Connell see reason. And if you all can't ..

(*He frowns at the alternative.*)

CANTELUPE: Didn't you say she came to you first of all?

WEDGECROFT: I met her one morning at Trebell's.

FARRANT: Actually *at* Trebell's!

WEDGECROFT: The day he came back from abroad.

FARRANT: Oh! No one seems to have noticed them together much at any time. My wife .. No matter!

WEDGECROFT: She tackled me as a doctor with one part of her trouble .. added she'd been with O'Connell in Ireland, which of course it turns out wasn't true .. asked me to help her. I had to say I couldn't.

HORSHAM: (*echoing rather than querying*) You couldn't.

FARRANT: (*shocked*) My dear Horsham!

WEDGECROFT: Well, if she'd told me the truth! .. No, anyhow I couldn't. I'm sure there was no excuse. One can't run these risks.

FARRANT: Quite right, quite right.

WEDGECROFT: There are men who do on one pretext or another.

FARRANT: (*not too shocked to be curious*) Are there really?

WEDGECROFT: Oh yes, men well known .. in other directions. I could give you four addresses .. but of course I wasn't going to give her one. Though there again .. if she'd told me the whole truth! .. My God, women are such fools!

And they prefer quackery . . look at the decent doctors they simply turn into charlatans. Though, there again, that all comes of letting a trade work mysteriously under the thumb of a benighted oligarchy . . which is beside the question. But one day I'll make you sit up on the subject of the Medical Council, Horsham.

(HORSHAM *assumes an impenetrable air of statesmanship.*)

HORSHAM: I know. Very interesting . . very important . . very difficult to alter the status quo.

WEDGECROFT: Then the poor little liar said she'd go off to an appointment with her dressmaker; and I heard nothing more till she sent for me a week later, and I found her almost too ill to speak. Even then she didn't tell me the truth! So, when O'Connell arrived, of course I spoke to him quite openly and all he told me in reply was that it wouldn't have been his child.

FARRANT: Poor devil!

WEDGECROFT: O'Connell?

FARRANT: Yes, of course.

WEDGECROFT: I wonder. Perhaps she didn't realise he'd been sent for . . or felt then she was dying and didn't care . . or lost her head. I don't know.

FARRANT: Such a pretty little woman!

WEDGECROFT: If I could have made him out and dealt with him, of course, I shouldn't have come to you. Farrant's known him even longer than I have.

FARRANT: I was with him at Harrow.

WEDGECROFT: So I went to Farrant first.

(*That part of the subject drops.* CANTELUPE, *who has not moved, strikes in again.*)

CANTELUPE: How was Trebell's guilt discovered?

FARRANT: He wrote her one letter which she didn't destroy. O'Connell found it.

WEDGECROFT: Picked it up from her desk . . it wasn't even locked up.

FARRANT: Not twenty words in it . . quite enough though.

HORSHAM: His habit of being explicit . . of writing things down . . I know!

(*He shakes his head, deprecating all rashness. There is another pause.* FARRANT, *getting up to pace about, breaks it.*)

FARRANT: Look here, Wedgecroft, one thing is worrying me. Had Trebell any foreknowledge of what she did and the risk she was running and could he have stopped it?

WEDGECROFT: (*almost ill-temperedly*) How could he have stopped it?

FARRANT: Because . . well, I'm not a casuist . . but I know by instinct when I'm up against the wrong thing to do; and if he can't be cleared on that point I won't lift a finger to save him.

HORSHAM: (*with nice judgment*) In using the term Any Foreknowledge, Farrant, you may be more severe on him than you wish to be.

(FARRANT, *unappreciative, continues.*)

FARRANT: Otherwise . . well, we must admit, Cantelupe, that if it hadn't been for the particular consequence of this it wouldn't be anything to be so mightily shocked about.

CANTELUPE: I disagree.

FARRANT: My dear fellow, it's our business to make laws and we know the difference of saying in one of 'em you *may* or you *must*. Who ever proposed to insist on pillorying every case of spasmodic adultery? One would never have done! Some of these attachments do more harm .. to the third party, I mean .. some less. But it's only when a ménage becomes socially impossible that a sensible man will interfere. (*he adds quite unnecessarily*) I'm speaking quite impersonally, of course.

CANTELUPE: (*as coldly as ever*) Trebell is morally responsible for every consequence of the original sin.

WEDGECROFT: That is a hard saying.

FARRANT: (*continuing his own remarks quite independently*) And I put aside the possibility that he deliberately helped her to her death to save a scandal because I don't believe it is a possibility. But if that were so I'd lift my finger to help him to his. I'd see him hanged with pleasure.

WEDGECROFT: (*settling this part of the matter*) Well, Farrant, to all intents and purposes he didn't know and he'd have stopped it if he could.

FARRANT: Yes, I believe that. But what makes you so sure?

WEDGECROFT: I asked him and he told me.

FARRANT: That's no proof.

WEDGECROFT: You read the letter that he sent her .. unless you think it was written as a blind.

FARRANT: Oh .. to be sure .. yes. I might have thought of that.

> (*He settles down again. Again no one has anything to say.*)

CANTELUPE: What is to be said to Mr O'Connell when he comes?

HORSHAM: Yes .. what exactly do you propose we shall say to O'Connell, Wedgecroft?

WEDGECROFT: Get him to open his oyster of a mind and ..

FARRANT: So it is and his face like a stone wall yesterday. Absolutely refused to discuss the matter with me!

CANTELUPE: May I ask, Cyril, why are we concerning ourselves with this wickedness at all?

HORSHAM: Just at this moment when we have official weight without official responsibility, Charles ..

WEDGECROFT: I wish I could have let Percival out of bed, but these first touches of autumn are dangerous to a convalescent of his age.

HORSHAM: But you saw him, Farrant .. and he gave you his opinion, didn't he?

FARRANT: Last night .. yes.

HORSHAM: I suppose it's a pity Blackborough hasn't turned up.

FARRANT: Never mind him.

HORSHAM: He gets people to agree with him. That's a gift.

FARRANT: Wedgecroft, what is the utmost O'Connell will be called upon to do for us .. for Trebell?

WEDGECROFT: Probably only to hold his tongue at the inquest tomorrow. As far as I know there's no one but her maid to prove that Mrs O'Connell didn't meet her husband some time in the summer. He'll be called upon to tell a lie or two by implication.

FARRANT: Cantelupe .. what does perjury to that extent mean to a Roman Catholic?

(CANTELUPE'S *face melts into an expression of mild amazement.*)

CANTELUPE: Your asking such a question shows that you would not understand my answer to it.

FARRANT: (*leaving the fellow to his subtleties*) Well, what about the maid?

WEDGECROFT: She may suspect facts but not names, I think. Why should they question her on such a point if O'Connell says nothing?

HORSHAM: He's really very late. I told .. (*He stops.*) Charles, I've forgotten that man's name again.

CANTELUPE: Edmunds, you said it was.

HORSHAM: Edmunds. Everybody's down at Lympne .. I've been left with a new man here and I don't know his name. (*He is very pathetic.*) I told him to put O'Connell in the library there. I thought that either Farrant or I might perhaps see him first and –

> (*At this moment* EDMUNDS *comes in, and, with that air of discreet tact which he considers befits the establishment of a Prime Minister, announces,* 'Mr O'Connell, my lord'. *As* O'CONNELL *follows him,* HORSHAM *can only try not to look too disconcerted.* O'CONNELL, *in his tightly buttoned frock coat, with his shaven face and close-cropped iron grey hair, might be mistaken for a Catholic priest; except that he has not also acquired the easy cheerfulness which professional familiarity with the mysteries of that religion seems to give. For the moment, at least, his features are so impassive that they may tell either of the deepest grief or the purest indifference; or it may be, merely of reticence on entering a stranger's room. He only bows towards* HORSHAM'S *half-proffered hand. With instinctive respect for the situation of this tragically made widower the men have risen and stand in various uneasy attitudes.*)

HORSHAM: Oh .. how do you do? Let me see .. do you know my cousin Charles Cantelupe? Yes .. we were expecting Russell Blackborough. Sir Henry Percival is ill. Do sit down.

> (O'CONNELL *takes the nearest chair and gradually the others settle themselves;* FARRANT *seeking an obscure corner. But there follows an uncomfortable silence, which* O'CONNELL *at last breaks.*)

O'CONNELL: You have sent for me, Lord Horsham?

HORSHAM: I hope that by my message I conveyed no impression of sending for you.

O'CONNELL: I am always in some doubt as to by what person or persons in or out of power this country is governed. But from all I hear you are at the present moment approximately entitled to send for me.

> (*The level music of his Irish tongue seems to give finer edge to his sarcasm.*)

HORSHAM: Well, Mr O'Connell .. you know our request before we make it.

O'CONNELL: Yes, I understand that if the fact of Mr Trebell's adultery with my wife were made as public as its consequences to her must be tomorrow, public opinion would make it difficult for you to include him in your cabinet.

Lympne: an ancient town near the Kent coast.

HORSHAM: Therefore we ask you .. though we have no right to ask you .. to consider the particular circumstances and forget the man in the statesman, Mr O'Connell.

O'CONNELL: My wife is dead. What have I to do at all with Mr Trebell as a man? As a statesman I am in any case uninterested in him.

> (*Upon this throwing of cold water,* EDMUNDS *returns to mention even more discreetly ..*)

EDMUNDS: Mr Blackborough is in the library, my lord.

HORSHAM: (*patiently impatient*) No, no .. here.

WEDGECROFT: Let me go.

HORSHAM: (*to the injured* EDMUNDS) Wait .. wait.

WEDGECROFT: I'll put him *au fait*. I shan't come back.

HORSHAM: (*gratefully*) Yes, yes. (*then to* EDMUNDS *who is waiting with perfect dignity*) Yes .. yes .. yes.

> (EDMUNDS *departs and* WEDGECROFT *makes for the library door, glad to escape.*)

O'CONNELL: If you are not busy at this hour, Wedgecroft, I should be grateful if you'd wait for me. I shall keep you, I think, but a very few minutes.

WEDGECROFT: (*in his most matter-of-fact tone*) All right, O'Connell.

> (*He goes into the library.*)

CANTELUPE: Don't you think, Cyril, it would be wiser to prevent your man coming into the room at all while we're discussing this?

HORSHAM: (*collecting his scattered tact*) Yes, I thought I had arranged that he shouldn't. I'm very sorry. He's a fool. However, there's no one else to come. Once more, Mr O'Connell .. (*He frames no sentence.*)

O'CONNELL: I am all attention, Lord Horsham.

> (CANTELUPE *with a self-denying effort has risen to his feet.*)

CANTELUPE: Mr O'Connell, I remain here almost against my will. I cannot think quite calmly about this double and doubly heinous sin. Don't listen to us while we make light of it. If we think of it as a political bother and ask you to smooth it away .. I am ashamed. But I believe I may not be wrong if I put it to you that, looking to the future and for the sake of your own Christian dignity, it may become you to be merciful. And I pray too .. I think we may believe .. that Mr Trebell is feeling need of your forgiveness. I have no more to say. (*He sits down again.*)

O'CONNELL: It may be. I have never met Mr Trebell.

HORSHAM: I tell you, Mr O'Connell, putting aside Party, that your country has need of this man just at this time.

> (*They hang upon* O'CONNELL'S *reply. It comes with deliberation.*)

O'CONNELL: I suppose my point of view must be an unusual one. I notice, at least, that twenty four hours and more has not enabled Farrant to grasp it.

FARRANT: For God's sake, O'Connell, don't be so cold-blooded. You have the life or death of a man's reputation to decide on.

O'CONNELL: (*with a cold flash of contempt*) That's a petty enough thing nowadays

---

put him au fait: bring him up to the minute.

it seems to me. There are so many clever men .. and they are all so alike ..
surely one will not be missed.

CANTELUPE: Don't you think that is only sarcasm, Mr O'Connell?

> (*The voice is so gently reproving that* O'CONNELL *must turn to him.*)

O'CONNELL: Will you please to make allowance, Lord Charles, for a mediaeval
scholar's contempt of modern government? *You* at least will partly understand
his horror as a Catholic at the modern superstitions in favour of popular
opinion and control which it encourages. You see, Lord Horsham, I am not a
party man, only a little less enthusiastic for the opposite cries than for his own.
You appealed very strangely to my feelings of patriotism for this country; but
you see even my own is – in the twentieth century – foreign to me. From my
point of view neither Mr Trebell, nor you, nor the men you have just defeated,
nor any discoverable man or body of men will make laws which matter .. or
differ in the slightest. You are all part of your age and you all voice – though in
separate keys, or even tunes they may be – only the greed and follies of your
age. That you should do this and nothing more is, of course, the democratic
ideal. You will forgive my thinking tenderly of the statesmanship of the *first*
Edward.

> (*The library door opens and* RUSSELL BLACKBOROUGH *comes
> in. He has on evening clothes, complicated by a long silk comforter
> and the motoring cap which he carries.*)

HORSHAM: You know Russell Blackborough.

O'CONNELL: I think not.

BLACKBOROUGH: How d'you do?

> (O'CONNELL *having bowed,* BLACKBOROUGH *having nodded,
> the two men sit down,* BLACKBOROUGH *with an air of great
> attention,* O'CONNELL *to continue his interrupted speech.*)

O'CONNELL: And you are as far from me in your code of personal morals as in
your politics. In neither do you seem to realise that such a thing as passion can
exist. No doubt you use the words Love and Hatred; but do you know that
love and hatred for principles or persons should come from beyond a man? I
notice you speak of forgiveness as if it were a penny in my pocket. You have
been endeavouring for these two days to rouse me from my indifference
towards Mr Trebell. Perhaps you are on the point of succeeding .. but I do not
know what you may rouse.

HORSHAM: I understand. We are much in agreement, Mr O'Connell. What can a
man be – who has any pretensions to philosophy – but helplessly indifferent to
the thousands of his fellow creatures whose fates are intertwined with his?

O'CONNELL: I am glad that you understand. But, again .. have I been wrong to
shrink from personal relations with Mr Trebell? Hatred is as sacred a
responsibility as love. And you will not agree with me when I say that
punishment can be the salvation of a man's soul.

---

the first Edward: Edward I raised the monarchy to new heights in the thirteenth century by his
military and political leadership and devotion to justice. This clear and slighting reference to
the current monarch, the seventh Edward, even coming from the mouth of an Irishman,
certainly did nothing to endear *Waste* to the censor.

FARRANT: (*with aggressive common sense*) Look here, O'Connell, if you're indifferent it doesn't hurt you to let him off. And if you hate him . . ! Well, one shouldn't hate people . . there's no room for it in this world.

CANTELUPE: (*quietly as ever*) We have some authority for thinking that the punishment of a secret sin is awarded by God secretly.

O'CONNELL: We have very poor authority, sir, for using God's name merely to fill up the gaps in an argument, though we may thus have our way easily with men who fear God more than they know Him. I am not one of those. Yes, Farrant, you and your like have left little room in this world except for the dusty roads on which I notice you beginning once more to travel. The rule of them is the same for all, is it not . . from the tramp and the labourer to the plutocrat in his car? This is the age of equality; and it's a fine practical equality . . the equality of the road. But you've fenced the fields of human joy and turned the very hillsides into hoardings. Commercial opportunity is painted on them, I think.

FARRANT: (*not to be impressed*) Perhaps it is, O'Connell. My father made his money out of newspapers and I ride in a motor car and you came from Holyhead by train. What has all that to do with it? Why can't you make up your mind? You know in this sort of case one talks a lot . . and then does the usual thing. You must let Trebell off and that's all about it.

O'CONNELL: Indeed. And do they still think it worth while to administer an oath to your witnesses?

> (*He is interrupted by the flinging open of the door and the triumphant right-this-time-anyhow voice in which* EDMUNDS *announces* 'Mr Trebell, my lord'. *The general consternation expresses itself through* HORSHAM, *who complains aloud and unreservedly.*)

HORSHAM: Good God . . No! Charles, I must give him notice at once . . he'll have to go. (*He apologises to the company.*) I beg your pardon.

> (*By this time* TREBELL *is in the room and has discovered the stranger, who stands to face him without emotion or anger.* BLACKBOROUGH'S *face wears the grimmest of smiles,* CANTELUPE *is sorry,* FARRANT *recovers from the fit of choking which seemed imminent and* EDMUNDS, *dimly perceiving by now some fly in the perfect amber of his conduct, departs. The two men still face each other.* FARRANT *is prepared to separate them should they come to blows, and indeed is advancing in that anticipation when* O'CONNELL *speaks.*)

O'CONNELL: I am Justin O'Connell.

TREBELL: I guess that.

O'CONNELL: There's a dead woman between us, Mr Trebell.

> (*A tremor sweeps over* TREBELL; *then he speaks simply.*)

TREBELL: I wish she had not died.

O'CONNELL: I am called upon by your friends to save you from the consequences of her death. What have you to say about that?

TREBELL: I have been wondering what sort of expression the last of your care for

---

hoardings: 'billboards' in American English.
Holyhead: port in north Wales where the Irish ferry lands.

her would find . . but not much. My wonder is at the power over me that has been given to something I despised.

 (*Only* O'CONNELL *grasps his meaning. But he, stirred for the first time and to his very depths, drives it home.*)

O'CONNELL: Yes . . If I wanted revenge I have it. She was a worthless woman. First my life and now yours! Dead because she was afraid to bear your child, isn't she?

TREBELL: (*in agony*) I'd have helped that if I could.

O'CONNELL: Not the shame . . not the wrong she had done me . . but just fear – fear of the burden of her womanhood. And because of her my children are bastards and cannot inherit my name. And I must live in sin against my Church, as – God help me – I can't against my nature. What are men to do when this is how women use the freedom we have given them? Is the curse of barrenness to be nothing to a man? And that's the death in life to which you gentlemen with your fine civilization are bringing us. I think we are brothers in misfortune, Mr Trebell.

TREBELL: (*far from responding*) Not at all, sir. If you wanted children you did the next best thing when she left you. My own problem is neither so simple nor is it yet anyone's business but my own. I apologise for alluding to it.

 (HORSHAM *takes advantage of the silence that follows.*)

HORSHAM: Shall we . .

O'CONNELL: (*measuring* TREBELL *with his eyes*) And by which shall I help you to a solution . . telling lies or the truth tomorrow?

TREBELL: (*roughly, almost insolently*) If you want my advice . . I should do the thing that comes more easily to you, or that will content you most. If you haven't yet made up your mind as to the relative importance of my work and your conscience, it's too late to begin now. Nothing you may do can affect *me*.

HORSHAM: (*fluttering fearfully into this strange dispute*) O'Connell . . if you and I were to join Wedgecroft . .

O'CONNELL: You value your work more than anything else in the world?

TREBELL: Have I anything else in the world?

O'CONNELL: Have you not? (*with grim ambiguity*) Then I am sorry for you, Mr Trebell. (*Having said all he had to say, he notices* HORSHAM.) Yes, Lord Horsham, by all means . .

 (*Then* HORSHAM *opens the library door and sees him safely through. He passes* TREBELL *without any salutation, nor does* TREBELL *turn after him; but when* HORSHAM *also is in the library and the door is closed, comments viciously.*)

TREBELL: The man's a sentimentalist . . like all men who live alone or shut away. (*then surveying his three glum companions, bursts out*) Well . . ? We can stop thinking of this dead woman, can't we? It's a waste of time.

FARRANT: Trebell, what did you want to come here for?

TREBELL: Because you thought I wouldn't. I knew you'd be sitting round, incompetent with distress, calculating to a nicety the force of a scandal . .

BLACKBOROUGH: (*with the firmest of touches*) Horsham has called some of us here to discuss the situation. I am considering my opinion.

TREBELL: You are not, Blackborough. You haven't recovered yet from the shock

of your manly feelings. Oh, cheer up. You know we're an adulterous and
sterile generation. Why should you cry out at a proof now and then of what's
always in the hearts of most of us?

FARRANT: (*plaintively*) Now, for God's sake, Trebell . . O'Connell has been going
on like that.

TREBELL: Well then . . think of what matters.

BLACKBOROUGH: Of you and your reputation in fact.

FARRANT: (*kindly*) Why do you pretend to be callous?
> (*He strokes* TREBELL'S *shoulder, who shakes him off impatiently.*)

TREBELL: Do you all mean to out-face the British Lion with me after tomorrow . .
dare to be Daniels?

BLACKBOROUGH: Bravado won't carry this off.

TREBELL: Blackborough . . it would immortalise you. I'll stand up in my place in
the House of Commons and tell everything that has befallen soberly and
seriously. Why should I flinch?

FARRANT: My dear Trebell, if your name comes out at the inquest –

TREBELL: If it does! . . whose has been the real offence against society . . hers or
mine? It's I who am most offended . . if I choose to think so.

BLACKBOROUGH: You seem to forget the adultery.

TREBELL: Isn't Death divorce enough for her? And . . oh, wasn't I right? . . What
do you start thinking of once the shock's over? Punishment . . revenge . .
uselessness . . waste of me.

FARRANT: (*with finality*) If your name comes out at the inquest, to talk of anything
but retirement from public life is perfect lunacy . . and you know it.
> (HORSHAM *comes back from the passage. He is a little distracted;
> then the more so at finding himself again in a highly-charged
> atmosphere.*)

HORSHAM: He's gone off with Wedgecroft.

TREBELL: (*including* HORSHAM *now in his appeal*) Does anyone think he knows
me now to be a worse man . . less fit, less able . . than he did a week ago?
> (*From the piano-stool comes* CANTELUPE'S *quiet voice.*)

CANTELUPE: Yes, Trebell . . I do.
> (TREBELL *wheels round at this and ceases all bluster.*)

TREBELL: On what grounds?

CANTELUPE: Unarguable ones.

HORSHAM: (*finding refuge again in his mantelpiece*) You know, he has gone off
without giving me his promise.

FARRANT: That's your own fault, Trebell.

HORSHAM: The fool says I didn't give him explicit instructions.

FARRANT: What fool?

HORSHAM: That man . . (*The name fails him.*) . . my new man. One of those
touches of Fate's little finger, really.
> (*He begins to consult the ceiling and the carpet once more.* TREBELL
> *tackles* CANTELUPE *with gravity.*)

---

dare to be Daniels: Daniel outfaced the Persian lions in the den, convinced of his rectitude in
God's eyes (Daniel 6).

TREBELL: I have only a logical mind, Cantelupe. I know that to make myself a capable man I've purged myself of all the sins .. I never was idle enough to commit. I know that if your God didn't make use of men, sins and all .. what would ever be done in the world? That one natural action, which the slight shifting of a social law could have made as negligible as eating a meal, can make me incapable .. takes the linch-pin out of one's brain, doesn't it?

HORSHAM: Trebell, we've been doing our best to get you out of this mess. Your remarks to O'Connell weren't of any assistance, and ..

> (CANTELUPE *stands up, so momentously that* HORSHAM'S *gentle flow of speech dries up.*)

CANTELUPE: Perhaps I had better say at once that, whatever hushing up you may succeed in, it will be impossible for me to sit in a cabinet with Mr Trebell.

> (*It takes even* FARRANT *a good half minute to recover his power of speech on this new issue.*)

FARRANT: What perfect nonsense, Cantelupe! I hope you don't mean that.

BLACKBOROUGH: Complication number one, Horsham.

FARRANT: (*working up his protest*) Why on earth not? You really mustn't drag your personal feelings and prejudices into important matters like this .. matters of state.

CANTELUPE: I think I have no choice, when Trebell stands convicted of a mortal sin, of which he has not even repented.

TREBELL: (*with bitterest cynicism*) Dictate any form of repentance you like .. my signature is yours.

CANTELUPE: Is this a matter for intellectual jugglery?

TREBELL: (*his defence failing at last*) I offered to face the scandal from my place in the House. That was mad wasn't it ..

> (BLACKBOROUGH – *his course mapped out* – *changes the tone of the discussion.*)

BLACKBOROUGH: Horsham, I hope Trebell will believe I have no personal feelings in this matter, but we may as well face the fact even now that O'Connell holding his tongue tomorrow won't stop gossip in the House, club gossip, gossip in drawing rooms. What do the Radicals really care so long as a scandal doesn't get into the papers! There's an inner circle with its eye on us.

FARRANT: Well, what does that care as long as scandal's its own copyright? Do you know, my dear father refused a peerage because he felt it meant putting blinkers on his best newspaper.

BLACKBOROUGH: (*a little subtly*) Still .. now you and Horsham are cousins, aren't you?

FARRANT: (*off the track and explanatory*) No, no .. my wife's mother ..

BLACKBOROUGH: I'm inaccurate, for I'm not one of the family circle myself. My money gets me here and any skill I've used in making it. It wouldn't keep me at a pinch. And Trebell .. (*He speaks through his teeth.*) .. do you think your accession to power in the party is popular at the best? Who is going to put out a finger to make it less awkward for Horsham to stick to you if there's a chance of your going under?

> (TREBELL *smiles at some mental picture he is making.*)

TREBELL: Can your cousins and aunts make it so awkward for you, Horsham?

HORSHAM: (*repaying humour with humour*) I bear up against their affectionate attentions.

TREBELL: But I quite understand how uncongenial I may be. What made you take up with me at all?

FARRANT: Your brains, Trebell.

TREBELL: He should have enquired into my character first, shouldn't he, Cantelupe?

CANTELUPE: (*with crushing sincerity*) Yes.

TREBELL: Oh, the old unnecessary choice .. Wisdom or Virtue. We all think we must make it .. and we all discover we can't. But if you've to choose between Cantelupe and me, Horsham, I quite see you've no choice.

(HORSHAM *now takes the field, using his own weapons.*)

HORSHAM: Charles, it seems to me that we are somewhat in the position of men who have overheard a private conversation. Do you feel justified in making public use of it?

CANTELUPE: It is not I who am judge. God knows I would not sit in judgment upon anyone.

TREBELL: Cantelupe, I'll take your personal judgment if you can give it me.

FARRANT: Good Lord, Cantelupe, didn't you sit in a cabinet with .. Well, we're not here to rake up old scandals.

BLACKBOROUGH: I am concerned with the practical issue.

HORSHAM: We know, Blackborough. (*Having quelled the interruption he proceeds.*) Charles, you spoke, I think, of a mortal sin.

CANTELUPE: In spite of your lifted eyebrows at the childishness of the word.

HORSHAM: Theoretically, we must all wish to guide ourselves by eternal truths. But you would admit, wouldn't you, that we can only deal with temporal things?

CANTELUPE: (*writhing slightly under the sceptical cross-examination*) There are divine laws laid down for our guidance .. I admit no disbelief in them.

HORSHAM: Do they place any time-limit to the effect of a mortal sin? If this affair were twenty years old would you do as you are doing? Can you forecast the opinion you will have of it six months hence?

CANTELUPE: (*positively*) Yes.

HORSHAM: Can you? Nevertheless I wish you had postponed your decision even till tomorrow.

(*Having made his point he looks round almost for approval.*)

BLACKBOROUGH: What had Percival to say on the subject, Farrant?

FARRANT: I was only to make use of his opinion under certain circumstances.

BLACKBOROUGH: So it isn't favourable to your remaining with us, Mr Trebell.

FARRANT: (*indignantly emerging from the trap*) I never said that.

(*Now* TREBELL *gives the matter another turn, very forcefully.*)

TREBELL: Horsham .. I don't bow politely and stand aside at this juncture as a gentleman should, because I want to know how the work's to be done if I leave you what I was to do.

BLACKBOROUGH: Are we so incompetent?

TREBELL: I daresay not. I want to know .. that's all.

CANTELUPE: Please understand, Mr Trebell, that I have in no way altered my good opinion of your proposals.

BLACKBOROUGH: Well, I beg to remind you, Horsham, that from the first I've reserved myself liberty to criticise fundamental points in the scheme.

HORSHAM: (*pacifically*) Quite so .. quite so.

BLACKBOROUGH: That nonsensical new standard of teachers' salaries for one thing .. you'd never pass it.

HORSHAM: Quite easily. It's an administrative point, so leave the legislation vague. Then, as the appropriation money falls in, the qualifications rise and the salaries rise. No one will object because no one will appreciate it but administrators past or future .. and they never cavil at money. (*He remains lost in the beauty of this prospect.*)

TREBELL: Will you take charge of the bill, Blackborough?

BLACKBOROUGH: Are you serious?

HORSHAM: (*brought to earth*) Oh no! (*He corrects himself smiling.*) I mean, my dear Blackborough, why not stick to the Colonies?

BLACKBOROUGH: You see, Trebell, there's still the possibility that O'Connell may finally spike your gun tomorrow. You realise that, don't you?

TREBELL: Thank you. I quite realise that.

CANTELUPE: Can nothing further be done?

BLACKBOROUGH: Weren't we doing our best?

HORSHAM: Yes .. if we were bending our thoughts to that difficulty now..

TREBELL: (*hardly*) May I ask you to interfere on my behalf no further?

FARRANT: My dear Trebell!

TREBELL: I assure you that I am interested in the Disestablishment Bill.
(*So they return readily enough from the more uncomfortable part of their subject.*)

BLACKBOROUGH: Well .. here's Farrant.

FARRANT: I'm no good. Give me Agriculture.

BLACKBOROUGH: Pity you're in the Lords, Horsham.

TREBELL: Horsham, I'll devil for any man you choose to name .. feed him sentence by sentence..

HORSHAM: That's impossible.

TREBELL: Well, what's to become of my bill? I want to know.

BLACKBOROUGH: (*casting his care on Providence*) We shall manage somehow. Why, if you had died suddenly .. or let us say, never been born..

TREBELL: Then, Blackborough .. speaking as a dying man .. if you go back on the integrity of this scheme, I'll haunt you. (*Having said this with some finality, he turns his back.*)

CANTELUPE: Cyril, I agree with what Trebell is saying. Whatever happens there must be no tampering with the comprehensiveness of the scheme. Remember you are in the hands of the extremists .. on both sides. I won't support a compromise on one .. nor will they on the other.

---

spike your gun: make you useless.
in the Lords: the Disestablishment Act is a money bill and must be introduced in the House of Commons.

HORSHAM: Well, I'll confess to you candidly, Trebell, that I don't know of any man available for this piece of work but you.

TREBELL: Then I should say it would be almost a relief to you if O'Connell tells on me tomorrow.

FARRANT: We seem to have got off that subject altogether. (*There comes a portentous tap at the door.*) Good Lord! .. I'm getting jumpy.

HORSHAM: Excuse me.

(*A note is handed to him through the half opened door; and obviously it is at EDMUNDS whom he frowns. Then he returns fidgeting for his glasses.*)

HORSHAM: Oh, it turns out .. I'm so sorry you were blundered in here, Trebell .. this man .. what's his name .. Edwards .. had been reading the papers and thought it was a cabinet council .. seemed proud of himself. This is from Wedgecroft .. scribbled in a messenger office. I never can read his writing .. it's like prescriptions. Can you?

(*It has gradually dawned on the three men and then on TREBELL what this note may have in it. FARRANT'S hand even trembles a little as he takes it. He gathers the meaning himself and looks at the others with a smile before he reads the few words aloud.*)

FARRANT: 'All right. He has promised.'

BLACKBOROUGH: O'Connell?

FARRANT: Thank God. (*He turns enthusiastically to TREBELL who stands rigid.*) My dear fellow .. I hope you know how glad I am.

CANTELUPE: I am very glad.

BLACKBOROUGH: Of course we're all very glad indeed, Trebell .. very glad we persuaded him.

FARRANT: That's dead and buried now, isn't it?

(*TREBELL moves away from them all and leaves them wondering. When he turns round his face is as hard as ever; his voice, if possible, harder.*)

TREBELL: But, Horsham, returning to the more important question .. you've taken trouble, and O'Connell's to perjure himself for nothing if you still can't get me into your child's puzzle .. to make the pretty picture that a cabinet should be.

(*HORSHAM looks at BLACKBOROUGH and scents danger.*)

HORSHAM: We shall all be glad, I am sure, to postpone any further discussion ..

TREBELL: I shall not.

BLACKBOROUGH: (*encouragingly*) Quite so, Trebell. We're on the subject, and it won't discount our pleasure that you're out of this mess, to continue it. This habit of putting off the hour of disagreement is .. well, Horsham, it's contrary to my business instincts.

TREBELL: If one time's as good as another for you .. this moment is better than most for me.

HORSHAM: (*a little irritated at the wantonness of this dispute*) There is nothing before us on which we are capable of coming to any decision .. in a technical sense.

BLACKBOROUGH: That's a quibble. (*Poor HORSHAM gasps.*) I'm not going to pretend either now or in a month's time that I think Trebell anything but a most dangerous acquisition to the party. I pay you a compliment in that, Trebell. Now, Horsham proposes that we should go to the Country when Disestablishment's through.

HORSHAM: It's the condition of Nonconformist support.

BLACKBOROUGH: One condition. Then you'd leave us, Trebell?

HORSHAM: I hope not.

BLACKBOROUGH: And carry with you the credit of our one big measure. Consider the effect upon our reputation with the Country.

FARRANT: (*waking to* BLACKBOROUGH'S *line of action*) Why on earth should you leave us Trebell? You've hardly been a Liberal, even in name.

BLACKBOROUGH: (*vigorously making his point*) Then what would be the conditions of your remaining? You're not a party man, Trebell. You haven't the true party feeling. You are to be bought. Of course you take your price in measures, not in money. But you are preeminently a man of ideas .. an expert. And a man of ideas is often a grave embarrassment to a government.

HORSHAM: And vice-versa .. vice-versa!

TREBELL: (*facing* BLACKBOROUGH *across the room*) Do I understand that you for the good of the Tory party .. just as Cantelupe for the good of his soul .. will refuse to sit in a cabinet with me.

BLACKBOROUGH: (*unembarrassed*) I don't commit myself to saying that.

CANTELUPE: No, Trebell .. it's that I must believe your work could not prosper .. in God's way.

> (TREBELL *softens to his sincerity.*)

TREBELL: Cantelupe, I quite understand. You may be right .. it's a very interesting question. Blackborough, I take it that you object first of all to the scheme that I'm bringing you.

BLACKBOROUGH: I object to those parts of it which I don't think you'll get through the House.

FARRANT: (*feeling that he must take part*) For instance?

BLACKBOROUGH: I've given you one already.

CANTELUPE: (*his eye on* BLACKBOROUGH) Understand there are things in that scheme we must stand or fall by.

> (*Suddenly* TREBELL *makes for the door.* HORSHAM *gets up concernedly.*)

TREBELL: Horsham, make up your mind tonight whether you can do with me or not. I have to see Percival again tomorrow .. we cut short our argument at the important point. Good-bye .. don't come down. Will you decide tonight?

HORSHAM: I have made up my own mind.

TREBELL: Is that sufficient?

HORSHAM: A collective decision is a matter of development.

TREBELL: Well, I shall expect to hear.

HORSHAM: By hurrying one only reaches a rash conclusion.

TREBELL: Then be rash for once and take the consequences. Good-night.

> (*He is gone before* HORSHAM *can compose another epigram.*)

BLACKBOROUGH: (*deprecating such conduct*) Lost his temper!

FARRANT: (*ruffling considerably*) Horsham, if Trebell is to be hounded out of your cabinet .. he won't go alone.

HORSHAM: (*bitter-sweet*) My dear Farrant .. I have yet to form my cabinet.

CANTELUPE: You are forming it to carry Disestablishment, are you not, Cyril? Therefore you will form it in the best interests of the best scheme possible.

HORSHAM: Trebell was and is the best man I know of for the purpose. I'm a little weary of saying that.

> (*He folds his arms and awaits further developments. After a moment* CANTELUPE *gets up as if to address a meeting.*)

CANTELUPE: Then if you would prefer not to include me .. I shall feel justified in giving independent support to a scheme I have great faith in. (*And he sits down again.*)

BLACKBOROUGH: (*impatiently*) My dear Cantelupe, if you think Horsham can form a Disestablishment cabinet to include Trebell and exclude you, you're vastly mistaken. I for one ..

FARRANT: But do both of you consider how valuable, how vital Trebell is to us just at this moment? The Radicals trust him ..

BLACKBOROUGH: They hate him.

HORSHAM: (*elucidating*) Their front bench hates him because he turned them out. The rest of them hate their front bench. After six years of office, who wouldn't?

BLACKBOROUGH: That's true.

FARRANT: Oh, of course, we must stick to Trebell, Blackborough.

> (BLACKBOROUGH *is silent; so* HORSHAM *turns his attention to his cousin.*)

HORSHAM: Well, Charles, I won't ask you for a decision now. I know how hard it is to accept the dictates of other men's consciences .. but a necessary condition of all political work; believe me.

CANTELUPE: (*uneasily*) You can form your cabinet without me, Cyril.

> (*At this* BLACKBOROUGH *charges down on them, so to speak.*)

BLACKBOROUGH: No, I tell you, I'm damned if he can. Leaving the whole high church party to blackmail all they can out of us and vote how they like! Here .. I've got my Yorkshire people to think of. I can bargain for them with you in a cabinet .. not if you've the pull of being out of it.

HORSHAM: (*with charming insinuation*) And have you calculated, Blackborough, what may become of us if Trebell has the pull of being out of it?

> (BLACKBOROUGH *makes a face.*)

BLACKBOROUGH: Yes .. I suppose he might turn nasty.

FARRANT: I should hope he would.

BLACKBOROUGH: (*tackling* FARRANT *with great ease*) I should hope he would consider the matter not from the personal, but from the political point of view .. as I am trying to do.

HORSHAM: (*tasting his epigram with enjoyment*) Introspection is the only bar to such an honourable endeavour. (BLACKBOROUGH *gapes.*) You don't suffer from that as – for instance – Charles here, does.

BLACKBOROUGH: (*pugnaciously*) D'you mean I'm just pretending not to attack him personally?

HORSHAM: (*safe on his own ground*) It's only a curious metaphysical point. Have you never noticed your distaste for the colour of a man's hair translate itself ultimately into an objection to his religious opinions .. or what not? I am sure – for instance – I could trace Charles's scruples about sitting in a cabinet with Trebell back to a sort of academic reverence for women generally which he possesses. I am sure I could .. if he were not probably now doing it himself. But this does not make the scruples less real, less religious, or less political. We must be humanly biased in expression .. or not express ourselves.

BLACKBOROUGH: (*whose thoughts have wandered*) The man's less of a danger than he was .. I mean he'll be alone. The Liberals won't have him back. He smashed his following there to come over to us.

FARRANT: (*giving a further meaning to this*) Yes, Blackborough, he did.

BLACKBOROUGH: To gain his own ends! Oh, my dear Horsham, can't you see that if O'Connell had blabbed tomorrow it really would have been a blessing in disguise? I don't pretend to Cantelupe's standard .. but there must be something radically wrong with a man who could get himself into such a mess as that .. now mustn't there? Ah! .. you have a fatal partiality for clever people. I tell you .. though this might be patched up .. Trebell would fail us in some other way before we were six months older.

> (*This speech has its effect; but* HORSHAM *looks at him a little sternly.*)

HORSHAM: And am I to conclude that you don't want Charles to change his mind?

BLACKBOROUGH: (*on another tack*) Farrant has not yet allowed us to hear Percival's opinion.

> (FARRANT *looks rather alarmed.*)

FARRANT: It has very little reference to the scandal.

BLACKBOROUGH: As that is at an end .. all the more reason we should hear it.

HORSHAM: (*ranging himself with* FARRANT) I called this quite informal meeting, Blackborough, only to dispose of the scandal, if possible.

BLACKBOROUGH: Well, of course, if Farrant chooses to insult Percival so gratuitously by burking his message to us..

> (*There is an unspoken threat in this.* HORSHAM *sees it and without disguising his irritation ..*)

HORSHAM: Let us have it, Farrant.

FARRANT: (*with a sort of puzzled discontent*) Well .. I never got to telling him of the O'Connell affair at all. He started talking to me .. saying that he couldn't for a moment agree to Trebell's proposals for the finance of his bill .. I couldn't get a word in edgeways. Then his wife came up..

> (HORSHAM *takes something in this so seriously that he actually interrupts.*)

HORSHAM: Does he definitely disagree? What is his point?

FARRANT: He says Disestablishment's a bad enough speculation for the party as it is.

BLACKBOROUGH: It is inevitable.

FARRANT: He sees that. But then he says .. to go to the Country again having

---

burking: suppressing or hushing up.

bolstered up Education and quarrelled with everybody will be bad enough . .
to go having spent fifty millions on it will dish us all for our lifetimes.

HORSHAM: What does he propose?

FARRANT: He'll offer to draft another bill and take it through himself. He says . .
do as many good turns as we can with the money . . don't put it all on one
horse.

BLACKBOROUGH: He's your man, Horsham. That's one difficulty settled.

> (HORSHAM'S *thoughts are evidently beyond* BLACKBOROUGH,
> *beyond the absent* PERCIVAL *even.*)

HORSHAM: Oh . . any of us could carry that sort of a bill.

> (CANTELUPE *has heard this last passage with nothing less than
> horror and pale anger, which he contains no longer.*)

CANTELUPE: I won't have this. I won't have this opportunity frittered away for
party purposes.

BLACKBOROUGH: (*expostulating reasonably*) My dear Cantelupe . . you'll get
whatever you think right for the Church to have. You carry a solid thirty eight
votes with you.

> (HORSHAM'S *smooth voice intervenes. He speaks with finesse.*)

HORSHAM: Percival, as an old campaigner, expresses himself very roughly. The
point is, that we are after all only the trustees of the party. If we know that a
certain step will decimate it . . clearly we have no right to take the step.

CANTELUPE: (*glowing to white heat*) Is this a time to count the consequences to
ourselves?

HORSHAM: (*unkindly*) By your action this evening, Charles, you evidently think
not. (*He salves the wound.*) No matter, I agree with you . . the bill should be a
comprehensive one, whoever brings it in.

BLACKBOROUGH: (*not without enjoyment of the situation*) Whoever brings it in
will have to knuckle under to Percival over its finance.

FARRANT: Trebell won't do that. I warned Percival.

HORSHAM: Then what did he say?

FARRANT: He only swore.

> (HORSHAM *suddenly becomes peevish.*)

HORSHAM: I think, Farrant, you should have given me this message before.

FARRANT: My dear Horsham, what had it to do with our request to O'Connell?

HORSHAM: (*scolding the company generally*) Well then, I wish he hadn't sent it. I
wish we were not discussing these points at all. The proper time for them is at
a cabinet meeting. And when we have actually assumed the responsibilities of
government . . then threats of resignation are not things to be played about
with.

FARRANT: Did you expect Percival's objection to the finance of the scheme?

HORSHAM: Perhaps . . perhaps. I knew Trebell was to see him last Tuesday. I
expect everybody's objections to any parts of every scheme to come at a time
when I am in a proper position to reconcile them . . not now.

> (*Having vented his grievances he sits down to recover.*
> BLACKBOROUGH *takes advantage of the ensuing pause.*)

BLACKBOROUGH: It isn't so easy for me to speak against Trebell, since he
evidently dislikes me personally as much as I dislike him . . but I'm sure I'm

doing my duty. Horsham .. here you have Cantelupe who won't stand in with
the man, and Percival who won't stand in with his measure, while I would
sooner stand in with neither. Isn't it better to face the situation now than take
trouble to form the most makeshift of cabinets, and if that doesn't go to pieces,
be voted down in the House by your own party?

> (*There is an oppressive silence.* HORSHAM *is sulky. The matter is
> beyond* FARRANT. CANTELUPE, *whose agonies have expressed
> themselves in slight writhings, at last, with an effort, writhes himself to
> his feet.*)

CANTELUPE: I think I am prepared to reconsider my decision.

FARRANT: That's all right then!

> (*He looks round wonderingly for the rest of the chorus to find that
> neither* BLACKBOROUGH *nor* HORSHAM *have stirred.*)

BLACKBOROUGH: (*stealthily*) Is it, Horsham?

HORSHAM: (*sotto voce*) Why did you ever make it?

> (BLACKBOROUGH *leaves him for* CANTELUPE.)

BLACKBOROUGH: You're afraid for the integrity of the bill.

CANTELUPE: It must be comprehensive .. that's vital.

BLACKBOROUGH: (*very forcefully*) I give you my word to support its integrity, if
you'll keep with me in persuading Horsham that the inclusion of Trebell in his
cabinet will be a blow to the whole Conservative Cause. Horsham, I implore
you not to pursue this short-sighted policy. All parties have made up their
minds to Disestablishment .. surely nothing should be easier than to frame a
bill which will please all parties.

FARRANT: (*at last perceiving the drift of all this*) But good Lord, Blackborough ..
now Cantelupe has come round and will stand in ..

BLACKBOROUGH: That's no longer the point. And what's all this nonsense about
going to the Country again next year?

HORSHAM: (*mildly*) After consulting me Percival said at Bristol ..

BLACKBOROUGH: (*quite unchecked*) I know. But if we pursue a thoroughly safe
policy and the bye-elections go right .. there need be no vote of censure
carried for three or four years. The Radicals want a rest with the Country and
they know it. And one has no right, what's more, to go wantonly plunging the
Country into the expenses of these constant general elections. It ruins trade.

FARRANT: (*forlornly sticking to his point*) What has all this to do with Trebell?

HORSHAM: (*thoughtfully*) Farrant, beyond what you've told us, Percival didn't
recommend me to throw him over.

FARRANT: No, he didn't .. that is, he didn't exactly.

HORSHAM: Well .. he didn't?

FARRANT: I'm trying to be accurate! (*Obviously their nerves are now on edge.*) He
said we should find him tough to assimilate – as he warned you.

> (HORSHAM, *with knit brows, loses himself in thought again.*
> BLACKBOROUGH *quietly turns his attention to* FARRANT.)

BLACKBOROUGH: Farrant, you don't seriously think that .. outside his
undoubted capabilities .. Trebell is an acquisition to the party?

FARRANT: (*unwillingly*) Perhaps not. But if you're going to chuck a man .. don't
chuck him when he's down.

BLACKBOROUGH: He's no longer down. We've got him O'Connell's promise and jolly grateful he ought to be. I think the least we can do is to keep our minds clear between Trebell's advantage and the party's.

CANTELUPE: (*from the distant music-stool*) And the party's and the country's.

BLACKBOROUGH: (*countering quite deftly*) Cantelupe, either we think it best for the country to have our party in power or we don't.

FARRANT: (*in judicious temper*) Certainly, I don't feel our responsibility towards him is what it was ten minutes ago. The man has other careers besides his political one.

BLACKBOROUGH: (*ready to praise*) Clever as paint at the Bar – best Company lawyer we've got.

CANTELUPE: It is not what he loses, I think .. but what we lose in losing him.
(*He says this so earnestly that* HORSHAM *pays attention.*)

HORSHAM: No, my dear Charles, let us be practical. If his position with us is to be made impossible it is better that he shouldn't assume it.

BLACKBOROUGH: (*soft and friendly*) How far are you actually pledged to him?
(HORSHAM *looks up with the most ingenuous of smiles.*)

HORSHAM: That's always such a difficult sort of point to determine, isn't it? He thinks he is to join us. But I've not yet been commanded to form a cabinet. If neither you – nor Percival – nor perhaps others will work with him .. what am I to do? (*He appeals to them generally to justify this attitude.*)

BLACKBOROUGH: He no longer thinks he's to join us .. it's the question he left us to decide.
(*He leaves* HORSHAM, *whose perplexity is diminishing.* FARRANT *makes an effort.*)

FARRANT: But the scandal won't weaken his position with us now. There won't be any scandal .. there won't, Blackborough.

HORSHAM: There may be. Though, I take it we're all guiltless of having mentioned the matter.

BLACKBOROUGH: (*very detached*) I've only known of it since I came into this house .. but I shall not mention it.

FARRANT: Oh, I'm afraid my wife knows. (*he adds hastily*) My fault .. my fault entirely.

BLACKBOROUGH: I tell you Rumour's electric.
(HORSHAM *has turned to* FARRANT *with a sweet smile and with the air of a man about to be relieved of all responsibility.*)

HORSHAM: What does she say?

FARRANT: (*as one speaks of a nice woman*) She was horrified.

HORSHAM: Of course. (*Once more he finds refuge and comfort on the hearthrug, to say, after a moment, with fine resignation*) I suppose I must let him go.

CANTELUPE: (*on his feet again*) Cyril!

HORSHAM: Yes, Charles?
(*With his query he turns an accusing eye on* CANTELUPE, *who is silenced.*)

BLACKBOROUGH: Have you made up your mind to that?

FARRANT: (*in great distress*) You're wrong, Horsham. (*then in greater*) That is .. I *think* you're wrong.

HORSHAM: I'd sooner not let him know tonight.

BLACKBOROUGH: But he asked you to.

HORSHAM: (*all show of resistance gone*) Did he? Then I suppose I must. (*He sighs deeply.*)

BLACKBOROUGH: Then I'll get back to Aylesbury.
> (*He picks up his motor-cap from the table and settles it on his head with immense aplomb.*)

HORSHAM: So late?

BLACKBOROUGH: Really one can get along quicker at night if one knows the road. You're in town, aren't you, Farrant? Shall I drop you at Grosvenor Square?

FARRANT: (*ungraciously*) Thank you.

BLACKBOROUGH: (*with a conqueror's geniality*) I don't mind telling you now, Horsham, that ever since we met at Shapters I've been wondering how you'd escape from this association with Trebell. Thought he was being very clever when he crossed the House to us! It's needed a special providence. You'd never have got a cabinet together to include him.

HORSHAM: (*with much intention*) No.

FARRANT: (*miserably*) Yes, I suppose that intrigue was a mistake from the beginning.

BLACKBOROUGH: Well, good-night. (*As he turns to go he finds* CANTELUPE *upright, staring very sternly at him.*) Good-night, Cantelupe.

CANTELUPE: From what motives have we thrown Trebell over?

BLACKBOROUGH: Never mind the motives if the move is the right one. (*Then he nods at* HORSHAM.) I shall be up again next week if you want me.
> (*And he flourishes out of the room; a man who has done a good hour's work.* FARRANT, *who has been mooning depressedly around, now backs towards the door.*)

FARRANT: In one way, of course, Trebell won't care a damn. I mean, he knows as well as we do that office isn't worth having .. he has never been a place-hunter. On the other hand .. what with one thing and the other .. Blackborough is a sensible fellow. I suppose it can't be helped.

HORSHAM: Blackborough will tell you so. Good-night.
> (*So* FARRANT *departs, leaving the two cousins together.*
> CANTELUPE *has not moved and now faces* HORSHAM *just as accusingly.*)

CANTELUPE: Cyril, this is tragic.

HORSHAM: (*more to himself than in answer*) Yes .. most annoying.

CANTELUPE: Lucifer, son of the morning! Why is it always the highest who fall?
> (HORSHAM *shies fastidiously at this touch of poetry.*)

HORSHAM: No, my dear Charles, let us above all things keep our mental balance. Trebell is a most capable fellow. I'd set my heart on having him with me .. he'll be most awkward to deal with in opposition. But we shall survive his loss and so would the country.

CANTELUPE: (*desperately*) Cyril, promise me there shall be no compromise over this measure.

HORSHAM: (*charmingly candid*) No .. no unnecessary compromise, I promise you.

CANTELUPE: (*with a sigh*) If we had done what we have done tonight in the right spirit! Blackborough was almost vindictive.

HORSHAM: (*smiling without amusement*) Didn't you keep thinking .. I did .. of that affair of his with Mrs Parkington .. years ago?

CANTELUPE: There was never any proof of it.

HORSHAM: No .. he bought off the husband.

CANTELUPE: (*uneasily*) His objections to Trebell were – political.

HORSHAM: Yours weren't.

CANTELUPE: (*more uneasily still*) I withdrew mine.

HORSHAM: (*with elderly reproof*) I don't think, Charles, you have the least conception of what a nicely balanced machine a cabinet is.

CANTELUPE: (*imploring comfort*) But should we have held together through Trebell's bill?

HORSHAM: (*a little impatient*) Perhaps not. But once I had them all round a table .. Trebell is very keen on office for all his independent airs .. he and Percival could have argued the thing out. However, it's too late now.

CANTELUPE: Is it?

> (*For a moment HORSHAM is tempted to indulge in the luxury of changing his mind; but he puts Satan behind him with a shake of the head.*)

HORSHAM: Well, you see .. Percival I can't do without. Now that Blackborough knows of his objections to the finance he'd go to him and take Chisholm and offer to back them up. I know he would .. he didn't take Farrant away with him for nothing. (*Then he flashes out rather shrilly.*) It's Trebell's own fault. He ought not to have committed himself definitely to any scheme until he was safely in office. I warned him about Percival .. I warned him not to be explicit. One cannot work with men who will make up their minds prematurely. No, I shall not change my mind. I shall write to him.

> (*He goes firmly to his writing desk leaving CANTELUPE forlorn.*)

CANTELUPE: What about a messenger?

HORSHAM: Not at this time of night. I'll post it.

CANTELUPE: I'll post it as I go.

> (*He seeks comfort again in the piano and this time starts to play, with one finger and some hesitation, the first bars of a Bach fugue.*
> *HORSHAM'S pen-nib is disappointing him and the letter is not easy to phrase.*)

HORSHAM: But I hate coming to immediate decisions. The administrative part of my brain always tires after half an hour. Does yours, Charles?

CANTELUPE: What do you think Trebell will do now?

HORSHAM: (*a little grimly*) Punish us all he can.

> (*On reaching the second voice in the fugue CANTELUPE'S virtuosity breaks down.*)

CANTELUPE: All that ability turned to destructiveness .. what a pity! That's the paradox of human activities ..

> (*Suddenly HORSHAM looks up and his face is lighted with a seraphic smile.*)

HORSHAM: Charles .. I wish we could do without Blackborough.

CANTELUPE: (*struck with the idea*) Well .. why not?

HORSHAM: Yes .. I must think about it. (*The both get up, cheered considerably.*) You won't forget this, will you?

CANTELUPE: (*the letter in* HORSHAM'S *hand accusing him*) No .. no. I don't think I have been the cause of your dropping Trebell, have I?

> (HORSHAM, *rid of the letter, is rid of responsibility and his charming equable self again. He comforts his cousin paternally.*)

HORSHAM: I don't think so. The split would have come when Blackborough checkmated my forming a cabinet. It would have pleased him to do that .. and he could have, over Trebell. But now that question's out of the way .. you won't get such a bad measure with Trebell in opposition. He'll frighten us into keeping it up to the mark, so to speak.

CANTELUPE: (*a little comforted*) But I shall miss one or two of those ideas..

HORSHAM: (*so pleasantly sceptical*) Do you think they'd have outlasted the second reading? Dullness in the country one expects. Dullness in the House one can cope with. But do you know, I have never sat in a cabinet yet that didn't greet anything like a new idea in chilling silence.

CANTELUPE: Well, I should regret to have caused you trouble, Cyril.

HORSHAM: (*his hand on the other's shoulder*) Oh .. we don't take politics so much to heart as that, I hope.

CANTELUPE: (*with sweet gravity*) I take politics very much to heart. Yes, I know what you mean .. but that's the sort of remark that makes people call you cynical. (HORSHAM *smiles as if at a compliment and starts with* CANTELUPE *towards the door.* CANTELUPE, *who would not hurt his feelings, changes the subject.*) By the bye, I'm glad we met this evening! Do you hear Aunt Mary wants to sell the Burford Holbein? Can she?

HORSHAM: (*taking as keen, but no keener, an interest in this than in the difficulty he has just surmounted*) Yes, by the will she can, but she mustn't. Dear me, I thought I'd put a stop to that foolishness. Well now, we must take that matter up very seriously..

> (*They go out talking arm in arm.*)

ACT IV

SCENE 1. *At* TREBELL'S *again; later, the same evening. His room is in darkness but for the flicker the fire makes and the streaks of moonlight between the curtains. The door is open, though, and you see the light of the lamp on the stairs. You hear his footstep too. On his way he stops to draw back the curtains of the passage-way window; the moonlight makes his face look very pale. Then he serves the curtains of his own window the same; flings it open, moreover, and stands looking out. Something below draws his attention. After leaning over the balcony with a short 'Hullo' he goes quickly downstairs again. In a minute* WEDGECROFT *comes up.* TREBELL *follows, pausing by the door a moment to light up the room.* WEDGECROFT *is radiant.*

TREBELL: (*with a twist of his mouth*) Promised, has he?

WEDGECROFT: Suddenly broke out as we walked along, that he liked the look of

you and that men must stand by one another nowadays against these women.
Then he said good-night and walked away.
TREBELL: Back to Ireland and the thirteenth century.
WEDGECROFT: After tomorrow.
TREBELL: (*taking all the meaning of tomorrow*) Yes. Are you in for perjury, too?
WEDGECROFT: (*his thankfulness checked a little*) No .. not exactly.
        (TREBELL *walks away from him.*)
TREBELL: It's a pity the truth isn't to be told, I think. I suppose the verdict will be
    murder.
WEDGECROFT: They won't catch the man.
TREBELL: You don't mean .. me.
WEDGECROFT: No, no .. my dear fellow.
TREBELL: You might, you know. But nobody seems to see this thing as I see it. If I
    were on that jury I'd say murder too and accuse .. so many circumstances,
    Gilbert, that we should go home .. and look in the cupboards. What a lumber
    of opinions we inherit and keep!
WEDGECROFT: (*humouring him*) Ought we to burn the house down?
TREBELL: Rules and regulations for the preservation of rubbish are the laws of
    England .. and I was adding to their number.
WEDGECROFT: And so you shall .. to the applause of a grateful country.
TREBELL: (*studying his friend's kindly encouraging face*) Gilbert, it is not so much
    that you're an incorrigible optimist .. but why do you subdue your mind to
    flatter people into cheerfulness?
WEDGECROFT: I'm a doctor, my friend.
TREBELL: You're a part of our tendency to keep things alive by hook or by crook
    .. not a spark but must be carefully blown up. The world's old and tired; it
    dreads extinction. I think I disapprove .. I think I've more faith.
WEDGECROFT: (*scolding him*) Nonsense .. you've the instinct to preserve your
    life as everyone else has .. and I'm here to show you how.
TREBELL: (*beyond the reach of his kindness*) I assure you that these two days while
    you've been fussing around O'Connell – bless your kind heart – I've been
    waiting events, indifferent enough to understand his indifference.
WEDGECROFT: Not indifferent.
TREBELL: Lifeless enough already, then. (*Suddenly a thought strikes him.*) D'you
    think it was Horsham and his little committee persuaded O'Connell?
WEDGECROFT: On the contrary.
TREBELL: So you need not have let them into the secret?
WEDGECROFT: No.
TREBELL: Think of that.
        (*He almost laughs; but* WEDGECROFT *goes on quite innocently.*)
WEDGECROFT: Yes .. I'm sorry.
TREBELL: Upsetting their moral digestion for nothing.
WEDGECROFT: But when O'Connell wouldn't listen to us we had to rope in the
    important people.
TREBELL: With their united wisdom. (*Then he breaks away again into great
    bitterness.*) No .. what do they make of this woman's death? I saw them in that
    room, Gilbert, like men seen through the wrong end of a telescope. D'you

think if the little affair with Nature .. her offence and mine against the conveniences of civilization .. had ended in my death too .. then they'd have stopped to wonder at the misuse and waste of the only force there is in the world .. come to think of it, there is no other .. than this desire for expression .. in words .. or through children. Would they have thought of that and stopped whispering about the scandal?

    (*Through this* WEDGECROFT *has watched him very gravely.*)

WEDGECROFT: Trebell .. if the inquest tomorrow *had* put you out of action..

TREBELL: Should I have grown a beard and travelled abroad and after ten years timidly tried to climb my way back into politics? When public opinion takes its heel from your face it keeps it for your finger-tips. After twenty years to be forgiven by your more broad-minded friends and tolerated as a dotard by a new generation..

WEDGECROFT: Nonsense, What age are you now .. forty-six .. forty-seven?

TREBELL: Well .. let's instance a good man. Gladstone had done his best work by sixty-five. Then he began to be popular. Think of his last years of oratory.

    (*He has gone to his table and now very methodically starts to tidy his papers,* WEDGECROFT *still watching him.*)

WEDGECROFT: You'd have had to thank Heaven for a little that there were more lives than one to lead.

TREBELL: That's another of your faults, Gilbert .. it's a comfort just now to enumerate them. You're an anarchist .. a kingdom to yourself. You make little treaties with Truth and with Beauty, and what can disturb you? I'm a part of the machine I believe in. If my life as I've made it is to be cut short .. the rest of me shall walk out of the world and slam the door .. with the noise of a pistol shot.

WEDGECROFT: (*concealing some uneasiness*) Then I'm glad it's not to be cut short. You and your cabinet rank and your Disestablishment Bill!

    (TREBELL *starts to enjoy his secret.*)

TREBELL: Yes .. our minds have been much relieved within the last half hour, haven't they?

WEDGECROFT: I scribbled Horsham a note in a messenger office and sent it as soon as O'Connell had left me.

TREBELL: He'd be glad to get that.

WEDGECROFT: He has been most kind about the whole thing.

TREBELL: Oh, he means well.

WEDGECROFT: (*following up his fancied advantage*) But, my friend .. suicide whilst of unsound mind would never have done .. The hackneyed verdict hits the truth, you know.

TREBELL: You think so?

WEDGECROFT: I don't say there aren't excuses enough in this miserable world, but fundamentally .. no sane person will destroy life.

TREBELL: (*his thoughts shifting their plane*) Was she so very mad? I'm not thinking of her own death.

WEDGECROFT: Don't brood, Trebell. Your mind isn't healthy yet about her and –

TREBELL: And my child.

(*Even* WEDGECROFT'S *kindness is at fault before the solemnity of this.*)

WEDGECROFT: Is that how you're thinking of it?

TREBELL: How else? It's very inexplicable . . this sense of fatherhood. (*The eyes of his mind travel down – what vista of possibilities. Then he shakes himself free.*) Let's drop the subject. To finish the list of shortcomings, you're a bit of an artist too . . therefore I don't think you'll understand.

WEDGECROFT: (*successfully decoyed into argument*) Surely an artist is a man who understands.

TREBELL: Everything about life, but not life itself. That's where art fails a man.

WEDGECROFT: That's where everything but living fails a man. (*drifting into introspection himself*) Yes, it's true. I can talk cleverly and I've written a book . . but I'm barren. (*Then the healthy mind re-asserts itself.*) No, it's not true. Our thoughts are children . . and marry and intermarry. And we're peopling the world . . not badly.

TREBELL: Well . . either life is too little a thing to matter or it's so big that such specks of it as we may be are of no account. These are two points of view. And then one has to consider if death can't be sometimes the last use made of life.

(*There is a tone of menace in this which recalls* WEDGECROFT *to the present trouble.*)

WEDGECROFT: I doubt the virtue of sacrifice . . or the use of it.

TREBELL: How else could I tell Horsham that my work matters? Does he think so now? . . not he.

WEDGECROFT: You mean if they'd had to throw you over?

(*Once again* TREBELL *looks up with that secretive smile.*)

TREBELL: Yes . . if they'd had to.

WEDGECROFT: (*unreasonably nervous, so he thinks*) My dear fellow, Horsham would have thought it was the shame and disgrace if you'd shot yourself after the inquest. That's the proper sentimental thing for you so-called strong men to do on like occasions. Why, if your name were to come out tomorrow, your best meaning friends would be sending you pistols by post, requesting you to use them like a gentleman. Horsham would grieve over ten dinner-tables in succession and then return to his philosophy. One really mustn't waste a life trying to shock polite politicians. There'd even be a suspicion of swagger in it.

TREBELL: Quite so . . the bomb that's thrown at their feet must be something otherwise worthless.

(FRANCES *comes in quickly, evidently in search of her brother. Though she has not been crying, her eyes are wide with grief.*)

FRANCES: Oh, Henry . . I'm so glad you're still up. (*She notices* WEDGECROFT.) How d'you do, Doctor?

TREBELL: (*doubling his mask of indifference*) Meistersinger's over early.

FRANCES: Is it?

TREBELL: Not much past twelve yet.

FRANCES: (*the little gibe lost on her*) It was Tristan tonight. I'm quite upset. I

Tristan: it is characteristic of the subtle irony of *Waste* that Frances has been to *Tristan und Isolde*, Wagner's tragic opera about sexual passion and adultery, just after Amy has played out her own *liebestod*.

heard just as I was coming away . . Amy O'Connell's dead. (*Both men hold their breath.* TREBELL *is the first to find control of his and give the cue.*)

TREBELL: Yes . . Wedgecroft has just told me.

FRANCES: She was only taken ill last week . . it's so extraordinary. (*She remembers the doctor.*) Oh . . have you been attending her?

WEDGECROFT: Yes.

FRANCES: I hear there's to be an inquest.

WEDGECROFT: Yes.

FRANCES: But what has been the matter?

TREBELL: (*sharply forestalling any answer*) You'll know tomorrow.

FRANCES: (*the little snub almost bewildering her*) Anything private? I mean . .

TREBELL: No . . I'll tell you. Don't make Gilbert repeat a story twice . . He's tired with a good day's work.

WEDGECROFT: Yes . . I'll be getting away.

> (FRANCES *never heeds this flash of a further meaning between the two men.*)

FRANCES: And I meant to have gone to see her today. Was the end very sudden? Did her husband arrive in time?

WEDGECROFT: Yes.

FRANCES: They didn't get on . . he'll be frightfully upset.

> (TREBELL *resists a hideous temptation to laugh.*)

WEDGECROFT: Good-night, Trebell.

TREBELL: Good-night, Gilbert. Many thanks.

> (*There is enough of a caress in* TREBELL'S *tone to turn* FRANCES *towards their friend, a little remorseful for treating him so casually, now as always.*)

FRANCES: He's always thanking you. You're always doing things for him.

WEDGECROFT: Good-night. (*seeing the tears in her eyes*) Oh, don't grieve.

FRANCES: One shouldn't be sorry when people die, I know. But she liked me more than I liked her . . (*This time* TREBELL *does laugh, silently.*) . . so I somehow feel in her debt and unable to pay now.

TREBELL: (*an edge on his voice*) Yes . . people keep on dying at all sorts of ages, in all sorts of ways. But we seem never to get used to it . . narrow-minded as we are.

WEDGECROFT: Don't you talk nonsense.

TREBELL: (*one note sharper yet*) One should occasionally test one's sanity by doing so. If we lived in the logical world we like to believe in, I could also prove that black was white. As it is . . there are more ways of killing a cat than hanging it.

WEDGECROFT: Had I better give you a sleeping draught?

FRANCES: Are you doctoring him for once? Henry, have you at last managed to overwork yourself?

TREBELL: No . . I started the evening by a charming little dinner at the Van Meyer's . . sat next to Miss Grace Cutler, who is writing a *vie intime* of Louis Quinze and engaged me with anecdotes of the same.

FRANCES: A champion of her sex, whom I do not like.

---

vie intime: private life of Louis XV.

WEDGECROFT: She's writing such a book to prove that women are equal to anything.

> (*He goes towards the door and* FRANCES *goes with him.* TREBELL *never turns his head.*)

TREBELL: I shall not come and open the door for you .. but mind you shut it.

> (FRANCES *comes back.*)

FRANCES: Henry .. this is dreadful about that poor little woman.

TREBELL: An unwelcome baby was arriving. She got some quack to kill her.

> (*These exact words are like a blow in the face to her, from which, being a woman of brave common sense, she does not shrink.*)

TREBELL: What do you say to that?

> (*She walks away from him, thinking painfully.*)

FRANCES: She had never had a child. There's the common-place thing to say .. Ungrateful little fool! But..

TREBELL: If you had been in her place?

FRANCES: (*subtly*) I have never made the mistake of marrying. She grew frightened, I suppose. Not just physically frightened. How can a man understand?

TREBELL: The fear of life .. do you think it was .. which is the beginning of all evil?

FRANCES: A woman must choose what her interpretation of life is to be .. as a man must too in his way .. as you and I have chosen, Henry.

TREBELL: (*asking from real interest in her*) Was yours a deliberate choice and do you never regret it?

FRANCES: (*very simply and clearly*) Perhaps one does nothing quite deliberately and for a definite reason. My state has its compensations .. if one doesn't value them too highly. I've travelled in thought over all this question. You mustn't blame a woman for wishing not to bear children. But .. well, if one doesn't like the fruit one mustn't cultivate the flower. And I suppose that saying condemns poor Amy .. condemned her to death .. (*then her face hardens as she concentrates her meaning*) and brands most men as .. let's unsentimentally call it *illogical*, doesn't it?

> (*He takes the thrust in silence.*)

TREBELL: Did you notice the light in my window as you came in?

FRANCES: Yes .. in both as I got out of the cab. Do you want the curtains drawn back?

TREBELL: Yes .. don't touch them.

> (*He has thrown himself into his chair by the fire. She lapses into thought again.*)

FRANCES: Poor little woman.

TREBELL: (*in deep anger*) Well, if women will be little and poor..

> (*She goes to him and slips an arm over his shoulder.*)

FRANCES: What is it you're worried about .. if a mere sister may ask?

TREBELL: (*into the fire*) I want to think. I haven't thought for years.

FRANCES: Why, you have done nothing else.

TREBELL: I've been working out problems in legal and political algebra.

FRANCES: You want to think of *yourself.*

TREBELL: Yes.

FRANCES: (*gentle and ironic*) Have you ever, for one moment, thought in that sense of anyone else?

TREBELL: Is that a complaint?

FRANCES: The first in ten years' housekeeping.

TREBELL: No, I never have .. but I've never thought selfishly either.

FRANCES: That's a paradox I don't quite understand.

TREBELL: Until women do they'll remain where they are .. and what they are.

FRANCES: Oh, I know you hate us.

TREBELL: Yes, dear sister, I'm afraid I do. And I hate your influence on men .. compromise, tenderness, pity, lack of purpose. Women don't know the values of things, not even their own value.

    (*For a moment she studies him, wonderingly.*)

FRANCES: I'll take up the counter-accusation tomorrow. Now I'm tired and I'm going to bed. If I may insult you by mothering you, so should you. You look tired and I've seldom seen you.

TREBELL: I'm waiting up for a message.

FRANCES: So late?

TREBELL: It's a matter of life and death.

FRANCES: Are you joking?

TREBELL: Yes. If you want to spoil me find me a book to read.

FRANCES: What will you have?

TREBELL: Huckleberry Finn. It's on a top shelf towards the end somewhere .. or should be.

    (*She finds the book. On her way back with it she stops and shivers.*)

FRANCES: I don't think I shall sleep tonight. Poor Amy O'Connell!

TREBELL: (*curiously*) Are you afraid of death?

FRANCES: (*with humorous stoicism*) It will be the end of me, perhaps.

    (*She gives him the book, with its red cover; the '86 edition, a boy's friend evidently. He fingers it familiarly.*)

TREBELL: Thank you. Mark Twain's a jolly fellow. He has courage .. comic courage. That's what's wanted. Nothing stands against it. You belittle yourself by laughing .. then all this world and the last and the next grow little too .. and so you grow great again. Switch off some light, will you?

FRANCES: (*clicking off all but his reading lamp*) So?

TREBELL: Thanks. Good-night, Frankie.

    (*She turns at the door, with a glad smile.*)

FRANCES: Good-night. When did you last use that nursery name?

    (*Then she goes, leaving him still fingering the book, but looking into the fire and far beyond. Behind him through the open window one sees how cold and clear the night is.*)

SCENE 2. *At eight in the morning he is still here. His lamp is out, the fire is out and the book laid aside. The white morning light penetrates every crevice of the room and shows every line on* TREBELL'S *face. The spirit of the man is strained past all reason. The door opens suddenly and* FRANCES *comes in, troubled, nervous. Interrupted in her dressing, she has put on some wrap or other.*

FRANCES: Henry . . Simpson says you've not been to bed all night.
>(*He turns his head and says with inappropriate politeness –*)

TREBELL: No. Good morning.

FRANCES: Oh, my dear . . what is wrong?

TREBELL: The message hasn't come . . and I've been thinking.

FRANCES: Why don't you tell me. (*He turns his head away.*) I think you haven't the right to torture me.

TREBELL: Your sympathy would only blind me towards the facts I want to face.
>(SIMPSON, *the maid, undisturbed in her routine, brings in the morning's letters.* FRANCES *rounds on her irritably.*)

FRANCES: What is it, Simpson?

SIMPSON: The letters, Ma'am.
>(TREBELL *is on his feet at that.*)

TREBELL: Ah . . I want them.

FRANCES: (*taking the letters composedly enough*) Thank you.
>(SIMPSON *departs and* TREBELL *comes to her for his letters. She looks at him with baffled affection.*)

FRANCES: Can I do nothing? Oh, Henry!

TREBELL: Help me to open my letters.

FRANCES: Don't you leave them to Mr Kent?

TREBELL: Not this morning.

FRANCES: But there are so many.

TREBELL: (*for the first time lifting his voice from its dull monotony*) What a busy man I was.

FRANCES: Henry . . you're a little mad.

TREBELL: Do you find me so? That's interesting.

FRANCES: (*with the ghost of a smile*) Well . . maddening.
>(*By this time he is sitting at his table; she near him watching closely. They halve the considerable post and start to open it.*)

TREBELL: We arrange them in three piles . . personal . . political . . and preposterous.

FRANCES: This is an invitation . . The Anglican League.

TREBELL: I can't go.
>(*She looks sideways at him as he goes on mechanically tearing the envelopes.*)

FRANCES: I heard you come upstairs about two o'clock.

TREBELL: That was to dip my head in water. Then I made an instinctive attempt to go to bed . . got my tie off even.

FRANCES: (*her anxiety breaking out.*) If you'd tell me that you're only ill . .

TREBELL: (*forbiddingly commonplace*) What's that letter? Don't fuss . . and remember that abnormal conduct is sometimes quite rational.
>(FRANCES *returns to her task with misty eyes.*)

FRANCES: It's from somebody whose son can't get into something.

TREBELL: The third heap . . Kent's . . the preposterous. (*talking on with steady monotony*) But I saw it would not do to interrupt that logical train of thought which reached definition about half past six. I had then been gleaning until you came in.

FRANCES: (*turning the neat little note in her hand*) This is from Lord Horsham. He writes his name small at the bottom of the envelope.

TREBELL: (*without a tremor*) Ah . . give it me.

> (*He opens this as he has opened the others, carefully putting the envelope to one side. FRANCES has ceased for the moment to watch him.*)

FRANCES: That's Cousin Robert's handwriting. (*She puts a square envelope at his hand.*) Is a letter marked private from the Education Office political or personal?

> (*By this he has read HORSHAM'S letter twice. So he tears it up and speaks very coldly.*)

TREBELL: Either. It doesn't matter.

> (*In the silence her fears return.*)

FRANCES: Henry, it's a foolish idea . . I suppose I have it because I hardly slept for thinking of her. Your trouble is nothing to do with Amy O'Connell, is it?

TREBELL: (*his voice strangled in his throat*) Her child should have been my child too.

FRANCES: (*her eyes open, the whole landscape of her mind suddenly clear*) Oh, I . . no, I didn't think so . . but . .

TREBELL: (*dealing his second blow as remorselessly as dealt to him*) Also I'm not joining the new cabinet, my dear sister.

FRANCES: (*her thoughts rushing now to the present – the future*) Not! Because of . . ? Do people know? Will they . . ? You didn't . . ?

> (*As mechanically as ever he has taken up Cousin Robert's letter and, in some sense, read it. Now he recapitulates, meaninglessly, that his voice may just deaden her pain and his own.*)

TREBELL: Robert says . . that we've not been to see them for some time . . but that now I'm a greater man than ever I must be very busy. The vicarage has been painted and papered throughout and looks much fresher. Mary sends you her love and hopes you have no return of the rheumatism. And he would like to send me the proof sheets of his critical commentary on First Timothy . . for my alien eye might possibly detect some logical lapses. Need he repeat to me his thankfulness at my new attitude upon Disestablishment . . or assure me again that I have his prayers. Could we not go and stay there only for a few days? Possibly his opinion –

> (*She has borne this cruel kindness as long as she can and she breaks out . .*)

FRANCES: Oh . . don't . . don't!

> (*He falls from his seeming callousness to the very blankness of despair.*)

TREBELL: No, we'll leave that . . and the rest . . and everything.

> (*Her agony passes.*)

FRANCES: What do you mean to do?

TREBELL: There's to be no public scandal.

FRANCES: Why has Lord Horsham thrown you over then . . or hasn't that anything to do with it?

TREBELL: It has to do with it.

FRANCES: (*lifting her voice; some tone returning to it*) Unconsciously . . I've known for years that this sort of thing might happen to you.

TREBELL: Why?

FRANCES: Power over men and women and contempt for them! Do you think they don't take their revenge sooner or later?

TREBELL: Much good may it do them!

FRANCES: Human nature turns against you . . by instinct . . in self-defence.

TREBELL: And my own human-nature!

FRANCES: (*shocked into great pity, by his half articulate pain*) Yes . . you must have loved her, Henry . . in some odd way. I'm sorry for you both.

TREBELL: I'm hating her now . . as a man can only hate his own silliest vices.

FRANCES: (*flashing into defence*) That's wrong of you. If you thought of her only as a pretty little fool . . Bearing your child . . all her womanly life belonged to you . . and for that time there was no other sort of life in her. So she became what you thought her.

TREBELL: That's not true.

FRANCES: It's true enough . . it's true of men towards women. You can't think of them through generations as one thing and then suddenly find them another.

TREBELL: (*hammering at his fixed idea*) She should have brought that child into the world.

FRANCES: You didn't love her enough!

TREBELL: I didn't love her at all.

FRANCES: Then why should she value your gift?

TREBELL: For its own sake.

FRANCES: (*turning away*) It's hopeless . . you don't understand.

TREBELL: (*helpless; almost like a deserted child*) I've been trying to . . all through the night.

FRANCES: (*turning back enlightened a little*) That's more the trouble then than the cabinet question?

> (*He shakes himself to his feet and begins to pace the room; his keenness coming back to him, his brow knitting again with the delight of thought.*)

TREBELL: Oh . . as to me against the world . . I'm fortified with comic courage. (*then turning on her like any examining professor*) Now which do you believe . . that Man is the reformer, or that the Time brings forth such men as it needs and lobster-like can grow another claw?

FRANCES: (*watching this new mood carefully*) I believe that you'll be missed from Lord Horsham's cabinet.

TREBELL: The hand-made statesman and his hand-made measure! They were out of place in that pretty Tory garden. Those men are the natural growth of the time. Am I?

FRANCES: Just as much. And wasn't your bill going to be such a good piece of work? That can't be thrown away . . wasted.

TREBELL: Can one impose a clever idea upon men and women? I wonder.

FRANCES: That rather begs the question of your very existence, doesn't it?
>   (*He comes to a standstill.*)
TREBELL: I know.
>   (*His voice shows her that meaning in her words and beyond it a threat.*
>   *She goes to him, suddenly shaking with fear.*)
FRANCES: Henry, I didn't mean that.
TREBELL: You think I've a mind to put an end to that same?
FRANCES: (*belittling her fright*) No .. for how unreasonable ..
TREBELL: In view of my promising past. I've stood for success, Fanny; I still stand
>   for success. I could still do more outside the cabinet than the rest of them,
>   inside, will do. But suddenly I've a feeling the work would be barren. (*His eyes*
>   *shift beyond her; beyond the room.*) What is it in your thoughts and actions
>   which makes them bear fruit? Something that the roughest peasant may have
>   in common with the best of us intellectual men .. something that a dog might
>   have. It isn't successful cleverness.
>   (*She stands .. his trouble beyond her reach.*)
FRANCES: Come now .. you've done very well with your life.
TREBELL: Do you know how empty I feel of all virtue at this moment?
>   (*He leaves her. She must bring him back to the plane on which she can*
>   *help him.*)
FRANCES: We must think what's best to be done .. now .. and for the future.
TREBELL: Why, I could go on earning useless money at the Bar .. think how nice
>   that would be. I could blackmail the next judgeship out of Horsham. I think I
>   could even smash his Disestablishment Bill .. and perhaps get into the next
>   Liberal cabinet and start my own all over again, with necessary modifications. I
>   shan't do any such things.
FRANCES: No one knows about you and poor Amy?
TREBELL: Half a dozen friends. Shall I offer to give evidence at the inquest this
>   morning?
FRANCES: (*with a little shiver*) They'll say bad enough things about her without
>   your blackening her good name.
>   (*Without warning, his anger and anguish break out again.*)
TREBELL: All she had .. all there is left of her! She was a nothingness .. silly ..
>   vain. And I gave her this power over me!
>   (*He is beaten, exhausted. Now she goes to him, motherlike.*)
FRANCES: My dear, listen to me for a little. Consider that as a sorrow and put it
>   behind you. And think now .. whatever love there may be between us has
>   neither hatred nor jealousy in it, has it, Henry? Since I'm not a mistress or a
>   friend but just the likest fellow-creature to you .. perhaps.
TREBELL: (*putting out his hand for hers*) Yes, my sister. What I've wanted to feel
>   for vague humanity has been what I should have felt for you .. if you'd ever
>   made a single demand on me.
>   (*She puts her arms round him; able to speak.*)
FRANCES: Let's go away somewhere .. I'll make demands. I need refreshing as
>   much as you. My joy of life has been withered in me .. oh, for a long time
>   now. We must kiss the earth again .. take interest in common things, common
>   people. There's so much of the world we don't know. There's air to breathe

everywhere. Think of the flowers in a Tyrol valley in the early spring. One can walk for days, not hurrying, as soon as the passes are open. And the people are kind. There's Italy .. there's Russia full of simple folk. When we've learned to be friends with them we shall both feel so much better.

TREBELL: (*shaking his head, unmoved*) My dear sister .. I should be bored to death. The life contemplative and peripatetic would literally bore me into a living death.

FRANCES: (*letting it be a fairy tale*) Is your mother the Wide World nothing to you? Can't you open your heart like a child again?

TREBELL: No, neither to the beauty of Nature nor the particular human animals that are always called a part of it. I don't even see them with your eyes. I'm a son of the anger of Man at men's foolishness, and unless I've that to feed upon .. ! (*Now he looks at her, as if for the first time wanting to explain himself, and his voice changes.*) Don't you know that when a man cuts himself shaving, he swears? When he loses a seat in the cabinet he turns inward for comfort .. and if he only finds there a spirit which should have been born, but is dead .. what's to be done then?

FRANCES: (*in a whisper*) You mustn't think of that woman..

TREBELL: I've reasoned my way through life..

FRANCES: I see how awful it is to have the double blow fall.

TREBELL: (*the wave of his agony rising again*) But here's something in me which no knowledge touches .. some feeling .. some power which should be the beginning of new strength. But it has been killed in me unborn before I had learnt to understand .. and that's killing me.

FRANCES: (*crying out*) Why .. why did no woman teach you to be gentle? Why did you never believe in any woman? Perhaps even I am to blame..

TREBELL: The little fool, the little fool .. why did she kill my child? What did it matter what I thought her? We were committed together to that one thing. Do you think I didn't know that I was heartless and that she was socially in the wrong? But what did Nature care for that? And Nature has broken us.

FRANCES: (*clinging to him as he beats the air*) Not you. She's dead, poor girl .. but not you.

TREBELL: Yes .. that's the mystery no one need believe till he has dipped in it. The man bears the child in his soul as the woman carries it in her body.

> (*There is silence between them, till she speaks low and tonelessly, never loosing his hand.*)

FRANCES: Henry, I want your promise that you'll go on living till .. till..

TREBELL: Don't cry, Fanny, that's very foolish.

FRANCES: Till you've learnt to look at all this calmly. Then I can trust you.

> (TREBELL *smiles, not at all grimly.*)

TREBELL: But, you see, it would give Horsham and Blackborough such a shock if I shot myself .. it would make them think about things.

FRANCES: (*with one catch of wretched laughter*) Oh, my dear, if shooting's wanted .. shoot them. Or I'll do it for you.

> (*He sits in his chair just from weariness. She stands by him, her hand still grasping his.*)

TREBELL: You see, Fanny, as I said to Gilbert last night .. our lives are our own

and yet not our own. We understand living for others and dying for others.
The first is easy .. it's a way out of boredom. To make the second popular we
had to invent a belief in personal resurrection. Do you think we shall ever
understand dying in the sure and certain hope that it really doesn't matter ..
that God is infinitely economical and wastes perhaps less of the power in us
after our death than men do while we live?

FRANCES: I want your promise, Henry.

TREBELL: You know I never make promises .. it's taking oneself too seriously.
Unless indeed one has the comic courage to break them too. I've upset you
very much with my troubles. Don't you think you'd better go and finish
dressing? (*She doesn't move.*) My dear .. you don't propose to hold my right
hand so safely for years to come. Even so, I still could jump out of a window.

FRANCES: I'll trust you, Henry.

> (*She looks into his eyes and he does not flinch. Then, with a final grip
> she leaves him. When she is at the door he speaks more gently than
> ever.*)

TREBELL: Your own life is sufficient unto itself, isn't it?

FRANCES: Oh yes. I can be pleasant to talk to and give good advice through
the years that remain. (*Instinctively she rectifies some little untidiness in the
room.*) What fools they are to think they can run that government without
you!

TREBELL: Horsham will do his best. (*then, as for the second time she reaches the
door*) Don't take away my razors, will you? I only use them for shaving.

FRANCES: (*almost blushing*) I half meant to .. I'm sorry. After all, Henry, just
because they are forgetting in personal feelings what's best for the country ..
it's your duty not to. You'll stand by and do what you can, won't you?

TREBELL: (*his queer smile returning, in contrast to her seriousness*)
Disestablishment. It's a very interesting problem. I must think it out.

FRANCES: (*really puzzled*) What do you mean?

> (*He gets up with a quick movement of strange strength, and faces her.
> His smile changes into a graver gladness.*)

TREBELL: Something has happened .. in spite of me. My heart's clean again. I'm
ready for fresh adventures.

FRANCES: (*with a nod and answering gladness*) That's right.

> (*So she leaves him, her mind at rest. For a minute he does not move.
> When his gaze narrows it falls on the heaps of letters. He carries them
> carefully into WALTER KENT'S room and arranges them as carefully
> on his table. On his way out he stops for a moment; then with a sudden
> movement bangs the door.*)

SCENE 3. *Two hours later the room has been put in order. It is even more full of
light and the shadows are harder than usual. The doors are open, showing you
KENT'S door still closed. At the big writing table in TREBELL'S chair sits
WEDGECROFT, pale and grave, intent on finishing a letter. FRANCES comes to
find him. For a moment she leans on the table silently, her eyes half closed. You
would say a broken woman. When she speaks it is swiftly, but tonelessly.*

FRANCES: Lord Horsham is in the drawing room .. and I can't see him, I really
    can't. He has come to say he is sorry .. and I should tell him that it is his fault,
    partly. I know I should .. and I don't want to. Won't you go in? What are you
    writing?
>   (WEDGECROFT, *with his physicianly pre-occupation, can attend,*
>   *understand, sympathise, without looking up at her.*)
WEDGECROFT: Never mind. A necessary note .. to the Coroner's office. Yes, I'll
    see Horsham.
FRANCES: I've managed to get the pistol out of his hand. Was that wrong ..
    oughtn't I to have touched it?
WEDGECROFT: Of course you oughtn't. You must stay away from the room. I'd
    better have locked the door.
FRANCES: (*pitifully*) I'm sorry .. but I couldn't bear to see the pistol in his hand. I
    won't go back. After all he's not there in the room, is he? But how long do you
    think the spirit stays near the body .. how long? When people die gently of age
    or weakness .. But when the spirit and body are so strong and knit together
    and all alive as his ..
WEDGECROFT: (*his hand on hers*) Hush .. hush.
FRANCES: His face is very eager .. as if it still could speak. I know that.
>   (MRS FARRANT *comes through the open doorway. FRANCES*
>   *hears her steps and turning falls into her outstretched arms to cry there.*)
FRANCES: Oh, Julia!
JULIA: Oh my dear Fanny! I came with Cyril Horsham .. I don't think Simpson
    even saw me.
FRANCES: I can't go in and talk to him.
JULIA: He'll understand. But I heard you come in here ..
WEDGECROFT: I'll tell Horsham.
>   (*He has finished and addressed his letter, so he goes out with it.*
>   FRANCES *lifts her head. These two are in accord and can speak their*
>   *feelings without disguise or preparation.*)
FRANCES: Julia, Julia .. isn't it unbelievable?
JULIA: I'd give .. oh, what wouldn't I give to have it undone!
FRANCES: I knew he meant to .. and yet I thought I had his promise. If he really
    meant to .. I couldn't have stopped it, could I?
JULIA: Walter sent to tell me and I sent round to ..
FRANCES: Walter came soon after, I think. Julia, I was in my room .. it was nearly
    breakfast time .. when I heard the shot. Oh .. don't you think it was cruel of
    him?
JULIA: He had a right to. We must remember that.
FRANCES: You say that easily of my brother .. you wouldn't say it of your
    husband.
>   (*They are apart by this.* JULIA FARRANT *goes to her gently.*)
JULIA: Fanny .. will it leave you so very lonely?
FRANCES: Yes .. lonelier than you can ever be. You have children. I'm just
    beginning to realise ..
JULIA: (*leading her from the mere selfishness of sorrow*) There's loneliness of the
    spirit, too.

FRANCES: Ah, but once you've tasted the common joys of life .. once you've proved all your rights as a man or woman..

JULIA: Then there are subtler things to miss. As well be alone like you, or dead like him, without them .. I sometimes think.

FRANCES: (*responsive, lifted from egoism, reading her friend's mind*) You demand much.

JULIA: I wish that he had demanded much of any woman.

FRANCES: You know how this misery began? That poor little wretch .. she's lying dead too. They're both dead together now. Do you think they've met ..?

> (JULIA *grips both her hands and speaks very steadily to help her friend back to self control.*)

JULIA: George told me as soon as he was told. I tried to make him understand my opinion, but he thought I was only shocked.

FRANCES: I was sorry for her. Now I can't forgive her either.

JULIA: (*angry, remorseful, rebellious*) When will men learn to know one woman from another?

FRANCES: (*with answering bitterness*) When will all women care to be one thing rather than the other?

> (*They are stopped by the sound of the opening of* KENT'S *door.*
> WALTER *comes from his room, some papers from his table held listlessly in one hand. He is crying, undisguisedly, with a child's grief.*)

KENT: Oh .. am I in your way ..?

FRANCES: I didn't know you were still here, Walter.

KENT: I've been going through the letters as usual. I don't know why, I'm sure. They won't have to be answered now .. will they?

> (WEDGECROFT *comes back, grave and tense.*)

WEDGECROFT: Horsham has gone. He thought perhaps you'd be staying with Miss Trebell for a bit.

JULIA: Yes, I shall be.

WEDGECROFT: I must go too .. it's nearly eleven.

FRANCES: To the *other* inquest?

> (*This stirs her two listeners to something of a shudder.*)

WEDGECROFT: Yes.

JULIA: (*in a low voice*) It will make no difference now .. I mean .. still nothing need come out? We needn't know why he .. why he did it.

WEDGECROFT: When he talked to me last night, and I didn't know what he was talking of..

FRANCES: He was waiting this morning for Lord Horsham's note..

JULIA: (*in real alarm*) Oh, it wasn't because of the cabinet trouble .. you must persuade Cyril Horsham of that. You haven't told him .. he's so dreadfully upset as it is. I've been swearing it had nothing to do with that.

WEDGECROFT: (*cutting her short, bitingly*) Has a time ever come to you when it was easier to die than to go on living? Oh .. I told Lord Horsham just what I thought.

> (*He leaves them, his own grief unexpressed.*)

FRANCES: (*listlessly*) Does it matter why?

JULIA: Need there be more suffering and reproaches? It's not as if even grief would do any good. (*suddenly with nervous caution*) Walter, you don't know, do you?

>   (WALTER *throws up his tear-marked face and a man's anger
>   banishes the boyish grief.*)

KENT: No, I don't know why he did it .. and I don't care. And grief is no use. I'm angry .. just angry at the waste of a good man. Look at the work undone .. think of it! Who is to do it! Oh .. the waste ..!

APPENDIX A: BARKER'S COSTUME NOTE FOR *THE MARRYING OF ANN LEETE*

This note was included as an opening stage direction in the 1902 typescript of *The Marrying of Ann Leete*, which Granville Barker prepared for the Stage Society production. (The typescript is now housed in the British Library, C.116.g.8.) He omitted it from the 1909 printed text, and it is published here for the first time, with the permission of the Society of Authors. Since the note explains the dramatist's attitude to the social background of the play, its value goes beyond the dressing and coiffuring of the actors.

Opie is not the Mrs Opie of the play but John Opie (1761–1807), 'the Cornish wonder', a self-taught painter whose portraits strove for realistic depiction rather than the classical dignity characteristic of the eighteenth century. His self-portrait in the National Portrait Gallery in London shows him with untied and unpowdered hair, natural in color and styling, just covering the ears and reaching the top of the collar in back. In the front it is brushed forward and down over the forehead. *The Lady's Monthly Museum* was a miscellany magazine which began publication in 1798 and which included color-tinted fashion plates each month. Barker adapted his three dresses from the issues of October 1799 (3:312), July 1800 (5:72), and November 1798 (1:397).

A NOTE UPON THE COSTUME AND MANNER OF WEARING THE HAIR

I make this note here because the period seems to have been in costume as well as in manners a transitional one, one in which not only a man's nature, but his opinions were very much to be known by the fashions he followed. The general tendency, of course, was from the ornate to the simple; silks and satins were going out, and the rougher, more sober-looking materials coming in.

Men's hair was worn long, tied back or in a queue; for full dress, frizzed and powdered; wigs in imitation apparently by older men whose hair had failed them; this for social conservatives. But those pretending to advanced and republican opinions forswore powder, cut their hair fairly short and kept it none too tidily. By some, slight side whiskers were cultivated. Sir George Leete should wear a wig; so should Carnaby, though perhaps not such an obvious one. Lord John Carp and Tatton – their long hair tied back and in the first act powdered. George has his hair unpowdered and untied (see Opie's portrait of himself). The two clergymen should wear wigs. Mr Crowe – I think – his own hair, close-cropped.

Lace was no longer worn. Three cornered hats had passed almost out of use; tall hats of beaver and felt, bell-topped with wide flapping brims took their place. For the younger men, breeches now came below the knee to be met by boots, worn when walking or on a journey; for the house, pumps tied with ribbon. Buckles were much out of fashion.

Except for Court functions hoops and powder had been abandoned by the ladies for some years past. The prevailing style was a sort of bastard Greek. Morning dress ran into the extreme of modesty; evening dress into quite the other extreme. Muslin, cambric, and such like were the most used stuffs.

Powder was not worn at all in the fashionable world (there may have been a very few exceptions to this rule). Hair was curled into ringlets, filleted, turbaned, in many cases entirely covered. If a woman had a good head of hair she would naturally exhibit it, but I think that in many cases women's hair had been so ruined by the powder treatment that it was not fit to be seen.

I copy below three fashion plate descriptions from the 'Lady's Monthly Museum'.

Morning dress 1799. Helmet bonnet of straw or chip, white or lilac muslin crown, tied under chin with yellow handkerchief, orange bow. Cambric muslin dress drawn close round the neck, buttoned half way then forming a train; trimmed with orange coloured epaulets on the shoulders and small puckered cuffs trimmed with lace. Orange coloured gloves and shoes.

Morning dress 1800. A plain blue muslin gown. A tippet of white muslin plain over the breast and shoulders and drawn round the neck. Braces of the same fixed on each shoulder, crossing on the breast and tied on the right side, the whole trimmed with lace.

Full dress 1798. A white gown wrapping over one side, cut in an angle, drawn up a little with white cord and tassels, so as to be equal to the opening on the other and forming a point in front. Headdress – bandeaux of muslin, crossing each other.

APPENDIX B: THE REVISED OPENING SCENE OF *WASTE* (1927)

Granville Barker completely rewrote *Waste* in 1926. (The revision was published the next year, though not performed until 1936.) As I explain in the textual note, the new version has substantial differences from the original; the first scene of act 1 was altered the most, and even though Trebell does not appear it will serve well as an example. Aside from the changes in style and a general updating of the references, Barker made the scene more accessible by clarifying the political backdrop. He thus attacked one of the chief difficulties of the original opening, which often seems impenetrable. How he accomplished this should be of interest to any director of the 1907 text.

A few mechanical matters: Horsham is no longer an earl; Lord Charles now spells his surname Cantilupe; Lady Davenport is elevated in rank and called Countess Mortimer in the cast list; her daughter Julia, now a thorough snob, has the title of Lady. Barker abandoned his earlier habit of the two-dot ellipsis and consistently used three dots in this version, which I have reproduced.

WASTE (1927 version)

ACT I

SCENE 1. *Shapters, which is thirty miles or so from London, is a typically English house. Its kitchens are Tudor; it faces the world looking seventeenth century; from the garden you would call it Queen Anne. But the sanctity of age is upon even this last and not least ruthless of its patchings and scrappings, and the effect of the whole is beautiful.*

It is a Sunday evening in summer, and in one of the smaller sitting-rooms LADY JULIA FARRANT *has been playing to some of her week-end guests. She is a woman of fifty; she plays very well for an amateur; she has just launched into Chopin's shortest prelude (Op. 28, No. 20). Her listeners are her mother,* LADY MORTIMER, *a genuinely old lady and dowered with all the beauty of age;* FRANCES TREBELL, *a woman in the fifties who has nothing smart about her, her face showing more thought than feeling;* MRS [AMY] O'CONNELL, *a charming woman, who takes care she does charm;* LUCY DAVENPORT, *a girl in her twenties, more grave than gay; and* WALTER KENT, *just such a young man as the average English father would wish his son to be. They are all attentive. The room is not so brightly lit but that one can see in the moonlight – for the curtains are drawn back and the long windows are open – a paved garden set in a courtyard of some sort, and lights in the rooms beyond. The room is evidently a woman's room, and its owner's taste, one*

would guess, was formed in the school of Burne-Jones. Having finished the prelude,
LADY JULIA *shuts the piano and, after a moment, leaves it.*

KENT: Oh . . . was that 'God save the King'? I'd have stood up.
LADY MORTIMER: Thank you, my dear Julia.
JULIA: Thank you for listening, mamma. That's the polite reply, isn't it?
FRANCES: Chopin for a finish, Julia . . . after John Sebastian!
JULIA: Allow us that much emotional indulgence.
KENT: Romantic moonrise into a starlit sky.
LUCY: Five marks to you for an epigram, Walter.
KENT: Don't be so frightfully surprised when I say something clever.
FRANCES: I prefer the stars.
AMY: And I'd been wondering what was missing.

> (LADY JULIA *finds herself a chair; it happens not to be very near*
> AMY O'CONNELL.)

JULIA: Don't you like Bach? Why didn't you say so?
AMY: I respect the old gentleman . . . but he makes me feel a demi-semi-quaver of a
creature.

> (LADY JULIA *catches sight of a book – a quite severe-looking book*
> *– upon* LUCY DAVENPORT'S *lap.*)

JULIA: Lucy . . . were you reading while I played?
LUCY: No, indeed, Cousin Julia. But I keep hold of it . . . it soaks in up the arm.
AMY: I spent half a fugue trying to make out the title.

> (*The book is handed to her;* LUCY'S *arm at full stretch will just do it.*)

AMY: Walter Bagehot . . . the English Constitution. Bagehot and Bach! What
company I'm in! Dear Lucy, are you doing it for a bet?
LUCY: No; it's good stuff.
AMY: So all the authorities declare. Yes . . . and one ought to be able to say: I've
read Bagehot. You can say that, Julia, can't you?
JULIA: I can . . . even truthfully. But I don't.
AMY: And Frances has lectured on Bagehot.
FRANCES: No. Mathematics were my bread and butter.
AMY: And Lady Mortimer will tell us that she once saw Bagehot plain. And I'm
sure he was plain.
LADY MORTIMER: Yes . . . he used to come to my father's house . . . with Mr
Richard Hutton . . . when I was small. They had long beards . . . which
frightened me.
AMY: That's better. Now, Mr Kent . . . what's your contribution?
KENT: I have been lectured on Bagehot . . . and examined on Bagehot. And it
never, please Heaven, can happen again.

Burne-Jones: Edward Burne-Jones (1833–98) was one of the chief Pre-Raphaelite painters and
designers; his dreamy medievalism greatly influenced domestic taste.
Bagehot: (1826–77), editor of *The Economist* and author of a number of works on society and
economics. *The English Constitution* (1867) is a classic analysis of the British political system.
Hutton: (1826–97), theologian, man of letters; a life-long friend of Bagehot's, they worked on
The National Review and *The Economist* together.

LUCY: Shame!

AMY: Well ... if I'd only thought of it I might have put all you clever, well-brought-up people in the shade by protesting loudly at dinner to the distinguished statesmen each side of me that I'd never even heard of Bagehot! Though I have ... oh yes, in my hot youth, I have!

JULIA: Who did bring you up, Amy?

> (*Her tone is ever so slightly tart, as* MRS O'CONNELL *is quick to hear – and she counters.*)

AMY: Dear Julia ... there's no scandal about it! I was orphaned at two and bequeathed to a great-uncle, who was a parson and an atheist and too clever for his job and too conceited to ask for a better one. And he thought the whole duty of woman was to be pretty...

LADY MORTIMER: You gave him no trouble there, my dear.

AMY: Kind Lady Mortimer! Pretty and agreeable and helpless. He drank casks of Madeira ... and that was old-fashioned, too ... and had a dreadful temper.

FRANCES: Cause and effect, possibly.

AMY: I think suppressed atheism was worse for it. So I married at seventeen and turned Catholic and went to Ireland with Justin. Then Justin turned Sinn Fein and I came back ... and every one was so kind. And that's enough about me. But if I'd only been sent to Cambridge instead ... and been lectured at by Frances, perhaps, on mathematics and morals ... what a very different woman I should be! More like Lucy ... though never so nice. Or I might have gone in for politics and been a power in the land.

FRANCES: I don't see you tramping the Lobbies in those pretty shoes.

AMY: No, no ... a power behind the throne ... like Julia. But, of course, never so powerful.

JULIA: (*a shade wryly; only a shade*) I'm not so powerful, I fear.

AMY: (*who can be very innocent at times*) Aren't you? Don't you make history? I thought all the diaries that can't possibly be published for heaven knows how long must be full of you. I thought we were all here this week-end helping you make history. The election coming ... this horrid hypocritical Lib-Labour government to be beautifully beaten ... dear Mr Horsham to be sent for again to save the country ... with Mr Blackborough to find the money and Mr Trebell to find the brains. And that you were arranging it all, Julia.

JULIA: I wish the country's salvation were so simple a matter.

> (*This may sound a little smug; but* LADY JULIA *does not like you to chaff her unless she likes you very much.* GEORGE FARRANT'S *arrival breaks the conversation. He is about his wife's age; a pleasant, very honest fellow, bred to big affairs, but with no other particular qualification for them. Yet this, allied to his honesty and good-nature, has let him hold his place among them respectably enough.*)

Sinn Fein (*shin faine*): society founded *c.* 1905 to work for the political, cultural, and economic independence of Ireland.

Lib-Labour: the Labour Party, with Liberal support, formed a minority government under Ramsay MacDonald in Dec. 1923 which lasted only ten months, when the Conservatives were returned to power. But Barker has probably fictionized the political situation, as he did in the 1907 version.

FARRANT: Blackborough's going, Julia.
JULIA: I thought he must have gone. What time is it?
FARRANT: Ten past eleven.
JULIA: Well . . . you've had something of a talk, you four.
AMY: What about . . . or can't we be told?
FARRANT: About the Goths in Italy and the Normans in Sicily . . . Maltese fever . . . Marriage in Morocco . . . Witchcraft . . . Oliver Cromwell and the Jews . . . William III's love affairs and Bergson's philosophy. I forget what else.
> (RUSSELL BLACKBOROUGH *follows his host into the room. One might more suitably say that he arrives. For to arrive is his vocation, and he by no means agrees with the proverb-maker that to travel is better. He is an able man; he has all the virtues that make for success, and, if sensitiveness is not among them, yet he is not an unkindly man. His voice, perhaps, is louder than it need be; and even when he is silent you always know he is there.*)
BLACKBOROUGH: Good-bye, Lady Julia. A delightful week-end.
JULIA: Whatever hour will you be home?
BLACKBOROUGH: Not before the moon's down. But I'm due in Birmingham bright and early tomorrow. Good-bye, Lady Mortimer.
> (*He is rounding the room with his good-byes.*)
LADY MORTIMER: You're a marvel, Mr Blackborough. And never a holiday, you were telling me.
BLACKBOROUGH: I hate holidays. Want to know my secret?
AMY: Oh . . . please!
BLACKBOROUGH: Learn to sleep at odd moments.
AMY: In public?
BLACKBOROUGH: Yes.
AMY: That's no advice to give a woman.
BLACKBOROUGH: Why not?
AMY: I saw you asleep after tea. Good-bye.
> (*The pin-point does not prick him. Thick-skinned he may be, but, to do him justice, he has no unmanly vanities.*)
BLACKBOROUGH: Besides . . . we poor politicians must work double shifts for our bread and butter while we're in opposition. It's hardly safe when you're in office to hold on to a share . . . much less a directorship. How's the wretched capitalist to live? We can't all have Copper magnates for great-grandfathers like you, Farrant . . . or be Company lawyers like your brother . . . and they'd not have him in public life in America, Miss Trebell. Sorry I missed the music.
> (*He really is. He likes music and the vigour of it. He sang in the Leeds choir in his young days.*)
JULIA: I left you alone. I thought you'd be talking shop.
BLACKBOROUGH: No, no, no . . . we'd no shop to talk. And when will Horsham talk shop if he can help it? Idealist philosophy we finished with. That counts me out . . . I don't know the jargon. But I strongly suspect there's not too much sense in anything that can't be discussed in language the ordinary educated man can understand.
> (*The BUTLER has entered.*)

BUTLER: Mr Blackborough's car, my lady.
> (BLACKBOROUGH *has finished his round, but for* WALTER
> KENT. *Standing by him, he addresses* LADY JULIA.)

BLACKBOROUGH: Do you go campaigning? No ... Farrant's seat is safe. Come
and speak for me.

JULIA: (*as who should say, with all courtesy: The impudence!*) I have never spoken
in public in my life ... and I never shall.

BLACKBOROUGH: (*almost welcoming the snub;* LADY JULIA *can impress him,
though it would not become him to own it*) Ah ... that's the true Tory
tradition. We've to leave it to you ladies, though, to keep it up nowadays.

FARRANT: A September dissolution, too! Labour *would* let us in for that.

LADY MORTIMER: Is it to please the partridges? But they have no votes yet, have
they?

AMY: Poor partridges ... with nobody but nobodies left to shoot at them!

FARRANT: I mean to get a fortnight, though ... whatever happens.

BLACKBOROUGH: We shall come back this time, I don't doubt. (*Then with
masterful suddenness to* WALTER.) Are we to find you a seat, young man?

KENT: Not yet, thank you. I've my trade to learn.

BLACKBOROUGH: Trebell's taking you on.

KENT: Yes.

BLACKBOROUGH: (*though somehow he doesn't seem to mean quite – quite –
what he says*) Lucky fellow! You'll learn a lot.

FARRANT: Classical tripos at Cambridge. Now he has to go to Pitman's for
shorthand and type-writing.

BLACKBOROUGH: A year at the Central Office would have done you some good.
I could have got you in there. Our young men in the House don't start by
learning ... as they ought ... how a Party is run and how votes are got.

KENT: (*very simply: one likes him for it*) I think I'm more interested in ideas.

BLACKBOROUGH: Then why go in for politics?

JULIA: Really, Mr Blackborough!

BLACKBOROUGH: (*genially*) I know, I know ... that raises a laugh from the
intellectual snobs. Ideas have their place, undoubtedly. We need them to draw
upon. But the statesman's task is the accommodation of stubborn fact to
shifting circumstance ... and in effect to the practical capacities of the average
stupid man. Democracy involves the admission of that.

JULIA: (*whose patience is being tried*) I am at least not a democrat, Mr
Blackborough.

BLACKBOROUGH: Nor I ... more of a democrat than I need to be. We've all to
bow down a bit nowadays in the House of Rimmon. But, stampede a people
with ideas ...! Why ... look at the Russian Revolution ... look at the

---

dissolution: of Parliament.
tripos: the curricular and examination system at Cambridge University.
Pitman's: a popular method of shorthand, and a clerical school in London.
bow down ... in the House of Rimmon: follow the prescribed observances without belief, as
Naaman must perform the ceremonies of the god Rimmon of the Syrians, even after conversion
by Elisha in 2 Kings 5.

Chinese Revolution . . . look at India . . . look at Poplar. We live in dangerous times.

LADY MORTIMER: So my dear grandfather used to say.

BLACKBOROUGH: And no doubt he was right. The salvation of this country so far has been its imperviousness to abstract ideas. The difficulty of doing anything definite by party politics . . . strange as this sounds . . . is what keeps us sane and lets us get on with our business. I am a good enough democrat to wish to save democracy from itself . . . and from the ideologue and the doctrinaire. And I wish very much that this present government weren't leaving us such a crop of problems to deal with. The Dominion Treaties . . . the Emigration muddle . . . Disestablishment! They've shown great political wisdom in leaving us to tackle them. Well . . . we must just keep our heads and go slow . . . go slow. Good-night . . . good-night.

> (*These last farewells have the savour of businesslike blessings. He departs, and* FARRANT *hardly allows himself a smile as he follows him to see him off. But the rest of the company is visibly relieved.*)

LADY MORTIMER: Most impressive.

AMY: Shouldn't we have cheered, or said 'Order' or 'Divide' or something?

FRANCES: Alas . . . one must never suppose a man a fool because he *talks* nonsense.

JULIA: And I begged George to see he had his say after dinner. He'd been saving that up for *them* . . . and he empties it over *us*. I will not be called an intellectual snob by Mr Blackborough. Is he out of my house yet?

KENT: I expect so.

JULIA: Then I consider him a hog of a man.

> (*Having said so, she forgives* MR BLACKBOROUGH.)

LADY MORTIMER: But why have you let the Blackboroughs of this world become a power in your Party, Julia?

JULIA: They think they are.

LADY MORTIMER: I should give this one a peerage without more delay.

JULIA: Heavens . . . he wouldn't take it. I know . . . we used to quiet them that way. He wants the Treasury . . . and he'll get it someday, I suppose. He's useful . . . he knows where the votes come from . . . and he does raise funds from people that one really couldn't truckle to oneself. And if it pleases him to imagine that he 'bosses' us . . .

LADY MORTIMER: Julia, don't be complacent. The man rattles you in his pocket with the rest of his loose change.

JULIA: Well, mamma . . . if you'll tell me how to prevent undesirable people joining a Party . . . we'll all be very much obliged to you.

> (FARRANT *has returned, and finds himself opposite* MRS O'CONNELL.)

FARRANT: How's the headache?

AMY: Oh, had I a headache? So I had. No one pitied me. That must have cured it.

Poplar: squalid and overcrowded dock district in the East End of London, rife with social unrest in the period.
peerage: which would of course remove him from his seat in the House of Commons.

FARRANT: Come and play one game of pool. Good exercise. Come along, you
two.

> (*This last is to* LUCY *and* WALTER. LADY JULIA'S *eyebrows go
> up.*)

JULIA: Dear George ... at this hour!

LUCY: I'll play.

JULIA: Send Mr Trebell in to us. He won't, I'm sure.

FARRANT: He said he'd a brief to look through. Shocking Sabbath-breaking!

AMY: What a wonderful moon!

> (*The suggestion of pool has shifted* AMY O'CONNELL *and* LUCY
> *from their chairs; and* AMY *is standing half in, half out of one of the
> windows.* LADY JULIA *can ask her husband just a little more
> confidentially* ...)

JULIA: Did he and the dear departed ...?

FARRANT: Who's that? Oh, Blackborough.

JULIA: Did they get on any sort of terms, d'you think?

FARRANT: I daresay. There's often more gained by not talking about a thing than
just by talking.

JULIA: We really ought to have got one step further.

FARRANT: Don't scold me ... I did my devilmost. Why didn't you ask his
Eminence Charles Cantilupe down? Then we'd have had Disestablishment hot
for breakfast and cold for lunch ... and Disestablishment nicely warmed up
again for dinner.

JULIA: Yes ... just what we didn't want at this juncture.

FARRANT: Oh! Sorry I'm not subtle. (*grumbling contentedly*) I'm sick of politics.
Nothing but a safe seat and devotion to my country...

LUCY: Why don't you take a peerage, Cousin George?

FARRANT: I'd love it. Julia won't let me.

FRANCES: Oh ... why not?

FARRANT: Julia, the daughter of a hundred earls ... Julia, the wife of a pinchbeck
modern peer! No, no! She married me for my money ... and I must keep in
my place.

JULIA: George ... your humour is old-fashioned. Run away.

> (*The two of them must be very happy together if he can joke with the
> truth like that. He turns towards the window.* MRS O'CONNELL *is
> standing right out in the moonlight now, but when he speaks to her she
> frames herself in the window again to answer him.*)

FARRANT: Come and take a cue, dear lady.

AMY: Kind gentleman ... did you never remark that I have a pointed elbow?

FARRANT: (*who is perhaps not quite so simple as he seems*) No ... have you?

AMY: If I took a cue, you would. My headache's back ... and the moon's very good
for it. I shall stroll once round the fountain. And so to bed, Julia?

JULIA: Yes ... biscuits are by the billiard-room. We'll pick you up there.

AMY: I may be rude and not wait for you.

> (*She vanishes into the moonlight and the garden.* FARRANT *departs.*
> LUCY *and* WALTER *are about to follow him.*)

JULIA: Oh dear, oh dear! I'm growing old ... I'm growing clumsy. Here's the week-end over ... and nothing has happened. And I thought I'd made up the mixture so nicely too. Lucy! Take Amy O'Connell her lace ... or she'll catch a cold next.

    (LUCY *returns and picks up the lace scarf as if, it would seem, she had a certain contempt for it.*)

LUCY: Colds are unbecoming.

JULIA: Lucy!

LUCY: Sorry! My claws need cutting. Here, Walter ... you take it. Be gallant. You're forgetting how ... hob-nobbing with me.

KENT: That's your fault.

    (*There is a happy, triumphant confidence in his voice which can have nothing to do, surely, with what he says. He goes after* MRS O'CONNELL *and* LUCY *after her Cousin* GEORGE. *The three women left together settle at once into cosier friendliness.*)

LADY MORTIMER: Are those two young people engaged or are they not, Julia?

JULIA: No ... but they settled when they were children that neither of them would ever marry anybody else. They haven't twopence. He thinks he ought to go into the City for a few years. She won't have that ... he's to start for a career straight away. She's to have babies ... two boys and a girl, she tells me.

LADY MORTIMER: Science is so accommodating nowadays.

JULIA: She has the brains really ... but he wants to please her. He'll be somebody before she has done.

LADY MORTIMER: It was good of your Henry to give him such a chance.

FRANCES: My Henry wanted to please. And likes Walter. He doesn't like many people.

JULIA: Your Henry has been very naughty this week-end.

FRANCES: Julia, I did warn you ... you may be wasting your time.

LADY MORTIMER: Julia ... if a brutal question is permissible: What are you up to?

JULIA: I hoped it was obvious. The successful intriguer, mamma, does nothing underhand. If Cyril Horsham forms a cabinet, Mr Trebell must be in it.

LADY MORTIMER: But he doesn't belong to your Party.

JULIA: He doesn't belong to any other. He sits as an Independent ... Ellesmere's his pocket borough. He always has got in as an Independent, hasn't he, Frances?

FRANCES: During the war...

JULIA: Oh, that doesn't count. And I want him to have charge of the Disestablishment Bill.

LADY MORTIMER: That'll be a bold stroke.

JULIA: It's high time we made one ... if we're not to be Blackboroughed to death.

LADY MORTIMER: But won't it be Cyril's own affair?

JULIA: He can't ... he must take the Foreign Office. Do you mean to tell me, Frances, that if Henry's made the offer point-blank, he'll say no?

FRANCES: I think it quite likely.

JULIA: But what is he in public life for at all, then? He can't stay in the House and

---

Ellesmere: market town in Shropshire, a safe seat for Trebell.

make speeches that count . . . count for votes! . . . and always refuse office. It's
not right. He needn't join the Party even. Disestablishment is an exceptional
thing . . . there'll be a lot of cross voting.

LADY MORTIMER: But sanctified by office, he might stay in it, you think?

JULIA: (*countering her mother with perfect frankness*) Yes . . . I hope. Practical
politics are Party politics. And we'd be the better off for him. Can't you use
your influence, Frances?

FRANCES: Julia . . . though such a thing must seem to you against nature . . . I have
no influence with Henry . . . and never have had, from the days when we
played in our suburban nursery together.

JULIA: But what does he want of life? He doesn't like society . . .

FRANCES: No.

JULIA: He dislikes women, apparently.

FRANCES: He's pretty indifferent to them.

JULIA: He can't suspect *me* of wanting to flirt with him, I hope. But whenever I try
to talk to him the temperature drops.

LADY MORTIMER: He flattered an old lady at tea-time yesterday with some very
pleasant attentions.

JULIA: He considers you safe, mamma.

LADY MORTIMER: Then he has no right to. Mine is the perfect age for a love
affair.

JULIA: How old is he, Frances?

FRANCES: Fifty-one.

JULIA: Well . . . he has made himself a unique position. If it's going to be a barren
one . . . what a pity! And here's a chance of the premiership for him . . .
nothing less in the end. Isn't that good enough? If you can't do better with
him, Frances . . . marry him off to some vulgar ambitious woman who will.

FRANCES: I think I have never really known what Henry believed in. We all
disbelieve in so much . . . and believe in so little nowadays.

 (*The* BUTLER *comes in.*)

BUTLER: Dr Wedgecroft has telephoned, my lady. His thanks . . . they stopped the
express for him and he reached town in good time.

JULIA: Thank you.

 (*The* BUTLER *goes.*)

LADY MORTIMER: Was he sent for?

JULIA: No . . . it's his point of honour not to sleep out of town during what he calls
his duty months.

FRANCES: Gilbert can do as much with Henry as anyone.

JULIA: I know. That's why I fetched him down today. They had a talk before
dinner. Bed, mamma?

LADY MORTIMER: I think so.

JULIA: I must go by the billiard-room. Is our lovely Amy still star-gazing? Mr
Blackborough didn't seem to be very 'took' with her.

LADY MORTIMER: He eyed her as if he thought she'd try to borrow money from
him.

FRANCES: I don't see her.

 (*The suggestion of bed has brought them to their feet;* LADY

MORTIMER *is collecting her spectacles and such-like;* FRANCES *has moved out into the courtyard, she now comes back.*)

JULIA: I only asked her in the hope that she'd amuse him.

FRANCES: Julia ... how brutal!

JULIA: People must expect to be made use of. She sets out to be amusing ... to men. A house-party needs just a dash of ... her sort of thing.

LADY MORTIMER: Your cunning is too consistent, Julia. You really should do something single-minded occasionally. Why, by the way, did you ask *me*?

JULIA: I love you, mamma.

LADY MORTIMER: That may be your salvation yet.

JULIA: But the lovely Amy bores me. I wonder you like her so, Frances.

FRANCES: I like all sorts of people.

JULIA: Why doesn't she go back to her Justin?

FRANCES: He's impossible.

JULIA: I doubt it.

FRANCES: My dear ... with a housemaid for his mistress ... even an Irish housemaid!

JULIA: She could give her a month's notice.

LADY MORTIMER: And this is the result of bringing up my daughter upon the novels of Miss Charlotte M. Yonge!

FRANCES: But for all Amy's airs and graces one feels sorry for her at times. There's something of the waif about her.

LADY MORTIMER: Good-night, dear Miss Trebell.

FRANCES: Good-night.

JULIA: I'll come in and kiss you, mamma. And I will not sit up watching Lucy play pool...

(*And so they talk themselves out of the room.*)

Yonge: (1823–1901), leading novelist of the Anglo-Catholic revival or Oxford Movement, best known as a prolific writer of historical romances for children.

THE PLAYS OF HARLEY GRANVILLE BARKER

When known, the date of composition is given in parentheses, followed by details of first production and first publication. Except where noted, the place for both is London; when the first production was elsewhere, details of the London première are also included. 'Unproduced' means that no record of professional performance has been discovered. A complete list of productions directed by GB is contained in my *Granville Barker and the Dream of Theatre*. [Sources: Nicoll, Purdom, and Wearing (see Bibliography for full citations); relevant editions of *Who's Who in the Theatre*; press reports in *The Times*, *The Stage*, *The Era*, and *The New York Times*.]

I. UNPUBLISHED EARLY PLAYS (typescripts in the British Library)

The Family of the Oldroyds (written with Berte Thomas, *c*. 1895–6). Unproduced.

The Weather-Hen (with Berte Thomas, 1897). Terry's Theatre, 29 June 1899.

Our Visitor to 'Work-a-Day' (with Berte Thomas, 1898–9). Unproduced.

A Miracle (short play in verse, *c*. 1900). Terry's Theatre, 23 March 1907, Literary Stage Society, directed by Robert Farquharson (on bill with Aeschylus' *The Persians*, directed by Lewis Casson).

Agnes Colander (1900–1). Unproduced.

II. MAJOR PLAYS

The Marrying of Ann Leete (1899). Royalty Theatre, 26 January 1902, directed by GB for Stage Society. Sidgwick & Jackson, 1909 (in *Three Plays*).

Prunella, or Love in a Dutch Garden (with Laurence Housman, 1904). Court Theatre, 23 December 1904, directed by GB for Vedrenne–Barker management. A. H. Bullen, 1906.

The Voysey Inheritance (1903–5). Court Theatre, 7 November 1905, directed by GB for Vedrenne–Barker. Sidgwick & Jackson, 1909 (in *Three Plays*).

Waste (1906–7). Imperial Theatre, 24 November 1907, directed by GB for Stage Society. Sidgwick & Jackson, 1909 (in *Three Plays*).

The Madras House (1909). Duke of York's Theatre, 9 March 1910, directed by GB for Charles Frohman's repertory season. Sidgwick & Jackson, 1911.

Rococo (one-act farce, 1911). Court Theatre, 21 February 1911, directed by GB for Lillah McCarthy (on bill with John Masefield's *The Tragedy of Nan*). Sidgwick & Jackson, 1917.

The Voysey Inheritance, first revised version (1912). Kingsway Theatre, 7 September 1912, directed by GB for Lillah McCarthy–Granville Barker management. Sidgwick & Jackson, 1913.

The Harlequinade (one-act, with Dion Clayton Calthrop, 1913). St James's Theatre, 1 September 1913, directed by GB for McCarthy–Barker (on bill with Shaw's *Androcles and the Lion*). Sidgwick & Jackson, 1918. (Though GB is credited as co-author, he had little to do with the writing of this piece.)

Vote by Ballot (one-act, 1914). Court Theatre, 16 December 1917, Stage Society (on bill with *Fêtes Galantes* by Mme Donnet and *The Philosopher of Butterbiggens* by Harold Chapin). Sidgwick & Jackson, 1925.

Farewell to the Theatre (one-act, 1916). Unproduced. Sidgwick & Jackson, 1925.

The Secret Life (1919–23). Unproduced. Chatto & Windus, 1923.

The Madras House, revised version (1925). Ambassador's Theatre, 30 November 1925, directed by GB. Sidgwick & Jackson, 1925.

Waste, revised version (1926). Westminster Theatre, 1 December 1936, directed by GB and Michael MacOwan. Sidgwick & Jackson, 1927.

His Majesty (1923–8). Unproduced. Sidgwick & Jackson, 1928.

The Voysey Inheritance, second revised version (1934). Sadler's Wells Theatre, 3 May 1934, directed by GB and Harcourt Williams. Sidgwick & Jackson, 1938.

III. TRANSLATIONS AND ADAPTATIONS

Anatol by Arthur Schnitzler. Little Theatre, 11 March 1911, directed by GB for McCarthy–Barker. Sidgwick & Jackson, 1911.

The Dynasts, adaptation of verse drama by Thomas Hardy. Kingsway Theatre, 25 November 1914, directed by GB for McCarthy–Barker. Unpublished (typed promptscript in Harvard Theatre Collection).

The Morris Dance, adaptation of *The Wrong Box* by R. L. Stevenson and Lloyd Osbourne. Little Theatre, New York, 13 February 1917, directed by Winthrop Ames. Unpublished (typescript in New York Public Library).

The Romantic Young Lady by Gregorio Martinez Sierra, trans. Helen and Harley Granville Barker. Royalty Theatre, 16 September 1920, jointly directed by translators. Published in *Collected Plays of Martinez Sierra*, vol. 2, Chatto & Windus, 1923.

The Two Shepherds by Martinez Sierra, trans. Helen and Harley GB.
Birmingham Rep., 29 October 1921; Old Vic Theatre, 11 February
1935. In *Collected Plays* as above.

Deburau by Sacha Guitry. Belasco Theatre, New York, 23 December 1920,
directed by David Belasco; Ambassador's Theatre, 2 November 1921,
(probably) directed by GB. Heinemann, 1921.

The Kingdom of God by Martinez Sierra, trans. Helen and Harley GB.
Abbey Theatre, Dublin, 21 October 1923; Strand Theatre, 26 October
1927, directed by A. E. Filmer. In *Collected Plays* as above.

Wife to a Famous Man by Martinez Sierra, trans. Helen and Harley GB.
Aldwych Theatre, 25 May 1924, directed by A. E. Filmer. In *Collected
Plays* as above.

Doctor Knock by Jules Romains. Royalty Theatre, 27 April 1926, directed
by Peter Godfrey. Ernest Benn, 1925.

Six Gentlemen in a Row by Jules Romains. Liverpool Playhouse, 2 October
1927. Sidgwick & Jackson, 1927.

A Hundred Years Old by Serafin and Joaquin Alvarez Quintero, trans.
Helen and Harley GB. Theatre Royal, Glasgow, 30 April 1928; Lyric
Theatre, Hammersmith, 21 November 1928, directed by A. E. Filmer.
In *Four Plays* by the Alvarez Quinteros, Sidgwick & Jackson, 1927.

Fortunato and *The Lady from Alfaqueque* by the Alvarez Quinteros, trans.
Helen and Harley GB. Court Theatre, 22 October 1928, directed by
James Whale. In *Four Plays* as above.

The Women Have Their Way by the Alvarez Quinteros, trans. Helen and
Harley GB. Oxford Playhouse, 26 November 1928; Everyman
Theatre, 1 June 1933, directed by George More O'Ferrall. In *Four
Plays* as above.

Take Two from One by Martinez Sierra, trans. Helen and Harley GB.
Haymarket Theatre, 16 September 1931, directed by Theodor
Komisarjevsky. Sidgwick & Jackson, 1931.

Love Passes By by the Alvarez Quinteros, trans. Helen and Harley GB.
Unproduced. In *Four Comedies* by the Alvarez Quinteros, Sidgwick &
Jackson, 1932.

Doña Clarines by the Alvarez Quinteros, trans. Helen and Harley GB.
Webber-Douglas Theatre, 12 July 1934, directed by Susan Richmond
(on bill with Martinez Sierra's *The Lover*, trans. G. J. Underhill). In
Four Comedies as above.

Peace and Quiet by the Alvarez Quinteros, trans. Helen and Harley GB.
Webber-Douglas Theatre, 25 November 1935, directed by Susan
Richmond. In *Four Comedies* as above.

Don Abel Wrote a Tragedy by the Alvarez Quinteros, trans. Helen and
Harley GB. Arts Theatre, 13 January 1944, directed by Denys
Blakelock. In *Four Comedies* as above.

SELECT BIBLIOGRAPHY

Unless otherwise specified, the place of publication is London.

CHIEF NON-DRAMATIC WORKS BY GRANVILLE BARKER

A nearly complete list of GB's writings is appended to Purdom (see below), prepared by Margery Morgan and Frederick May.

Associating with Shakespeare. Humphrey Milford, 1932.
A Companion to Shakespeare Studies, ed. with G. B. Harrison. Cambridge: Cambridge Univ. Press, 1934.
The Exemplary Theatre. Chatto & Windus, 1922.
Granville Barker and His Correspondents, ed. Eric Salmon. Detroit: Wayne State Univ. Press, 1986.
'The Heritage of the Actor', *Quarterly Review* 140(1923):53–73. Abridged version rpt. in *Actors on Acting*, ed. Toby Cole and Helen K. Chinoy (New York: Crown, 1949).
More Prefaces to Shakespeare, ed. Edward M. Moore. Princeton: Princeton Univ. Press, 1974. [Contains short uncollected introductions and prefaces, and the essay 'From Henry V to Hamlet'.]
A National Theatre. Sidgwick & Jackson, 1930.
A National Theatre: Scheme and Estimates (with William Archer). Duckworth, 1907. Rpt. Port Washington, NY: Kennikat Press, 1970.
'Notes on Rehearsing a Play', *Drama* 1(1919):2–5.
On Dramatic Method. Sidgwick & Jackson, 1931.
On Poetry in Drama. Sidgwick & Jackson, 1937.
Prefaces to Shakespeare. 2 vols. Princeton: Princeton Univ. Press, 1946–7. 1 vol. issue by Batsford, 1971.
'Repertory Theatres', *The New Quarterly* 2(1909):491–504.
'Shakespeare's Dramatic Art', in *A Companion to Shakespeare Studies* (see above).
The Study of Drama. Cambridge: Cambridge Univ. Press, 1934.
'The Theatre: The Next Phase', *The English Review* 5(1910):631–48.
'Two German Theatres', *Fortnightly Review* 89(1911):60–70.
The Use of the Drama. Princeton: Princeton Univ. Press, 1945.

SOME IMPORTANT WORKS ON GRANVILLE BARKER

Archer, William. *The Old Drama and the New*. Heinemann, 1923.
Bridges-Adams, W. 'Granville Barker and the Savoy', *Drama* N.S. 52(1959):28–31.

The Lost Leader. Sidgwick & Jackson, 1954.

Casson, Lewis. 'Granville Barker, Shaw and the Court Theatre', in Mander & Mitchenson, *A Theatrical Companion to Shaw*. Rockliff, 1954.

Downer, Alan S. 'Harley Granville-Barker', *Sewanee Review* 55(1947):627–45.

Dukes, Ashley. *Modern Dramatists*. Frank Palmer, 1911.

Gielgud, John. *Stage Directions*. Heinemann, 1963.

Henderson, Archibald. *European Dramatists*. Cincinnati: Steward & Kidd, 1913.

Howe, P. P. *Dramatic Portraits*. Martin Secker, 1913.

The Repertory Theatre: A Record and a Criticism. Martin Secker, 1910.

Kennedy, Dennis. *Granville Barker and the Dream of Theatre*. Cambridge: Cambridge Univ. Press, 1985.

'Granville Barker's Sexual Comedy', *Modern Drama* 23 (1980):75–82.

MacCarthy, Desmond. *The Court Theatre 1904–1907*. A. H. Bullen, 1907. Rpt. Coral Gables, Florida: Univ. of Miami Press, 1966, ed. Stanley Weintraub.

McDonald, Jan. 'New Actors for the New Drama', *Drama and the Actor*, ed. James Redmond (Themes in Drama 6). Cambridge: Cambridge Univ. Press, 1984.

The 'New Drama' 1900–1914. Macmillan, 1986.

Morgan, Margery M. *A Drama of Political Man: A Study in the Plays of Harley Granville Barker*. Sidgwick & Jackson, 1961.

'Edwardian Feminism and the Drama: Shaw and Granville Barker', *Cahiers Victoriens et Edouardiens* 9–10(1979):63–85.

Intro. to GB's *The Madras House* (ed. Morgan). Methuen, 1977.

Nicoll, Alardyce. *English Drama 1900–1930*. Cambridge: Cambridge Univ. Press, 1973.

Pearson, Hesketh. *The Last Actor–Managers*. Methuen, 1950.

Modern Men and Mummers. Allen & Unwin, 1921.

Purdom, C. B. *Harley Granville Barker*. Barrie & Rockliff, 1955. Rpt. Westport, Conn: Greenwood Press, 1971.

Ritchie, Harry M. 'Harley Granville Barker's *The Madras House* and the Sexual Revolution', *Modern Drama* 15(1972–3): 150–8.

Salenius, Elmer W. *Harley Granville Barker*. Boston: Twayne, 1982.

Salmon, Eric. *Granville Barker: A Secret Life*. Heinemann, 1983.

Scott, Dixon. 'Granville Barker', *The Bookman* 44(1914):153–62.

Shaw, G. B. *Bernard Shaw's Letters to Granville Barker*, ed. C. B. Purdom. Phoenix House, 1956.

Collected Letters, ed. Dan H. Laurence. 3 vols. Max Reinhardt, 1965–85. [A final vol. is projected]

Styan, J. L. *The Shakespeare Revolution*. Cambridge: Cambridge Univ. Press, 1977.

Trewin, J. C. *The Edwardian Theatre*. Oxford: Blackwell, 1976.
Weales, Gerald. 'The Edwardian Theatre and the Shadow of Shaw', *Edwardians and Late Victorians*, ed. Richard Ellmann (English Institute Essays, 1959). New York: Columbia Univ. Press, 1960.
Wearing, J. P. *The London Stage 1890–1929*. 9 vols. Metuchen, NJ: Scarecrow Press, 1976–84.